Can socialism make sense?

An unfriendly dialogue

Sean Matgamna

With additional texts by Ernest Belfort Bax, August Bebel,
Eugene Debs, Hal Draper, Albert Einstein, Frederick
Engels, Henry Hyndman, Paul Lafargue, Vladimir Lenin,
Rosa Luxemburg, David Marsland, Kenneth Minogue,
William Morris, Roger Scruton, Max Shachtman, Martin
Thomas, Leon Trotsky, and Clara Zetkin

Can socialism make sense?

Sean Matgamna

Printed by Imprint Digital, Exeter EX5 5HY

ISBN: 978-1-909639-27-0

Published 2016 by Workers' Liberty
20E Tower Workshops
Riley Road
London SE1 3DG
020 7394 8923
awl@workersliberty.org
www.workersliberty.org

Labour

While the ages changed and sped
I was toiling for my bread.
Underneath my sturdy blows
Forests fell and cities rose.
And the hard reluctant soil
Blossomed richly from my toil.
Palaces and temples grand
Wrought I with my cunning hand.
Rich indeed was my reward —
Stunted soul and body scarred
With the marks of scourge and rod.
I, the tiller of the sod,
From the cradle to the grave
Shambled through the world — a slave.
Crushed and trampled, beaten, cursed,
Serving best, but served the worst,
Starved and cheated, gouged and spoiled.
Still I builded, still I toiled,
Undernourished, underpaid
In the world myself had made.
Up from slavery I rise,
Dreams and wonder in my eyes.
After brutal ages past
Coming to my own at last.
I was slave — but I am free!
I was blind — but I can see!
I, the builder, I, the maker,
I, the calm tradition breaker,
Slave and serf and clod no longer,
Know my strength — and who is stronger?

"BB"

The cover pictures are of Rosa Luxemburg (front) and Karl Marx (back). The verse on the previous page is by "BB", from *Young Spartacus*, youth paper of the US Trotskyists, 1932.

Graphics: p.168, *The Militant* (USA), 4 November 1944; p.186, *Socialist Appeal* (USA), 29 January 1938; p.235, *Daily Worker* (USA), 3 March 1928; p.236, *Labor Action* (USA), 11 May 1942; p.320, *Socialist Appeal* (USA), 21 March 1939.

German socialist poster for International Women's Day 1914

Contents

Introduction

The first step in the revolution by the working class is to raise the proletariat to the position of ruling class, to win the battle of democracy — Marx and Engels, *The Communist Manifesto*

THE STARTLING economic crisis of 2008 and its aftershocks have cracked the tremendous mystique which the world capitalist system had built in the two decades after the collapse of Russian and European Stalinism. They had been decades of accelerated globalisation; of great capitalist expansion; of the US hyper-power bestriding the world; and of mass belief in markets as the regulator of economic and therefore of all social, all human, affairs.

Something else startled the world. In an era of globalisation and worship of the market-as-god, it was revealed that in the US and Britain we were ruled by "social-istic" governments, selectively social-istic but social-istic all the same. Governments intervened fundamentally in the operation of the markets. The right wing US government took over, or engineered the taking-over, of the biggest insurance company in the world, of most of the big banks, and of the two corporations that guarantee around 90% of household mortgages in the USA. In Britain, the neo-Thatcherite Blair-Brown government temporarily took over the banks. The US administration of George W Bush and the Blair-Brown government of Britain assumed the social role which the failing banks had played, the role of financial organiser and regulator of the entire economy. They used the government power to channel many billions of dollars and pounds from tax-paying society to subsidise the banks.

The British prime minister, Gordon Brown, explained that if they had not intervened, if they had not played the role of organiser, financier, and guarantor of the financiers, then the high street cash-point machines, the fuelling-points of commercial and social activity, would have closed down. "Society" would have seized up, as the US economy did when the banks closed their doors in the early 1930s. Or worse. This was an acknowledgement that uncontrolled markets and privately-owned banks had led us to the brink of social disaster. In the last resort, the all-ruling banks depended on social action by the overall representatives of society, the governments, to avert disaster, to cancel out the natural consequences for the bankers and for society of free markets. But if this "socialism", or "social-ism", or "society-ism", was in the interests of society, it was also pointedly in the direct and immediate interests of the bankers and those who own,

5

control, and benefit most from the capitalist economy. If it was "socialism", it was bankers' social-ism, fat-cat social-ism. Bourgeois social-ism. In Marxist terms, state capitalism. It did, however, point to the fundamental rationale of Marxist socialism, the thing that makes it good sense and, essentially invulnerable to the defeat, subversion or destruction of socialist parties, despite the often terrible human cost of those defeats: capitalism itself prepares and continually develops towards the socialist transformation of society. As Frederick Engels put it: the future socialist society "invades", infiltrates, large-scale modern capitalism. Marxist socialism is only the conscious expression of this objective reality.

Capitalism grows from small-scale production to ever more gigantic concentrations of the means of production in huge society-wide enterprises. Capitalism has developed from a world where markets regulated the affairs of small commodity production to a world of giants whose size modifies the workings of markets and whose needs — and society's needs in relation to them — can, as in 2008 and after, only be met by social, society-wide, governmental action. But these gigantic social enterprises are still organised and run to produce the maximum private profit. The fate of the workers within them, and the role they play in society as a whole — all that is determined not by broad social interests, social considerations, social consequences, but by the imperative to produce profit for private shareholders and enormous salaries and bonuses for the corporate bosses who run these great chunks of social activity and social labour.

A polemicist in the liberal *Observer* dismissed as foolish the idea that Marx, writing early in industrial capitalism, could have understood its essentials. In fact Marx, according to himself, based his analysis of capitalist society on over 400 years, before his time, of capitalism in history (as distinct from industrial capitalism). In any case the question is: did he or did he not see into the essentials of our system? A writer in the right-wing *Daily Telegraph* in 2008 gave a forthright and truthful answer: "the world now corresponds more to the expectation of Karl Marx than of any other economist or social philosopher." Does capitalism continue to have the basic characteristics which Marx anatomised? Do we live in a world dominated by capitalist companies, entities whose driving force and goal is to wring the maximum profit out of their operations — that is, out of those who work in them — no matter what the human and social consequences of that may be? Yes, we do. Of course we do! It would not be too fanciful to say that the shareholders in each company — even though their democratic control is normally more theoretical than

6

real — bear the same sort of relationship to those employed by the companies, and to society as a whole, as the minority of citizens in the ancient Greek democratic city-state did to the four or five times more numerous slaves, women and foreigners who made their lives there. The great paradox in political and social life is that though this social development corresponds to the bedrock Marxist expectations of the way capitalism, in accordance with its inner drives and needs, had to develop, nonetheless the case for socialism today, socialism in general and Marxist socialism in particular, is marginal, more than at any time in the last one hundred years.

Commentators point to the absence of a credible socialism, that is, of a compellingly-made case for the democratic control of the economy and society, as one of the great assets which capitalism possesses in this still not-fully-resolved crisis. There is no denying it. That is how things stand with socialism. Authentic socialism is still buried under the ruins of Stalinism, the fraudulent, counterfeit, anti-socialist "socialism" of the 20th century. Socialism is in eclipse, everywhere.

What is socialism? To paraphrase one of its founders, socialism is the democratic organisation of production for use, of production for abundance, of plenty for all, without the exploitation of human beings. Socialism is the union of the whole world into an international federation of free and equal peoples, disposing in common of the natural resources and wealth, the highways and sea-lanes and airways, of our earth. It means the working class, in the name and in the interests of society as a whole, taking the huge monopolies and trusts out of the hands of the capitalist monopolists and placing them under the democratic control of society as a whole, led by this same working class. Socialists organise to make the working class conscious of the part it must play in leading and reorganising society. Socialists are part and parcel of the working class and the labour movement, fighting not only for its great future, but also for its present, for its interests and demands today. Socialists support every fight and every demand of labour today which strengthens the working class, which gives it a stronger position in society, which increases its self-confidence and militancy, which pits it against its mortal enemy capitalism and the capitalist class — which strengthens its political independence, and which, therefore, brings it a step further along the road of struggle for the socialist future.

The Alliance for Workers' Liberty offers this book as a contribution to the urgent work of rebuilding a mass working-class socialist consciousness, perspective, and a movement that embodies and fights for them. *Sean Matgamna, April 2016*

Can socialism make sense? An unfriendly dialogue

I pondered all these things, and how men fight and lose the battle, and the thing that they fought for comes about in spite of their defeat, and when it comes turns out not to be what they meant, and other men have to fight for what they meant under another name...

— William Morris, *A Dream of John Ball*

Part 1: Socialism and Stalinism

CAPITALISM AND SOCIALISM TODAY

B. Say what you like in criticising capitalism, that doesn't positively make the case for socialism as an alternative.

A. Yes; but, nevertheless, look around you. Look at the crisis we are in. And why? Because the bankers, everywhere, lent money, and borrowed money from each other, wildly and recklessly. The story of the banks here is not only about the banks. It is the summing-up, the epitome, of the whole capitalist system, of which the banks are so central a part. The people fall victim to the ruthless, reckless, heedless competitive drive for private profit by a small minority which dominates economic life.

B. Many "ordinary" people benefited. They were able to buy their homes because the banks were generous.

A. An awful lot of them now have found that their homes are owned by the banks, impatient for their loot. In America the promised land of capitalism, by 2015 six million households had lost their homes in an epidemic of bank foreclosures. What they had already paid was confiscated — by the "generous" bank! — because they couldn't meet the monthly mortgage-money repayments. The bankers were driven to make reckless loans not by generosity but greed. They went mad for money. Like the Gadarene swine in the bible story, in their frenzy they stampeded over a cliff — pulling vast numbers of home-owners with them. They got madder the more

8

money they got. Without the services the bankers operate, this society would seize up. But they run the banks as their private property. Astonishingly, if you pause to think of it, the banks *are* their private property! An international class of billionaires, united in an attitude of disdain or hostility to the working class, ran the credit system essential to the whole of society for their own benefit, to make the maximum profit for themselves. In thier blinkered, aggressive, self-serving, they came not to care about anything else. Social need? What's that? Me and mine! Then in 2007-8 some American bankers — like a man who suddenly realises that he is sleep-walking on the edge of an abyss — panicked at the realisation that vast numbers of mortgages would never be paid off, and as a consequence reams and reams of financial paper issued by banks and indirectly based on those mortgages might be valueless. The panic spread. The whole system was convulsed. The governments had to step in to take on the role that the banks had played. They propped them up.

B. Because the alternative was to let the whole system seize up, even to the extent that High Street cash-points would close.

A. Yes, because the great social engines of finance, on which everything in the social economy depends, were the billionaires' private property, and run as engines of their own private enrichment. The necessary social role of the banks was tied to, merged with, and regulated by the exigencies of private ownership. They were operated to make profits for private owners. That brought society across the world to a convulsive, juddering crisis. Then "society" had meekly to pay to rescue those whose greed had brought us close to disaster. As someone aptly said: this is a system of privatised profit and socialised loss. That in a nutshell sums up what is wrong with capitalism as a whole.

Vast social complexes of production, exchange, communication, without which this society could not function, and on which the livelihoods of untold millions depend, are run as private property for the benefit of private owners, no matter what it means for the others in society, or for society as a whole. It would be hard to invent a cleverer parable to illustrate what is wrong with capitalism than this true story, which affects all our lives, pitching us into the worst slump for nearly a century.

I put it to you that such a system is insane. The ways the governments responded — the right-wing Bush administration in the USA as well as the New Labour neo-Thatcherite government in Britain —

proves how nonsensical and crazy it is. The governments took over and guaranteed the functions of the banks — "temporarily". In Ireland, where we go to extremes, the government took responsibility for all the banks' debts. Governments "nationalised" the losses of the banks, made "society" responsible for them. They took over the banks, but only temporarily. They will be returned to private owners once the storm is weathered, that is, when they become profitable again. A mad way to run society — running it for the rich by the rich in the service of the rich! The government intervention in the crisis proved how important social action is, and how necessary — but this was social-ism for the billionaires. Socialists want a socialism for all working-class people.

B. Oh, I agree that the bankers' vast bonuses should not be allowed.

A. "Everyone" agrees on that — and nobody can do anything very much about it. That neatly sums up our situation. Yes, the bonuses are obscene. But the bigger obscenity is the power we let them have over us and society. And it is not confined to the bankers. All through society it's the same. Vast institutions on which all our lives depend are run not in the interests of society, of the people, but of private owners.

B. You exaggerate. There's been big trouble since 2008, but in the long view that is just a blip.

A. Do I exaggerate? The world in which we live is wracked by terrible crises. It is plagued by local wars, by famine and malnutrition in Africa and elsewhere, by ecological disasters now and the certainty of even worse ecological disasters to come, by the "routine" death of about eight million children under the age of five, each year, from preventable or curable diseases. There are many other such things.

In the USA, the richest country in the world, and one of the most democratic, sprawling "Third World" slums and ghettos for large parts of the working class are part of the most modern cities. In that country, and others, many of the rich live in ghettos — fenced-off, privately-policed compounds.

In such cities, and in the cities of poorer countries like Stalino-capitalist China, people live in varieties of want, and are cut off by poverty from modern medicine. In the most advanced society on earth, the USA, tens of millions of people exist without adequate medicine and medical care. Vast numbers in the cities are homeless.

In an era of wonderful, almost-miraculous mass communications, tens and hundreds of millions live educationally in a world of ignorance, pseudo-knowledge, intellectual, spiritual, and moral barbarism, internet-legend and internet-scuttlebut. Just glance at the programme lists on satellite TV, where so much is on what used to be the level of kids' comics and the old film serials like Batman and Superman, a mixture of science-fiction and tongue-in-cheek pseudo-supernatural drivel. The most popular movies are on the same level. We see immensely developed technology in the service of profit-chasing commercial moronism and lowest-common-denominator social idiocy. We live in what someone satirically called an "idiocracy" run with no consideration in mind other than to make money for the already very rich. Commerce, and its needs and conveniences, are the givers of morality in our world, and its great exemplars. *Protestanism + capitalism?*

The breakdown of old religious-based ethics and morality creates an urgent need for a rational, humanity-centred system of private and public morality, a morality based on human solidarity. But that morality requires a society compatible with it. The culture of commercial capitalism eats at the ties, linkages, and functioning of capitalist society. The prevailing morality, "the war of all against all", is the natural spirit and morality of capitalism. This account-book morality is radically at odds with the needs of a reasonable, responsible and humane society. It sheds all human considerations, everything other than the imperatives of trade, commerce, and money. Capitalist market-modelled culture — do whatever will benefit you — is irredeemably at odds with human solidarity. As Karl Marx and Frederick Engels put it in the Communist Manifesto: "the bourgeoisie has left remaining no other nexus between man and man than naked self-interest, than callous 'cash payment'."

B. You prefer the morality of the old religious mumbo-jumbo, laid down by the priests of a supposedly all-ruling but incredibly stupid God, obsessed with trivialities?

A. No. I prefer a morality based on reason and human solidarity. Everywhere in society we have the twisted wrecks of old aspirations. Democracy? We have only shallow political democracy, and an anaemic version of it at that, not social or economic democracy. Vast areas of life are outside any sort of democratic control. In theory, democracy makes the government, the state, and "society" the supervisor of over-mighty economic subjects. In reality, the government is under the control of the rich and powerful. We have what Marxists have called bourgeois democracy or pluto-democracy. Our bourgeois democracy is increasingly emptied of much of its never very robust democratic content.

A. Who else should the government serve? They serve the job creators, the big business which generates near abundance. You want to go back to the immense waste and low productivity of small business? Anyway, everyone has a vote. You're just sore that people mostly vote for what you call bourgeois parties. But that's democracy.

A. The existing democratic systems fall a great deal below their own nominal value. Where wealth gives such enormous advantages, the votes of all citizens are not, cannot be, equal. Inequality in our world is grotesque and all-pervasive. The poor pay, proportionately, as much or more tax than the rich.

Because of VAT, council tax, and other regressive taxes, a household in the bottom ten per cent pays 43% of its income in tax, while a household in the top ten per cent pays 35%.

The horrible paradox is in the same sort of class matrix as the privileges of the pre-1789 French nobility. Among the rich, the ethos of paying only what cannot be helped, and evading as much as possible, is dominant.

B. Maybe you have a point. But your comparison with the French aristocracy is typically grotesque socialist hyperbole.

A. The private ownership of city land allows the charging of immense "taxes" on everybody who rents, or uses the services of those who rent. The Duke of Westminster and the Earl of Cardogan own much of central London and the Mosley family, the family of the old Fascist leader, Sir Oswald Mosley, much of central Manchester. This amounts to a system of robbery administered for the robbers by the state.

B. Ah — Henry George! Tax the landlords out of existence?

A. In itself not a bad idea. But we'll need a lot more than that to get rid of capitalism. There is an attitude of Aztec-fatalistic, superstitious helplessness towards the depredations of the market and its capitalist priests tearing out human hearts.

B. The Stalinists who dispensed with the market tore out a lot of hearts.

A. Yes, but don't use old horrors to excuse the ones around you. In Aztec times you'd have been the person singing the praises of religious heart-ripping because it was quicker and more merciful than the practice of the folk down the river who tortured prisoners to death.

B. Yes, and socialists like you would have argued that a mercifully quick ripping out of hearts and the slowly torturing to death of prisoners were identical things.

A. The decline of old Christian churches gives place not to enlightenment, but to regression to more primitive forms of "wild" religion, tarotry, "horoscopolatry", and half-baked nature-worship, which is a form of rejection of modern society. Reason and knowledge, and respect for reason and knowledge, are at an immense disadvantage. In the USA, a politician cannot get elected unless he or she professes and practises a religion, or pretends to. Baptists and other Christian sects from the most developed and most powerful country on earth export their reason-defying, emotion-driven, barbarous beliefs to Africa. One result of that is ultra-savage repression and legislation against homosexuality in Uganda and other African countries. In the Muslim world, the immense oil-wealth of the rulers of such places as Saudi Arabia combines with the pressures, contradictions, and explosive amalgamations of cultures in modern life to trigger volcanic eruptions of petrified, ignorantly self-righteous, murderously militant jihadist superstition.

B. That's not capitalism! It's an irruption from the dark ages!

A. Yes, it is. But it is a result of the cultural and economic interactions in world capitalism and it is fuelled by the great oil wealth of Arab rulers — some of whom foster primitive Muslim religious sects. The Islamists are entwined with world capitalism. It's a malign example of what Marxists call "combined and uneven development".

B. Spare me the Marxist gobbledegook!

A. To resume: ecological catastrophe looms, for lack of rational planning of economic and social development.

On such issues, the direct involvement of international corporations and their tame pre-paid scientists poisons public discourse. The profit-fuelled corporations must go on driving for profit, even though their system now threatens ecological ruin, and their own ruination too. We are like ignorant and primitive farmers who do not know enough not to work the soil to an exhaustion which means destruction for themselves and their community — except that here the problem is not lack of knowledge, but the inability of knowledge, or considerations about the general interests of humankind, to control the profit-mongers, themselves caught in the terrible rush of profit-seeking and often profit-mad capitalism. The profit drive here puts out the social, ethical, historical, and forward-looking eyes of modern humankind.

B. And what did socialism in power...

A. Stalinism in power! Neither the USSR after Stalin's counter-revolution, nor any of the many states tightly or loosely modelled on it, were socialism. Not as I understand socialism, or as Marxist working-class socialists understood socialism before the rise of Stalinism.

B. ... what did socialism in power do?

A. Exploitative capitalism, which dominates the world, and Stalinism, which used to dominate one-third of it and still controls China, in alliance with spectacularly vicious forms of capitalist exploitation — these are the causes of those horrors. To both capitalism and Stalinism, the people are essentially what farm beasts are to the farmer — creatures to be either worked, exploited, and used up, or banished to the wild margins of society and beyond.

Socialism is the plain and obvious answer to the problems our world faces. By that I mean the very opposite of Stalinism: rational, democratic planning of our social and economic affairs, which means also of our ecological affairs; the application of consistent reciprocal democracy (instead of war) to the solution of the economic, national, and religious conflicts of our world.

IS SOCIALISM DISCREDITED BY STALINISM?

B. All through history there have been people like you — recklessly putting at risk what has been achieved, what is, in pursuit of untried and allegedly better alternatives — the benefits that supposedly might come to be in the future. That some innovations have worked out well does not prove that all innovations do, or have done! In fact, the experience is that they don't. Look at socialism in practice, in the old USSR, or in China! Socialism is the bogeyman my mother threatened me with — except that socialism was real.

A. Yes, look at the old USSR — but understand it, the whys and wherefores of it! It was not socialism; it was Stalinism, the rule of a privileged, exploitative, collectivist-bureaucratic ruling class over the people. Right now, in your head, socialism is mainly a shadowy, and thereby all the more terrifying a bogeyman.

B. Ah yes, nobody understands it but you. And Stalinism had nothing to do with socialism!

A. Marxists base their socialism on certain social and economic achievements of capitalism — in the first place the development of the productive forces to a very high level of productivity. The Stalinist system emerged, proclaiming itself to be building socialism in one country, by overthrowing working-class rule, and in circumstances in which, according to Marx and according to the leaders of the Russian Revolution, the basic social and economic prerequisites of their socialism were not present. Backward Russia was way behind the advanced capitalist countries. So what is wrong about refusing to accept Stalinism as "socialism" in the Marxist sense? The perversity here is yours. I don't know about you personally, but in many anti-socialists these arguments are post-Stalinist jitters and political-philosophical funk. Get over Stalinism! Look around you at the foulness that immerses us all under capitalism, and the squandering of the opportunities that capitalism's development of the productive forces gives us for creating a better social world.

B. But facts are facts. Every thoroughgoing attempt to make socialism has resulted in tyranny. Maybe the intentions of the socialists were good. But the results were horrific. Every time. It's a truly terrible story, the story of 20th century socialism...

A. Of Stalinism!

B. ...And yet you still advocate "socialism"! Socialism? Why on earth should I be a socialist? Why should anyone in the 21st century be a socialist? What socialism? There is no viable, clean, uncontami-

15

nated socialism left. Jumping out of the capitalist frying pan into the Stalinist fire, or risking that we will end up again in the totalitarian Stalinist fire, makes no sense. Learn from history! Socialists today are people incapable of learning from history — fond and fixated sentimentalists, fantasists, masochists, or political fuckwits, or all of them together. The much-cited quotation puts it neatly: those who do not learn from history are likely to repeat it. That's you, mate, and the count-them-on-one-hand little tribe of your co-thinkers.

A. Yes, socialism is less of a political force now than it has been for over a hundred years. Stalinism, which Trotsky called the "syphilis" or, again, the "leprosy" of the labour movement, undermined, sapped, butchered, and discredited the old socialist movement. It turned the Stalinist-controlled part of the labour movement into a confused enemy of liberty, equality, fraternity, and unfettered reason — in short, into an enemy of socialism as it was before Stalin. Today the socialists must live and do their political work amidst the ideological ruins, the discouragement, the revulsion, and the poisonous ideological vapours that constitute the legacy of Stalinism. Old socialism, pre-Stalinist and anti-Stalinist socialism, has been buried beneath the ruins of the collapsed Stalinist, but self-named socialist, system.

We live under an incessant bombardment of anti-socialist propaganda from the capitalists and their collaborators in the labour movements. The burden of their message is this: because Stalinism has failed, therefore socialism has failed. They say that Stalinism was authentic socialism, and the only possible socialism, although in fact Stalinism killed more honest socialists than German, Italian, and Spanish fascism put together.

In the early and mid 1920s most of the surviving Bolsheviks came out against Stalinism at one point or another — that is, against the bureaucratic dictatorship taking shape. From late 1927 Stalin drove the Bolshevik opposition into exile, then into labour camps. To establish its full control, in the 1930s the Stalin gang massacred most of the surviving revolutionaries of 1917, leaders and rank-and-file members alike. It massacred both those in internal exile or in the labour camps, and those who had capitulated to Stalin in the vain hope that capitulation would win them a chance to do positive work inside the bureaucratic machine.

It massacred even those who in the disputes of the 1920s had made up the Stalin faction. Of the 1,996 party delegates at the 100%-Stalinist "Congress of Victors" in 1934, Stalin's gang had 1,108 ar-

16

rested, and maybe 700 killed, within three years. Of the 139 members elected to the "Central Committee" at that Congress, Stalin would kill 98. And yet you insist that Bolshevism and Stalinism, the murdered and their murderers, are identical!

The defenders of capitalism take over, turn around, and use for their own purposes the great lie of the Stalinists. Stalinism, they say, was socialism; Stalinism was Bolshevism; the Stalinist states were Marxism come to life — and therefore socialism, Bolshevism, and Marxism are now deservedly dead and rotting. This is the United Front of the Liars Against Socialism!

B. No, it's the United Front of the Truth-Tellers Against Socialism! As anyone who knows modern history can tell you, Stalinism was socialism. The Stalinists told the truth about socialism and their relation to it. They gave their system its true name: socialism.

A. Unscrupulously, you annex and deploy the old lies of old Stalinism, putting them work for the bourgeois enemies of socialism. In fact, of course, the leaders of the Stalinist counter-revolution in the USSR in the 1920s and '30s wrote and rewrote history to suit themselves, threading and weaving a mass of totalitarian lies into its very fabric, and centrally the cardinal lie that Stalinism was socialism, the natural and necessary outcome of the Russian workers' socialist revolution of 1917.

The Stalinists in their time claimed, and the bourgeois enemies of socialism claim today, that Stalinism or something like it would be the inevitable result of any effort to establish a socialist society. We anti-Stalinist socialists know that Stalinism had nothing in common with the aims, the modes, the methods, and the objectives of real communism and socialism; that communism and Stalinism were, as Trotsky put it, like Cain and Abel (the two brothers in the bible Book of Genesis, one of whom murdered the other). The triumph of the lie that Stalinism and socialism were identical played an enormous part for decades in hypnotising would-be communist workers throughout the world into accepting Stalinism.

B. It's not a lie that Stalinism was socialism, and socialism was Stalinism. It is the plain truth.

A. Today the only rational answer to the urgent needs of society for economic and political democracy, for rational planning of the economy, and for responsible ecological politics, is socialism, real socialism. It is the precondition of continued human progress, and, maybe, for the survival of civilisation itself.

You insist that the self-naming as socialism by the rulers of the to-talitarian Stalinist states entitle you to identify socialism with all the horrors of Stalinism and to proclaim that the historical regressiveness and all-around corruption of Stalinism means the bankruptcy of so-cialism and the end of the road for honest socialist aspirations.

OK. What's sauce for the goose is sauce for the gander, as they say. The rulers of the Stalinist states didn't only call themselves commu-nists and socialists; they also called themselves democrats, and their system democratic. The official name of the satellite states — Poland, Czechoslovakia, Hungary, etc. — was "People's Democracies". Their international magazine in the 1940s and 50s was, believe it or not, called: *For a Lasting Peace, for a People's Democracy*. Stalin proclaimed the advent of "full democracy" in the new Stalinist constitution of 1936. It was "the most democratic Constitution in the world", its ad-mirers said, and they were not all fully paid-up dyed-in-the-lies Stal-inists. They included the venerable British Fabians, Beatrice and Sidney Webb, and many such Stalinist "non-Stalinists". If the Stalin-ists' fraudulent claim to be socialists damns and stigmatises all so-cialists for ever after, and Stalinism's collapse proves socialism impossible — why does their no less fraudulent claim to be democ-rats not discredit democracy?

B. Because real democracies — what you call bourgeois, pluto-cratic democracies — existed side-by-side with the Stalinist "democ-racies", and continue to exist and multiply long after the collapse of European Stalinism. Show me an example of working class socialism side-by-side with what you call the fraudulent socialism of the Stal-inists! Then I might accept the point you're trying to make.

A. There was no socialist state or society existing in parallel to Stal-inism; but there were socialist movements, including those who fought against Stalinism in the name of the socialist ideas which ex-isted before Stalinism and continued side by side with it. The anti-Stalin socialists counterposed that socialism to Stalinism, and based a radical critique of Stalinism on it. If you want to say that there was no socialist state side by side with the USSR to contrast to it, that's true. But it is not the whole truth. My case for socialism is not that it has been put into practice already. It is that humanity must go for-ward to something new, and that must be socialism, the socialism of the socialists who fought against Stalinism, and many of whom died fighting Stalinism. The Stalinist states had nothing to do with democracy of any kind. But they had nothing to do with socialism, either. Think about the fact that masses and masses of people believed in the democracy proclaimed by the Stalinists, just as many people believe that the truncated and severely limited democracy we have in countries like Britain is the best democracy possible. The Stalinist ideologists argued, when they deigned to argue, and convincingly to a lot of people, that things like housing, assured employment, public health care, etc., were the real stuff of democracy in the USSR. Conflating distinct things, they redefined democracy as no unemployment and things like that.

B. The virtues they claimed for the USSR — housing, for example — were not really there either, any more than democracy was.

A. Indeed! But leave that aside, for now.

B. On democracy those socialist...

A. Stalinist!

A.... arguments ducked the issue. They were sleights of mind. They substituted something else for the thing under debate — democracy, self-rule by the demos, the people. People politically enslaved may have all the social amenities you like, though of course they didn't, and in a society of scarcity couldn't; but they don't have democracy.

A. Again, yes indeed. We can agree on that. But mark you this: a major reason why people thought Stalinism democratic was the social shallowness of bourgeois democracy — how little real control over society it gives us. That's what made them receptive to the Stalinist demagogues who substituted lying patter about jobs and housing, etc., for political democracy.

B. Socialism is the eternal virgin in its own head but — excuse my old-fashioned, politically-incorrect language — a scabby whore in reality. Yours is Blanche Du Bois socialism! Good works, not good intentions! Socialism? All fine words and intentions, and, once in power, something else entirely. Give it up! You're not fooling anyone any more. The idea that socialism can revive, or even survive as a set of ideas among sensible people is preposterous. It is a bit like the Trinity (three persons in one god), or the Real Presence (the little bit of communion bread is literally, not symbolically, the body and blood of Christ). You will get believers still, but not among seriously rational people.

To believe in the revival of socialism, you need to have a very low opinion of people's intelligence. You can fool some of the people all of the time, and all the people some of the time, but not with "socialism", any more, thank God! People learn, albeit painfully. And they don't forget. They remember.

A. Yes! People learn, and will go on learning. And nothing is more obvious now, in the still unresolved world capitalist crisis that opened in 2007-8, than that capitalism, which was the dominant system even in the 20th century world that included Stalinism (Stalinism, not socialism!), has contradictions which it cannot quell or resolve.

B. Capitalism has contradictions? Yes — but it is not dead. The capitalists learn. You refuse to learn.

A. Capitalism supposedly learned from the great slump after the stock-market crash of 1929. Governments imposed restrictions on bankers and devised new state-spending and credit policies designed to avoid similar things in the future. Has it worked? It hasn't..

B. It worked for a long time. Like democracy, capitalism may be riddled with faults — but all the alternatives are worse. That is what history tells us. You refuse to listen.

A. Listen to *yourself!* Your argument is essentially that because some people calling themselves socialists and communists acted in ways that contradicted all the promise of something better than capitalism which old socialism seemed to offer, and created Stalinism — something worse than capitalism — therefore socialism is and deserves to be discredited. The underlying assumption is that capitalism is thereby rendered acceptable and that the socialist critique of capitalism can be brushed aside. But it can't be. Why? Because we live still in the grip of a crazily rapacious and anti-human capitalism.

B. I think most people would say my conclusion about socialism being discredited is common sense. Your "socialism" is a picture of the Virgin Mary on the walls of a brothel — or of Gandhi or Tolstoy on the walls of a homicide chamber!

The pictures would not affect what went on in those places — and only fools would define the places by the pictures on the wall.

On the actual history of real socialism as the 20th century knew it, you offer evasion, special pleading, and bad faith. Socialism? Socialism is what *you* say it is, and therefore you reject responsibility for any other socialism, and for the real, historical socialism, what you try to insist was Stalinism. As the fond mother said when she saw her son marching in a platoon of soldiers: "Oh look — they're all out of step except my Johnny!"

A. Socialism and Marxism existed long before Stalinism. It is perfectly sensible not to define socialism by Stalinism, but to measure Stalinism by the earlier socialist goals, norms, and aspirations, and by the Marxist and Bolshevik criticism of Stalinism.

PUBLIC OWNERSHIP

B. Stalinism grew out of socialism, out of what you think was a workers' revolution — I would rather say: the myth that the October 1917 Bolshevik coup was a workers' revolution. Stalinism did what socialists advocated and "nationalised", statised, the economy, eliminated the bourgeoisie, the Tsar and the old aristocracy.

You imagine yourself pure because you say that "socialism" and "left" are just what you say they are, and not what everyone else says they are!

A. Would you accept being equated with all those who call themselves "right-wing" or "conservative"? You wouldn't. The self-definition of the left, in capitalist society, is always and inevitably a struggle against rabid misrepresentation and unreasoning prejudice.

B. The leftists who see future socialism as a modified version of what you call Stalinism have logic on their side. Those 20th century socialist states had what even you see as the main condition of socialism, public ownership of the main means of production.

A. Do you seriously think that for socialists nationalisation is socialism, irrespective of everything else in society? Of who rules in society? But it isn't. It never was. What do you think those who made the Russian Revolution believed? In common with all Marxists then, they believed:

"State ownership and control is not necessarily socialism — if it were, then the Army, the Navy, the police, the judges, the gaolers, the informers, and the hangmen, all would all be socialist functionaries, as they are state officials — but the ownership by the state of all the land and materials for labour, combined with the co-operative control by the workers of such land and materials, would be socialism... An immense gulf separates the 'nationalising' proposals of the middle class from the 'socialising' demands of the revolutionary working class. The first proposes to endow a class state... with certain powers and functions to be administered in the common interest of the possessing class; the second proposes to subvert the class state and replace it with the socialist state, representing organised society — the socialist republic.

"To the cry of the middle class reformers, 'make this or that the property of the government', we reply, 'yes, in proportion as the workers are ready to make the government their property'."

B. Who are you quoting?

A. That was James Connolly. He was shot by the British state after trying to establish the right of the Irish nation to democratic self-rule, 18 months before the October Revolution. Nationalisation without democracy and without a workers' state, so Marxist socialists thought then, would produce only the tyranny of an elite. George Plekhanov declared: "There will not be any self-government by the people and the revolution which has taken place may lead to a political monster similar to the ancient Chinese or Peruvian empires, i.e., to a renewal of tsarist despotism with a communist lining".

B. Plekhanov opposed the Bolsheviks in 1917

A. Yes. But Trotsky was a central leader of the Bolsheviks in 1917. He wrote in 1936, of Russian "socialism": "The means of production belong to the state. But the state, so to speak, 'belongs' to the bureaucracy." In fact, the nationalisation of everything, even the street corner shops, was specific to Stalinism. It came out of the Stalinist bureaucracy's drive in a backward country to eliminate all rivalry for control of the surplus product, even that of small shopkeepers, artisans and so on. In this also Stalinism was a product of backwardness.

B. Such concentration of economic, social, and political power in the hands of the state inevitably produces tyranny. You say there were people in the Russian revolution who did not like what the state created by the revolution became? I'll admit that socialists often have good intentions. But those intentions are not realisable. The attempt to realise them will always produce tyranny.

A. Why?

B. Because widespread public ownership inevitably gives great power to those who control the government machine. They will inevitably use that power in their own interests. Democracy can exist stably only in an economy where ownership is dispersed. It is bound to perish where it is concentrated.

A. That doesn't augur well for capitalism, then, does it? The big corporations are becoming more and more dominant. Under modern capitalism, ownership is becoming more and more concentrated.

B. With a free market there are always limits to that concentration. There are always new competitors.

A. The big businesses dominate, even if from time to time one big corporation declines and another takes its place at the top. Maybe capitalist competition stops the general administration of society being dominated by a single fixed cartel of leading capitalists. Nonetheless it remains dominated by the general interests of all big business.

B. Not as completely as with public ownership of all the major enterprises.

A. That depends on democracy, or the absence of it. Your argument about the inevitability of tyranny with widespread public ownership is really an argument that democracy is impossible. Or rather, you concede that present-day parliamentary democracy is too weak to stop big-business bosses dominating; you assume that no better democracy is possible; and so you "prove" to your satisfaction that public ownership can only be bureaucratic ownership, and never democratic collective ownership.

That could not be true under a regime of all-pervading social and economic democracy. With the abolition of privileges for representatives and officials. With a system which allows everyone the same access to the means of information, and to free time for political activity, which the well-off monopolise today. With a state in the process of withering away, losing its coercive tools and functions. With a functioning socialist economy, society, and politics.

B. You hope!

A. Yes, but with more than uninformed, unintelligent, and merely passive hope. Socialists fight for that fuller democracy. We can and will achieve it. It is central to our socialist political program.

B. You ignore history: you juggle frivolously and irresponsibly with abstract theory, fond ideals, early socialist utopian blueprints! It's irrelevant. Stalin was the real socialist. Stalinism was the real socialism, the practical consequence of a socialist coup.

A. What I'm telling you is what socialism meant before Stalinism, and to the Marxist critics and enemies of Stalinism, in the first place, to Trotsky. This is a straightforward question of fact. The choice is: either measure Stalinism against socialist politics and socialist theory before Stalinism and thus put Stalinism in historical perspective. Or arbitrarily set up Stalinism not only as socialism, but as the only possible socialism. That is shoddy polemic, not serious discussion. You rest entirely on the fact that Stalin said it was socialism, and said, no less falsely, that it was rooted in the October Revolution. Yet the Stalinists slaughtered the Bolshevik party. I repeat: the Stalinists killed more socialists than Hitler and Mussolini and Franco combined! You use Stalinism to rule out, wipe out, crush all serious discussion of socialism and the real history of the Russian workers' revolution and its fate, of the Stalinist counter-revolution that destroyed it. It could be said that here you use the historical fact of Stalinism in a totalitarian way — indeed, in a Stalinist way!

You bury yourself in the crassest know-nothing anti-socialist claptrap, using Stalinism as your excuse! Why you make the historical experience of Stalinism the greatest thing in any discussion of socialism is, of course, no mystery: you can be self-righteous about Stalinism and avoid discussing socialism beyond making that false identification.

STALINISM IN HISTORY

B. It is no mystery why you repudiate the idea that Stalinism was the socialism it undoubtedly was and proclaimed itself to be.

24

A. The history of Stalinism was simultaneously the history of socialist anti-Stalinism. Stalinism was not the only self-proclaimed socialism. Authentic working-class socialists measured the USSR against socialist hopes, perspectives, norms, basic Marxist theory; against the programme in the name of which the Russian Revolution was made; against the socialist commitment to working-class freedom and democracy. Those critics included the leaders of the Russian Revolution, which you think evolved smoothly into Stalinism!

B. It did evolve smoothly. The same party remained in power. There was no coup.

A. Vladimir Lenin, with his last dying strength, tried to remove Joseph Stalin from his central place in the Communist Party of the Soviet Union and in the state. Trotsky led the Bolshevik opposition to Stalin and Stalinism. To defeat that opposition, Stalin had to destroy the real Bolshevik party, and keep only its name. Trotsky kept up a running commentary on Stalinism for 17 years, criticising it, denouncing and damning it, and putting forward programs and strategies for the working class struggle against it. He measured its deepening degeneration against the program of the October Revolution and the Bolsheviks who led it.

He criticised the forced collectivisation and the breakneck industrialisation, the enslavement of the working class, driven like cattle by the Stalinists, the degradation of Marxism into a mere bureaucratic pidgin-religion, a system of rationalising whatever Stalin did. He tried to organise the USSR workers to make a new working-class revolution against Stalinism. He led a whole generation of Bolsheviks who fought Stalinism to the death. The very least any honest anti-Bolshevik can say in face of these facts is that something more is involved in this history than the smooth evolution of Vladimir Lenin's and Leon Trotsky's Bolshevism into its own opposite, and its own murderer, Stalinism.

The grim joke here is that Stalinism lied and misrepresented itself and its history to claim continuity with Bolshevism — and long after European Stalinism is in its grave the bourgeoisie takes over, cherishes, nurtures, and disseminates this part of the legacy of Stalinism!

B. But Stalin and his friends decided what happened — and that's what is historically important. That is the history! If there was a struggle within Bolshevism, and of course everybody knows that there was, the Stalinists won, and that was no accident. Stalin and his followers never ceased to call themselves socialists and Marxists.

A. I might call myself the true king of Ireland, but you wouldn't believe me if I did, would you? In fact Trotsky and the Opposition embodied Bolshevism counterposing itself to Stalinism and fighting against it. They were leaders of both the revolution — Trotsky organised the insurrection in St Petersburg in 1917 — and of the fight to stop, destroy, undo the Stalinist counter-revolution against the working class.

B. But they did not shape what happened! Stalin developed the real-world practice and theory of 20th century socialism. What Stalin did was socialism — full stop!

A. In other words, what Stalin and his successors and emulators *said*, or *thought*, they were doing, when they did what they did, made it socialism! What Stalin did was socialism, because he said it was. It was Bolshevism, because he said it was. It was Marxism, because he said it was. What he did, the semi-slave society he created, was Marxist, Bolshevik Socialism — because he said it was! (Though somehow, even though he said it was democracy incarnate, that doesn't matter: you know it wasn't.)

B. Because it wasn't democracy.

A. Who anointed Stalin Pope, who appointed him Caliph?

B. He anointed himself Pope! He sanctified and empowered himself. He made himself dictator and Pope of the socialist and Marxist world, and that's what counts. Stalin in his own way was a great man.

A. Yes, of course: he'd have been a great capitalist entrepreneur and a millionaire had he had the good fortune to be born in the USA or Britain! The Stalinists proclaimed themselves the only socialists — and you rush in to back them up. You won't hear a word said against that proposition! If you had lived and decided to be a socialist...

B. God forbid!

A. ... in Stalin's time you would have been a Stalinist! God protect us from political simple-mindedness and shell-armoured ignorance!

B. God protect us from people in a state of political and historical denial!

A. The Stalinists always were the bourgeoisie's ideal socialists and they still are! And you and your similars sput the lies of the Stalinist state about socialism and Marxism and Bolshevism: the great lie that they were the only socialists, Marxists, Bolsheviks, Leninists. The Stalinists had one sort of role for that compound lie; you have another one. In both cases you target the truth about Bolshevism, socialism, Marxism, the Russian workers' revolution. In this you are, so to speak, in a retrospective alliance with the Stalinists. You malign the memory of those who led the most democratic revolution in history, and those Bolsheviks who fought Stalin as long as they were alive.

The Stalinists' lie that they were democrats you ignore. You haven't explained why.

B. Obviously they weren't.

A. What in logic and consistency gives you the right to pick and choose like that? To say that the Stalinists' claim to be the only social-ists damns socialism, but their claim to be the best democrats leaves democracy untainted? You can't have it both ways.

B. Not everything they said was lies! And in proclaiming them-selves the socialists, they told the truth. They were the people who made socialism work — for a while. You deny that because you want to slough off the responsibility that goes with acknowledging that Stalinism was socialism epitomised.

A. Large numbers of people of my political persuasion "sloughed off" Stalinism when it was at its acme. They lived in its Gulag or died fighting it outside Russia — in Spain, Greece, France, Vietnam, and other places — in the name of socialism, of working-class commu-nism, of the October 1917 revolution and of social and political democracy.

B. You can't wipe socialism clean with such weasel words!

A. You — you use the Stalinists' anthraxed "socialism" to make the capitalists seem clean and healthy by contrast with the Stalinists. Historical truth is the casualty.

B. Aren't they clean, by comparison?

A. Are they? Depends which capitalists, at which stage of capitalist development, you take. Nothing was dirtier than German capitalism under the geno-maniacal Nazis.

B. Now you are using criticism of capitalism to excuse Stalinism

A. I don't "excuse" Stalinism! I reiterate: the real socialists and Marxists criticised and condemned the crimes of the Stalinists, from forced collectivisation at the beginning of the 1930s, through China's Cultural Revolution (from 1966), to the invasion of Afghanistan in December 1979. In the historically short time of its existence, Stalinism was worse than capitalism. I don't deny that, or weasel-word my way around it. I deny that socialism has anything in common with those horrors. I deny that those horrors justify and exonerate capitalism.

B. Yes, of course you deny it. You have to, in order to resist the necessary logical conclusion from that terrible experience!

A. Logic! Logical reasoning needs to be a valid chain: you create an artificial chain of your own. You ignore everything that speaks against the identity of working-class socialism and Stalinism.

B. You simply won't accept what is obvious to all sensible people: Stalinism killed socialism. First it corrupted the old socialist ideals. They're not my ideals, but they were not negligible or contemptible ideas and ideals. Then Stalinism destroyed socialism — the scorpion eating its own poisoned tail. Socialism is dead.

A. The way you damn socialism by accepting every claim to be socialist by those whose behaviour you dislike is sleight of mind, evasion, and, essentially, political cowardice and irresponsibility.
In the 20th century, Hitler, Stalin, David Ben Gurion, Clement Attlee, Fidel Castro, Leon Blum, Gamal Abdul Nasser, Saddam Hussein, Mao Zedong, Leon Trotsky, Rosa Luxemburg, Buenaventura Durruti — they all called themselves "socialists" — socialists, or Arab socialists, national socialists, Ba'th socialists, Zionist socialists, anarchist socialists, etc. All of them except the anarchist socialists had a common element of sorts in the word "socialism", namely state and social action. But, if they are defined by what they did, or by the doctrine

28

they proclaimed and under whose banner they mobilised to act, or by the social classes for which they acted, they can't all have been equally socialist. Say they were all socialists because they all said they were, and you reduce socialism to a meaningless word. Yes, that, I suppose, is pretty much what the 20th century itself did to the word "socialism". But it is not the end of the story.

The Stalinists in power insisted they were socialists. Their anti-socialist opponents agreed wholeheartedly that yes, the Stalinists were socialists, and, yes, they were the only possible socialists. That settles it: there is nothing more to think about or say. I'll tell you why your glib abuse of socialism is a foolish brake on perception, thought, and understanding: it functions as special pleading for capitalism. That's the point of it. It works to crowd out discussion of capitalism as what it is: a particular historical socio-economic formation, one of a number. To crowd out discussion of whether or not a better system than capitalism can exist. Whatever capitalism is, however horrible aspects of it are, there is, you insist, no better alternative, because Stalinism was worse. You say Stalinism was the socialist alternative to capitalism, and therefore there is no real alternative.

On the level of historical fact and of serious argument it is a frame-up. Marxist socialism, communism, cannot just be sunk into a mere vague word, "socialism", and equated with what Stalin or Mao or Hitler did in power. It cannot be made responsible for everything done by people calling themselves socialists or prefix-socialists. Marxist socialism was never just a matter of general aspirations and wishes for a better or an ideal world, such as many "socialisms" had been across the centuries as far back as classical Greece and Plato, most likely even earlier. It was never a "utopia", an ideal, arbitrary blueprint worked out in someone's head to be imposed on reality. It was a thoroughly worked-out account of social history, an analysis of capitalism, of its laws of motion, its history, its tendencies, and its necessary evolution. The socialism of Marx — our socialism — was, in its analysis and its expectations from that analysis, based on the history of capitalism, its evolution, the concentration and socialisation of production and distribution which capitalism brings through its own development. That is still true.

B. If socialism is inevitable, if it exists, so to speak, in the "genes" of capitalist society, then why didn't it break through the barriers in the 20th century?

A. Because the economic dynamic works itself out, and can only

29

work itself out, through people — through the class struggle between the exploited, the have-nots, and the exploiters, the "haves". And we were defeated in that struggle in the 20th century. The owners dispose of great wealth and the services of many people tied to them by privileges and pay-outs. The "haves" are tied to the system that gives them wealth and the power of shaping and reshaping society now. Naturally they defend it. An individual here and there from among them may change sides in the conflict and come over to socialism, but this powerful class stands like a gigantic series of rocks across the highway of history, across the logical and necessary development of humanity further along the road capitalism itself has already built, and indicates still.

B. Indicates?

A. The inner conflict of capitalist society is about how the *socialised*, but not yet *socialist*, forces of production should be operated, and for whom. For the owners' private profit, or for the good of society as a whole? This ruling class has inflicted defeat, again and again, on those who tried to resolve the contradiction between society and the private ownership of the social means of production, exchange, and communications.

Societies do not only go forward. The class struggle can lead, and in history has led, to stagnation and regression, to a lesser society — to what Marx and Engels as long ago as the Communist Manifesto of 1848 called "the mutual ruination of the contending classes". Much of the history of the 20th century is the history of the partial or temporary ruination of the contending classes: the utter ruination of Germany and other parts of Europe in the 1940s, for instance. A progressive solution to the inner conflict of capitalism requires the victory over the ruling class of the opposite group — the triumph of the non-owners of the means of production.

B. More double-talk. The idea of the working class as the protagonist of the socialist revolution is a mystical-religious elevation of the poor and the downtrodden and exploited in someone's well-meaning head.

A. The proletariat was a product of capitalism, and is so now. Around the world, there are greatly more of us now than there ever were. We say that the proletariat, the wage-labour class of people who, to live, must sell their labour-power, is the bearer of socialism.

30

Why? Because it alone can resolve the contradiction within capitalism between private ownership and socialised production. And how? By establishing collective social control, democratic control, over the production processes that knit together vast social networks. The working class will do that because it needs to free itself from exploitation and social mistreatment and general social mismanagement by the buyers of labour-power. In the French and similar revolutions the land of the great landlords could be divided up by their former serfs, the peasantry. Modern industry can not be divided up like that. It can only be owned by the working class and by all the working people collectively. And that also, necessarily, means democratically.

B. So you say. But in the 20th century collective ownership meant tyranny!

A. You can't have real collective ownership without democracy. I mean collective ownership by the working class, by the people. Not "collective ownership" by a small minority, by a ruling bureaucracy. Collectively-controlled economy without democracy is a contradiction in terms: either the people own collectively, and that means democratically, or it is the sham collectivism of Stalinist state ownership. As Trotsky puts it: if the state owns the economy, then the question is, who "owns" the state? Who has political power?

That is the decisive question. The working class, in aspiring to own the great enterprises produced by capitalism, can only aspire to own them collectively and thus democratically (unlike the peasants, who could divide up the land taken from the big landlords).

B. In actual history, socialism...

A. Stalinism!

B. Let me finish! In actual history, socialism is the enemy of democracy.

A. In the early 19th century, many would have said that in actual history, democratic republics had only produced tyrannies like Napoleon Bonaparte's; that they were the enemies of a freedom possible only with a constitutional monarchy and a right to vote restricted to a propertied minority. In the 20th century, there were regimes which called themselves "socialist", as they also called themselves "democratic", which were the enemies of democracy. But when they called themselves "socialist", they lied in order to camouflage what in fact they were. If the Stalinists, the Maoists, the Ba'thists, were "the socialists", then the socialism and communism of Marx and Lenin need another name. The eruption of those alien formations, Nazi or Stalinist, which took on the name socialist because it was popular, did not mean that authentic socialism sank into being just one of the variants of "socialism" or "prefix-socialism" (Ba'thist Arab socialism, national socialism, Zionist socialism, etc.) The criticism of these political formations by their contemporary Marxist socialists is enough to establish that.

B. Sheer evasion! Intellectual dishonesty!

A. There is nothing evasive or in-bad-faith about taking those things into account. There is evasion, special pleading, self-blinding, and vicious know-nothing bad faith in doing what you do. You damn Marxist socialism, working-class socialism, on the basis of the history of the most powerful groups that called themselves socialist or communist in the 20th century. In fact, of political formations that oppressed the workers and did not meet the criteria of working-class or Marxist socialism. Least of all the key criterion: self-liberation of the working-class.

Marxists had never said that state control of the economy, implemented by no matter whom, would bring progress. They had said the opposite. Those so-called "socialist" political formations developed in societies which lacked the economic precondition for working-class socialism which Marxism named in its most basic doctrine — advanced capitalist economy. They developed on social bases very different from the politically-aware working class to which Marxists looked as agency; and without the democracy which Marxists saw as an essential political precondition for socialism. They were political formations whose ideas had been rejected and denounced in advance by Marxists, Bolsheviks, socialists, and which massacred a vast number of Marxist socialists. It is a frame-up!

B. It tags you fair and square for what you are!

A. If you insist, use *words* like socialism and communism to describe the horrors of the 20th century, and choose another name for what I'm calling socialism — "democratic collectivism", or a less clumsy term, if you can think of one. But stop fooling yourself with the pretence that Stalinism and its like were what Marx and Lenin

32

talked about and acted for. Or what they defined as scientific social-ism. Stop blinding yourself! Stop misleading those who take your misrepresentations as intellectual good coin. Stop brandishing Stal-inism as a scarecrow against those who fought Stalinism and, of course, fascism, to the death. Stop using the old horrors of Stalinism to excuse the present horrors of capitalism. Stop pretending that the fundamental and explosive contradictions generated by the very de-velopment of capitalism have gone away, or that they will go away of their own accord.

B. Of course I want to resist your socialistic conclusions from the faults and crimes of capitalism! Suicide is not a solution to the prob-lems that go with being alive. Socialist suicide is not a solution to the social and economic problems of life under capitalism.

The only possible economic basis for social liberty is market cap-italism. "Liberticide" is too self-murdering and others-murdering a price for eliminating the faults and difficulties of capitalism.

Whatever those difficulties, under capitalism we have democracy, liberty, the right to life and to pursue happiness.

A. What you and others like you do is a form of ideological bully-work, or intellectual terrorism, in the first place against yourselves. Stop frightening yourself into know-nothing mindlessness and a-his-torical accounts of capitalism and Stalinism both! Your approach has inhibited god knows how many people of good will from drawing socialist conclusions from the crisis of world capitalism since 2007. Socialism? they think. No, that is that Stalinist horror story we all know so well. Stop using Stalinism as the great scarecrow of history to frighten away all serious discussion of capitalism and its place in history, as well as of socialism. Stop pretending that liberty and the right to pursue happiness are tied to and inseparable from capitalist exploitation and de facto plutocratic rule.

WHAT IS SOCIALISM?

B. You political Houdinis of socialism are good at criticising and rubbishing the society we live in. You are less forthcoming about your own positive alternative to it. You say that the elaboration of a picture of a socialist society would be "unscientific", arbitrary, and pointless, because you don't know in detail how things will evolve. That puts people like me at a disadvantage. We defend what is, what we know, what critics also can see and know and denounce. You "defend" the vague and shadowy future, and say that in detail it is unknowable. What, positively, would a socialist society as you conceive of it be like?

A. Socialism is human solidarity raised from a system of working class bonding in resistance to our exploiters to be the guiding principle of all society. It is the enthronement of unfettered reason armed with enlightenment and democracy in all the social, economic and political affairs of society.

Society will collectively own and democratically control and administer the bulk of productive wealth. Every major industry will be reorganised roughly like the National Health Service at its ideal best — with full provision for need as its reigning principle. It will be democratically controlled by workers, by consumers, and by the overall community.

The privileges and perks of managers, officials, bureaucrats and shareholders will be abolished. There will be democratic self-rule in all aspects and on all levels of society and in the economy, in short, in all the circumstances and conditions of our lives — democratic self-rule that will be far more flexible, responsive and accountable than any government is today. Each electorate will control its representatives and be able to use a right of recall and re-election at any time. There will be a living democracy in the social and economic affairs of humankind, where now there exists only pluto-democracy, money-dominated democracy — shallow, often socially and economically impotent, mere-political democracy. The whole industrial structure can thus be planned, in broad outline, to meet human need.

That means no rich and no poor, no profit-as-goal and no wage-slavery, no palaces and no homeless, no jobless and no-one overworked on the treadmills of profit. The working week will be cut to a level which enables all to have ample free time to devote to social and political affairs and to self-development as individuals — by study, sport, art, handicrafts, friendship, travel, or whatever they wish that does not harm or hinder others. Socialism means liberty as well as economic planning.

B. Still too vague and shadowy.

A. There is nothing vague or shadowy about what socialists propose. Maybe the vagueness and shadowiness you perceive are an aspect of your refusal to see this clearly.

B. Or maybe it's a result of built-in imprecision and vagueness in the ideas you expound.

A. Socialist ideas are an accumulation from Marx's analysis, from the history of capitalism, and from working-class struggle and experience. Socialism would build on the science, the technology, the economic cooperation, the working-class solidarity, and more, developed within capitalism, but free them from being poisoned by exploitation and all that goes with it, and thwarted by the profit-drive. The economy would be run in a cooperative way, for the benefit of society, and not for private profit. The economy would be operated in the interests not of a few but of everyone. Socialism would end the compulsion inbuilt in capitalist society for the workers to sell their labour power — their active lives, most of their conscious hours of life — to people intent on making money out of their labour power, that is, on exploiting them. Employers put them to work, on the employer's terms, for a certain time each day during which the workers create for the employer much more than the value of the wage they cost the employer. The bedrock class struggle — the workers' struggle for higher wages and shorter hours, and the bosses' resistance to that — is a tussle over possession of the surplus product created by workers which becomes the property of the buyer of labour power.

B. You are talking not about capitalist society as people like me experience it and see it, but about a picture of reality, a "construing" of facts in a way that is peculiar to yourself and a few others. It is fond and blatant ideologising. That is why that view is unpopular now. People have seen through it.

A. Well, yes, of course. Marx and Engels put it well: the ruling ideas in every society are the ideas of the ruling class. The class struggle also takes place on the level of ideas and conceptions of class and of society.

B. And the fact that so many of us see it differently settles your hash, the socialist hash!

A. Not forever! Events such as the 2008 economic semi-collapse of capitalism speak powerfully for our picture of reality, the Marxist picture. But you asked what socialism would be like.

B. And you gave me a litany of things socialist society won't be!

35

A. I gave you much more than that, but what's wrong with capitalism is fundamental to the case for socialism. Positively, at the most basic level, I see socialism as a world run like a good, caring family is run now: sharing, taking care of everyone's needs, treating all the children of the society equally, educating everyone, fully and properly. A world run according to human solidarity, without racism, sexism, or built-in disadvantage for anyone or for any groups or classes of people.

B. What you call working-class solidarity is narrow, obtuse, and limited solidarity.

A. Working-class solidarity here and now is a weapon in the class war. It is also a manifestation inside capitalism of the human solidarity of the socialist society we will build without disadvantaging any subsection of humankind, as women and people of colour are disadvantaged now, even after the progress made towards gender and race equality in the 20th century. Working-class solidarity embodies here and now the humanity of human beings living under the dog-eat-dog conditions of capitalism. As I've said, socialism will be a world run according to what William Morris called "fellowship".

B. That day-dreaming old medievalist poseur!

A. He was a Marxist! You know, much of your slant on society and on socialism depends on sheer shell-backed prejudice and self-righteous ignorance. The socialist world would be governed by the idea of unlimited and unstinting human solidarity and fellowship, whereas in capitalist society, the dominant ethos is that each person seeks ways to rob the neighbours, to steal an advantage, to monopolise possession of a desirable job. It is what Frederick Engels and earlier socialists described as the war of all against all.

SOCIALISM AND THE NATIONAL HEALTH SERVICE

A. Let's get down to cases in contemporary Britain. What do you think of the NHS?

B. What's that got to do with anything?

A. The battle between "socialism" and market capitalism, which we fight here with skirmishing words, is being fought out in life in the NHS.

B. Now you are being silly!

A. For the sake of argument, how do you see the NHS?

B. I see the NHS the way most people do. Undoubtedly a good thing.

A. And the way it has been undermined, tunnelled-under, sapped, and set up to "collapse"?

B. Has it? I don't know what you are talking about.

A. The internal market, contracting-out, cuts, and so on.

B. Necessary reforms, ensuring value for money; necessary and worthwhile economies, knitting it properly into the market system.

A. But you accept the anti-market principle of the NHS set up for the Labour government by Nye Bevan in 1948 — medical care for everyone, free at the point of delivery?

B. Well, yes. Probably the only good thing a Labour government ever did.

A. Even now, after all the changes, and despite the cost of pre-scribed medicines, the NHS is still a socialist island in a capitalist sea.

B. No, it isn't: health care is a special case, demanding special measures.

A. Why is it a special case? And if it is a special case in Britain, why not in, say, America, where lack of health care for those who can-not pay is an enormous disgrace on US society — an outrage! Obama's reforms have reduced the numbers without health insur-ance in the USA, but only down to about 11% of the population (33 million people!) in 2015. And the Republicans want to reverse Obama's reforms. If the uninsured can't pay, they go without proper medical attention.

B. The US has its own ethos, its own way of doing things.

A. Or not doing things… It has an ultra-capitalist market-is-the-one-true-god ethos. So, though you approve of the NHS, you wouldn't advocate a British style NHS for the USA?

B. No. Things could be improved, I suppose, but…

A. Things are being worsened in Britain now by the internal market. Without a good NHS, vast numbers in Britain would fall out of health care when they need it, as in America.

B. That's life!

A. That's death, often — if you can't pay, if you do not have insurance, or enough insurance. If you think about it, that's the greatest inequality imaginable, the inequality between the healthy and the sick, between the living and the dying.

B. It's a natural inequality. Nothing you can do about it. Or do you think that socialism will abolish physical decrepitude and death?

A. You can treat ill-health with state-of-the-art medical care. You can't abolish death, but you can fight it, you can fend it off, and you can enable many people to live in good health who would otherwise languish in permanent pain and impairment or die early. Without a proper health-care system — "socialised medicine" — a vast amount of needless suffering and avoidable early death is our lot. Millions of babies all over the world die for lack of medicine because their parents can't afford it, and, very often, for lack of adequate food.

B. It's a case of the glass half-full or half-empty. Think of the vast numbers saved and nurtured.

A. What that makes me think of is all the dead babies, all the avoidable sufferings and deaths, unpardonable because they are unnecessary. The problem is not uncontrollable raw nature, or uncontrollable diseases — though there are as yet uncontrollable diseases — but the paucity or withholding of technically available medical counters to nature. Those people could be saved.

B. We don't live in an ideal world.

A. But we can change it! In medicine, we do that all the time. The 1948 NHS changed things radically for most people. In Britain now the capitalist politicians are working to make the world a great deal less ideal — by undermining the NHS, with the longer-term objective of breaking it up. The Tory party has never put that to the electorate. Polls consistently show that a big majority favour the NHS.

B. You're imagining things. The Tories are not trying to break up the NHS!

A. They push to create and extend internal market relations — selling and buying between different parts of the NHS — and to contract out more and more of the service to private companies, at greatly increased cost, by the way! They push, manoeuvre, manipulate, and do things stealthily and bit by bit which will destroy the NHS. Bit by bit they are working to increase the inequalities, to make people even less equal than they are now, with the NHS.

B. The NHS is safe with the Tories! The Tory promise is the truth.

A. Suppose for the sake of argument that it isn't. If the Tories go openly for breaking up the NHS, and creating a two or three tier system of health care, with the poor on the bottom tier, will you be against that?

B. You're going to say that if I am against it, therefore I'm a socialist?

A. No, you are a socialist — sort of! -- just for a "special case"! Only, so to speak, a "conjunctural socialist".

B. Thanks — that takes a weight off my mind.

A. Why is health the only "special case"?

B. It's obvious!

A. I mean, why not other sectors? Why not social housing, for instance? Why not everything basic? Right now, isn't education another special case? Or do you think children should be unable to go to school unless their parents pay? Of course you don't.

B. But health care *is* special. Other sectors, maybe excepting education, aren't.

A. The implication of breaking up the NHS, of "rationing" essential medicine by ability to pay, of moving to a situation like that in the USA and other places, is that the sick poor are not considered equal to the better-off and the rich. Your chance of life and health depends on how much money you have. That's an attack on everything you as a democrat claim to believe.

B. Resources are limited.

A. There are vast resources. Some could be re-channelled from the rich to the NHS. Not doing that means that those without money are excluded from the best medicine society can offer. In Britain, to mess up the NHS (and ultimately to abolish it and replace it by a fully "market medicine") is to push people out of adequate health care. It is an obscenity. It is a direct assault, on the most fundamental level, on the idea of human equality. A "democracy" that can't do better than that is a pretty miserable and feeble specimen of democracy.

B. But people aren't equal, you fool!

A. Under the NHS, in health care, people in Britain were made equal, more or less. They are incrementally being made less equal, and at the most fundamental level, that of the chance of life and good health. In a plebiscite people would reject that, as they do in opinion polls. Yet it is happening — has been happening, piece by piece, for many years.

The only way it could be done, given mass support for the NHS, was piece by piece, stealthily, unacknowledgedly. What they are doing to the NHS, sapping and undermining it, flies in the face of even your democracy. It's an obscenity! It's pluto-democracy in action!

B. It's common sense. It embodies and makes explicit the reality of human inequality. As the old song has it: "If life were a thing that could buy, then the rich would live and the poor would die". Nothing you can do about it!

A. There's a lot we can do about it! Equality in health care was created by working-class political action. It can be defended and extended by working-class action.

B. Dream on! If you want equality in health care, buy yourself a good private insurance scheme.

A. And if I can't afford it?

B. Tough!

THE BOLSHEVIKS AND SOCIALISM

B. You try to separate your socialism from the historical record of Stalinism. And your better model for both socialism and democracy is what — the "Trotskyist tradition"? A feeble Bolshevik anti-Stalinist tradition? Like the good intentions of Lenin and Trotsky, and poor old Rosa Luxemburg, that counts for nothing. It is the Cheshire Cat's hologram-smile after it has vanished and been replaced by a rabid, snarling wild beast. Their good intentions are confined to the margins of the story! Your retrospective good intentions count for even less. For nothing but obfuscation and self-bamboozlement.

A. It is plain fact that the system that got locked into place at the end of the civil war, at the 10th congress of the Bolshevik party in March 1921, and the controlled unleashing then of market forces, led straight into Stalinism. It could even be argued that, with their forced collectivisation and breakneck command-industrialisation, the Stalinists, or some of them, may have drawn some of their inspiration and models from the "war communism" of the civil war. And, yes, by, let us say, 1930, Stalinism was a full-fledged, though not yet stabilised, totalitarian system

B. Being Bolsheviks, the civil-war leaders cleared the way for Stalinism!

A. The banning of factions in the party in 1921 was a tremendous Bolshevik mistake, even though it was seen as a temporary emergency measure.

B. Bolshevism was its own first mistake!

A. Bolshevism was much more than its mistakes. One of the first things the Bolsheviks did in power was abolish the death penalty!

41

And on 8 November 1917, the day after the Bolshevik-led soviets seized power, with Europe drowning in blood and the world war set to go on for another year, they issued an appeal for immediate peace, an end to the war on the basis of free self-determination for all nations and peoples.

B. Appeals are cheap — cheap as paper! Cheap as the airwaves to broadcast such things!

A. A pity the other belligerent parties didn't respond with their own "cheap" appeals for peace, but went on slaughtering. In just two of the biggest battles of the war between the time of the Bolsheviks' appeal and the eventual armistice of 11 November 1918, 804,100 men were killed and wounded in the second battle of the Somme, and 319,200 killed and wounded in the second battle of the Marne. About 160,000 soldiers were killed in those two battles.

B. At least the other governments were honest.

A. Honest imperialist butchers? No, not even that: they said they fought the war "to end war", and for the self-determination of small nations. It was the Bolsheviks who published the secret treaties that guided the imperialists at war. Listen:
"The workers' and peasants' government... calls upon all the belligerent peoples and their government to start immediate negotiations for a just, democratic peace. By a just or democratic peace... the government means an immediate peace without annexations (i.e., without the seizure of foreign lands, without the forcible incorporation of nations in states alien to them) and without indemnities...
"The government proposes an immediate armistice to the governments and people of all the belligerent countries, and, for its part, considers it desirable that this armistice should be concluded for a period of not less than three months, i.e., a period long enough to permit the competition of negotiations for peace..."

B. They didn't stick to that peaceful approach, though, did they? Therefore, it was not for them a code they lived by — it was hypocrisy.

A. They could not, in a fierce civil war, confine themselves to pacifist rules for living in a future world not yet realised. They had to fight for that future against the ruling-class gangs that had been stifling Europe, and Russia, in blood since 1914. They lived and fought in a society where to make a religious code of behaviour out of peace and forbearance would be to disarm their side, the side of the slaves in revolt, the side fighting to remove violence, oppression and exploitation from human society, the working-class side — to disarm them in face of the enemies of those ideals.

B. Don't you see the irony, the absurdity, in what you have just said?

A. To abjure force and violence in the struggle would be to let their own side be overwhelmed by the force, violence, and homicide of the other side. They lived and fought in a pre-socialist world, a world plunged death-deep into neo-barbarism, in order to act upon it and change it for the better. The Bolsheviks did not make a lifestyle out of their aspirations: they made their aspirations the inspiration for a determined battle in their here-and-now, as we do today.

B. So their ideals were meaningless! And by dropping out of the war, they strengthened German militarism against the Allies.

A. Their ideals gripped the minds of workers and soldiers in the warring countries and especially affected Germany, where there was a great socialist tradition. They helped foment the German revolution which in October-November 1918 brought down the Kaiser and brought the great capitalist slaughter to an end.

B. They just did whatever would help them keep the power they had grabbed.

A. Someone, arguing that Bolshevik and Stalinist were the same because the Bolsheviks, too, used violence, once said that the Bolsheviks had the morality of "Kaffirs". Trotsky responded: "First of all such a contemptuous reference to the Kaffirs is hardly proper from the pen of 'socialists'... If we should tell the toiler-Kaffir how the workers arose in a part of our planet and caught their exploiters unawares, he would be very pleased".

B. The Bolsheviks built an authoritarian state! That is the verdict of history on Lenin and Trotsky.

A. Yes, but whose history? Whose verdict is that?

B. The verdict of all decent people who know the facts.

A. Of prejudiced and impregnably ignorant people like you. The Bolsheviks, knowing they had a majority in the great congress of Soviets due to start on 25 October (on the old calendar; 7 November on the new), seized power on 24-25 October. On 25-26 October the Congress of Soviets, the most democratic parliament in Russian or any other history, endorsed the Bolshevik uprising and set up a new government.

B. What the Bolsheviks did was organise a coup. The idea that there was a working-class revolution is only a myth to comfort people like you. It was a Bolshevik coup; a seizure of power by the incipient totalitarians.

A. It was a seizure of power from an unelected government, which had minority support, and dwindling support at that, by people who led the majority of the most democratic parliament in history, a workers' and farmers' parliament — the Soviet. That was a revolution, not a coup. It licensed and triggered a great revolution made by the workers and peasants all through Russian society. Do you know that in 1918, the workers seized the factories and drove out the employers, ignoring the plea of the government, which wanted to move much more slowly? Coup, indeed!

B. So what? Working-class action is not self-sanctifying! To call it the most democratic parliament anywhere, more democratic than Britain, the USA, or France, is ridiculous!

A. US democracy even today is shackled by entrenched plutocratic rule and 18th century Whig "safeguards" and restraints against too precipitate democracy. The unelected Supreme Court has as much and maybe more power than Congress! In all the countries you list, in 1917 the vote was restricted. Women lacked the right to vote in all of them, with the exception of votes for state affairs in some recent frontier states of the USA. French and Belgian women did not get the right to vote until 1945. In Switzerland, believe it or not, women got the right to vote as late as 1971. In Britain large sections of the men of the working class could not vote until 1918 because they did not meet property qualifications. Women over 30 got the vote in 1918, and the vote on the same terms as those men got in 1918, at the age of 21, a decade later.

The elections in the Soviets had no constraints of property or gender. The Soviet Congress could not be vetoed by an appointed-not-elected Supreme Court. Nowhere else did the electorate have the right to recall their deputies at will, and elect new ones. The Congress of Soviets which met on 25 October (7 November) 1917 and appointed a government was indeed the most democratic parliament in history. The Bolshevik and Left-SR government it appointed was, therefore, the most democratic government in history.

B. They overthrow the previous government in a coup!

A. If the Bolsheviks had not overthrown the unelected Kerensky government, then it would probably soon have been overthrown by some would-be military dictator. An attempted military coup, by General Kornilov, had been defeated in August 1917. It was in defeating that coup that the Bolsheviks gained a great deal of the political strength that they used in October.

B. It was the Bolsheviks, not the working class, that took power.

A. Representative bodies of the working class and the peasants took power and elected a government. Bolshevik-led workers backed by the peasants and their Congress of Soviets took power. It is possible to argue, as anarchists do, that "representative government" is a contradiction in terms, and that the individuals who "hold power" are always just individuals, just themselves, and that the working class as such cannot hold power, ever. But that is an argument against representative government in general. Apply it to Britain today!

B. Not a class, but a whole nation, stands behind British governments!

A. No. A majority of elected MPs stands behind British governments, but that is all, and the majority among MPs is in its turn shaped and formed by the power and patronage of the government. Up until the Falklands war of 1982, the Thatcher government that wrought such changes in British society, presiding from mid-1979 over the destruction of much of the old industries, imposing legal shackles on trade unionism, banning solidarity strikes, condemning a generation of working-class youth to the social scrapheap — that government had only minority support according to the opinion polls of the time. In 1980-1 Labour led the Tories in the polls by usually around 10%, often around 15 or even 20%.

B. But it was the elected government!

A. No matter who had voted for it, and even if most workers had voted for it (they didn't), the Thatcher government functioned as a government of the capitalist class, an especially vicious one. So too did the Tory/ Lib-Dem government after 2010. Socialists thought — and argued at the time — that working-class direct action to resist the Thatcher government was democratically legitimate, and, indeed, a healthy part of a functioning democracy, no matter how big a majority in Parliament Thatcher had.

B. Those socialists were not democrats!

A. In fact, we were. The weekly paper *Socialist Organiser* campaigned for an extension of existing democracy. But we recognised the social and political realities of the time. Irreversible social and economic damage was being done to the working class and to British society as a whole. As it happened, that was without an electoral sanction, but, irrespective of that, the victims had a right to resist a tyrannous government of the capitalist class. Even the American constitution asserts and upholds the right of revolt against a tyrannical government.

B. That sort of direct action is against democracy! The leader of the Labour Party, Michael Foot, said so at the time.

A. That's what he said as he surrendered before the class-war Tories. He was wrong even on democracy. People of your political persuasion will resort, and have resorted, to "direct action" to resist working-class or left-wing governments that "interfere with" the capitalist system. Michael Foot simply threw in the towel. In fact, one of his urgent motives was fear of a British military coup such as had erupted in Chile in 1973 against a moderately left-wing elected government.

B. The Bolsheviks dispersed the real democratic parliament in Russia! In January 1918 they closed down the elected Constituent Assembly.

A. Yes, they did. But the idea that the Constituent Assembly was more democratic than the Soviets, with their right to recall and to replace their delegates at any time — that's preposterous. And ignorant. The Constituent Assembly was elected on lists of candidates finalised before the Soviet Congress of October-November 1917. The biggest bloc of elected deputies was that of the "Socialist Revolutionary" party, but in October the "Socialist Revolutionaries" had split into "Left SRs", who in November formed a coalition government with the Bolsheviks, and "Right SRs", who walked out of the Congress of Soviets. If they'd had the strength, the "Right SRs" would have dispersed the Congress of Soviets as the Soviets dispersed the Constituent Assembly in 1918. The "Left SRs", who were the majority of the old SR party, were underrepresented on the Constituent Assembly lists drawn up before their party split, and the "Right SRs" overrepresented.

B. They should not have dismissed the elected parliament.

A. Even if one agrees with Rosa Luxemburg, an ardent supporter of the Bolsheviks, that it would have been better for the Soviet majority not to dismiss the Constituent Assembly — and I'm not saying that I do — democracy is not the issue. It was the democracy of the Soviets, led politically by the Bolsheviks and initially the Left SRs, against the democracy of the Constituent Assembly, led by the Right SRs. When the English bourgeoisie was fighting Stuart absolutism, to make a beginning of parliamentary rule, Oliver Cromwell too dismissed a Parliament.

B. The Constituent Assembly was more representative. All classes, not just the workers and peasants, were represented in it.

A. And that would have given it the right to override the Soviet majority, which certainly represented the majority of the people, peasants and workers alike? The point was that the working class and most of the peasants were in the process of overthrowing the bourgeoisie and the landlords and their rule. The exigencies of class struggle were decisive, not the notion that everybody's vote was equal to everyone else's. Your idea of what is democratic and anti-democratic defines itself here, and plainly, as a conception of limited democracy. Your democracy means the right of the ruling class and their supporters to override even a democratic majority. (A bit like the US Constitution, in fact.) You call the necessary action of the representatives of that majority, when they act as the majority, a coup!

47

B. The Constituent Assembly was the supreme Parliament. It had the duty, as well as the right, to oppose the Soviet pretend-parliament!

A. Who but the people, the workers and farmers, could say which was the real and which the pretend parliament? They backed the soviet Government, which legislated in favour of what they were already doing in the factories and on the land. The limited democracy you advocate is, as I've already said, bourgeois democracy, plutocratic democracy. The idea of economic, social, democracy does not even occur to you. Your "democratic" face is set against it.

B. I am against the robbery of one class by another under the flag of democracy.

A. Are you? In fact, no, you're not! You side with the landlord and capitalist robbers of the people. In Russia then, and in Britain now. Essentially, your position is that representative democracy, the election of deputies, is no real democracy. But for the Russian Revolution only. For Britain, France, the USA, etc., you raise no objection to it. Against the working-class regime set up in 1917 you postulate — by implication, I mean — some undefined super-democracy, and counterpose it as an ideal to the real, historically-evolved, Soviet democracy.

Part 2: The working class

THE WORKING CLASS

B. The working class? The proletariat? Ha! That is the best example of the falseness and foolishness running through your pretended "objectivity" and the allegedly "scientific" character of your Marxist socialism! Your view of the working class is absurd.

A. Someone, John Maynard Keynes, I think it was, once asked why he should look to the social equivalent of mud, the working class, as saviour against the educated ruling classes. Why should he look for social salvation to the most ignorant, the least accomplished, the demonstrably least able class in the society — to its human beasts of burden? To its "vocal tools" (as the ancient Romans described their slaves)?

B. Why indeed? You want a solution to what you call the economic and social contradictions of capitalism — and you make it a precondition of that solution that the beasts of burden, the "vocal tools" of that society, should first, within this society, rise above it, above the best educated in the society. It is absurd. It is like proposing to play tennis not with a net between the players, but an unsurpassable 30 foot high solid brick wall. It is rank sentimentality — or transmuted Christianity, with its cult of the humble — on the part of middle-class socialists, and ridiculous narcissism on the part of working-class socialists like you! Socialists from working-class backgrounds, above all, should know better. Working-class quiescence now shows that most workers know it too.

A. Yes, the unreadiness of the working class to do in history what it alone can do is part of the contradictions in advanced — not to say senile! — capitalism that we have to overcome if society is to go forward. Other solutions, reactionary, regressive, ruinous solutions, are possible too. The Thatcherite solution was possible from the 1980s because of the political failure of the powerful working class movement of the 1970s to settle accounts, properly and finally, with the ruling class.

B. Looking to the working class is whimsical and arbitrary. In a way, that in itself shows up the hopelessness of the socialism you espouse. That is your version of what in others you call utopian socialism. It is deeply senseless and scarcely believable foolishness. Look at the history of the 20th century, for Christ's sake!

A. A lot less absurd that looking to the ruling class, as you, like the snob Keynes, do. To those who as a social group are tied, hand, foot, mind, and morality, to the existing system? Those who have in the 20th century resorted to Hitler, Mussolini, Peron, Chiang Kai Shek, Pinochet, and all their many similars, against letting the working class reorganise society? That strikes me as the ultimate foolishness. That is the real equivalent of the so-named utopian romantic socialists of the early 19th century, such as the immensely great Robert Owen in Britain, appealing to the upper classes and the rich to rescue the wage slaves of capitalist society by benignly creating a fair society. That is, by expropriating their class and themselves —

collectively cutting their own throats. Or of the confused post-Trotsky neo-Trotskyists who in "open letters" appealed at various times in the 20th century to Stalinist dictators like Mao and Tito to abolish Stalinist rule, or to "democratise" it, which, for them, would mean the same thing as abolishing it.

B. Exactly! That is why socialism is an impossibility, an ever-shifting mirage.

A. Against the ruling class as a class — or its majority, or even a sizeable minority of it — ever wanting or peacefully agreeing to an egalitarian reorganisation of society, there is an impassable barrier: deep-rooted self-interest. There is no such barrier to the working class wanting it. And eventually winning it, by defeating the ruling class. Not only is there no objective barrier. There is a strong incentive for working-class people to want socialism. Leaving aside maybe sections of society that have been pauperised and pushed into long-term unemployment, the working class finds no class in society lower than itself. It can exploit no-one. It must own the means of production in order to emancipate itself from the position of a class forced to sell its labour-power in order to exist. As I've said, it can only own the means of production collectively — and, therefore, only democratically, because there is no other way to own and administer collectively. The barriers to the working class achieving this are many. It must first come to understand the need for it — that is, it must break through the domination in its minds of the ideas of the ruling class and the habit of seeing capitalist society as normal and the only possible system. It must organise and educate itself, and defeat the ruling class — a ruling class armed as it always is with every sort of weapon, from propaganda and brainwashing to the regular armies of the bourgeois state and, in acute crises, its auxiliary irregular shock troops such as fascist thugs.

B. A tall order! An impossibility, in fact.

A. A tall order indeed! But it is not an impossibility, like the idea of the capitalist class transforming capitalism into a system without its chronic contradictions. It can be done. That isn't just blind faith or socialist wish-thinking. We know for sure that it can be done because it has been done, mostly importantly in Russia in 1917.

The fundamental fact of capitalism is that it exploits the workers. The workers, in the process of working for a wage, create new value greater than the cost of their wage. This so-named "surplus value" becomes the property of the capitalist who controls the enterprise. That happens whether the worker receives high or low wages. The worker is robbed.

In turn, the capitalists are forced to compete with each other to squeeze and grind as much surplus as possible out of the workers. The most successful can grow, re-equip, and make themselves more profitable. Those who fall behind in competition are gobbled up by their successful competitors.

B. That's too fatalistic and too cynical. Even the worst people, and I don't say that they are, can be reformed. Bad systems can be reformed. The Britain we have was shaped by many reforms.

A. Reforms forced through by the revolt and pressure of the workers — for instance the revolt that created the Labour landslide in 1945, from which came the modern welfare state. It didn't come from the good will of the capitalist rulers. No matter how good-willed or good-intentioned a capitalist may be, he or she is locked into this competitive system. The rule is: exploit, accumulate wealth, expand — or die. Be predator or prey. The profit drive is therefore the all-controlling mainspring, regulator, and determinant in the system. It will remain so until conscious overall planning replaces profit and competition as the mainspring — until the workers who are now the basic exploited class take collective ownership and substitute free cooperation for what Marx called "wage slavery". The fundamental relation of capitalist exploitation also, by its very nature, generates the integration of workers into large collective workforces, and constant conflicts between workers and capitalists over working hours, pay, and conditions. It pushes workers towards organising for those conflicts, and educating themselves politically and socially, in the process.

B. That credo of unreconstructed socialists and Marxists like you, that stupid fetish of the working class, is self-stupefying, brain-pickling dogma! I repeat: it is simply absurd.

A. And what is your eyes-shut-tight unwillingness to simply see the working class as it really is in history? There has been a great history of day-to-day struggle, heroic drives to build trade unions, general strikes, insurrections. Of course, there are also periods, sometimes long periods, of working-class passivity in the aftermath of defeats and pyrrhic victories — seeming, but unreal and empty, victories like the one we won over the Tories in the mid-70s, only to have the Labour government we put into office demobilise the working class.

B. Defeated, or part-defeated, always. Always. Yes! For ever and ever, amen. Good!

A. Defeats go with the territory. Rosa Luxemburg truly observed that the socialist revolution "is the only form of 'war'... in which the ultimate victory can be prepared only by a series of 'defeats'. What does the entire history of socialism and of all modern revolutions show us? The first spark of class struggle in Europe, the revolt of the silk weavers in Lyon in 1831, ended with a heavy defeat; the Chartist movement in Britain ended in defeat; the uprising of the Parisian proletariat in the June days of 1848 ended with a crushing defeat; and the Paris Commune ended with a terrible defeat.

"The whole road of socialism — so far as revolutionary struggles are concerned — is paved with nothing but thunderous defeats. Yet, at the same time, history marches inexorably, step by step, toward final victory! Where would we be today without those 'defeats', from which we draw historical experience, understanding, power and idealism?... We stand on the foundation of those very defeats; and we can not do without any of them, because each one contributes to our strength and understanding".

B. She should know, with her poor silly head smashed in!

A. She knew it from the history of the workers' movement. We know it from history, including the defeat of the German communists in 1919 and the murder of Luxemburg, Liebknecht, Jogiches, and many thousands of others. Class-struggle socialists, who try to be the memory of the working class, know it all too well. There is no denying that the working class and its political movements have to operate under very unfavourable conditions.

B. Against an insuperable enemy!

A. Not an *insuperable* enemy. A formidable and strong one, which has enormous built-in advantages. That enemy has all the wealth. It has control of the propaganda and education machines in society. It has the power and wealth to buy over some of our people. I think it was the Liberal Imperialist Joseph Chamberlain who sneered to the

Fabian Beatrice Webb, about working-class trade-union and political leaders: "You train them, and we'll buy them".

B. Exactly! Your whole project is hopeless and ridiculous. You are hypnotising yourself! Look around you! All around you is the evidence of working-class defeat and indifference — sensible indifference! — to your message and your cause. You believe far more preposterous things than the Christians, Muslims, Jews and other such self-hypnotisers and addicts of fairy stories for grown-ups, whom you mock and deride. You believe that a too-often defeated class can be victorious at some unknown future time. That is a fairy story for immature adults who can't come to terms with social reality. The future belongs to the working class? Yes, and the dead will get up and walk the streets on an appointed day! And the trumpet will sound to announce the imminence of the kingdom of God on earth! You believe in miracles.

A. Not quite. There is a rational basis for our "miracles". Dead men and women don't get up and walk. In society, defeated classes do rise again.

In all societies and in all history, the basic exploited class revolts. Revolts again and again. In the history of the working class, we have risen from defeat again and again and again. That is the other side of the defeats. Every victory of the bourgeoisie is incomplete. It can't win outright, because it needs to preserve the working class to do the work. Even while British capitalism was defeating the British working class in the 1980s, capitalism was vastly increasing the number of workers in other areas of the world. Capitalism creates its own gravediggers — the proletariat.

B. It is its own grave that the "proletariat" digs! Again and again and again. And a good thing too!

A. Don't let wish father feeble thoughts on you. The long history of the working class, of its defeats, its declines, and its revivals, shows us what will happen in the future, though not of course in exact detail. It is sure and certain that the working class will revive. The working-class socialist movement will revive. Everything in history shows that it will. Why? Because capitalism can live only by exploiting the "labour force". There are many working-class struggles around the world now. We, the working-class socialists, will build new working-class political parties, on the foundations of working-class struggle!

B. Yeah, and Atlantis will rise again!

A. Atlantis of the legends never existed. But even the legends offer us some lessons... Atlantis was where the Minoan civilisation of Crete and Homeric Greece was supposed to come from, borne by survivors — as socialists now bear socialist culture and historical awareness for the future.

B. Minoan socialism! Not "scientific", but legend-founded, myth-rooted socialism! A socialist Theseus lost in the capitalist maze! I like it.

A. The history of working-class mobilisation, struggle, sustained effort, prolonged resistance, outright revolt — that is neither myth nor merely legend!

B. That is all it is *now* — self-consoling legend. There may have been big, threatening, socialist movements in the past, but you can't win now.

A. We'll see. Naturally I have no guarantees to offer to you, or to those attracted to socialism, about exactly when the working class will revive, or when or where it will next be victorious.

And nobody is saying that we should wait for the working class to revive on a world scale before we can do anything. I do say that the full solution — the creation of a world-wide democratically-planned economy controlled by those who work it — can only be achieved by the working class. Humankind will not sink into passive acceptance of looming, or perhaps-looming, catastrophe. Beyond that, it is a fight; right now, a battle on what someone called "the ideological front" (as distinct from the political and economic fronts of the class struggle).

The one thing that is certain is that the working-class struggle on its lower or higher levels will go on, as it is going on now — and that serious socialists will work to help those fighting in that struggle to find their way through the political and ideological mazes of capitalism.

B. The fact that you admit that you can offer no guarantees shows how confident you really are in your expectations and predictions.

A. It shows that I know the limits of my own or anyone else's power to predict in detail, to know in advance the strength of our enemies, the obstacles we must overcome, the complexities and intractabilities of history. And, therefore, that I am not a charlatan or a megalomaniac.

B. Just an unteachable fool, trying to mislead others to join you in your foolishness.

A. What is it that makes Marxist socialism "scientific"? ...

B. Nothing!

A. ... It is that Marxists base ourselves on the socialising logic of capitalist economy. We say that humanity still faces the choice of socialism or of some variety of barbarism. We propose to honest and responsible people that they join us in the socialist struggle. We ask them to struggle when and where possible against the rulers of today and their system, and to help rebuild a working-class socialist movement that can overthrow capitalism and emancipate society from wage-slavery.

B. If you were truly confident in what you say, you would offer something more!

A. And if you knew what you are talking about, you would not expect me, or any rational Marxist, to offer either guarantees or detailed blueprints.

B. But, really, look at the historical record. When you demand, as you do, miraculous changes in attitudes and moralities - and first of all from the wretched "proletariat" — is it any wonder that socialists have not succeeded?

A. It is not a matter of miracles. We build on what already exists in the working class. Inside capitalism, the labour movement has always been and is now a repository of values other than those of the surrounding society — of the values of class and human solidarity. Characteristically we have argued, for example, for changing environments that produce crime rather than severely punishing criminals. Trade unions fight the capitalists for a better share of the product, or to stop the workers' share being diminished. They fight on bread-and-butter questions to benefit the workers. But in the trade unions you will also find tremendous stores of benevolence, benign fellow-feeling, selfless devotion to the common good. Workers sacrifice wages to their spirit of solidarity with other workers. The drive to change things for the better triggered by the elemental "trade union" struggle over the effects of dog-eat-dog capitalism tends to nourish the manifold values of solidarity. Not perfectly and instantly; but the contrast between the labour movement and the society around it is always one between greater civilisation and solidarity, and a more predatory culture. We build on that, just as we build our perspective on the inner logic of capitalism's own development.

B. You want it to be so, that I understand. What you want is impossible. Foolishness! Dreaming! Dangerous dreaming that might again damage what we have now.

A. Only those who actively and perseveringly want such transformations can bring them about. But the fact that such things have happened before is a proof that they can be made to happen again. Mass socialist labour movements have been built before and therefore they can be built again. Or, putting it at its weakest, there is no absolute reason why such movements can't be built again, in conditions which have changed in many ways but are the same in fundamentals — capitalist exploitation; working-class resistance to it; and the socialising drives, tendencies, and needs of capital.

Labour movements can be, and, I say, will be again converted to socialism, which is the natural expression of what the working class is, and the necessary negation of the capitalist class and its system.

B. Those mass socialist labour movements were crushed and defeated. You know that. They have gone the way that other such would-be benevolent schemes have gone. All in all, I say that is a good thing.

A. What hasn't "gone" is capitalism, its modes of operating, and the effects it produces in working-class people. It is capitalism that breeds socialism! The wolves running wild in society evoke class and human solidarity in self-protection and in revolt and revulsion against them.

RADICAL DECLINE OF THE WORKING CLASS?

B. The truly dangerous wolves are the self-proclaimed anti-wolves, the socialists! In any case, your cherished working class is diminishing. It is now too weak to revolutionise society or anything else.

A. The opposite is true. Now is probably the first time in history that the wage-workers and their immediate families are the largest class in the population of the world.

According to the International Labour Organisation, the world's waged workforce increased from 0.9 billion in 1991 to 1.7 billion in 2014. Even though a large number of those, in the poorer countries, are "semi-proletarians", who scrape a living by varying combinations of petty trade, self-employment, theft, begging, domestic work, and straightforward wage-work, the actual number of wage-workers has increased sharply.

B. But that's not the real working class, manual workers in factories.

A. Your idea of "working class" is far too narrow. The working class is not only manual workers. It never has been. What defines workers is their relation to capital. This is how Marx put it: "With the development of... the specifically capitalist mode of production, the real lever of the overall labour process is increasingly not the individual worker. Instead, labour-power socially combined and the various competing labour-powers which together form the entire production machine participate in very different ways... one as a manager [Marx means a low-level administrator or organiser], engineer, technologist, etc., the other as overseer, the third as manual labourer or even drudge... It is quite immaterial whether the job of a particular worker, who is merely a limb of this aggregate worker, is at a greater or smaller distance from the actual manual labour".

B. Teachers, technicians, and so on — they're middle class.

A. No, they are part of the working class.

B. Most of them would say you are wrong.

A. Most manual workers in the USA call themselves "middle

class". Such labels don't change their place in the economy, or the way they relate to the hirer of their labour, the capitalist. They are working-class. They are the US proletariat.

B. A "class" as diverse as the working class now is can never unite. Inequalities in wages and living standards have increased since the early 1980s within the working class as well as between the working class and the capitalist class.

A.That diversity is not new either, though of course you'll believe what you want. Inequalities within the working class were large in Marx's day too. The central divide remains the one between the working class and the capitalist class. That is not diminishing!

B. Better-off workers share more with what you call the petty bourgeoisie than with the working class. The worse-off workers are a minority in society. Any politics which appeals only to them cannot succeed. And in any case your socialist ideas have little support even among them.

A. We don't confine our appeal only to the worst-off sections of the working class. A mass socialist labour movement would have a wider appeal even beyond the working class properly defined. You are also mistaken in your sociology of the working class. There is a fundamental difference between better-off workers and the "petty bourgeoisie". You can see it in the fact that the small business owner or the "middle manager" votes much more right-wing than the teacher or nurse well up on their pay scale.

B. You are flamming to yourself, using political voting allegiances instead of the proper economic and social criteria.

A. The social and economic difference between better-off workers and the petty bourgeoisie remains enormous. For instance, in times of higher class struggle, the well-off workers are drawn into (and quite often they lead) the general workers' struggle; the petty bourgeois are still petty bourgeois.

B. The relative decline of factory labour cuts away what you see as the revolutionary potential of the working class.

A. It does not cut it away, though it may relocate it to a certain extent. Certain sections of the working class have greater strategic weight than others: those who directly produce the bulk of socially-useful products, those who can hit capital hardest, those who are concentrated in big workplaces and large cities, those most bitterly hurt by capitalist exploitation. Shop-floor workers in factories and in extractive industry are central — but also warehouse workers, goods-transport workers, and those in such sectors as post and telecom, and maybe even bank workers or teachers.

The factory working class is expanding fast on a world scale. In the older-industrialised capitalist countries, it has declined as a part of the total workforce, but even there it is still large in absolute terms.

B. It is not what Marx expected to happen, is it?

A. Isn't it? Your Marx is a "Marx" for the superficial and shoddy polemicist. You are simply wrong to think that Marx's perspective was based on a vision of a population almost all made up of factory workers. Marx's own analysis of the English census of 1861 showed only 1.7 million workers in factories, mines, gasworks, and railways, out of a population of 20 million.

B. Yes, but Marx saw the numbers of industrial workers as increasing, and they did up to, say, World War One. Not now.

A. In Germany, the country Marxists cited as the epitome of high capitalist development around World War One, 34% of the labour force were self-employed or working for their families. Capitalist society is more "proletarianised" now than then in the fundamental sense of the proportion of people drawn into the capital-labour nexus.

B. But students are middle-class.

A. Even here you are wrong. It is no longer accurate to call students, as a social category, "middle class". Many of them come from working-class families (usually better-off), and will go into (usually better-paid) wage-labour on finishing their studies. Students are a fluid social group without clear class anchoring. They can be a vital leaven for democratic struggles and even sometimes for socialist struggles.

IMPERIALISM

B. The left's attitude to "imperialism" repels me.

A. We should be for it? The denial of self-rule and self-determination to most of humankind across the globe was a good thing?

B. Try not be silly! British imperialism was...

A. A foul and dirty thing! An international system of brigandage!

B. No — or anyway, not just that. It was not just about plunder and exploitation. It modernised the countries it ruled, with railways, trade, even education. Indian democracy and African democracies were also works of British imperialism.

A. It would be strange if the economically most advanced country in the world, as Britain was into the 20th century, did not bring technical and economic improvements to the countries it ruled and exploited. But the prime purpose of British imperialism was to extract wealth from their colonies. Their "modernisation" was a means to that end.

B. Whatever may have been their motives, they nonetheless made tremendous changes, and for the better. You Marxists ignore the facts.

A. Not quite! Karl Marx himself saw the breaking up by capitalism of the old Indian system, stagnant for millennia, as good work — but he denounced the inhumanity and the brutality with which that was done. He wrote that the fruits of the "good work" would only be harvested by the Indian people winning self-rule. Looking back at the Empire through a haze of nostalgia, romance, and self-approbation is, by this date in history, absurd.

B. In any case, imperialism is history.

A. One form of imperialism. There are many forms of imperialism in history.

B. Even Russian imperialism fell with the USSR.

A. And yet the powerful countries still throw their weight around.

Russia, against its neighbours, most spectacularly against the Ukrainians. America, too — usually with its British hunting dogs trotting behind its tanks. The invasion of Iraq was an example of 19th century style gunboat interventionism, but on a gigantic airborne scale. The result has been a manifold disaster.

B. America — and Britain — engaged in humanitarian intervention. Their intentions were good.

A. They wrecked Iraq. The way they did what they did was characterised by immense imperialistic arrogance and naive overconfidence. In the world after the collapse of Russian imperialism, they felt omnipotent. They were the gods of war and peace! They acted accordingly. Some at least of their objectives were old style imperialist aims — to gain control over Iraqi oil, to eliminate a regional-imperialist competitor, to increase America's power and prestige in the region.

B. If those were their aims, they didn't do it very well, did they?

A. No, indeed. Nonetheless, those aims were central to their reason for intervening. The extent of their arrogant, imperialistic bungling and incompetence still boggles the mind.

B. When the great powers do something like that against a dictatorial regime, they should be supported, not denounced in outmoded anti-imperialist rhetoric.

A. Nobody with any sense would trust the US plutocracy to do "the right thing" anywhere. Or to do it in a way that can be supported.

B. By socialist nitwits, you mean.

A. By consistent democrats or by socialists. When the imperialist powers do something like bombing Serbia to stop attempted genocide in Kosova, then, I'll grant you, they should not be denounced in ways that imply support for regional imperialisms far worse than theirs — in Kosova, Slobodan Milosevic's ethnic imperialism, with its attempt at genocide in Kosova.

B. The big powers should be positively supported!

A. By wish-thinking fools!

B. By honest democrats. In any case, the worst fools have been the socialists backing the clerical-fascist "resistance" in Iraq and half-backing Islamist terrorist organisations by making "political" excuses for them.

A. Some socialists. Yes, large parts of the left are politically, historically, and intellectually disoriented. Perhaps terminally so. We'll see.

B. Once again, you duck out of the line of fire by saying that these are not really socialist idiocies and crimes. Yet again, they are all out of step but you!

A. No, these are socialists all right. Socialists who have let themselves be disoriented by a comprehensive nay-saying to the capitalist world around them, so that on issues like Iraq and ex-Yugoslavia they become perfect negative imprints of the capitalists they attack.

B. To the point of political idiocy.

A. There are examples of political idiocy. On many other questions they continue to do something like good socialist work.

B. It must be hard for you, forever out of step with the self-proclaimed socialists you try feebly to defend. No: you don't have my sympathy!

A. For us, the fundamental thing is to maintain independent working-class socialist politics. That includes the denunciation of the imperialist activities of the big states. We do not let ourselves be fooled by the good democratic reasons they give for their activities. And neither do we let ourselves be pushed by mechanical negativism towards the capitalist great powers, by a thoughtless and often reactionary "anti-imperialism", into becoming merely negative imprints of their politics.

Part 3: Democracy

DEMOCRACY AND SOCIALISM

B. I say that your socialist ranting will never achieve anything positive. All such wild talk may do is undermine the real democracy we have now. You socialists simply do not understand or appreciate democracy.

A. Codswallop! For socialists — serious socialists, Marxian socialists — democracy is a central, all-conditioning and all-defining, principle and central value of socialism. Without democracy, genuinely socialist collective ownership is impossible. The socialist criticism of parliamentary democracy is not an opposition to democracy or a rejection of it. We want a better democracy. We say that the pluto-democracy, money-bourgeois-democracy we have now, under capitalism, is the shallowest, emptiest version of democracy.

B. It's a damn sight better than any form of authoritarianism or absolutism!

A. Our different ideas about the necessary economic basis for liberty and democracy are what divides us here. Of course we are for liberty and democracy! The socialist who is not for democratic self-rule and liberty in relation to the state and society is not a socialist but a walking contradiction in terms. And the other way round, too. The anti-socialist who is against extending democracy to the economic conditions in which people's lives have to be lived is not really a democrat.

B. You want to tear down the real democracy we have in the name of unrealistic dreams of some ideal future democracy?

A. What strikes me most is how unambitious you and your sort are for the democracy and liberty you claim as your guiding principles, your political lodestone. For a start you praise what we call bourgeois democracy for such things as liberty. These are distinct and separable things. You conflate democracy and liberty. Thereby you obscure the relationship between them and block discussion of the most important questions: democracy, yes, but how and for whom? Liberty — whose liberty? You settle for a miserably reduced, diminished, docked, stultified, dwarf, and often mere token version of the liberty and democracy you glorify. We have a deeper, older, and more comprehensive idea of democracy.

B. Older?

A. The common meanings of both democracy and liberty today are catastrophically diminished versions of ideas put forward 100, 150 or 200 years ago by the pioneer fighters for liberty and democracy. The Jacobin zealots of the great French revolution, or even the radical leaders of the American Revolution, such as Thomas Jefferson, or the mid-19th century Chartist labour-movement champions of democracy and liberty in Britain, or the leaders of the 1916 Rising in Dublin — Connolly, Pearse, and all the others for fought for liberty and democracy — none of them would recognise the extant version of liberty and democracy as the realisation of what they advocated under the same names. They would see it for what it is. Maximum freedom for the rich to do what they like to the poor throughout the world! None of them would accept as theirs what you in your militant-capitalist and fear-ridden Stalinophobic political idiocy champion and defend as democracy! They would call it a fraud.

B. As I've said: socialists don't defend real liberty and democracy. You now, for instance: you disparage and undermine it.

A. Some would-be socialists don't champion liberty and democracy. Serious socialists, consistently Marxist socialists, do. And we have for many decades. Trotsky did.

B. Socialists are usually in the vanguard — to use your jargon — of every "politically correct" attempt to control, regulate, stifle and suppress the free expression of ideas. Not just the horrible and insulting n-word and things like that...

A. Even the most repressive, or the silliest, of the "politically correct"-ists as a rule starts out with legitimate concern about real injustice against black people, women, gay people, physically or mentally disabled people...

You accept that the n-word, which encapsulates petrified age-old prejudice, and the memory of the enslavement of black people, should be suppressed. Yes, "politically correct" people are sometimes superstitious, authoritarian, repressive, regressive even. They sometimes make rational discussion impossible. They try to banish real injustices and bad attitudes by bits of what might be called "verbal engineering" . That should be opposed. But get your priorities right!

B. And your priorities?

A. For 30 years now, in Britain, privatisation has been very unpopular. A poll in 2013 found majorities for public ownership of 68% (energy companies), 67% (Royal Mail), 66% (rail), and 84% (NHS), with only small minorities positively for privatisation.

Yet for those same 30 years, government after government has continued to privatise. That happens because there is great pressure, through a million channels, on the larger parties that might oppose privatisation, like the Labour Party, to hew to big-business interests on issues which big business considers essential. Because it is very difficult for new parties to make way unless they have substantial backing in the moneyed classes. Because there is little way for the electorate to influence a government once it takes office, settles in to work with the permanent unelected state hierarchy, is immersed in the flows of big-business lobbying. The Blair Labour government came to office with a very popular promise to reverse the Tories' marketisation of the Health Service. Then it pushed the marketisation much further than the Tories had done; and the voters had no redress.

We have a very deficient, inadequate form of democracy. The truth is that, in the very broad historical sense in which the Liberals can claim to be of the left, the left has failed and failed first and last as democrats — that is, failed to secure a system that functions democratically in Abraham Lincoln's apt definition: "government of the people, by the people, for the people". Today's pluto-democracy is government of the rich, by the rich, for the rich, and a few sops sometimes for the people.

B. You are so negative — a destructive, subversive utopian.

A. I do the best I can! The question posed on democracy in historical experience is this: what is the economic basis needed for democracy to exist in reality as well as in name, democracy all through the economy and society as well as in politics — as the early democrats advocated it.

Today's democracy means a society in which the means of production, exchange, and communication are monopolised by a small class of vastly rich people, and administered for their benefit, not that

65

of society or of the workers, one in which economic decisions of vast and shaping importance are taken by that small class — look at the bankers, for god's sake! That system cannot honestly be called democratic. Saying that it is preferable to outright dictatorship — which is true — doesn't get you off the hook.

B. You are the one who is on the hook!

A. In such a system democratic political structures cannot but be a facade for the autocrats who own industry and make the fundamental social decisions that shape the lives of all of us.. The government, in the fundamental things, is their "executive committee". I repeat: this "pluto-democracy" is not what the great pioneer fighters for democracy and liberty would recognise as democracy if they could come and look at it..

B. History evolves, ideas are tempered and modified in experience. That's unavoidable. Usually it's good.

THE EVOLUTION OF DEMOCRACY

A. In the long-ago days of small enterprises and farm homesteads, in revolutionary 18th century America, democracy could in principle assume a society of more or less equal citizens who would exercise the democratic franchise. In our world, all in theory are equal, but some, in George Orwell's words satirising Stalinism, "are more equal than others". A lot more! In Britain today, just one thousand of the wealthiest people have between them more wealth than the poorest 40% of households. In the USA, the top 0.1% own as much household wealth as the lower 90%.

And the wealthy have more "liberty", too. When the freedom of the press in practice means freedom for newspaper and other media owners like Rupert Murdoch, Richard Desmond, or Berlusconi, that is liberty not of the people but against the people — the companion to a democracy that is a withered, mocking parody of real and full democratic self-rule.

B. There are shortcomings. Maybe some of them can be remedied, maybe most of them are inevitable limitations which arise from living in a complex society. In any case, actually existing democracy with its shortcomings is vastly better than the total suppression of democracy which you had under socialism.

A. Under Stalinism! If the memory of the horrors that went under variants of the name "socialism" in the past stop us, and inhibit us in drawing the necessary conclusions from what capitalism is, then people in the here and now are disarmed, ideologically and politically. Paralysed. The truth — and I repeat it — is that the demonisation of "socialism", the insistence that the murdering Stalinist liars were correct when they presented their system as the realisation of Marxist socialism — that is a central part of the bourgeoisie's "class struggle on the ideological front" now — in the battle of ideas. It functions to prevent people drawing the right *democratic* as well as socialist conclusions from Stalinism.

B. It's still a case of "they're all out of step except me and my comrade, Johnny"! You are trying to "deny", deconstruct, talk away the great fact that there is such a thing in our world as real democracy. It is real, whatever its limits, and however much you say it might be improved upon.

A. I probe and evaluate things democratic as part of advocating improved, or qualitatively better, democracy. If the existing forms of bourgeois democracy do not deserve criticism and debunking, then there is no need for improvement or transformation. If you insist on identifying criticism of "actually existing" democracy with hostility to democracy, and sneaky or overt promotion of authoritarianism of some sort, then you erect great barriers against critical examination and judgement, and any advocacy of improving it or finding a better model.

B. Your destructive criticism promotes an authoritarian socialist agenda!

A. You are being the poor silly guy in the old satire who, confronted with earthquakes, fires, and other catastrophes, insisted: "All is for the best in the best of all possible worlds". You are saying that existing democracy is the best of all possible democracies. You are also saying: please don't criticise it too roughly, lest it fall apart. Is it that fragile?

B. No, but I say: leave well enough alone.

A. As between the rich and the poor, bourgeois, plutocratic, "actually existing" democracy is not a "level playing field". It is less than democratic. The rich have immense advantages. Think of the repulsive and fascistic idiot Donald Trump in the 2016 US presidential race. He is there because he is rich. The great corporations and people like Trump have and use immense political weight in shaping public policy. The individual citizen is feeble in comparison with them, and on most things has no possibility of competing with them. The rich can spend tens of millions putting their candidates of choice into the House of Representatives and the Senate, and, usually, the Presidency — that is, buying them in advance, tying them by pre-election political "mortgages" on their expected future conduct.

And then they fund, to the tune of about $9 billion a year, a political lobbying industry which is estimated to employ 100,000 people in all its offshoots. Take averages, and each of the 500-odd members of Congress has an average of 200 lobby-industry people on her or his case. An average of $18 million a year spent on lobbying each member of Congress.

B. That's only the USA.

A. Not only the USA, by any means. A book published in 2014 estimated the lobbying industry in Britain at £2 billion a year, which is an average of £3 million a year per individual MP. And lobbying comes from the unelected supremos of the permanent state machine as well as from designated lobbyists. In his book about the experience of the Labour government from 1964 to 1970, Harold Wilson described how Lord Cromer, the Governor of the Bank of England, insisted on social cuts as soon as Labour came to office. "I asked him [Cromer, governor of the Bank of England] if this meant that it was impossible for any government, whatever its party label, whatever its manifesto or the policies on which it fought an election, to continue, unless it immediately reverted to full-scale Tory policies... We had now reached the situation where a newly elected government was being told by international speculators that the policy on which we had fought the election could not be implemented: that the government was to be forced into adoption of Tory policies to which it was fundamentally opposed... The Queen's First Minister was being asked to bring down the curtain on parliamentary democracy by accepting the doctrine that an election in Britain was a farce, that the British people could not make a choice between policies". But prime minister Wilson nevertheless did what Cromer asked. The number of people who see no point in bothering to vote in national elections testifies to their awareness of the limits of this democracy, even if their mood is often no more than a general feeling that politics is irrelevant, and all politicians are people on the make.

B. Obama proves the opposite.

A. Obama's election proves that the "little citizen" can sometimes assert herself against the corporate "Big Citizens". But look what happened when Obama tried to change things — the weight the pharmaceutical industry and the private health-insurance sellers throw against proper social medicine; the political clout the gun industry and its National Rifle Association deploy in preventing painfully necessary limits to the availability of guns, and so on.

Remember that it was known for decades that smoking caused cancer, and that information was obscured, diluted, and denied by the tobacco industry and on its behalf. It took decades before social regulation began.

B. That's democracy! That's pluralism.

A. No, that's pluto-democracy! Tremendous economic powers and social-financial forces dominate the democratic discourse, elections, the shaping of opinion and public policy. And they buy the legislators.

B. It's the best we've got. Your criticisms can only erode respect for it. Then we may get worse.

A. Don't raise a raucous dissenting voice in church, eh? Mere individual citizens or associations of citizens ordinarily have no chance of competing with the corporate "Big Citizens" and rich individual citizens.

B. You'd prefer it if all the "Big Citizens" confronted the "little citizens" as one giant state corporation, as one corporate "Big Brother Citizen"?

A. I'd prefer it if society ran what the "Big Citizens" now run in the interests of all instead of, as now, letting it be run in the private interests of the "Big Citizens". I'd prefer it if democracy were not a thing of politics only, if the power of the multiple-vote-possessing Big Citizens were taken from them.

B. They don't have more than one vote!

A. Through influence and wealth they dispose of many votes! If democracy included economic democracy, for the most important instance, then people could democratically control the conditions that shape their lives locally, nationally, and beyond the individual nations.

B. That's double-talk.

A. The wretched system you champion subsists on "double-talk"! For example, capitalist vested interests do their best to hide the facts about global warming. They have falsified the records and set up tame scientists, that is, bought-and-paid-for prostituted experts, to hinder the flow of real knowledge and real discussion. They have warped, diluted, and smothered serious discussion. To cliché it, they poison the wells of the public information which is irreplaceable for real democratic opinion-formation and decision-making. The social realities of capitalist class rule determine most of the time what really-existing democracy is in practice.

B. Yes, but democracy prevails.

A. No, it doesn't!

B. Not always and immediately. But in the long run democracy will prevail.

A. God is good, eh? Normally, usually, it takes tens of millions of dollars to run for any high national office in the USA.

B. People can club together small sums and pool money to back a candidate.

A. What kind of democracy is it with such enormous tariff walls against poorer people standing in elections? It is worse than the old system in Britain, before 1911, of not paying MPs, and thereby ensuring that only well-off people could be MPs. Normally less than half the US electorate votes.

B. People paid by private associations could be MPs. Trade unions and the early Labour Party financed their own MPs before 1911, people like Keir Hardie. And the point is, surely, that people in the USA have the choice of voting or not voting.

A. The point about so many, even of the registered voters, usually not bothering to vote is that so few people believe that their vote gives them a real voice in what's happening. And in the UK there are about seven million eligible people, about 13% of those eligible, not even registered to vote.

B. Nothing is perfect! I don't say it's perfect, only that it is better than any known alternative.

A. For sure, nothing in existing democracy — bourgeois democratic, plutocratic democracy — is perfect. The point is that it is not even adequate. Consider: everyone knows fictions like Anthony Hope's *The Prisoner of Zenda*, or Mark Twain's *The Prince and The Pauper*, in which in some "Ruritania" without democracy a commoner who looks like one of the rulers takes his place for a while. A decade or so ago, I saw an American "Ruritanian" equivalent of Twain and Hope, *Dave*, set in the USA in our times. Dave, a goodhearted, benign, socially responsible man, owns a small-town employment agency, and he happens to look like the President. A stroke makes the President a vegetable, and conniving politicians substitute Dave for him.
Dave, the good guy, sponsors all sorts of New-Deal-style Rooseveltian schemes to help the needy and uses his borrowed power to push them through the clogged-up democratic (or, so often in reality, pretendedly democratic) system.

B. Ah, you tell fairy stories, too, as light relief from socialist gobbledegook! Go on.

A. The film was far from being the biting satire it might have been, but think about what its production tells you about American democracy now. A lot of people feel so excluded that there is a market for an American-Ruritanian romance.

B. There have been lots of films like that, for example Frank Capra's *Mr Smith Goes To Washington*.

A. No, those were about citizens intervening into the "political process". *Dave* was about a good-king president bypassing or subverting the system, borrowing the king-president's power in order to do good with it that the real president would never have done.

B. As I said, it is not perfect. It is the best we've got, You know what Churchill, I think, said? The best argument for democracy is the alternatives. And of course it's secure. It's the future!

A. The enormous number of people normally not voting; the plutocratic costs of standing for office in the USA; the fact that a "free press" means freedom of billionaires to monopolise the means of forming public opinion — all those combine to make a serious atrophy in existing bourgeois democracy.

B. And what about the new social media?

A. That makes a difference, a big difference perhaps. It was a factor in Obama being able to stand for president, and Sanders being able to run in 2016. But that only modifies the main picture. The plain truth is that social evolution, the emergence over the last 150-200 years of economic "Giant Citizens", has rendered obsolete and inadequate the old forms of a democracy designed for a radically different age and society. Essentially it is the same social process that happened when the small-owner economy that went with the old democracy had economic-exploitative giants grow up inside it.

B. Nobody says there isn't room for improvement.

A. That's just waffle and evasion. I say we urgently need radical "improvement". We need something qualitatively different. You know what your big trouble here is? That you are so unambitious in your democratic aspirations, so hag-ridden with historical funk. Ridiculously, suicidally unambitious! You boast of "democracy", yet there is a glaring, obvious, timidity and uncertainty about it for you, isn't there?

B. Timidity? No, I'm just sticking to something real, in place of wild promises of something better which in fact, in history, so often led to something worse. A parliamentary democracy of all the people is better than a class-limited Soviet democracy (as you call it). By definition it is more democratic.

A. The truth is that such all-in democracy hides and disguises the rule of the bourgeoisie, and, in its pretensions to be an all-inclusive democracy, it functions mainly to evoke consent for bourgeois governments, or the pretence of such consent.

B. It is real consent.

A. Yes, manufactured consent, consent which is in large part resigned acceptance of what the power structures make seem inevitable. The Soviets of 1917 assumed the right to ride roughshod over the bourgeoisie and the landlords and what had seemed inevitable under their rule. That, by the way, is what the Bolsheviks understood by "dictatorship of the proletariat". They did not think of it as a single person's dictatorship, or as what the Stalinists created, but as the rule of a class acting "dictatorially" to override entrenched ruling-class laws, traditions, and state institutions.

B. Again: you are against parliamentary democracy!

A. I'm not against parliamentary democracy if the alternative is some sort of authoritarian or totalitarian political system. In 1934 Trotsky and his comrades advocated that the French working class defend parliamentary democracy, then under threat by fascists: "As long as the majority of the working class continues on the basis of bourgeois democracy, we are ready to defend it with all our forces against violent attacks from the Bonapartist and fascist bourgeoisie". At the time he put forward a program to improve that democracy, and we have the same approach today. "A single assembly must combine the legislative and executive powers. Members would be elected for two years, by universal suffrage at eighteen years of age, with no discrimination of sex or nationality. Deputies would be elected on the basis of local assemblies, constantly revocable by their constituents, and would receive the salary of a skilled worker. This is the only measure that would lead the masses forward instead of pushing them backward. A more generous democracy would facilitate the struggle for workers' power". That was and is our attitude to parliamentary democracy.

B. Trotsky was being hypocritical!

A. No. Why should he be? This was the guiding policy of the French Trotskyists in the crisis of parliamentary democracy

B. After what the Bolsheviks did to the Constituent Assembly?

A. In France in 1934 there was no alternative parliament, no Congress of Soviets as in Russia in 1917. Yes, we are against bourgeois parliamentary democracy when the alternative is the higher form of democracy expressed in soviets or workers' councils.

B. We? You are royal, or editorial, now, are you?

A. We, the socialists, the movement, the ideas that have continuity from the past to the present and will continue beyond — the tradition. Continuity and tradition are very important things. We can give a precise account of the evolution of our ideas. You can't give a true account of the evolution of your bourgeois ideas on democracy and of the break with earlier conceptions of democracy, in the eyes of its proponents and opponents alike then, which your system now embodies. That is also the answer to your question, why Trotsky? Trotsky was the Spartacus of the 20th century, the leader with Lenin of the people's revolt, and the Kepler, the scientist groping for a full and accurate understanding.

B. Groping, indeed: in your self-induced and self-sustained intellectual and moral darkness.

DEMOCRACY IN BRITISH HISTORY

A. If democracy doesn't go forward, develop and expand, then it atrophies, hollows out, loses vitality, and begins to regress. In Britain, democracy has expanded and improved in stages to take in most of the people. After the Revolution of 1688, Parliament, not the King, ruled, but it was a parliament on only a very limited franchise. As Marx analysed it, a Whig aristocratic caste ruled for the whole bourgeoisie. In 1832, 144 years after the 1688 Whig revolution, the new middle class was admitted to the vote and electoral boundaries were changed so as to allow representation to the new centres of manufacturing such as Manchester and Birmingham. Many of the male urban proletarians were admitted to the vote in 1867, and some of the rural poor in 1884. Property qualifications meant that large swathes of poor males were still without votes. And, of course, no women, not even very rich women, had a vote. In 1918 men who hadn't had the property to qualify for a vote under the old system got the vote, and so did women, but not yet on the same basis as men. Men could vote at 21, women only at 30. Women finally got franchise equality with men in 1929.

B. That's just what I need, a rehash of school-kid history.

A. Are you sure you don't?

B. You accept that democracy has progressively improved, don't you? Whatever the shortcomings in the past, it's good now, or anyway, a great deal better.

A. Have you ever come across the idea that the best de facto constitution Britain has had was in the 35 years between the admission of the bourgeoisie to the vote in 1832, and the admission of some of the urban working class in 1867?

B. Now you go on from school-kid history to eccentric glosses on the British constitution!

A. I was startled by the idea that 1832-67 was the ideal system of bourgeois democracy the first time I came upon it, in a book by a serious historian of democracy and other things, W E H Lecky, published at the end of the 19th century.

B. Serious historian? Crank, surely?

A. Serious and once very prominent historian. He wrote a multi-volumed history of Britain in the 18th century. He published a history of Ireland. Initially for Irish Home Rule, he ended up a Liberal Unionist MP in 1895-1903. His idea about the British constitution between the first and second Reform Acts was very simple and, I think, true from his point of view. It is a mirror of what Marxists say, from our point view, about bourgeois democracy. Before 1867, when some of the urban workers got the vote, there was an identity between the electorate and the men of property. Therefore, there could be a responsible self-administering democracy.

B. It wasn't what we call democracy today!

A. From our working-class point of view, control by the property-owners is exactly what we have today for most of the affairs of the country. Only in 1832-67 it was straightforward and transparent.

B. What do you find good in that system?

A. Nothing! The important thing to grasp is that there was then a transparent relation between economic and political power. That was altered by the electoral reforms after 1867 which admitted some of the "have-nots" into the old democracy of the "haves". In a sense Lecky merely explained and expounded the meaning of an old key idea in the case for democracy: "No taxation without representation". It also meant: no representation without taxation. Or, that politics should belong to those with a stake in the serious property of the country.

The great paradox in pluto-democracy is that political democracy and economic democracy are splintered. Successive expansions of the electorate admitted the "have-nots" to nominal rule over the property-owning "haves". The ownership of the country did not go with or fall in line with the new official political system. A gap like a pair of scissors opening came into being between notional political power and real economic and social power. That gap was dealt with by the opening of another gap: between notional political power and real political and social power.

Socialists want to restore the link between democracy, voting and property in the only way it can be restored, to reunite political forms and economic power in the only they can be reunited, by collective property and all-embracing political and social democracy. In the 1832-67 system, politics could be open and honest and frank, posing real issues before an educated electorate who were legislating for themselves, the property-owners of the country. You could say: legislation of the people of money, for the people of money, by the people of money. After 1867, politics was no longer, could no longer be, that. It was no longer a matter of self-administration by responsible property-holders. From that came the dominance in politics of demagogy, lies, "spinning", and political cloak-work with politicians acting as matadors to baffle the electoral bull.

For the first half or three quarters of the 19th century, the upper classes feared democracy — the democracy of Robespierre and St Just in the French Revolution, or of Thomas Jefferson after the USA achieved independence — seeing it as rule for the people by the people, and necessarily in their interests. Just as rule by the rich was rule in their own interests, so too would be rule by the people. That is how those clamouring for the vote saw it too. When, for example, the British Chartists of the 1830s and 40s demanded the vote, they understood the franchise to mean the gaining of political and economic control. The people who would gain the vote would have their bread-and-butter questions taken care of by an administration of their own

— just as those who already had the vote did.

B. That was primitive democracy, and impossible democracy if rich and poor were to coexist peacefully.

A. Yes, indeed. That is why in the political crisis of 1848 the British ruling class were willing to have civil war rather than concede what the Chartists demanded. They mobilised masses of special constables, as well as the army, to beat down the Chartists.

B. And what happened?

A. The Chartists retreated, and thereafter, as capitalism surged to new growth and expansion, Chartism went into a severe decline. Decades later the thread was picked up by the early Marxist organisations and the Independent Labour Party and then the Labour Party, and woven into the fabric of a renewed working-class political movement.

B. Well, evidently the Chartists were mature enough eventually to understand that democracy is and must be above class rule, and impossible if it's a case of "winner takes all" in the economy and society.

A. After 1867 the rich kept their economic and social power behind a facade of "pure democracy", that is, of democracy redefined to mean votes for the people but continued rule for the rich by the rich and their agents. The rich held to what they had and increased it. Bourgeois right and bourgeois norms remained in place, behind the allegedly "pure" democracy. Democracy became pluto-democracy, democracy not of the people, not for the people, not by the people.

B. So you say that the British constitution between the first and second Reform Acts, between 1832 and 1867, was the best democratic constitution?

A. No, I don't say that. Lecky says it. His point of view is not mine. But it is tremendously illuminating. It is what serious socialists say — from the other side of the class barricades. He said, from his own bourgeois point of view, what Marxist socialists say: that to be real, political democracy has to have a corresponding basis of economic and social democracy. Without that, political democracy is shallow, demagogic, and far less than its heralds say it is. And in times of crisis it becomes unstable. To be real and historically secure, democracy has to have a commensurate social and economic basis. It has to be coupled either with a restricted franchise or with an economy owned collectively — that is, democratically. In Britain after 1867, a state bureaucracy was built to act as a dual steering system with political democracy and democratically elected governments and usurp in fact the rights of any elected government the bourgeoisie did not agree with. Tony Benn told of an incident after Labour won a general election. By accident a file of papers was given him which had a note attached: "For the new minister, if he is not Tony Benn".

In 1848 the Chartists backed down before the concentrated force of the ruling class. They did not change their views on what democracy was, what it had to be if it was really to be democracy, and not a system of deception and bamboozlement of the people. Or, to put it at its weakest, a system with a large component of deception and bamboozlement.

B. Surely that was good? Without it we wouldn't have our existing democracy, "compromise democracy" if you like. When the lower orders threaten property, then society locks down. You get a Mussolini or Hitler or Franco regime.

A. You get naked and unashamed bourgeois rule through fascist or regular army gangsters.

B. Democracy above the conflicts and interests of class is preferable. "Pure democracy", if you like, is the only possible democracy.

A. The only form of democracy compatible with bourgeois property ownership and de facto political rule in society is that "pure" political democracy which leaves decisive day-to-day economic questions outside its normal scope. In the system administered by "pure democracy", the property of the rich is secure. The voting rights and other democratic reforms sought by the Chartists are gutted of the social and economic content of democracy as initially conceived by democrats and anti-democrats alike.

B. Democratic government *should* be free of the crude self-interest of classes.

A. You really believe that it is? If that is what you think democracy should be, then you implicitly condemn the existing democracy, which normally, in most respects, serves the crude self-interest of the rich. A welfare state may emerge out of a compromise between the mass of the people and the property-owners brokered by reform-socialists, as after 1945 with the British Labour government. In great social crises like that in France in 1936, when there was a general strike and the election of a Popular Front government, big concessions may be made to the workers, for a time. For a long time, even. They are taken back at the first chance that the bourgeoisie gets to do it in safety.

B. That's got nothing to do with the principles of democratic self-government and "pure democracy".

A. But don't kid yourself: we don't have "pure democracy". Such a thing is impossible. "Pure democracy" — democracy conceived apart from the economic and social rule of the demos, of the people, in their own interest — becomes "pluto-democracy", social and economic and political rule in the interests of the rich and very rich. It becomes the hybrid thing you see today in Britain and, more nakedly, in the USA.

Democratic governments fight class and social wars on behalf of the big property-owners. A generation ago, the Thatcher government fought a ferocious class war against the working people. For a year it waged brutal class war on the most rebellious section of the working class, the coal miners. After it beat the miners, it rampaged through society, against the interests and rights of the working people. The political and social world we live in has been shaped by the victories of the ruling class under Thatcher. The trade unions are still legally shackled as a result of those victories. Britain has the most restrictive and repressive trade-union laws in western Europe! "Pure democracy" is a mirage, a sham, in essence a lie or an inverted pyramid of lies.

B. So you dismiss the vote and civil liberties as shams?

A. In the most serious matters, yes. For instance, during the year-long miners' strike of 1984-5, the government directed the police to ignore the laws when expedient and necessary to control the miners. Police stopping miners on the highways to prevent them going picketing was illegal. They did it anyway.

B. So the vote and civil liberties are worthless?

A. I didn't say that. Limited though they may be, civil liberties and the franchise are precious rights won by the people, and worth fighting to preserve and extend.

B. Now you are being illogical, or hypocritical.

A. The vote — and civil liberties going back centuries — were won by the "common people" and the women and men of the working class. They are precious even in their diminished or undeveloped form. They are springboards for further advance and barriers against social regression. They should be defended when they are attacked. And extended, deepened, put on a better socio-economic foundation!

B. Defended even if they are attacked by the authoritarian left?

A. By Stalinists? If that is what you mean, then yes. Stalinism was not in fact a left-wing movement, despite what you, and people who share your point of view say, in your determination to maintain that Stalinism was the typical left-wing movement.

B. Determination to defend the truth! Stalinism was an anti-capitalist movement.

A. Yes it was, but not thereby a working-class or a liberating movement. Nor was it a progressive alternative to capitalism. It was simultaneously an anti bourgeois and an anti working class movement. It demonstrated in practice that not all anti-bourgeois movements are progressive or in the interests of the working class.

B. Stalinism was the only actual and viable supposedly-progressive alternative to what you call pluto-democracy.

A. One of the greatest political achievements in the history of the bourgeoisie was the enthronement of "pure democracy", the separation of democracy from the meaning it had up to the mid 19th century and beyond, which was, to use Abraham Lincoln's classic definition, "rule of the people, for the people, by the people".

B. So, democracy doesn't live up to romantic rhetoric from the 19th century? Of course it doesn't. That's human nature for you. All politicians lie and present false prospectuses to the electorate, and socialist politicians more than most.

A. Suddenly you turn cynic! You are an example of how political life under the existing system can make even a naive and credulous bourgeois democrat disablingly cynical. It corrupts your capacity to see possible futures — just as it blinds you to the realities around you now. The mystification and degradation of politics is a consequence of the separation of political democracy from social democracy. Politicians in this system can't tell the full social or political truth. Often they can't openly avow what is really being discussed in political debates. Because of the pretend-democracy to which they bow, they can't with candour speak of the bourgeois minority rule in society and economy and the subordination of the rest of society to their needs and interests. This system is, so to speak, the "democracy of the lie". The big lie that within the democratic shell, the bourgeoisie does not rule society, primarily in its own interests.

You get lies, double-talk, self-misrepresentation, demagogy, the noisy clash of parties over personalities and trivia. You get the political cesspool we live in. You can get the de facto disenfranchisement of large parts of the people, when they have no political party to express and defend their interests, as with the British working class from the Blair-Brown coup in 1994 to the Corbyn victory in 2015.

B. The way to find answers to social problems is through our existing real democracy, not through your chimerical future democracy.

A. Don't be so naïve! There was once something in some Third World countries, Indonesia and others, officially called "guided democracy". Present-day democracies are all, even the best, though to different extents, "guided democracies".

B. Better than your ideal of "guided socialist authoritarianism".

A. That isn't my ideal! Nor is it the logic of my socialism.

B. You disparage democracy at every turn! You conjure up a stupid day-dream and substitute it for a proper evaluation and appreciation of the great things we have already, now. You destructively counterpose a "should be" and a "might be" to the good that exists now. The inescapable implication is that the only possible alternatives to democracy are better.

A. Try not to be so "authoritarian" and "totalitarian" yourself in your way of arguing. And try not to be an idiot! Criticism of existing democratic systems implies neither a desire to destroy them, nor support for some sort of authoritarianism. The problem here is that you see "democracy" as an abstract, classless, a-historical democracy that does not in fact exist.

B. Of course democracy exists.

A. Of course different sorts and degrees of democracy exist. But so, again, do all sorts of limitations of specific democracies. Democracy is not something always equal to itself. No existing democracy is equal to even the better self of its own limited ideal.

If you are serious about democracy and about developing democracy, you need to stand back and look at it in historical perspective. It has not existed all that long in history, you know, and where it has existed in capitalist society it has sometimes unravelled and regressed. There have been various sorts and durations of parliamentary democracy. And other sorts of democracy have existed too.

B. Don't be ridiculous? You mean the old USSR "democracy"?

A. No. I mean real soviet democracy — the democracy of the workers' councils that emerged in Russia in 1917, and then in Germany and Austria and Hungary. And even in Ireland between 1919 and 1922.

B. Ah! The island of saints, scholars, sorrows and soviets! Don't be perverse! In any case, it didn't last long, did it?

A. No. But it did tremendous things while it existed.

B. Not as good as the USA's democracy, for example, which you call mere bourgeois democracy.

DEMOCRACY IN U.S. HISTORY

A. Take the USA's democracy, then. Over 200 years old — or: in historical time a *mere* 200 years old! — it was designed for a population of small and medium farmers and urban producers and slave-plantation owners. It was an elite democracy, as of course the original Athenian democracy of slave-owners was. There were a lot of exclusions from the franchise: by religion until 1828, by property requirements until 1856, by race until 1869-70, and by gender until 1919-20. There were also many exclusions from civil liberty, for slaves in the first place and also for indentured servants, people who were white semi-slaves for a set time.

There were vast numbers of black slaves, captured in Africa and put to work in America, or, later, when Britain suppressed the international slave trade after 1807, produced on US slave-breeding farms. Children bred to slavery would never, so long as the slave system existed, have any rights at all. Not even the right to life, or the right not to be worked to death under the slave-driver's whip.

So-called Indians, the Native Americans, had few right too. Amerindians did not get the right to be US citizens until 1924. The last state laws excluding them from voting were not abolished until 1957.

B. So marauding savages should have had the vote! That would reconcile them! Great for democracy, too! Citizen Indian, aim your arrow, bullet, knife, or tomahawk at the slit in that little ballot box over there!

A. You think bonehead prejudice is funny? Even "civilised" Native Americans had no rights. Early in the 19th century, the so-called "five civilised tribes", including the well-known Cherokees, were forcibly removed from the south-east of the United States and set down in "Indian Territory" in Oklahoma.

B. US society was being formed, absorbing vast numbers of immigrants. "Give me your poor, your huddled masses..." What do you want to do — roll back the spool of history and give America back to the Amerindians? That would also mean undoing the effects of America's interaction with the rest of the world, rolling back the last 500 years of world history.

A. No. That isn't possible.

B. It is desirable?

A. Not desirable, either.

B. Your attitude is reactionary romanticism! The exclusion of Native Americans from the emerging American society and civilisation was not only something done to them. They were self-excluding, because they were in the grip of an all-shaping cultural inertia and conservatism. Tribes fought to maintain their way of life. Do you think that the great plains and prairies should have been left to a handful of Native Americans as hunting grounds? That we should give the USA and Canada back to them?

A. "We"?

B. Yes, we. Something of the same order of things was done to the aboriginal Irish in the 16th and 17th centuries. But going back and undoing history — "give Ireland back to the aboriginal Irish" — is absurd. We can undo some of the consequences of history, but that is all.

A. "The Irish" have taken it back!

B. Come to think of it, was that a good thing?

A. Yes. I agree that there are tragic things in history which nonetheless in fact entered importantly into historical progress. They are a large part of what Marxists think of as human "pre-history" — the history of class society. They can't be undone or reversed and they shouldn't be if they could. Their effects have entered into and shaped irreversible histories. The English plunder and would-be genocidal massacres of my ancestors in Ireland played a part in the primitive accumulation of English capital, which revolutionised the world, Ireland too eventually, and for the better. We can wish that things had been done less murderously and with fewer victims. At this remove we can only try to mend some of the consequences.

B. With democracy. As we do.

A. Democracy itself worked to destroy the Amerindians in the USA. The Native Americans did much better in Canada and even in South America, even though terrible things were done to them there, than in the USA. In the USA there was no authoritative central state (like the British power in Canada or the Spanish power in South America). There was no government which would have the power, if it had the will, to coerce the settlers who repeatedly invaded territory allotted by treaty to the Native Americans in pursuit of gold and good land.

84

B. OK. We've all seen the Western movies!

A. The democratic, self-governing, weak-state aspects of US society worked to create a relentless pressure on Amerindian territories and their Amerindian peoples. As you sneer, it's the sort of thing you see in many old Western movies.

B. Unpleasant. An oft-repeated tragedy. It can't be, and in its fundamentals shouldn't be, undone.

A. No. But note the part played in the tragedy of the Amerindians by the democratic nature of society in the territory of the USA.

B. All right. Democracy enables, but does not ennoble. It does not necessarily produce the ideal good society. Women and black people and Amerindians eventually got the vote — a stake and a role in US democracy. The original democracy was improved, adapted, and expanded. It evolved according to its benign democratic nature.

A. The USA's transformation was not just a peaceful evolution, a mere "democratic process". The slave states weren't quiet and passive passengers in the American body politic, waiting to be sorted out by democratic evolution. They shaped US foreign policy for a long time. We read of the American "Texicans'" fight for freedom in Texas against the Mexican military dictator Santa Ana.

B. Seen that film, too. Remember the Alamo!

A. In fact one of the grievances of American-Texicans like Jim Bowie against Mexico was that it forbade the black slavery that they wanted to introduce, and did introduce when they had control. They were not just martyrs in the fight of Americans in Texas for democratic self-rule. They were martyrs in the cause of extending slavery beyond the borders of the existing American slave states. You haven't see that film yet...

B. That was then. This is the democratic now!

A. It took a very bloody civil war to free the slaves. And then, after less than a decade in which the Federal government encouraged "Black Reconstruction", the political and social emancipation of the freed slaves, the ex-slaves were again plunged down into helotry, in

85

practice deprived of the vote for a hundred years. Then it took the great civil rights struggle — initiated by a brave pioneering black woman, Rosa Parks, who in 1955 refused to give her seat on a bus to a white man — to begin to give substance to the formal democratic rights of African-Americans and end segregation, or at least some aspects of segregation. The post-slavery century of black helotry is a terrible story. African-Americans are still having to fight right now against being casually shot down in the street by nervous cops.

B. Nevertheless, democracy and liberty allow progress. A civil rights movement was possible.

A. Yes. I don't say otherwise. But can we get back to the point I was trying to make? The "good things" in the early American democracy were designed for a society of small and medium producers. Thomas Jefferson thought slavery would simply wither away, but that was before the 19th century expansion of the Lancashire cotton trade, the world's most advanced power-driven industry, and the consequent expansion of the market for slave-produced raw cotton on which the Lancashire mills depended.

The physiognomy of society changed, and at an accelerated pace after the Civil War. Giant industrial enterprises emerged — railroads, mines, oil, steel, cars, etc. In a democracy designed for 18th century communities of small and medium-sized producers, these giants and their owners bestrode society like the proverbial Colossus.

B. So, society evolves. Do you want to stop that?

A. I want you to understand what happened to US democracy as a result of those social changes.

B. You want to devalue, disqualify, and disparage actually existing democracy. That's what you are trying to do!

A. I want you to see that US social evolution has devalued and disparaged and in effect disqualified its original democratic ideal, and to an enormous extent.

WOMEN AND DEMOCRACY

A. You know, of course, that even in the most democratic countries, women were long excluded from democracy and from equal citizenship? No vote, no right to personal property as against their husbands, no rights over their children. That was the underside of the great democratic progress for humankind over centuries. The political and social "rights of man and the citizen" which were won, more or less, in the French Revolution and the other bourgeois revolutions did not exist for women for many decades after they existed for men, or at least for some men. Women have had to fight for their own "bourgeois" revolution. And that fight is still going on.

B. No, democracy prevails.

A. If it does, it didn't come to prevail peacefully. Women had to fight, and some women to die, to win even approximations to equality and democracy.

B. That crazy suffragette throwing herself under the hooves of the king's horse at a racetrack? Advance for women would have come anyway, as a result of their role in the factories during the First World War.

A. Don't be such a bonehead! Women workers were exploited as workers, and doubly exploited as workers without substantial social rights.

B. Letting women into many jobs previously the preserve of men liberated them.

A. It opened up great possibilities, while also systematically blocking off those possibilities. Capitalism provoked people to fight for the equality it promised but could not deliver. Women have had to fight a double fight. Women need socialism as much as, maybe more than, men. To an enormous extent, in practice unequal pay continues. So does the channelling of women workers into usually lower-paid jobs. So do glass ceilings. So does the main burden of child-care and housework.

B. Modern domestic equipment and fast foods, all products of capitalism, have already "liberated" women.

A. Not even remotely enough! To liberate women fully, socialism would reorganise domestic work on a collective basis.

B. Capitalism has already done some real things to lighten the load. Why do you think the working class would do more?

A. Because most women are working class, and in a general forward movement of the whole working class, the female half of the class would want to liberate itself fully. It would cut away the barriers which restrict women's equality outside the home. Women's status would rise.

B. Don't you think it has risen enough? Spectacularly, in fact.

A. There are many things still to fight for: equal pay; equal respect; free, state-of-the-art health care that meets women's needs; safe pregnancy, safe childbirth, safe abortion; freely available social childcare.

B. Isn't there a choice to be made between your silly socialism on the one hand, and feminism, anti-racism, etc. on the other? You are trying to boost your socialism by selling it as something else. If you were really sure of your socialism, you would concentrate on that. Logically, you should argue against women's organisations on the grounds that they divide the workers' movement.

A. Then we'd be your ideal socialists! Narrow, stupid, and not in touch with real life. Socialists are honest participants in the battles of women, black people, refugees, and others, because what their zealots fight for is part of what we fight for. There is a logical and natural link between their battles and our socialism. In any case, it is not really "us" and "them": "they" are an equal part of our people, of the human and working-class solidarity for which we fight.

B. The idea that women in Britain today are oppressed is wild exaggeration. Demagogy. Socialists who were serious in their socialism would have no truck with such ideas.

A. Only bigoted fools would oppose campaigns for women's rights, or against oppression of gay people, or denounce such activists with the claim that their campaign is "divisive". Serious fighters for solidarity get involved, help the campaigns to grow, and contribute to political discussions about how best to go forward. And in fact, of course, we do not just join in; socialists initiate action for women's rights. These are complementary parts of the cause of solidarity in society, not alternatives.

B. When we had a good woman as prime minister, bigoted socialists spat hate at her. That was anti-woman!

A. Thatcher was a disgrace to womankind as well to humanity. She offered negative proof that "womanism" is not enough in a world where women are part of the bourgeoisie as well as of the exploited class, the working class. If not proof, at least evidence that "womanism" — feminism that is not socialist — cannot finally emancipate women. The women's "bourgeois" revolution must be fused with the general socialist revolution if it is to win its great liberating objectives.

Part 4: Socialism and human nature

CAPITALISM AND "THE INVADING SOCIALIST SOCIETY"

A. Karl Marx once defined his socialism as a consciousness of the unconscious social processes. It is a good description of it. Socialism — political, social, and economic communality, generalised human solidarity and fellowship — is of course a good idea. It was a good idea hundreds of years and millennia before Karl Marx. Marxists called themselves "scientific socialists" because their advocacy of socialism was more than a mere good idea about how things might be or should be. It was an idea of how the economy, society, and human thinking about how to organise social life, were tending to go — were compelled by their own logic to go. An idea of how the contradictions in capitalist society would propel society forward — like the contradiction we see in the case of the modern bankers, between the private ownership and owner-serving operation of the means of production and exchange, and the gigantically social nature of production and finance.

B. Your claim that Marxist socialism is rational and "scientific", not merely utopian, is just a dream, pure delusion.

A. Marx and Engels grasped the underlying tendency of capitalism to develop from smaller to ever larger concentrations of capital.

Today we have reached the overripe stage of global corporations so powerful that they can sometimes override governments and they ordinarily exercise a great deal of control over them. Routinely they evade the control of elected governments. They have the economic and political strength of medium-sized states. In certain boardrooms, the elect of capitalist civilisation can decide to move whole industries, employing thousands of workers, from one country to another, in search of cheaper labour-power or more docile workers.

B. But they are controlled by us all through the market.

A. The market is a good enough substitute for democracy?

B. Political control over all these economic operations is impossible. To attempt it would bring only bureaucratic bungling. The market may not be a perfect mechanism, but it works to make sure that economic activity serves the majority.

A. Capitalism socialises and centralises the processes of production, of exchange, and of communication. The plans and policies of a small number of companies govern what happens to many millions of people. In the 18th century great commercial entities like the British East India Company fought wars — sometimes against their French or Dutch equivalents — and conquered countries such as India. They ran ahead of governments. We have not quite come full circle here, but we aren't all that far from it either.

Frederick Engels once spoke of this phenomenon of capitalism's inbred tendency and need to "socialise" production, when it was a very early stage compared to now, as "the invading socialist society". Capitalism itself, in accordance with the unfolding logic of the market-profit mechanisms on which it operates, is the main engine of the evolution of capitalism towards socialism. It prepares the ground for socialism by its component units' relentless drives for growth, profit, monopolisation, annexation, the eating-up of competitors.

Marx's view was right or wrong as a picture of the social and economic reality of capitalism, and an expectation and advocacy about where it could go, but there was nothing vague and undefined about it, no arbitrary project-mongering, no utopianism. That, by the way, was why we call ourselves "scientific socialists".

B. Alchemistic socialists, surely! It has a better ring to it...

A. You need to prattle less, and think about things a little more! Socialism is the anticipatory shadow that capitalism casts ahead of itself.

B. No matter how big a corporation gets to be, there are competing corporations. Even giant corporations can go bust.

A. Yes. But some of today's global corporations control as much already as a hundred years ago a whole developed country's government could have controlled by nationalising industry. Some of the big and medium superstores contain whole towns'-worths of shops, organised and brought under one roof. But let me continue.

This state of affairs means that a tremendous degree of socialisation of the means of production, exchange, and communication already exists now. Each of the giant international conglomerates is a sort of island of "socialism", that is, of a planned economy. All this is the bedrock for our advocacy of socialism now. Socialists criticise pluto-democracy because it can't function as the multi-dimensional democracy that is required by these developments. The running of the great corporations needs to be put under democratic control. Here, democracy and socialism merge.

B. That is nonsensical! These corporations, no matter how big they are, are run for the private profit of the owners. They are governed by the self-interest, as they perceive it, of the office holders and shareholders. They are run democratically too. Each share carries a vote.

So too is the whole economy run democratically. Each purchase, so to speak, is a vote which almost mechanically regulates supply and demand in the economy. Adam Smith's so-called "hidden hand" is really the operation of an unseen subterranean exchange of information and exercise of choice by way of a market. Of a hidden rationality, if you like.

self-regulating market

A. In the market, the rich have much more "voting power" than the rest of us! But you think everything is for the best, in the best world you can imagine? Then how came 2008 and after...?

B. It is better than the world you imagine and advocate and say you "fight" for, and what socialism comes to in reality — Stalinism, or some similar -ism.

A. The point is that present-day capitalist reality has created

mountains of evidence for the basic Marxist thesis on which everything else depends — the spontaneous concentration of capital into
gigantic social entities. Even Marx might be momentarily astonished
at the extent of it now and the continued growth of the scope of the
multinational corporations. You are loud in insisting that you are a
democrat, yet you glory in the fact that these tremendous enterprises
operate outside democratic control and for the private profit of a
few...

B. Only to show that they have nothing to do with socialism!
These things are capitalist.

A. Yes, they are capitalist. No denying that! No-one who knows
what socialism is would say otherwise. You glory in the fact that these
great social and economic entities are run for private interests.

B. That's the only possible economic basis of democracy.

A. Each big corporation is, so to speak, an island of democracy!
You think the corporations are democratically run by the shareholders? And you conclude that that makes the whole thing democratic,
the totality of multinationals and conglomerates? In fact, as everyone
knows, the great "socialised" capitalist enterprises are dominated by
the owners of big concentrations of capital, not by a demos of small
and very small investors.

B. There are "shareholder revolts".

A. Not many, and not decisive. In any case, even if "shareholder"
democracy were real, it is a strange idea that the system is made democratic as a whole by some elements being internally democratic, no
matter how many of those there are. You probably know that the
Caribbean pirates in the 17th and 18th centuries, who roamed the
seas robbing, burning, and murdering, sometimes organised their
shipboard communities democratically, discussing and deciding big
questions by vote. I never heard anybody argue that therefore they
were not pirates, or that their shipboard democracy should be reck-
oned as a contribution to the progress of democracy in the world.

B. The equation of the great commercial enterprises of today to
those pirates is ludicrous! They operate legally, not outside the law.

A. Do they? They make and remake law, or flout and ignore it. Essentially, it is their law. We have yet to see one of these pirates hanged in chains at Marble Arch (which is the site of the old-time hanging ground, Tyburn)!

B. But their rule is not a lawless tyranny

A. Tell that to communities suddenly deprived of jobs by ukase of an international corporation seeking higher profits or more docile and more exploitable workers. Often, now, the rule of the corporations is a lawless tyranny. My point here, though, is that the development of the giant corporations has greatly strengthened the Marxist idea, that capitalism by its own operation, on its own laws of motion, erects the mechanical underpinnings of the future socialist economy. Stalinism did not destroy that trend. It did not kill that aspect of the socialist programme. To do that, it would have had to conquer the advanced capitalist world.

B. The viability of the existing social, political, and economic system within which the concentration of capital takes place — that is what kills socialism!

A. It isn't dead yet. In relation to the "social" character of the big corporations and conglomerates, what needs to be done was spelled out as long ago as 1848 by Karl Marx and Frederick Engels in the Communist Manifesto: the working class has to "win the battle of democracy".

B. We've won the battle of democracy already!

A. The world around you shows that that is not so. Most of the things that shape our lives are outside democratic control. International corporations make that more not less true. They can even decide what taxes they will deign to pay. They act in some ways like sovereign states.

B. We'll see.

A. We'll see. The widespread post-Stalinist sentiment against socialism solves nothing basic for capital. Capitalism exists objectively. Its laws operate objectively and go on operating. The fundamental political contradiction is that these comparatively few corporations, run for their owners' private profit, control the economy of the vast world wide society which everyone depends on and lives in, and they are largely outside democratic control. The gobbledegook about democratic corporations and the hidden-hand votes in the market does not change that one bit. In the great slump that began in 2008, people saw governments act to intervene and subsidise giant banks. We haven't "won the battle of democracy" yet; but we will.

B. You're whistling in the dark.

A. This is, for Marxists, the "objective" basis of our socialism. It operates, and goes on operating, no matter how weak or confused the forces conscious of the logic and needs of this process — the so-cialists — are. Only with the help of the conscious activity of socialists can we win the harmonious outcome of these social contradictions and dynamics. But the dynamic which creates conditions for social-ism goes on working even amidst the massacre of the socialists, and even if administered by those who condemn or massacre socialists. All they achieve, all they can achieve, is to confine the solution of the social contradictions, for a time, to stop-gap, pro-tem expedients. In recent times it has been the driving force behind globalisation, the concentration of the means of production, distribution, and commu-nication into gigantic, and ever yet more gigantic, enterprises, eco-nomically bigger, as is often said, than many nation states.

Today, across the world, there are enormous conglomerations of means of production, exchange, and communication, in corporations that relate to the existing states something like the smaller Duke and prince ruled sub-states of the Dark Ages and the Middle Ages to the monarchies to which they nominally owed allegiance. The corpora-tions' autonomy vis-a-vis national states increases as their strength increases.

These modern "commercial kingdoms" operate as lawless tyran-nies to those who work within them, and as looting brigands to the societies around them. All this is rooted in the spontaneous move-ment of the capitalist productive forces into ever bigger concentra-tions. To change the image, it is like a pool of piranha fish who over time eat each other up until there are far fewer, but bigger and fatter, piranha fish left. The contradictions that have grown in the two cen-turies since the Industrial Revolution from the continued private ownership and operation of the social means of production, and its ingrained perpetual conflict with the bulk of the people, do not lessen but become more acute.

94

PLANNING: WHO PLANS? IN WHOSE INTERESTS?

B. "Planning" is your answer? The old socialist panacea. But you can't "plan" a complex modern economy in every detail. The attempt to do that creates an enormous and inevitably incompetent bureaucracy, not a usable plan.

A. It is not case of plan or no plan. The great corporations have their plans, too. The issue is who plans, and in whose interest — the interests of society, or of the rich and super-rich?

B. No, the issue is between modest sectional plans by the great corporations, and an overblown, state-wide, cauterising, totalitarian, socialist economic plan.

A. This is a curious case of a myth erected upon a myth. Here too, the bourgeoisie and its apologists feed on the lies of Stalinism. It is also a sly substitution of something else for what is supposedly being discussed. Planning of every detail is impossible? Yes, I think that is true. Therefore? Therefore the exploitation that is central to capitalism as to all class society cannot be done away with? Therefore the market must be treated as a fetish, a god that can be overruled only at risk of catastrophe? It is a bit like the idea that socialists are against private property, and would therefore seize your house and your smartphone, when in fact socialists are only against private property in the means of production and the exploitation that goes with it.

You say that because it would be impossible to pre-plan all the complex details of a modern economy, therefore all planning is entirely impossible. Thereby you evade the decisive question: what is to be planned? What needs to be planned? How much needs to be planned if we are to escape the tyranny of the market and the capitalist class exploitation that goes with it?

Socialism does not need or presuppose a Stalinist-like "planning" or attempted planning of everything. It doesn't need the nationalisation of everything, either. What needs to be planned and integrated into coherence are the great basic decisions of production and distribution. There is no reason why in such planning there cannot also be free choice of what individuals consume, and production that is responsive to what people like or want.

B. In fact the "planned economies" were not responsive.

95

A. The Stalinists nationalised everything down to the proverbial corner shop because the Stalinist ruling class, the bureaucratic class, demanded for itself every possible scrap of wealth, in the painfully underdeveloped society over which they ruled. They viewed small enterprises as class competition from "the petty bourgeoisie" to possess the surplus product.

B. What's that, the surplus product, when it's at home?

A. All that can be leeched out of the producers; for the working class, all the value they add in their work, above the cost of their wages.

B. You mean the legitimate returns on investment!

A. Trotsky and his comrades such as Christian Rakovsky severely criticised the socially cauterising "nationalisation" of everything in the USSR, as they also criticised the blindly-bureaucratic, over-detailed, handed-down-from-above Stalinist attempts at planning. Trotsky described the command economy created by Stalinism in the first half of the 1930s as an exercise governed by "bureaucratic delirium". Such measures were specific to Stalinism. They were never part of a Marxist programme.

B. Trotsky had no effect on what happened! He was like a cat thrown out into the cold, mewling angrily outside the door.

A. He embodied old socialism, the October revolution and Bolshevism: read what he was "mewling"! You know what most expresses the spurious nature of the objection that you can't plan a modern economy? The fact that the great international and national conglomerates already plan now, for their own multifarious industries and networks.

B. Of course they do. That is why your "invading socialist society" is a delusion.

A. They plan. Except that they plan for maximising markets and profits in competition with each other. They plan to get the greatest volume of profit in their own interest, and not to serve the interests of society, or to do that only incidentally and on condition that they thereby serve their private interests. Socialist planning would inte-

96

grate and make complementary the sectional capitalist planning that is a central attribute of modern capitalism, and reorient it to serve the interests of the people and of society as a whole. That way we would overcome the crying contradiction at the heart of capitalism — social production with private appropriation of the fruits of the productive labour of vast numbers of people. I repeat: integrating and adapting the existing plans into human — as distinct from capitalist — coherence would not be all that difficult.

You're right that our capacity to predict is limited, and it is not possible to have a precise plan for every economic detail. But the argument for socialism does not depend in the least on future socialist economic plans being precise or minutely-detailed or error-free. It depends only on the claim that humanity can and must democratically and rationally plan the broad lines of the economic enterprises which now, after centuries of capitalist development, involve and affect us all, rather than leaving those broad lines to be decided by the outcome of chaotic competition driven by the greed of a few. As well as that basic argument, it is a fact that computers, which are continually being improved, do and will provide tremendous tools for planning.

B. Such an integrated central plan would inevitably lead to some species of authoritarianism. Increasing corporate power to plan points to the dangers. It is a danger that will increase, not lessen, with technological advance.

A. The question is not to plan or not to plan. It is not even one of what should or should not be centrally planned — but of who plans, how, and in whose interests. That is a question of democracy, of whether we continue to have the pluto-democracy we have now, or create a genuine three-dimensional democracy encompassing social, economic and political life. It is a question of whether or not the working class "wins the battle of democracy" against plutocratic bourgeois democracy.

State governed by wealthy

97

GLOBALISATION AND SOCIALISM

B. In any case, much of the old socialism was couched in terms of workers taking power in an existing state. Today the international conglomerates and the global financial markets are too much outside the power of national government for isolated national action to control an economy.

A. Yes, but also no. National governments do operate with cropped-down powers. Their economies are entwined with international economic operations over which they have little or no control. But national governments still have a lot of powers they don't use.

B. So, world government has to be in place first for a socialist transformation of even one country to be possible.

A. You should try to be consistent. Relate what you have just said to your claim that we already have a serviceable democracy, or maybe even the best possible democracy.

B. International conglomerates and global financial markets diminish democracy, true. But they do not destroy it — as socialists would.

A. No, we would expand and deepen democracy to take on the international conglomerates and the global financial markets! The problem you raise is new only in its form. Socialism have always conceived of working-class revolution as an international revolution. Wherever it started – France, Germany, Britain, or Russia – it would spread across Europe at least. That is what the Bolsheviks aimed to initiate: an international working-class revolution.

It is inconceivable that the political ferment that would lead to a workers' revolution in, say, France, would not also affect the workers in neighbouring countries; inconceivable that a working-class revolution in one country would not spur workers in other countries to do the same by lighting up perspectives and possibilities the workers had not seen before. And do that much faster now, with modern communications.

B. Yet that didn't happen for the Bolsheviks in 1917 and after, did it?

A. In fact it did, most notably in Germany in 1918-19. Pro-Bolshevik movements, strong or weak, emerged all over Europe. Short-lived soviet governments were established in Hungary and Bavaria in 1919. Factory occupations covered Italy in 1920. The workers were defeated, in large part because of the politics and character of their leaderships. There is never a guarantee of victory, but it would be very unlikely that a socialist revolution, wherever it started, would be isolated in one country for long. It would not be an isolated socialist state in a sea of capitalist power, or not for long. Relatively recent history shows a number of examples of revolutions spreading from country to country — in Eastern Europe during the collapse of the Russian empire in 1989 and after, in the Arab world in 2011. In your own way, you are right for once. Wherever a socialist revolution started, it would have to become an international revolution. Yes!

B. Instant world government or nothing! Another tall order.

A. A world government is not going to happen soon, or, if capitalism continues, ever. The emergence of a bloc of countries where the working class has set up socialist workers' governments is the likely great next step.

B. That's inconceivable — the remaining capitalist powers would be too hostile.

A. They were hostile to Bolshevik Russia. No fewer than 14 states intervened on the side of the counter-revolutionaries in the civil war that followed the 1917 revolution. But there was great working-class resistance to that at home in the countries that intervened. In 1920 British dockworkers refused to load munitions for the Polish army at war with revolutionary Russia.

B. Wishful thinking!

A. Illuminating precedent.

B. The Bolsheviks remained isolated. You people offer that as explanation for what you call the Stalinist degeneration of the USSR.

A. Before the Russian revolution, during it, and after it, we advocated international socialist revolution.

B. What if your revolution remained internationally isolated?

A. Then we would be defeated. But neither precedent nor probability says defeat would be inevitable.

B. You refuse to face up to the new conditions of international capitalist power, and the new arguments against socialism which flow from them.

A. I'd say that the growth of new global oligarchies outside even notional democratic control gives new arguments for socialism, not against. Your arguments against socialism are not new. For instance, in Britain in the mid-1920s, in a polemic with Leon Trotsky over his book *Where is Britain Going?*, Bertrand Russell rejected the idea of a British working-class revolution because Britain was so heavily dependent on foreign trade. He argued that a working-class Britain would be isolated and crushed.

B. Russell was just being responsible.

A. Not to the fight for socialism, to which he paid some lip-service in its reform-socialist form. In fact a British working-class revolution would probably have detonated similar revolutions in Germany, France, and Italy. Today, as I've said, a working-class revolution in one country would light up the world as the Bolshevik revolution did, only faster and more brilliantly, and let millions see and desire new possibilities.

HUMAN NATURE

B. You fly in the face of the natural laws of society and of human nature! Capitalism is an expression of humankind's deepest impulses, harnessed to produce good effects by the wonders-working market. You can't suppress or supersede that.

A. I know! Human beings are just animals? The naked ape?

B. Exactly. Nature itself is the opposite of your benign, or would-be benign, utopia-mongering. You can't change human nature. Humanity remains an animal. Human nature — competition, individualism, selfishness, predatoriness — produces, protects, and preserves capitalism.

100

A. If that were true, then why did we not have capitalism all back through history? We have had slave societies, feudal societies, "oriental-despotic" societies (ancient India and China, Inca Peru). The idea that capitalism is eternal is simply ignorant, or, for some, wish-thinking.

B. Don't be a smart-arse. You know what I mean: human beings are animals which prey on other animals. It's our deepest nature.

A. Society remoulds our animal natures and impulses to an enormous extent. You may be broke or hungry and have an impulse to rob someone or break a shop window to get what you want, but the great bulk of civilised humanity will not act on such impulses.

B. What about the riots four or five years back, when people looted electronic goods stores?

A. The rarity of things like that reinforces my point.

B. They are rare because of the fear that state reprisals instil in people. Fear rules, not social feeling or innate altruism.

A. It is not just fear, though in some people that may be the main inhibiting factor. Mostly it is the sense of right and wrong, the awareness that society could not run if many people behaved that way. A desire to keep faith with others in society.

B. And your point?

A. Human beings are self-aware, self-controlling, self-shaping, self-reshaping, as a rule. Natural animalist impulses are, for most people, most of time, educated into submission to the higher order we in society have made for ourselves and of ourselves. We can aspire to a society governed by something higher than the dog-eat-dog morality which capitalism teaches and which you accept and promulgate.

There is nothing in that aspiration which requires us to idealise human nature. Marx once said of himself that he identified with what an ancient Greco-Roman, Terence, said: Nothing human is alien to me.

B. Not everything he said or quoted is rubbish, then!

A. You could adapt that idea to: "Nothing animal is alien to humankind". At the start we are animals, and then animals who have developed themselves and gained consciousness of themselves — human beings. And not to slander our cousins, the animals, the fact is that much animal behaviour is altruistic. It is only human beings that prey systematically on their own kind.

To cite only one of many examples which the old anarchist Kropotkin collected in a whole book on the subject: "I was struck with the extent of mutual assistance which [crabs] are capable of bestowing upon a comrade in case of need. One of them had fallen upon its back in a corner of the tank, and its heavy saucepan-like carapace prevented it from returning to its natural position. Its comrades came to the rescue, and for [hours] they endeavoured to help".

B. Socialist solidarity for crabs! Now you are turning into a disciple of dear old St Francis, who preached to his brothers, the birds and the seals!

A. He probably got more sense out of them than I'm getting out of you! The process of evolution from ape to human, from hunter-gatherer to our present tremendous ability to manipulate and in some respects control inanimate nature, is a long process of self-construction and self-reconstruction, in which we have made and then again re-made ourselves. That is basic: humankind makes and remakes itself. Nurture refracts nature, shapes and determines its social manifestations. It does that now. It can do it differently.

B. The aspiration to the socialist world you want — as distinct from Stalinism: for the sake of argument, I'll concede that for the moment — a world governed by fellow-feeling and human solidarity...

A. What William Morris used to call "fellowship"...

B. ... is hopeless. That aspiration, too, in you is old Christianity disguised: "All things bright and beautiful... The Lord God made them all". No, he didn't! There is darkness, as well as light, and rather more of it. Learn from history! Accept the reality! Go with the grain! Not only the Stalinists, but the Nazis too, were what they were because they tried to reshape society according to an impossible, crazy ideal. Leave well enough alone!

A. Some wise old ape probably grunted that idea at another one

102

who swung down from the trees and tried to walk upright. Your ancestor, the mate of the woman who invented agriculture, probably beat her for wasting good eating-seed by putting it in little holes she made in the ground.

B. And the ape just down from the trees probably replied: We apes can do anything. As soon as I learn to walk, I'll climb to the top of the tree, flap my wings, and fly like the eagle. So, I haven't got wings? I'll grow a pair after I have learned to walk!

A. And yet the far distant descendants of that ape did learn to fly! Not by growing wings, it is true, but we fly nonetheless. The development of humankind's mastery of nature showed that growing fleshly wings, or adding bird-like wings to a mechanical structure, was not the way. There were other ways, and we discovered them. What that brave old ape wanted was realised, though not as she or he had imagined it could be.

As Trotsky put it: "The material premise of communism should be so high a development of the economic powers of man that productive labour, having ceased to be a burden, will not require any goad, and the distribution of life's goods, existing in continual abundance, will not demand — as it does not now in any well-off family or 'decent' boarding-house — any control except that of education, habit and social opinion. Speaking frankly, I think it would be pretty dull-witted to consider such a really modest perspective 'utopian'."

B. Said the man who slaughtered his enemies in the Russian civil war!

A. Enemies who slaughtered his comrades and who amidst other horrors organised the worst anti-Jewish pogroms known to history before Hitler's Holocaust. All your arguments that socialism is "against human nature" are proven false by history. It is true that basic human drives — hunger for survival, food, sex, putting self and family first — are instinctive and can't disappear. But Trotsky was right. People can be educated, and are educated and re-educated all the time. It is plain fact that prevailing conceptions of what is right or wrong, acceptable or unacceptable, have changed as society has changed. From age to age, the way that basic instinctual drives are harnessed, refracted, redirected, expressed in relations with other human beings, has changed. Brutus, Shakespeare's "noblest Roman of them all", thought it morally right that people who owed him money should be imprisoned: that is, deprived of freedom and the chance to earn a living, in a lot of cases condemned to starve to death. We know better. We have learned better.

B. Have we? Have we learned the right lessons? It is right that debtors should be penalised, and they are. One of the great bold statements of social law and the healthy society was made by an Irish government minister in the 1920s, Kevin O'Higgins, when he defined civilisation as a society in which the bailiff was able to function without fear of being shot.

A. The good part of that story is that he himself was shot dead on his way to Mass one Sunday morning in 1927.

B. You approve?

A. I don't weep. He had worked hard during the civil war of 1922-3 and after to earn what, finally, he got. It couldn't have happened to a man more deserving of it.

B. That means you approve.

A. Whatever. Take chattel slavery. In the ancient world, and long after, nobody, not philosophers, nor the early Christians, saw moral wrong in slavery, or in setting gladiators to fight and kill each other to provide spectators with sport. It's a myth that the Christians once in power stopped the gladiator-killing shows. There is some hidden chattel slavery in Britain now, and a lot of it in the wider world, but society frowns on it and punishes those who inflict it on other people.

Once we thought it right that kings should have absolute power of life and death and social regulation.

Not long ago in historical time it was thought right, and found to be morally acceptable, that children, even very small children, should go to work in dangerous factories or be made to crawl up sooty chimneys. When Parliament first regulated child labour, it cut the hours, but it was suggested that, instead, the morally upright Victorian capitalists should work double shifts of children on the shorter hours.

B. All those things have been rectified.

A. That's the point. They were once thought moral and necessary and good. The aspects of capitalism you defend and think normal will in future society be condemned as we condemn the now notorious old abuses.

B. Dream on! In fact, you prove only that the reform of abuses happens when enough people think it necessary.

A. I'm showing that moralities change. Pioneers began the work of changing the previous validation of existing social horrors. A large part of European and American society used to think it right to discriminate against Jews and persecute them; some, that it was a moral duty to persecute or murder them. For centuries, it was all right to enslave black people to forced labour. For a long time, it was all right in the USA to work them to death.

Not so long ago a woman's citizenship was subsumed into that of her husband. Legally, children had only one parent, the father; a woman's property became her husband's. What kind of "crank", what degree of crankiness, would it take now to advocate any of those things that were once prevalent? Or defend them? Take a case that shouldn't be forgotten, but is. At the end of the 19th century, a young couple, members of the Marxist Social Democratic Federation, announced that, not believing in marriage, they were going to live together without the blessing of priest or the licence of registrar. The woman's parents committed her to an asylum for the insane. The couple were eventually forced to legally marry. By the way, the daughter of that couple became a well-known actress, Elsa Lanchester.

B. Ah, the "Bride of Frankenstein" herself. That figures. Bet she was a socialist!

A. Less than a hundred years ago in Britain, women did not have the Parliamentary vote, and neither did vast numbers of men who lacked the minimum property requirements. Or take sexuality. The sexual freedom we have now is less than half a century old. We are foul and monstrous according to the old sexual morality. We live now in what used to be Sodom and Gomorrah. Not so long ago, tremendous restraints were placed on the expression of this basic human drive. Christian morality and social stigma imposed a terrible set of restraints on sexuality. People who believed that God made us, also believed that godly morality demanded that human beings fight to suppress the nature which they believe their god gave them. What changed? Essentially, there were changes in the technology and the possibilities of birth control — the pill — sexuality was uncoupled from procreation. Sexual liberation, a sex-morality revolution, followed. Today in Britain many people coming from Islamic societies look on typical women who follow the new sex-morality as being in effect prostitutes. Some Christians, too, are outraged, though in Britain they no longer count for much. There is a clash of two moralities: the new, and especially savage versions of the old sexual morality, come into conflict.

B. Moralities change. Human nature doesn't.

A. Morality "regulates" the expression of "human nature". People in the future will look at our capitalist society, in which, in order to work, people have to hire out to private individuals and companies and do their profit-hungry will for so many hours a week, as we now view slavery. They will see the private ownership of newspapers and TV stations as we now see a world in which prelates laid down the law on what people could think and vote, as absurd and radically incompatible with proper democracy. A lot less than half a century ago, it was considered right, moral, and necessary in Britain that school children should be beaten, frequently, regularly, by their teachers, and, at whim, by their parents and other "guardians". That isn't considered "right" any more, either, though a lot of bullying by parents still goes on. "Human nature" is channelled to new expressions as society evolves.

B. Not necessarily for the better. In any case, you exaggerate. Human nature is not as easy to modify and control as you wish-think it is.

A. The history of social behaviour and social morality, of shifting ideas of right and wrong, proves what I say to be true. What would be the opposite of wish-thinking — wish-armoured refusal-to-think? That's what you are doing here.

B. Again, you juggle irresponsibly with words — mere words! — and ideals. Reality is much harsher and more intractable than you think. Stubborn human individualism is the unsurpassable barrier to socialism.

A. Then let me tell you the strongest reason why the idea that capitalism corresponds to human nature is nonsense. In the oldest human societies we know about, long before capitalism, the sense of belonging to the collective is stronger than the sense of individual self. It was like that for god-knows how many hundreds of human generations. Individualism is itself a product of social and human development.

B. So now your socialist ideal takes as its model primitive groups of hunter-gatherers wandering in the primeval forests. We will go from primitive communism to... primitive communism!

A. This time, not primitive. This time, in a society which can exercise a tremendous degree of control over natural and social environments. In terms of the argument about human nature and capitalism and socialism, don't the facts about the earliest human societies say something to you?

B. Yes, thank god for rugged individualism!

A. Moving on from primitive collectivism and to the development of individualism was progress. But our instinctual "human nature" was not different in "primitive communism" from what it is now.

B. So it's back to the old Stone Age! That's your socialism for the 21st century?

A. Forward to a world in which the sense of human interconnectedness and interdependence is revived on an immensely higher level of human ability to produce and reproduce the material means of life.

B. And individualism? You concede that was progressive in its time.

A. Individualism and a strong and governing sense of belonging to a great social interconnectedness are not in contradiction: they are complementary.

B. You are feeding me gobbledegook "dialectics" again!

A. You know what the great paradox here is? Individuation that produces individualism, the development of diverse minds and personalities, is very limited under capitalism: that is one of the things socialists criticise in capitalist society. It is one of the great possibilities opened up by capitalism before humankind that capitalism does not deliver for most of its citizens. Under wage-slavery, most people are compelled to spend most of their energy being "cogs in the machine" of production-for-profit. At best they can hope to develop their individualism in a very limited way outside work hours. And there they are seized on by commercialised capitalist culture. The "mass media" work against individual, critical, creative thinking.

We live in the sugar-and-sex nexus of a commercial civilisation. Sugar in as many products as possible, sex used at varying conscious and subliminal levels to sell everything. Tremendous technologies of education, enlightenment, democratic participation, churn out Rupert Murdoch's news, commerce-ridden and commerce-corrupted spectator sport, pornography, programs like Jerry Springer's, exploiting ignorant, semi-literate victims of our educational system and of capitalism in general — the equivalent of the bear-baiting and lunatic-tormenting of old.

Everything is corrupted, tainted, and debased. Politics is reported as a branch of spectator sport or show business, a variant of fantasy football. People still see themselves in elective, notional, tribes of football clubs, rock star fanship, networkings, etc.

In terms of work and training for work, people are stereotyped mass products. A once very common expression amongst socialists, which I've come to dislike thoroughly, "the masses" sums that up. In a world of material well-being, of democratic collectivism, individualism would flower in a way it can never flower under capitalism.

B. So you say. In fact the herd mentality too is part of human nature. Not a good part, either. On one level, your socialism is an appeal to that herd mentality.

A. We have seen that operational human nature is not something static and fixed. That human nature includes many traits and possibilities. Remember that people in certain societies and with a certain conditioning are capable of eating, cannibalising, other people.

B. Tosh! We have gone so far beyond that.

A. Yes, of course we have. Sort of! But isn't exploiting people as wage labour a form of "cannibalising" people? What else is it to take someone's active life, qualities, and potential, and to use them to make money for yourself? You thereby consume a life, even if the idea of eating the flesh of those you exploit revolts you.

B. That's just a fanciful identification of vastly different things.

A. No, I do not say that they are the same thing. What I'm saying is that human nature is socially malleable and has all sorts of possibilities. The question is what a given society, or a given state, encourages to develop. Capitalist society prizes and rewards those who prey on other people.

That is not, or not just, human nature. That is also nurture — what capitalist society makes of a human nature that also has vastly different possibilities which capitalism inhibits and stifles.

B. Scratch a red, and you find a soft and stupid sentimentalist, oozing fond wet nonsense about humankind, an idiot who thinks that Christ's Sermon on the Mount or Kant's categorical imperative can govern society: "do to others as you would have them do to you". Have you never heard of the "Eleventh Commandment": Do to others as they would do to you, only do it first?

A. Yes, that sums up the morality of our capitalist society neatly and fully. But isn't the other idea — do to others as you would like people to do to you — far better, more desirable, and indeed more in line with full human nature, which is capable of so much more than preying on your neighbour? For instance, every decent, sane, well-bred person has an instinctive wish to protect and nourish small children, and facilitate their growth...

B. That's not the only reaction to children. Some psychologically maimed people have other, more predatory, instincts. Some have been abused in their own childhoods and, so to speak, pass it on.

A. Surely you're not basing any of your arguments on that? Let's put that aside. Why shouldn't the supremely benign human impulse of healthy human adults towards small children be generalised to all people? Why couldn't it be developed and trained and extended to humanity in general? In fact it is often generalised in that way.

B. Human beings, developing, growing, rely on the instinct that best serves them in order to guard and protect themselves, and allows them to develop their potential.

A. Yes, in the given conditions.

B. Historically developed conditions, which can't be changed at will.

A. No, not at will, not by abracadabra, hey-presto, or instant legislative change. But they can be changed. Proof of that? They are changed, all the time. Socialism is also a program of how society can be changed by those who make it up, changed deliberately and systematically over time, over a period of development. The overthrow of our successful super-predators, the bourgeoisie, is only the start of that process. The essential starting point.

B. But it can go wrong.

A. Capitalism goes wrong! Horrendously wrong. German capitalism bred Nazism, when it felt it needed it to defend itself against socialist revolution. And the "socialism" that "went wrong" went wrong in a way that was to be expected — not in detail, but in outline — by Marxists and in accordance with basic Marxist theory. The Marxists who led the 1917 revolution knew and said in advance that socialism could not be built in their conditions of economic and social backwardness. They adhered to Marx's basic doctrine about the place of socialism in history: that it had to come out of advanced capitalism, and the socialist possibilities it unleashes for the first time in history, and was impossible in a backward society like that of Russia.

B. Yet they seized power in Russia!

A. Expecting that the workers would also take power in the advanced European countries that were ready for socialist transformation. In the first place, Germany.

To get back to the point: the tremendously different socio-economic formations over the last seven thousand years or more; the many different forms taken, for instance, by the family in history; and the social moralities that went with them: those all rested on the basis of one human nature. It is a malleable human nature, a human nature of which different aspects, possibilities, can be fostered, developed, made to be dominant, encouraged, or discouraged or stamped on at different times. History proves that there is no such thing as one human nature; rather, if you want to put it that way, there are many "human natures", differing in their manifest characteristics according to the refraction and conditioning by the different socio-economic frameworks.

The "human nature" of those who ran Hitler's concentration camps and of the Allied soldiers who liberated the inmates in 1945, choking in horror and indignation as they did so, was, on the biological and instinctual level, the same human nature. One of the things that haunts my imagination about the Nazi horrors is the fact that the people who ran the camps were often in their private lives decent family men, fond and sentimental and cherishing to their own children — in the intervals between selecting for murder, and murdering, other children, women, and men.

B. Ah, but which was predominant, the private lives of the butchers, or the butchering public lives of those who were good parents to their own children?

A. Both, at different times and circumstances, in different socially approved roles, within the space of a single day. Mr Hyde could revert to being Dr Jekyll — and the other way round again. The point is that people with the same human nature could be both the one and the other. If the demonic Nazi regime had not licensed, encouraged, and fomented the bestiality, they would have lived out their lives, almost all of them, surely, as inoffensive clerks and mundane administrators. Would Adolf Eichmann have been what he was if the German government had not licensed, employed, paid, and encouraged him? The difference was in the traits of human nature brought out and encouraged and set to work in different systems. Socialism aims to create social conditions for a social morality that will cherish, reward, and develop the benign, socially-responsible, humanity-solidarising, child-cherishing elements and potentials of our instinctual "human nature".

CAPITALISM AND THE INVENTORS

B. The competitiveness and greed embedded in human nature can't be changed. Anyway, they shouldn't be. Without the stimulus of self-interest — greed for wealth, power, and status over and above other people — progress would grind to a halt. For instance, how are we going to discover new technologies, invent new procedures, make breakthroughs like penicillin or the internet or the microchip, if people do not have as stimulus the hope of riches and rewards? Without that everything would seize up.

A. It is a fact that under this system the hope of riches, prestige, and self-aggrandisement, and conversely the fear of poverty and of being someone else's prey, does spur people on to effort and perseverance. The "hope" of wages at the end of the week or month "spurs" most people on to "persevere", that is, to go to work! In a socialist society the knowledge of social necessity will spur people on. But if you think that wealth and power are the only spurs to action in humankind — my God, what a miserably diminished view you have of human beings! A bourgeois view. It is a piece of humanity-slandering social-Darwinist self-approving bourgeois superstition! You think capitalism and its characteristic traits can be read off from human nature. The opposite is true: your idea of human nature and human potentials is read off from, or is a projection of, capitalist modes and moralities around you.

B. I take a realistic view of history, and of society now. and of human nature. Facts speak louder than limp-witted sentimentality

A. All right: first, I'll take your point on its own terms. I don't know that anything necessary to a socialist society or to the work of building such a society rules out giving special material rewards or prestige to people who contribute important inventions and innovations to society. That stimulus need not disappear with capitalism. Certainly it doesn't depend on the whole of society being run for the private profit of a small minority, very few of whom contribute new inventions or, indeed, anything very much. Consider the Nobel Prizes, which confer status and financial reward on people in many fields of endeavour — science, literature, politics, and such intangible things as promoting "peace". How many people in all those fields work with the conscious objective of winning a Nobel Prize? How many would stop what they are doing when they don't get one?

B. Maybe a lot of them: how do you know?

A. There is a Nobel Prize for poetry, awarded in the past to such as William Butler Yeats. Yeats certainly needed the money, but do you think it was the hope of money which spurred Yeats on to do his wonderful work?

Or take penicillin, the discovery of which is attributed to Alexander Fleming in 1928. In fact he made observations of the antibiotic properties of a mould, published his observations in a scientific journal, got little attention, and was unable to see how to mass-produce penicillin.

The development of penicillin as an effective medicine was the work of others, over a decade later, stimulated and empowered by the need for medicine in World War Two. The invention of antibiotics was not driven by expectations of wealth or status, even though Fleming was eventually feted and knighted.

B. He wasn't indifferent to such things, was he?

A. The point is that he was not spurred or governed by the prospect of such things. The great work he did was not generated by hopes or expectations of money or glory. Or take a case more favourable to you: the great Thomas Edison, who ran a production-line for discoveries and new techniques. He was certainly greedy for money.

B. He was a great promoter of new inventions. Economic progress needs such entrepreneurs.

A. One of the reasons the nascent film industry moved from the East Coast of the USA to California was to escape the harassment of Edison's patent-enforcers. As you say, Edison was more an entrepreneur than an inventor. As a profit-hungry entrepreneur he was as likely to stifle inventions as to help them. That is often what capitalist "entrepreneurs" do.

B. Still, Edison brought many inventions into practical use. He couldn't have done that without being the sort of profit-seeker you want to stifle and render impossible in your socialist Utopia.

A. I don't know, can't know, but it seems possible to me that the American Thomas Edison, or another Thomas Edison, in a socialist society, would gain satisfaction and pleasure and self-approbation from sheer enterprise, from the practical realisation of inventions he picked up from others. The American Thomas Edison...

A. The real Thomas Edison...

B. ... was, so to speak, psychologically plugged in to late 19th century and early 20th century US capitalism and its typical drives and motivations. What would someone of his talents, drive, and interests have been like in an older society, say in ancient Greece? Or in a future society? It is surely possible to imagine someone like him "plugged in" to a different psychology, different drives, different moralities, different motivations, different satisfactions, different standards of self-judgement and self-measurement. Social service, benevolence towards his fellow citizens, the desire for recognition as a benefactor of humankind?

B. Things are what they are. Edison was what he was. In a socialist world he would be stifled and made an impossibility.

A. Because of lack of financial reward? But, as I've said, there are no reasons why a socialist society could not offer special material rewards for exceptional services, a sort of Great Human Benefactor Prize.

B. You concede my point, then!

A. Rewards and honours for innovators are not an issue in the argument between socialism and capitalism. There can be different mechanisms for rewarding them, so long as people want that sort of thing.

B. Capitalism is the tried and tested way. It works. Your socialist system simply wouldn't work. It would stifle and destroy.

A. The paradoxical truth is that innovators who are unrecognised and unrewarded cogs in present-day institutionalised technology, science, and research might well get more recognition and reward in a socialist society.

B. I may go to heaven when I die. But I'm not going to kill myself just to find out.

A. Your Heaven would be what? Eternity in a virtual bank counting imaginary money!

B. And yours? Sitting in a library dreaming up imaginary, impossible worlds — forever!

A. Your mistake is to think in great conglomerate blocks of ideas and associations. You do not separate out what was and is from what could be. The real Thomas Edison, a product of a certain time and environment, was greedy, therefore only greed can drive any person with his interests, abilities and capacities. No: people are shaped by their social environment, by what society values and holds up for emulation. "Human nature" is socially malleable.

B. Yes, it can produce and license socialist...

A. Stalinist!

B. ... concentration camp guards and murderers.

A. Of course, but what licensed what they did was not socialism but the Stalinist murder of socialists and of socialism. Ideas, drives, capacities are shaped, their innate traits encouraged or blocked, sublimated or diverted, by the different social and political regimes. Capitalism brings out, glorifies, rewards, and lauds the worst in people. But people are as capable of being gripped by benign drives and ideals of fellowship, social service, and, dare I say, empathy and love, as by the dog-eat-dog, war-of-all-against-all dreams of robbing their neighbours which capitalism conditions them into, from the cradle to the school to the workplace. Anyway, I think you have a false view of how science and scientific development work.

Research and development of drugs, for instance, is a large-scale capitalist activity. There is still sometimes the genius individual inventor or innovator. But mostly the development of science, inventions, and techniques is highly institutionalised and capitalised. That capitalist research and development is driven and regulated by the hope of gain — gain for the corporation and its shareholders, not for the inventors or for society in general, even though social benefits may ultimately come.

B. That makes no different. Greed and selfishness rule. That is the point, whether we are talking of an individual genius or inventor, or a whole corporation.

A. Do you really want to argue that the need to reward invention justifies, for example, the pharmaceutical industry and the way it prices new drugs, or incrementally improved versions of known drugs, beyond the range of vast numbers of people who need them? That is a great world-wide scandal, with anti-AIDS medicines, for example.

B. Oh, there may well be room, even great room, for improvement.

Despite your gibes, I don't think everything is always for the best. I want reform and modification; but not the abolition of the capitalist system to which we owe so much.

A. Take this recent case which shows just what the rule of profit means for medicine. In August 2015, the US businessman Martin Shrkeli bought the rights on an old drug called Daraprim, necessary to treat a parasitic infection that can kill people with HIV or cancer. He raised the price of the drug from $13.50 per tablet to $750. That was more shameless than bigger drug companies think they can get away with. Shkreli said he would lower the price. But then he changed his mind, and told a business conference that he would have raised the price higher if given the chance. "My shareholders expect me to make the most profit," he said. "That's the ugly, dirty truth." Indeed! Shkreli is just more shameless, more flamboyant, less cautious than the other drug-extortionists.

B. But Shkreli was arrested for securities fraud in December 2015!

A. Not for raising the price of the drug and pricing sick people out of being able to use it! He has been arrested for breaking some financial rules, not for being the living spirit of predatory capitalism in medicine. It's like the murderer Al Capone being jailed for tax evasion. Doesn't it even occur to you that someone capable of what Shkreli did is morally and mentally ill — a sociopath if not a full blown psychopath? He epitomises the capitalist system at its most dehumanised.

B. One extreme case proves nothing.

A. It is an extreme case which lights up the landscape of what is normally done. Drugs are patented, monopolies are created, drugs are priced as high as the corporations can get away with. Sick people and the NHS are held to ransom, or allowed to die when they could be saved. Even institutions like the NHS find some drugs beyond their capacity to pay for.

The "reward" goes to the shareholders and the top executives of companies like Roche. Those companies institutionalise "science" and "research". They put highly qualified technicians to work in certain areas. They direct collective scientific research, and decide how and where it may or may not be published. All inventions or improvements are their property. What guides their choice of research projects? Potential profitability. Not social need determines what they do, in this field which is so immensely important to us all, but their paramount private concern — revenue. The people being "rewarded" here are not the inventors of drugs that benefit humanity, but a section of the moneyed classes of capitalism. You will remember that not so long ago a company tried to copyright the map of the human genome — to put itself in a position to charge humankind a fee for all the multifarious uses of the new map.

B. As they say in America, they were "only trying to make a buck". You forget the trickle-down benefits of their activities.

A. I saw in a TV program recently that scientists are working on the carcasses of mammoths, tundra-frozen for thousands of years, with the intention of cloning a mammoth. They are financed by a South Korean company, to which their findings will belong by legally airtight contracts. This company already clones pet dogs — at $100,000 a time — for doting rich pet-lovers.

The vast social networks of science, invention, improvement of old means and methods does not, when you examine it, have much to do with rewarding great discoveries and encouraging others with the prospect of acclaim and wealth. In a sense invention is already "socialised", but for the financial benefit of certain shareholders, and not directly of society.

B. There is some healthy competition between companies. That is better than a state monopoly.

A. I repeat: there is no socialist reason why inventors should not get substantial rewards for great work. There is every reason why their inventions should not be turned into capitalist patent-monopoly products.

B. Better that than into state monopolies.

A. Again: I question your premiss. So does history. The people who developed penicillin for medical use out of Fleming's observations were driven, or mainly driven, by the needs of the British war effort, by the desire to help and heal wounded and sick soldiers. Theirs was part of a social effort, of a broad society-wide feeling of common purpose. Without that, the development of usable medicine from Fleming's observations probably wouldn't have happened for a long time. Here the drive for personal riches and aggrandisement was not central, and certainly not paramount in starting the great antibiotics revolution in medicine. Social need, social effort, social (in this case national) identification was (and very likely hostility to fascism and Nazism too). Why, in the name of common sense, and common decency, do you believe that social responsibility, and the desire to benefit society, would not be a sufficient spur to effort and invention in the future?

B. Experience. Look around you! Look at the precedent of the old Stalinist states!

A. In the last reduction, your picture of the individual being driven only by the prospect of being able to tax other human beings for the use of an invention on which their lives may depend is the stupidly dogmatic idea of human beings as only predatory animals. Of a society in which, in the words of Bartolomeo Vanzetti to the court that sentenced him, and his comrade Sacco, to be burned alive in the electric chair, as they duly were — "man is wolf to the man".

B. The facts don't lie.

A. Yes they do — especially through the mouths of fools interpreting them in a certain way. You, for instance!

B. There's no foolishness in facing reality.

WORKING-CLASS SOLIDARITY

A. People have motivations for action other than crude direct self-interest, certainly motivations other than monetary self-interest. Motives of social, class, and human solidarity, of doing good to other people, of benign sharing and being shared with, of being parts of a benign collective society.

In Britain before Thatcher you used to see that a lot in industrial disputes. Workers would lose wages rather than cross a picket line, that is, rather than sabotage other workers in their efforts to better themselves. More than once, other workers, coal-miners for instance, struck on behalf of hospital workers who were inhibited in taking action by the dependence on them of sick people.

You see that spirit in people responding to accidents and to the needs of accident victims. In war, people often sacrifice themselves for their comrades. You still see that spirit in industrial disputes now.

B. These are all atypical, extreme, freakish cases. The norm is what you denounce as the epitome of capitalism: enlightened self-interest.

A. In the most thoroughly capitalist-minded society in the world, the USA, between 25% and 30% of all people over 16 do organised voluntary work, a total of eight billion hours a year, and over 75% of them do informal voluntary work to help neighbours or friends.

B. God, what a stupid sentimentalist you are!

A. Am I? Isn't it that you are a stupid misanthrope? That you have a perversely one-sided idea of the nature of human beings. Here it is a question of the way real people behave, as distinct from your malign model of all-consuming selfishness. What you are saying is a libel on humankind. Your attitude to humankind is bred in you by the worst aspects of present-day human society. You are psychologically maimed, though you'd be the last to know it.

B. Bred in me by the realities of the world as it is and always has been. And your attitudes and ideals? Bred in you, most likely, by over-indulgent parents!

A. And you? I bet you were beaten, sent to bed without your supper, and locked in dark cupboards! Your parents probably gave you stingy pocket money and then made you pay for the meals you ate in their internal market family economy! Probably charged you separately for the use of a corner of their table and the chair you sat on. And for the use of cutlery and condiments!

B. At least I didn't grow up wet with sticky, false sentimentality.

A. Certainly the culture we live in, and the ideals and heroes held up to society, are all now of the predator-or-prey, the be-hammer-or-be-anvil type you describe. That can change. In fact it can change quickly. Take an example from working-class history: the port workers, dockers.

B. Must we?

A. Ships come, discharge their cargo, load another cargo, and go.

There is no continuity of work in such conditions. For a long time, thousands of years, I guess, gangs of dock workers would be hired as needed to hump cargo on and off ships. Entry into the work was unregulated. Anyone could turn up for a job on the docks. It was a buyer's market in labour. In late 19th century Britain, still, workers would compete with each other to get hired for half a day's work. They would crowd around the hiring foreman, and sometimes fight each other for preference. The big and burly men could push the weaker men aside. The foremen would pay wages in pubs — getting a cut from the landlords for it, so men would drink there. It was the social Darwinist's dream, or nightmare, world of dog-eat-dog individualism and the survival of the strongest. The weakest went down and were trampled, sometimes literally trampled, underfoot. The men were wolves fighting wolves, dogs fighting dogs, for scraps. Then at the end of the 1880s the British dockers formed a union, with the help of socialists like Tom Mann and John Burns, who were not dockers but skilled engineers, and Eleanor Marx. The docks were radically transformed, from every-man-for-himself to an all-shaping culture of working-class solidarity. The dockers learned the power they had when they stood together, and how much better it was when each docker looked out for himself by looking out for the others.

B. Holding the country to ransom! In fact, being pig-selfish.

A. You, who lauded capitalist greed a moment ago, think you can denounce "pig-selfishness" in workers fighting for a living wage!

B. I detest your sentimentalism, your idealisation of the lower depths of society.

A. My god, what a sad little snob you are! A Royal Commission on the ports reported in 1965 that dockers' solidarity was such that it only needed one docker running down a quay on which a line of ships were being worked, shouting the news that men on one ship, or in one warehouse, had a grievance and had stopped work, and all the others would come out in solidarity. That was the truth.

Inside a generation after the 1889 docks strike and the start of unionisation, the old culture had been turned upside down and inside out. Dockers used solidarity as a weapon in the never-ending strife with the bosses, and learned to hold up social solidarity as a socialist ideal to work for in politics.

As a dockworker in the 1960s, I saw and took part in things that

120

have sustained my belief in the working class and what it can and will do through decades of working-class defeat and retreat.

B. Shhh… Don't boast about your own stupidity! Your point in the here and now is what? That culture, if it really was as you say it was, has vanished. It doesn't exist any more. It didn't have much vitality then, did it?

A. It had great vitality. We were defeated, after long struggles.

B. Good! In any case, it proved unviable.

A. Or take the town labourers in my west-of-Ireland town, Ennis. In this farmers' market town which was also the administrative centre of County Clare, a place with schools and colleges and many priests and nuns, the town labourers were dirt. They lived in what were officially called "hovels". Many were illiterate. They were semi-outcasts to be hired as needed and then jettisoned to a regular condition of being half-starved. They relied for survival on big extended families that cared and shared for each other. And then, learning from the example of the tenant farmers' "trade union", the Land League, they organised a trade union, a one-town union five or six hundred strong. Soon the labourers, banded together, showed that solidarism can replace dog-eat-dog-ism. They stood by each other — walked off jobs they sorely needed to act in support of their fellow trade unionists. It was very like the culture on the docks. It was magnificent.

B. Mugs! At best a small footnote to history.

A. It was like that in other, similar, towns, such as Kilrush, for example. That sort of working-class solidarity had tremendous vitality, and over many decades.

B. What happened to it in the ports?

A. In the ports, there was a radical technological revolution. Giant containers were loaded away from the docks and delivered to them ready to be moved by cranes from the trucks to the ships. Incoming containers were lifted off ships by cranes to lorries or railway wagons. That was the precondition for everything. The tremendously militant dockers were defeated by bosses' governments, Labour as well as Conservative. So was the whole working class defeated in the 1980s.

The class struggle sometimes boils up, sometimes subsides from exhaustion, or after working-class defeat. But the class struggle is a fundamental fact of social life. It always revives. And the impulse to working-class solidarity is there still. It will make itself felt again.

B. They were beaten — and what makes you think they won't always be beaten? I've heard and read about the way things were in Britain before Margaret Thatcher came to power — the so-named "Winter of Discontent". Striking dust-cart workers and striking gravediggers left rubbish piled in the streets and dead bodies unburied. Those workers deserved what they got from Thatcher! She saved Britain from the wreckers.

A. Yes. She and her government had to wreck Britain in order to save it from the trade-unionist "wreckers"! A real heroine, that one. By the way, the "unburied bodies" is Tory spin-liar stuff, with little basis in fact.

THE SHIT JOBS

B. You talk about an idyllic future where everyone shares and shares alike. But who will do the shit jobs in socialist society? Who will clean the toilets, collect the rubbish, look after the hopelessly mad, the incontinent old?

A. Self-cleaning toilets have been commonplace for decades. In reality, most such work can be done now, or soon, by machines, robots, etc.

B. Old dodderers like you will be cared for by machines? And babies? That's your humane socialist solution? Aren't you "magicking" away a real problem? Even the most automated society will never eliminate all the unpleasant jobs.

A. Then they will be shared out. Isn't your objection best expressed as: "Who would spend their whole working lives cleaning the lavatories?" Isn't it? That is what makes the thing truly horrible: that some people for all their lives should do nothing else but the shit jobs, and others, the good jobs.
Oscar Wilde put it well: "To sweep a slushy crossing for eight hours, on a day when the east wind is blowing is a disgusting occupation. To sweep it with mental, moral, or physical dignity seems to

me to be impossible. To sweep it with joy would be appalling. Man is made for something better than disturbing dirt."

B. He was a socialist?

A. He was. One of the oddest things in our world, if you stand back and look at it, is that the good, interesting, capacity-employing, and developing, jobs are better paid than the bad, uninteresting, life-stifling jobs. Leave aside the obscene amounts of money that go to footballers and pop stars, bankers and speculators and asset-strippers — social cockroaches, thieving magpies, rats, wolves, and jackals like that. A surgeon who does interesting, rewarding, satisfying work earns so much more than the dirt-stirrer, the lavatory cleaner, the rubbish collector, whose working lives are almost devoid of satisfactions, and often very unpleasant as well as badly paid. In a humane, rational world, inhabited by equal people, the lavatory cleaner should have the high wage, in consideration of the damage, the suffering, the frustrating and dehumanising effects of the work, and the surgeon, who gets so much out of the work itself, the lesser wage.

B. That's economics for you!

A. That's capitalist economics for you. In reality the wage is regulated by the social costs of producing and reproducing the labour power of different jobs — what, respectively, it costs to train a surgeon and a lavatory cleaner — and by handed-down status.

B. It "shouldn't" be like that, but it is. Besides, don't forget that the surgeon will be a lot cleverer than the road-sweeper.

A. Not necessarily. Just better educated.

B. Senseless paradox-juggling! It is natural that people of wealth are the surgeons, and that people like you should clean the lavatories...

A. In a moral socialist world everybody could train to be a surgeon, or a classical musician, or a mathematician, or anything they want to be.

B. And some of those will sometimes clean the lavatories, or do similar menial jobs? Don't be silly!

123

A. Why not? The idea will disappear that some people are "too good", of too high a caste, too well-educated, their dignity too high, for them to do unpleasant work that other humans do. A socialist society will have a human ethos and morality. It will be governed by the central idea of human solidarity and intrinsic human worth. It will realise the great aspiration to human equality in society, in education, and in access to economic resources. It will thus lead to a flowering of things in which human beings are not and never can be entirely equal — capacity, interest, talent. It will provide for all the things that are now only for the well-off and the super-rich. It will enhance and develop every human life.

B. And the rivers will turn into lemonade, and some to champagne, and the Stakhanovite sturgeons will increase their production of eggs so that there will be caviare for everyone!

A. I've never had either, so I don't know or care. But in principle, if some people want champagne and caviare, why not?

B. Scarcity! So they have to be rationed, and rationing by price is better than rationing by government decree, in which the governors will always make sure they get first pick.

A. With technology as we have it now, most things don't need to be rationed at all. Food, clothes, public transport, for example: everyone could simply have what they want, and quite soon no-one would want excessive or wasteful consumption. Under capitalism, even in well-off Britain, one-third of lower-income parents skip meals in school holidays so that their children can eat, and hundreds of thousands have to ask for supplies from food banks, while a few dine in expensive restaurants. Of course, no way of organising society can enable everyone to live in the house with the best view. Some things will always be scarce. But why should that mean any more than that if you choose one scarce "prize", you must forego another? Why do you doubt that people can develop enough social solidarity and empathy to do that fairly? Attitudes change. Take the startling changes in sexual morality. Only five decades ago, the "conspicuous consumption" sort of sex life now available to more or less everybody who wants it in advanced capitalist societies was possible only for Hollywood film stars, some rich people, and small groups of libertines who believed in "free love" (you don't hear that expression any more. Why? It's from another world, vastly different to ours.)

124

B. Oh well, sex. That's human nature.

A. The same human nature used to be suppressed and shackled by religion-based moral and social codes. As recently as 1988, Thatcher's Tory government legislated "Section 28", branding homosexuality as contrary to human nature and making it illegal to "promote the teaching in any maintained school of the acceptability of homosexuality". Attitudes have changed so much since then that in 2013 a Tory-led government legislated for same-sex marriage. (Mind you, they still haven't made sex education compulsory in schools).

B. Progress, I suppose. But not everything can be changed.

A. Trotsky envisaged a world in which the average human being would be at the intellectual level of an Aristotle. Someone recently branded that as an element of romantic "utopianism" in Trotsky.

B. Or lunatic raving!

A. Who can say that it won't be so, still less that in terms of human capacity it can't be? We are still living in humankind's pre-history. History will not end, but this pre-history will. Humanity will rise to a level commensurate with our best benign possibilities and potentials. The citizen of that world will look back at ours as we look back on the stony cruelty and inhumanity of the ancient world, with its slaves, its gladiators killing each other to provide the citizens with sport, its mass ignorance, its stultified means of producing and reproducing the necessities of human life.

IS THERE AN ECOLOGICAL IMPERATIVE FOR SOCIALISM?

A. We live in the age of a "Great Fear", the fear that humankind has irreversibly fouled up its ecological nest. There have been other "Great Fears" in the past. For decades it seemed that world war, and then nuclear war, would wreck civilisation and open a new regressive dark age. At his death Trotsky was oppressed by the idea that because of the defeats and betrayals of the working-class movement's attempts to replace capitalism with socialism in the previous quarter-century, humankind faced a series of world wars that would be "the grave of civilisation".

B. A bizarre, esoteric idea, surely: personal despair...

A. Not so. At the end of the 1930s it was a commonplace fear and expectation. You'll find variants of it in a 1942 Papal Encyclical, in the historian E H Carr's editorials in *The Times*, even in the poetry and journalism of W B Yeats. So, not a case of "they are all out of step except Trotsky".

B. I find that hard to believe.

A. Like many of the other Great Fears of History, it was eclipsed. For many, including eventually the important American socialist, Max Shachtman, it transmuted into a paralysing fear of world Stalinism, seen as an encroaching barbarism likely to overcome both socialism and capitalism. The terrified horror with which so many people viewed the H Bomb in the 1950s and '60s was another Great Fear. That subsided with the test ban treaties of the early 1960s, and after the Cuban missile crisis, during which we lived for ten days with the seeming certainty that nuclear war was about to start.

B. Well, the groundless fear of ecological ruination of the planet will pass, too. We will muddle through.

A. Groundless? No. The justified, necessary and healthy fear of ecological ruination and social regression as a consequence faces us with stark urgency. There is a serious possibility that capitalism, which first opened up the socialist "option" in history, shifted it from wishful aspiration to practical possibility, will close it again by way of doing irreparable damage to the ecological system on which humankind depends. We cannot know, but there may be limited time in which to mount a socialist society, a fully democratic society, resting on the best achievements of capitalism. I repeat: it may be an option that is foreclosing on us. We cannot afford to be smug.

B. I'm not being smug! I'm refusing to follow you and the others into ecological panic and "the world may soon end" hysteria. Is it even proven that global warming is due to human activity?

A. The expert evidence is that it is. Much of the "debate" about that is people with vested interests and their bought and paid for hired "scientists" muddying the streams of debate.

B. But it isn't certain. Things will turn out all right.

A. We cannot afford to be smugly optimistic about it. What if you are wrong? Inactivity now will (or, to go some of your road with you, may) mean losing the chance to do something about it while there is still time. The reorganisation of the labour movement on a socialist basis is very urgent, because the task of confronting capitalism with a viable socialist alternative is very urgent, and getting more urgent.

B. Alarmism never did anybody any good. It's part of your utopian mindset. Only here it turns into a terrified dystopianism.

A. Contrast the unbelievably laid back and irresponsible way governments are responding to the prospect of irreversible ecological catastrophe with what they did in World War One and World War Two. Then, capitalist governments, faced with fighting major wars, took great powers of direction and control over industry. Britain and the USA were typical examples. Production had to be of whatever the war effort required. The allocation of resources, including labour-power, was subordinated to the governments' perceptions of what would promote or disrupt the waging of war. To a degree that is surprising, looked at from within the dominant ideology of our "new enlightenment", governments took control of the economy into their own hands. They had gone through the 1930s unable to eradicate unemployment, unable or unwilling to control economic forces. Now, when it was a matter of life or state-death, they did it wholeheartedly.

B. It was not socialism!

A. Of course it was not socialism. In both Britain and the USA, and also in Germany, it was a system of war state-capitalism. The capitalists kept their ownership, and made greatly enhanced profits out of the wars. But they operated under government control and direction. "Needs must when the devil drives". Now humankind is faced with the need to fight a new war, a prolonged and prodigious war, to avert a catastrophe immensely greater even than defeat in war would bring, greater even than was brought down upon the great loser in both wars, Germany.

It is a world-wide war to save, preserve, and as far as possible restore the ecological system on which human life and civilisation depends. Increasing numbers of people are becoming aware of that fact. Plainly we need a world economy that doesn't randomly cut down rain-forests for profit, or allow private interests to pollute the atmosphere, or loot irreplaceable resources, or measure things only in terms of profit for the exploiting class, without regard to ecological cost.

B. Jesus! Mel Gibson's Mad Max — the socialist! An ecological imperative for socialism? That's just a piece of opportunist special pleading by socialists who are proven political and ideological bankrupts.

A. The need for a planned economy has been central to socialism for many decades before we — socialists, and people in general — reached our present ecological awareness. That adds extra urgency to it. The economy of the world needs to be planned, brought under rational human control, freed from the tyranny of a market which is blind to human need and blind to the needs of the ecological system on which we depend. And only the working class can do that.

B. There are better answers to the problem than old socialism pinned as a tail onto the ecological donkey!

A. What are the alternative answers? The urgent task is to find a full and adequate answer to the looming ecological catastrophe towards which the capitalists…

B. Capitalists! The Stalinist systems were the worst polluters and the most wasteful industrialisers. Think of Chernobyl!

A. Indeed, think of Chernobyl. But you interrupted me: … towards which the capitalists and Stalinists have brought humankind. Little bits of tinkering simply won't do the job. Only rational, overall, world-wide planning according to the real costs of economic processes, including the ecological costs, will answer to the urgent need. Rational planning is by definition democratic planning on every level all through the economy.

B. Let me see if I understand you correctly. You want the governments to impose state controls on the economy such as they had in the World Wars?

A. No. I used that experience to illustrate what could be done when the rulers felt an urgent need, on pain of military defeat. It is a shocking contrast to the lackadaisical approach now to a far, far greater threat. I advocate a planned economy under democratic control. I mean by that workers' control in the industries as well as on the level of government, and democratic planning. The tiny minority of people who own our giganticist economic system must not be allowed to hold humankind to ransom or lead it by the nose to self-destruction. That is what they do now.

B. You want the governments to confiscate their property?

A. Not "the government". A *socialist workers' government*. Small shareholders should be pensioned off — but essentially, yes, big businesses should be expropriated. They themselves live by expropriating the value produced by the working class. The de-nationalisations in Britain under Thatcher were the biggest looting of public property since the common lands were enclosed and stolen from the 16th century to the 18th. The expropriators will be expropriated, as Karl Marx memorably put it.

B. For the sake of argument I'll accept your definition of the problem. Why not the wartime system you described?

A. A short answer is that it would not meet the scale and likely duration of the problem. And why leave proven incompetents — venal, self-serving, larcenous incompetents — in control and ownership in industry? The wartime arrangements were stop-gap short-term things by governments loyal to the capitalists. What we need is long-term planning, and not the sort of company-wide planning corporations have now, which is steered by the private interests of the owners. We need to eliminate profit-chasing as a consideration in economic and social activity. We need to eliminate the bourgeoisie.

B. God, you're absurd! Trade unions and trade-unionists are among the most bone-headed conservatives. They are "know-nothing" and "Luddite" defenders of vested interests in industry and politics. Any hope for doing something to overcome the ecological problem lies with enlightened employers and the governments they influence, most likely in the teeth of trade-union opposition.

A. And a great job those enlightened capitalists are making of it! Any solution to the ecological crisis adequate in scale and depth to the size of the problem has to be a society-wide and international solution. The big capitalists are not going to do that. It is in absolute antagonism with the necessary modes of capitalist functioning —

129

private ownership, competition, private interests of the capitalist owners in first place. At best they will tinker with it, fumbling and stumbling. Theirs is a world of corporate competition in which the loss of advantage in one country or sector is taken advantage of by competitors, and for that reason feared and shunned. Socialist ideas of society-wide transformation, by the suppression of crude capitalist economic advantage and profiteering, are the only ideas which can clear the way for action on the scale which the crisis demands.

B. You are saying that nothing can be done until the world is trans-formed by a socialist force which now exists only on a tiny scale — that is, for big politics, does not exist at all. Lobbying and pressure now are at least real things.

A. Lobbying and pressure may do some good. I am not counter-posing an ultimate solution to that. As the forces gather for a socialist solution, they will naturally put pressure on the powers that exist. They will massively increase the power and influence of lobbying. But no other class than the working class can break the market-profit nexus and replace it with something better, namely an economy run by human reason, to satisfy human need and bring sustainable human betterment, rather than by the market and the profit interests of the owners of capital. An economy that will put an end to the pro-duction of shoddy, short-lived goods with profitable built-on obso-lescence, to the tremendous waste of the present system, and produce solid, lasting goods.

Part 5: And what's in it for me?

THE "BIRD IN THE HAND"

B. But why should I want socialism? Capitalism has, despite the terrible events of the 20th century — and I'm not denying them — learned a great deal. We have been through a tremendous cycle of capitalist boom and expansion. Things have been getting better, pro-gressively, for a lot of people, for a sizeable portion of humankind, over decades.

And why should I want a social levelling-down, to a grey social uniformity and conformity? Why should I pretend that people as people are equal, when they are not equal in capacity, propensity, achievement, and possible achievement? The faults of capitalism, which I don't deny, and in honesty could not deny, are a necessary and therefore worthwhile price to pay for a society that creates wealth, unleashes and encourages personal initiative in all fields. It encourages social mobility, and allows easy entry into its elite ruling class. It promotes a thriving market in ideas, it offers choices, it fosters and rewards a free press. It nurtures rationality and realistic thinking and even, most of the time now, rational, democratic, and peaceful relations between states. At its best it promotes political democracy.

The bird in my hand is worth a lot more than the birds in the bush and the fields and the skies, no matter how enticing their plumage looks from a distance. The ideal here is the enemy of the possible and improvable. The imagined perfection is the enemy of bit-by-bit achievable improvement. You sacrifice that step-by-step improvement in pursuit of some ideal big-bang replacement that doesn't exist, is yet to be won, and may never be won, and you may bring down upon us stark ruination.

That you can think something up, and vividly envisage it in your head, doesn't necessarily mean that you can achieve it in reality. The unicorn is created in our imagination by combining characteristics of different animals, just as the creatures in the Star Wars films are. There are no unicorns in reality.

A. In fact, in today's state of knowledge and techniques of biological modifications, we could, I guess, now — or soon — create real unicorns! Dolly the sheep could be Dolly the unicorn.

B. Idiot! Cloning assumes that a unicorn already exists.

A. Genetic modification doesn't... In fact, of course, all domesticated animals, from the poor dumb sheep to the vast range of types of dogs, have been created over centuries by human activity in selective breeding. Existing species are the product of all-creative humankind. You sell us short with your fear to contemplate the creation of a society better than capitalism.

B. There — now you are fantasising about creating unicorns!

A. No. I'm pointing out that even when you invoke that polemical cliché, you lag behind the real social and biological possibilities of the world you live in.

B. Unicorn socialism! The Unicornists? The Impossibles? Not a bad name for your politics...

A. You are probably one of those who oppose stem cell research!

B. I don't.

A. Good! Your picture of capitalist reality is, to understate it, too one-sided. You attribute to "capitalism" and to the bourgeoisie things which the working class and the plebeians won against the bourgeoisie — the existing democracy is one example. It was won by plebeian struggle, but, along the way, progressively emptied of much of its old meaning by the entrenched ruling classes and their servants and tools. You assume that the desirable things and traits you list are inseparable from capitalism and cannot exist without the present arrangements of society. You assume that under capitalism the gains will continue to exist indefinitely, and go on improving. They will not regress as Europe regressed from progress, and belief in inevitable continuous progress, to Hitler's world, where the medieval ghetto for Jews reappeared in the cities of Europe, and factories were erected for killing human beings and disposing of their bodies.

Socialists believe that the social and human gains won under capitalism can survive capitalism, and that they can develop much more fully once the limits imposed on them by capitalism and private ownership of the economic bases of society are broken.

B. You believe, but there is no rational basis for your belief.

A. You are almost incredibly complacent. There were people making the same sort of conservative defence of the then status quo back in the old Stone Age! "If we get too reliant on this new-fangled craze for flint tools, may we not lose what we have had for tens of thousands of years?" "Iron? Ugly and foul-coloured stuff. Think of the beauties of bronze, and the artistry with which its forgers lift up society!" "Produce with steam power? Dirt, pollution, ruin lies that way — better stick to the handicraft manufactures we have!" "Democracy? How can the many-headed ignorant mass match the wisdom and learning and concentrated enlightenment, the best knitted to the best, as someone said, passed on from father to son through ages, of a good king enhanced in his personal rule by absolute power? Power to do good for his loyal people".

The things you praise were in their time opposed by people like you with similar arguments. "Remake society according to reason, champion what is rational and scrap what isn't? Don't be ridiculous! Tradition! Age-old tradition, the way our parents and great-grandparents and all our ancestors did things — that is the sure road of safety and of preventing society falling under a dictator like Cromwell or Napoleon Bonaparte". No socialist who knows history, and certainly no Marxist, will deny the great achievements of capitalism. The very possibility of socialism is created by capitalism as it develops the social productivity and social intermeshing of labour.

But today capitalism blocks the further logical development even of the good things it created in history, or allowed the people's struggles to create within it. And social regression is possible; if we don't avoid the ecological catastrophes that are a real and immediate threat to our societies, it is inevitable. Think back to the all-suffusing optimism, the confidence in steady improvement, in Europe and America before 1914, and what followed: war, the great slump, Hitler, and a second world war that killed 60 million people and brought physical ruination to large parts of Europe. Germany experienced worse than the devastation in the Thirty Years War in the 17th century.

B. What about the social catastrophes brought by socialism?

A. By Stalinism! But by capitalism, too. Much of capitalist progress is thin, thinner than it need be with the material possibilities of today. Take personal initiative, for instance. Most people are locked into economic and social situations that warp and mutilate them, stifle their development, and snuff out individuality. Their children too are locked in by disadvantages they suffer in their early years. In recent decades, in Britain, the child of a higher professional or managerial father has been twenty times more likely to end up in a similarly high status job than a child with a working-class father has been to end up in that sort of job. And "social mobility" is probably declining, not only here, but in the USA too.

B. But it exists. And we have freedom of the press. And choice.

A. The freedom of the press today in fact mostly means freedom for people like Rupert Murdoch to poison the streams of public information and informed debate. "Choice" is double-talk. Mostly it means choice, and wide choice, for the well-off. It is a thin ideological garment for the freedom of the moneyed behind which hides the cutting-off for most people of choice about most things, most of the time, including jobs, that is, about how they spend the main part of their entire lives. "For more choice you must have less choice for the rich", as Orwell or some other honest observer might have put it. Above all, the system corrupts humankind and keeps us at the level of predatory animals looking for options to rob each other.

The wise scientist Albert Einstein, who was a socialist, summed it up like this: "This crippling of individuals I consider the worst evil of capitalism... An exaggerated competitive attitude is inculcated... [we are] trained to worship acquisitive success... I am convinced there is only one way to eliminate these grave evils, namely through the establishment of a socialist economy, accompanied by an educational system which would be oriented toward social goals".

B. I'd listen to him about physics, but not on social organisation. What did he know?

A. The fundamental argument is that the whole capitalist system is crying out for change — for economic democracy, if you want to put it like that. It is devouring what you say are its great positive achievements. The growth of the multinational corporations massively undermines the very possibility of the democratic elected governments of most individual states controlling and regulating them.

B. You socialists are rather like the man who killed the gold-laying goose to get all its eggs at once. You don't understand how things work. The golden eggs only evolve, come into existence, in a certain way. Capitalism, the market, economic freedom

A. For the rich...

B. ... are tremendously productive forces. Look at the riches of the capitalist world which they have produced.

A. And you are rather like the man who worshipped a non-gold-laying goose strutting around the farmyard in the hope that one day she would lay a great big golden egg with his name on it.

B. Capitalism does lay golden eggs for quite a few people, you know.

A. The addled fantasy of many people, the paralysing passive hope that one day they will be rich themselves, is a major force in securing general consent for capitalism. It is the same psychology as waiting to win the lottery — and even less probable. The truth is that even limited upward mobility — forget about the dream of sudden riches — is beyond the reach of most people.

B. Even so, some people do move upwards. Some get rich. Look at Bill Gates and the other internet billionaires. And I'm not just talking about people becoming billionaires. Even if you don't move upwards socially, capitalism will give you higher living standards over time. Even if inequality increases in today's capitalism, still, even the worse-off gradually get better-off.

A. Not everywhere they don't. In the USA, working-class real wages have risen barely if at all since the 1970s. In the UK, median real wages fell 10% between 2008 and 2015, and have begun to rise again only slowly.

B. The period since 2008 is an exception, and the USA is an exception. Over the whole history of industrial capitalism, working-class living standards have risen a lot.

A. I'd be the last one to deny that working-class organisation and trade-union struggle can win gains under capitalism, and have won gains. Karl Marx, in his time, argued against the idea held by other socialists that working-class living standards were bound to be kept down to an absolute minimum by an "iron law of wages" which no working-class action could change. But he argued that capitalism has an organic tendency to increase inequality and insecurity for the working class. He was right.

Look at the cost in human terms of the system and its selectively bestowed bounties. Look at the world slump since 2007-8 and its tremendous human costs, all due to greed-mad bankers who ran the financial system on which so much in society depends for their private enrichment — for their own and shareholders' benefit. Look what results in the health service when profits and competition are introduced: the destruction of activities which are socially necessary even though economically unprofitable. That is true everywhere when private profit rules and regulates.

B. Yes, there are problems, social and ecological costs, if you want to dwell on that sort of thing, and of course socialists do. Even so, private profit, the drive for private enrichment, is the dynamo at the heart of what our society has produced. You would destroy that mainspring.

A. Ah, the Good, the Blessed, the all-shaping, law-giving, Divine Eternal Market!

B. I repeat: your objection to it is a form of kitsch-Christian morality, economically and socially ignorant. The harsh, or if you like, the sad, truth is that, as the man said, "Greed is good". It's not "nice", but it's good. That's the truth. Get used to it. Live with it, because it rules the world you live in.

A. Certainly, socialists want to live in a world governed by human solidarity — immediately, that means working-class solidarity — and not by the morality derived from brute-raw nature in which society is a jungle and everyone is a real or just-waiting-for-the-chance predator on everyone else. And the big, successful predators rule. As Albert Einstein put it, we see today "a community the members of which are unceasingly striving to deprive each other of the fruits of their collective labour", and we want to change that.

AND WHAT'S IN IT FOR ME?

B. So you hope! But it's plain that you are not at all certain you'll win. Why waste your life on this? Why invite me to do the same? Why fight for a cause that may suffer nothing but defeat, in your lifetime, or forever?

A. Because people should fight for what they know is right, is best, is necessary. The liberation of humankind from class society, and of the working class within that society, is, as someone said, the greatest cause in the world. That has been said often. It remains a fundamental truth to guide honest and responsible people.

B. Fools like you!

A. Yes, all the socialists in history were, like me, mere fools compared to your all-wise smug self... There are in the history of our movement people who cannot be bought, bullied, intimidated, brainwashed or demoralised into serving the rulers or going along with them passively. Rosa Luxemburg herself, and her comrades Karl Liebknecht and Leo Jogiches, who were murdered too, are good examples of those; and there have been immense numbers of them whose names we don't know, who didn't leave a written legacy. But they left a legacy all right. They augmented, gave life to, nurtured, and sustained the tradition of working-class socialist revolt and its written legacy from such as Rosa Luxemburg.

B. A big, lovely bunch of losers!

A. But they left us a social and political legacy, a great and enduring legacy. They augmented, gave life to, nurtured, and sustained the tradition and the culture of working people and working-class revolt.

B. Myths to comfort yourself! Even supposing I were to agree with you so far, what's in it for me? Why should I bother? Why spend even a small part of my life, waste even an instant of my too-short sentience, on advocating socialism? If it is as socially and historically necessary as you say it is, if the activity of the monopoly capitalists themselves works in favour of the "invading socialist society" — why, then it will inevitably come through without my help. And if it needs my help, then by implication I have no guarantee that we will succeed, so I'd most likely be wasting my life on something hopeless. The lesson of the 20th century here is that socialism is hopeless, and that your Marxist brand of socialism is doubly hopeless because of its absurd attachment to the daft idea that the working class and only the working class can bring it about.

A. If I offered you "guarantees", I would be a fool! There are no guarantees. And socialism may not come about "anyway". But let me focus on your question, "what's in it for me?" Here we need to go beyond mere political considerations into such questions as what life is all about — what should a life be about? We go into the world of ethical considerations and options.

B. Ah, philosophy! Monty Python-Trotsky and the Meaning of Life!

A. Are we nothing higher than a modern commercially-conducted and regulated rendition of animals, amongst them primitive humankind, spending an entire lifetime browsing and grubbing for food? That is the "shop until you drop" ethos which this society glorifies and depends on for dynamism. Leavened maybe with a bit of religious uplift, a half-tongue-in-cheek consultation with a horoscope to see what "the stars" are going to do to you? The small bacchanalia of a pop festival once a year or so?

If you are a worker, are you content to spend most of your work doing work you don't care about — or do care about, but are forced to do in a way you can't find fulfilling — for an employer whose only concern is to coin profit out of you? If you are a student, what are you going to do when leave college? If you are a one-time left-wing student, now working, what do you do?

Of course, you have to live, and you live in this society, not in the sort of society you might choose. You will have to get a job. If not an ideal one, you may still get a better job than you would have without your studies. Maybe one where (as some people say) you "love your work but hate your job". But can you, should you, put your best energies into "making a career"?

Will you teach? In a school in a low-income area, where you will participate in the heart-breaking reality of kids going through school and emerging semi-literate? When you know that only changes in society, not just the efforts of individual teachers, will change that? And where you will have to use more energy on complying with the box-ticking, exam-obsessed, impositions of school management and exam boards than on responding to the needs of your students?

Will you become a university teacher, retailing second and third hand opinion and received capitalist wisdom, with a bit of academic Marxist criticism, perhaps, for leaven and for the sake of your conscience? If you get an academic job with more scope, will you be a left-wing academic consumer of "revolutionary" anti-capitalist theory, but not do anything about it in practice by spreading understanding to the people at large, and helping them organise to fight for it?

Will you be a nurse? A doctor? You'll see the heartbreak of a National Health Service in chaos, with desperately needed medical care "rationed" by way of waiting times and increasingly by markets, and the enormous and crippling amounts of money paid out to the pharmaceutical companies. Will you become a chemist working for a pharmaceutical company? You might help invent a great medical step forward — and see it used as an expensive commodity, available only to those who can pay, in order to make profit for the bosses and shareholders of the company.

Will you go to a poorer country and make life a little better for people who, in a rich and supposedly civilised world, are dying for lack of money to buy even comparatively cheap medicines? Will you be a social worker? You will be providing inadequate help to the victims of poverty, poor education, unemployment, and migration far from home. At best you help them organise their lives a bit better with inadequate means and devastatingly arid prospects.

Will you be an immigration official? Help regiment migrant workers and their families; sort out the "legals" from the "illegals"; be part of a system which hunts down, imprisons, and deports the "illegals"?

Be a journalist? You won't be a privileged columnist, with some right to express a personal opinion (within the limits regulated by the choice of the newspaper and TV owners who can grant you that privilege). There are very few such jobs. As a run-of-the-mill newspaper or TV journalist, you can't help but contribute in some degree to the selection, slanting, and "balancing" of the millionaire-owned opinion-forming machine in which you will be a voice in a chorus singing what the others sing, what you are told to sing from the bourgeois hymnbook. You can't help but participate in a biased selection of what is "newsworthy", in presenting capitalism and "all its works and pomps" as something immutable and fixed, in suppressing discussion of the socialist alternatives that the crisis of capitalism has given a relevance which they seemed not to have in the days of the long capitalist boom before 2008.

Will you become a professional politician? Go from school and university, perhaps through office in a student union, on to be a "researcher" and maybe then a parliamentary candidate? That is, work to mould and shape yourself to fit into the political machinery that runs the system? The modern mainstream politician is a rancid mix of actor, reciting prescribed lines, and lawyer, arguing a brief from whichever side of the issue is indicated, without real conviction or real concern for what is true or best for society.

Will you become a trade-union official? You will be in the labour movement, but "professionally" barred from being able to tell workers openly what you think about the issues that arise and about the union leadership and its policies. Will you limit yourself to helping workers get a little more wages in the labour market — some of the time! — but also helping the union machinery and the top leaders regiment and limit working-class responses to their own exploitation, bamboozlement and degradation? Will you become a civil servant and keep your head down? Become some other sort of official, functioning as a cog in a bureaucratic machine?

You have to get a job. But to put your best energies into any of those jobs, or similar ones, is self-serving in the narrowest financial and consumerist sense. It would be, for you, self-submerging and self-destroying in the sense of destroying your critical overview of what is right and wrong. It would be, I put it to you, deeply irresponsible. Most students — most rebellious students too — go on as they get older to work an excising operation on themselves so that they can fit in to a career like those I've just surveyed. Don't you think that we socialist militants have a better idea? You have to live in society as it is, but you don't have to fool yourself and, as you get older, mutilate and repudiate your better, younger self. You don't have to prostitute yourself.

You can be better than that. You are better than that. You can be an enemy of capitalism and of its political machine and its opinion-industries. You can study the Marxist critique of capitalism — and maybe develop it — and be active, in your workplace, in your everyday life, on the streets, to prepare the working class to rise and make a better society, one free from the evils that make capitalism an abomination, all the more abominable because something better is possible now.

Individual life should not be clad in narrowly personal and familial asbestos-skinned egotism — "I'm all right, Jack, fuck the others" — conscience-salved perhaps with a donation here and there to charitable institutions such as War on Want or Oxfam. Anyway, "society" may not leave you alone. An awful lot of people hypnotised by the values of commercialism have had to wake up from that sleep to the fact that they have been like the legendary St Brendan, the Dark-Ages Irish monk who made his camp on a solid island in the sea, lit his fire to cook, and found it moving under him: it wasn't an island, it was a whale.

I put it to you that a better philosophy of life than the prevailing one is to face the fact that we are, each of us, part of a broader social entity, and that we should concern ourselves with its well-being as a necessary way of securing our own and our children's and grandchildren's well-being. I recently came across the following words, said to a journalist by the actress Marilyn Monroe, a woman of the left who had had to fight her way through the sewers of capitalist society. She summed up much of what socialists want in words that might have come from William Morris: "What I really want to say is that what the world really needs is a real feeling of kinship. Everybody, stars, labourers, Negroes, Jews, Arabs: we are all brothers. Please don't make me a joke. End the interview with what I believe".

We should concern ourselves with the moral climate around us, if only in the interests of our children and their children, and do something to counter the mind-rotting morality inculcated and reinforced by capitalism, for which, as someone well said, everything has a price but nothing an intrinsic or transcendent value. We should not fatalistically settle into accepting that a large part of humanity live in hunger and needless disease. We should not live without doing something about the slaughter of millions of Third World children on the altar of capitalist necessity. We should not be passive consumers only, but also try to create something better, or contribute to its creation.

All that aside, the root argument why you should join us is that you know that humankind lives in a world of savage, needless, shameful, damnable injustice. At stake here is the future of democracy, of equality, of all that is good in the society humankind has so far created, and of humankind itself. Have the courage to hope and to fight to realise your best hopes and desires. Slough off and break your paralysing sense of irony, unworthiness, absurdity, and, as James Connolly used to put it, dare to hope and fight. Take up the attitude expressed by one of Connolly's comrades in the 1916 Rising, Patrick Pearse:

"Did ye think to conquer the people,
Or that law is stronger than life,
And than our desire to be free?
We will try it out with you,
Ye that have harried and held,
Ye that have bullied and bribed.
Tyrants… hypocrites… liars!"

Underdogs and elites

DEBATE: SEAN MATGAMNA AND ROGER SCRUTON

Sean Matgamna

WHEN, RECENTLY, I DEBATED with Professor Kenneth Minogue, one important point he made against me was this: if you pin down a socialist about a particular regime in a particular country you invariably get the reply: this was not real socialism. Minogue made the point that it is very hard to know what we are arguing about. Ours is an idea which is never realised and therefore can never be criticised. On a certain level that is a reasonable point to make. So I will try to define what I mean by socialism.

Obviously, socialism is one of those words with a vast number of different meanings. Hitler was a socialist in his own designation, so was Clement Attlee. So was Ben Gurion. So was Nasser. What follows is that they cannot all be socialists. The people I mentioned are to a high degree mutually exclusive. You might try to find some socialist "essence" shared by them all — statism or whatever — but it strikes me that the word is so vague that it is best to start out by defining it. I understand it in terms of the ideas that Marx and Engels developed. According to Marx, socialism will grow out of capitalism, as capitalism grew out of the womb of feudalism. Socialism is being created inside capitalism by the spontaneous socialisation of production that is a natural part of capitalism, which ultimately spurs a rationalisation on a political level: the social property, now capitalist-owned, would become collectively owned social property. According to Marx, this socialism would differ from all previous socialisms, because it was based not just on a wish for an ideal, a perfect world, but on the natural development of our existing world. Socialism was the necessary outgrowth of advanced, developed capitalism.

Throughout history — and Marx was keen to admit this — ruling classes have emerged for particular reasons. Ruling classes have played progressive roles. The Communist Manifesto is full of praise for the bourgeoisie because capitalism had developed the means of production. Throughout history ruling classes have been necessary, because human beings have lived in a world of scarcity. That is the root of the class struggle. According to Marx capitalism had created, or was in the process of creating, a situation where there was no need for the struggle of classes, no longer a need for some people to rise to the top and create some sort

142

of civilisation on the basis of exploitation. Marx said socialism came out of advanced capitalism. This was Lenin's view also.

So why did Lenin — who insisted that socialism was not possible in backward Russia — make a revolution there? Why did Lenin and Trotsky make a revolution in a country where, though it was politically possible for the workers to take power there, socialism was not possible because the country was so backward? Lenin saw the Russian revolution as the first of a chain of revolutions in which the workers would take power in places like Germany and, eventually, America. The Bolsheviks did not see the Russian revolution as a socialist revolution in the sense that in Russia it was possible to create a better world than the world of advanced capitalism. The revolution was socialist only in so far as it was the beginning of an international working-class revolution.

This is fundamental. When Marxists insist that what happened in Russia from the 1920s on was not socialism, it is more than a way of saying that we do not like it — we are saying that it was an historical abortion, an historical cul-de-sac. If you look at what Lenin and the Bolsheviks said, nothing but an abortion could have been expected according to the bedrock ideas of Marxism. An historical abortion is what Lenin and Trotsky said would happen if the workers' power in the old Tsarist empire remained isolated. They did not foresee Stalinism. They expected that an isolated Russian workers' state would be overthrown by bourgeois forces. But they said in advance that socialism could not have been the result of the October 1917 Revolution unless October was the beginning of a series of victorious proletarian revolutions. And it was not. Socialism is the seizure of power by the working class in the advanced countries. It takes as its starting point the best that capitalism has achieved. From this point of view Russia was not socialist, and could not be socialist. I am not repudiating the revolution. We defend and stand by the Russian revolution. But the revolution was defeated by a bureaucratic, Stalinist counterrevolution — that is, a counter-revolution made by the state bureaucracy who came under the sway of the scarcity and backwardness which has dominated human history. The Stalinists created a totalitarian collectivism which most people take to be socialist. From the Marxist point of view, Russia was the opposite of socialism. In many ways it was further from socialism than the advanced capitalism we have in Western Europe is.

A second way of judging what real socialism is, is this: what does an alleged "socialism" mean to the working class? Did the workers rule in Stalinist Russia? No! Were the workers better off in Russia than in, say, Britain? No, they were not. I repudiate the idea that statification is socialism. Stalinist statification was the very opposite of socialism. All the conquests of the last few hundred years of human history — human rights, the slow spreading downwards of civilisation — were wiped away. They were not disposed of by socialism but by the Stalinist bureaucrats, behaving as ruling classes always do, in material conditions as backward and primitive as they were in the USSR. Therefore, the collapse of Stalinism does not mean the collapse of socialism. On the contrary.

For decades, the notion of socialism, which I have broadly defined, has been encrusted by a series of ideas which are alien to socialism. There are no shortage of quotes. James Connolly, for example, commenting on middle-class socialists like the Fabians, put it sharply: if state property is socialist property then the jails and enterprises like the Post Office are all socialist institutions; and the jailers, the hangmen and the police are all socialist officials. "Socialism" has long been encrusted with all sorts of statist ideas alien to socialism. Not all these ideas have come from Stalinism. During the last hundred years a collectivist wing of bourgeois liberalism — in this country in the past represented by the Fabians and the Labour Party — has grown up. These people also want statification. For example, Bismarck's state was the first attempt at a modern welfare state. He was not a socialist.

I want to take a different tack. We can all — Tories included! — agree that Stalinism is a bad thing. We will disagree when it comes to defining why Stalinism was a bad thing, what exactly was wrong with it. Socialists believe that there should be collective ownership of the means of production — I mean the basic means of production, rather than every single property — on the basis of a political democracy. Only on the basis of collective ownership of the means of production can there be a real, self-determining, self-controlling democracy. From this point of view, what was wrong with Stalinism? Stalinism could be seen as a grotesque caricature of every class society which ever existed. A state with unbridled power beat down the people. The state had such power that it could turn over the lives of tens of millions of peasants, wipe out millions of them, turn natural calamity to its advantage, and artificially intensify famine, as in the Ukraine, to break the peasants.

That state dominated the population in the interests of an elite. The elite, unlike the British elite, did not have private ownership of the means of production. The state had ownership of the means of production — but the Stalinists "owned" the state. You had exactly what you have in this country, in a different form! Stalinism had too many points in common — taken to a ridiculous caricature — with countries like Britain for people of Roger Scruton's persuasion to have a right to say: "That was the socialist future, and it did not work". It was the past of human his-

144

tory, the history of class society, encapsulated and intensified!

In Britain there is a ruling class which controls the lives of the people, not in a totalitarian fashion, not by direct force, but nevertheless for goals similar to those of Stalinism, and with immense powers of repression in reserve. Stalinism, in this respect, is only a grotesque caricature of what exists in Britain. In the Stalinist states, for example, education was formally accessible to the entire population, but in fact was semi-monopolised by the bureaucracy and their children. Exactly the situation that exists in Britain. Only the mechanisms of control differ. Now Mr Scruton would think this is a good idea, or something you have to live with because there can be nothing better. Socialists want neither Stalinism nor the system that Mr Scruton champions! We believe that we live in a world where objectively it is possible that elites can be dispensed with — whether they are Stalinist elites or British Tories and the class they represent. We believe we live in a world where it is now possible to realise democracy.

Although capitalism has been progressive, and did create possibilities for human beings that have not existed before, capitalism has raised possibilities that it cannot realise. Democracy is perhaps the clearest example. Democracy is necessary because the mass of the people cannot be liberated unless they can rule themselves democratically. The various political formations which developed capitalism — in Holland, Britain, France and America — put forward the idea of democracy. But at the very best this has only been realised in part, realised fully only for a section of the population. For example, in this country democracy is only a rough approximation to what democracy should be. It is not real, self-controlling political democracy. It is obviously better than that which exists under Stalinism. But there is not real self-rule in Britain.

If you are an elitist you believe democracy is not necessary. Desirable or useful, perhaps; necessary, no. But democracy is necessary if you believe in the rights of the vast majority of the people, that is, if you are a socialist. In capitalism there is only formal democracy and formal equality: formal equality before the law where some people are a lot more equal than others because they have property, and therefore, in fact, massively greater rights.

Without qualification, it is good that there are formal rules. The rule of law means that, most of the time, there are certain rules and certain rights. This is good and worth defending. Democratic socialists will defend these conquests of the people and achievements of bourgeois society (they were often achieved through mass action). We will defend these democratic gains against people like Mr Scruton! Nevertheless, those who are serious about liberty and democracy must realise that capitalism has failed to deliver what is possible. Right now you have a situation in Britain, after ten years of Thatcher, where a vast number of people sleep in doorways in central London. Capitalism has the possibility to create a real abundance on the basis of real self-rule. But what do we get? We get the rule of savages! This is a savage system. An elite rules on the back of the mass of the people and exploits the people. The bourgeois intellectuals act as sheep-herders of the people, defending the official ideological lies which lubricate the rule of the moneyed in the interests of the moneyed.

I do not know if Roger Scruton would say this, but certain critics of democracy from the right say that there are inbuilt features in bourgeois democracy which inevitably make it a system of lying. I think they are right. This system needs to lie. "Democracy" is its official ideology, in some ways now its religion; but democracy — real self-rule — is not its day-to-day reality. It is to a serious extent based on falsification. It has to be. It can only survive on the sort of trickery we have seen lately where the Tory government has, in the last few days, exempted students from the council tax because students form a sizeable part of a number of key marginal seats. This is blatant bribery! Our political world is comprehensively corrupt. It must depend on lies because it cannot deliver the democracy it promises, or be what it says it is. Within British democracy we have the actual rule of the minority through their control of the means of production.

Socialism says: this is wrong. Socialists have said that for 2000 years. Marxist socialists say it is now unnecessary. We do not need it. The people who do need it are the ruling class and their intellectuals, who defend their system and accept its unavoidable spiritual and cultural corruption. This is what it comes down to. One of the most awful things about modern Britain is the cultural exploitation and degradation inflicted on the people by some of the tabloid papers, for example. Stalinism's fall changes none of this! And the collapse of Stalinism allows real socialists, at least in the medium term, to be more likely to receive a hearing.

For a long time it was a legitimate response to ask socialists: what do you think of Russia? Do you want to create a Russia? That is no longer a question which, after this current burst of bourgeois triumphalism dies down, will dominate political life. So, the short answer to "Is socialism dead?" is no, because capitalism is not dead. Socialism is a reaction to the realities of capitalism that I have talked about. It is a reaction rooted in the class struggle of the workers; and that struggle will go on as long as capitalism goes on.

One of the reasons why people in Britain now ask "Is socialism dead?" is because for ten years the workers have been defeated in the

146

British class struggle. We have been defeated before. There have been downturns before. The labour movement will revive! It may revive initially by way of the election of a Labour government and what happens afterwards. When it revives, the possibility will exist for the spread of a renovated socialism, a socialism which has purged itself of the statist encrustations taken from bourgeois liberalism and Stalinist totalitarianism. Socialism will revive. Despite the pressure socialists feel now, and all the fashionable talk about the "bankruptcy of socialism", what we are seeing is the beginning of the rebirth of socialism. Roger Scruton knows that, I think, and he fears it.

Roger Scruton

MR MATGAMNA WAS ELOQUENT and forceful, covering a great deal of ground. I can not reply to everything he said, but when he spoke of "the cry of triumph" from the bourgeoisie which we have been hearing for the last ten years, I thought of my own childhood. I asked myself, not for the first time, whether I am a member of that class or not. When he spoke about the ruling class, in my father's accent and with all the venom with which it was said to me when I was a child by my father, I once again ask: do I really belong to that class? The answer, of course, is that I do not know. I thought then that I heard a voice from my own past, from my father, lecturing me, as he always did, on the injustices of the English class system. How he himself had been a victim and how I was destined to be a victim too — not having the money and the opportunities which only the upper class could enjoy. I have always borne in my heart the little thought that I am a member of the proletariat after all, despite all the accidents of circumstance which have followed. It is with that authority which I speak to you.

I do not accept the title of this debate, in the sense that I do not accept the phrase "collapse of Stalinism". What I think has collapsed in Eastern Europe at least, and in the Soviet Union too, is Leninism. I agree with Ken Minogue, insofar as I understand what Ken Minogue said to Mr Matgamna in a previous debate, that the roots of the evil we have seen are not in the personality of Stalin, but they go deeper into a project which Lenin himself introduced into Russia in 1917. This project has been introduced into many other parts of the world, by others unconnected with Lenin, and almost always with the same results. I am thinking of Ho Chi Minh, Mao Zedong, Pol Pot and a whole series of other people whose names perhaps one should not mention quite in the same breath as Lenin, but nevertheless had the same project in mind.

I am not sure whether socialism has a future. But I do believe that there is something else which does have a future which I want to define before beginning. This is: the leftwing attitude. I do not want to disparage it because I think it is a part of human nature, it will always exist. I was brought up in a family in which it was dominant. I would like to say, psychologically, what I think this attitude is, and why I think it will persist. I believe it is founded in sympathy for the underdog. Everyone recognises that there are people who lose out. The sight of them losing out is always heartrending and in decent people it gives rise to the question: what shall I do about it? The easiest thing to think in the light of this experience, of seeing people lose out, is that the underdog is a victim of the "overdog"; that wherever there is an underdog there is also an overdog that is doing him down. The ubermensch, or uberhund, rather. This overdog is a person who gets the good pay-off, the successful member of society, perhaps someone like myself, who, having started out in life as an underdog, has now enough money to drink a bottle of wine with my dinner. So, if one can believe that the fate of the underdog is somehow caused by the overdog, one has a political programme unfolding before one. Namely, to get rid of the distinction between underdog and overdog. Somehow, by whatever means, introduce a condition of equality, so there is no underdog any more, because there is no overdog ruling over him. Equality, then, becomes the primary goal.

Now, of course, one simple way of making everyone equal is to deprive everyone of everything. It is no exaggeration to say that this was the method adopted in the Soviet Union under Stalin. Almost everybody, as Mr Matgamna rightly said, not the elite who were doing the depriving. But even they were unsafe. From day to day they risked falling into just the same trap that they had built for the rest of mankind. Even Stalin himself never felt wholly secure — and rightly. So, we all recognise that there are ways of aiming at equality that threaten us all. I would simply say, without arguing for it, because this is a debate about other things, that I believe that the goal of equality is unachievable and that it would not be worth achieving if you could achieve it. I actually think, and Mr Matgamna rightly accuses me of this, that elites are necessary. They are also, in my view, the peaceful by-products of human society. They are not necessarily the evil and repulsive things that he believes they are.

I want to talk about the future of socialism, in particular this "leftwing attitude" that I have identified. It is obvious that the idea that the misery of the underdog is caused by the triumph of the overdog has a peculiar tenacity — not just intellectually. It has survived ever since the French Revolution, and of course had its origins long before that in medieval thinking. It is not just an intellectual tenacity, it is a moral tenacity.

People believe that if you deny such rights you are condoning the situation of those who lose out. You are part of the machinery of oppression which has caused them to be sleeping in that tin shed in Lincoln's Inn Fields. As a result, as all of you know, it does become very difficult to be open and honest about this very matter. If you are open and honest and say human equality is not achievable and not desirable, you can be the target of abuse. It is thought morally wrong even to think this. However, in my view, this is self-evidently true, as long as you clear your mind of the emotional need to think the opposite. This emotional need will survive because of human sympathy with the situation of those who lose out. I believe one should have that sympathy. But one should not take it to the extent of destroying the possibility of elites emerging. Because, in my view, it is only by the emergence of elites that the situation of everyone gets better. But elites have to emerge in the right way. Not by imposing themselves on others, but by the process once called by Adam Smith "the invisible hand".

Marxism, to which Mr Matgamna gave a very neat and elegant introduction, appeals not just because it conscripts this feeling of sympathy for the underdog, but for reasons he stated: it seems to give a scientific account of how that condition arose and how it will be bettered. It will be bettered by the natural processes of history, passing through capitalism to a socialist future. As he rightly said, that socialist future turned out after 1917 to have been betrayed. Well, he would say betrayed, I would say that was what it actually really was. At least it was not what was expected. Ever since 1917 people on the left have been exercised by what happened in Russia. They have wanted to explain it in a way which would enable them to maintain their own system of beliefs. The usual way out is the way out taken by Mr Matgamna, namely, that this was not real socialism. It was not real socialism because it was taken over (in his language) by a counter-revolution of Stalinist bureaucrats.

Now, I am not a historian, but I think if you were really interested in what went on in 1917 — most of you have socialist leanings, you ought to be — you should read the book by Heller and Neffs, *Utopia in Power*. It will prove to you, if you have an open mind, that the things that are normally blamed on Stalin had been consciously initiated by Lenin. In particular, the founding of the Cheka, which was to have all-encompassing power over the social processes. That is the sort of thing which was the most sinister development of the Russian Revolution. But it happened before Stalin and it happened in Lenin's thinking as part of the process of seizing power from the remnants of the bourgeoisie — from people like me, I suppose. Now, people on the left ought to feel some conscience about this. As I have said, the left-wing attitude is natural,

149

and will always remain, but it is also necessary to feel some conscience about what has been done in the name of it. If people like myself start saying of any particular conservative or reactionary regime which you disapprove of it was perhaps not real conservatism, you would all be, rightly, disapproving. You would say, come on, take some responsibility for things done in the name of your philosophy; show how you would separate yourself from it. You must give concrete historical detail and show you are aware of the evils and the dangers.

If anything should be learned from Stalinism, as Mr Matgamna called it — what I refer to as Leninism — it is that, whatever the future of socialism, whatever it is that you socialists think you should be doing, you must look at the past and take some responsibility for it. At least for having sympathised with it, for feeling it is going along the right lines. See how things went wrong and how you, seriously, would avoid the errors. I believe that many on the left, in Britain at least, have gone through this examination of conscience. I feel people, on the whole, agree about certain conclusions about the Great Socialist Experiment, as it was called.

First, and I think Mr Matgamna would probably agree with this, most people are sceptical about centralised planning. But their scepticism, I believe, does not go far enough. In particular, we should ask ourselves the question as to why centralised planning was thought of in the first place. It was instituted by Lenin as an instrument for equalising people, for destroying that old class structure and giving opportunities at the lower end of society. Is centralised planning in itself wrong, or is it only wrong when it is not used for the purpose of equalising people? If you can plan to equalise, how far can your planning go? What liberties would you allow yourself to trample on in order to achieve human equality? This is the real question I think all socialists — or rather all those with the leftwing attitude I have described — should ask themselves.

Most on the left have come to see that state control in itself is not a good thing. As Mr Matgamna said, what socialists, and in particular Marxists, have always argued for is not for control of the economy by the state but rather something else — collective ownership, what the 19th-century Marxists used to call social ownership, ownership by the people, not by the state. The problem, I think, is that the onus falls on you to define just what you mean by that. Is, for example, a modern capitalist firm, in which the workers can all acquire shares, social ownership or not? I see, from vibrations on my left, no. This is the kind of question you need to discuss. Just how do you bring it about? At a certain period people thought Yugoslavia was an ideal of social ownership, one that combined social ownership with a market economy. No-one would want to wish the destiny of Yugoslavia on the rest of the world. But also, the economic and social facts of Yugoslavia do not give a good record to that type of socialism either.

Let me say one thing further. I do not, again, want to give a definite view because it is for you in your hearts to decide. Mr Matgamna said that for him the idea of socialism was collective ownership, not state ownership, but ownership by the people or workers, based on political democracy. This raises for me the major question which all socialists have to confront in the post-Leninist world. Suppose it came to a choice between socialism, or collective ownership, and democracy — which way are you going to go? To the people who constantly manifest their desires for something which has the form of a capitalist economy, do you tell them that they are wrong and that their votes will be cancelled, or do you go along with it and accept the result? I think this is a paradox. All socialists I have known, not only my own father, believe that their doctrine, if understood, would have the spontaneous consent of all the people. But suppose it had the spontaneous dissent of all people, what then? Which way do you go?

Nevertheless, as I say, the left-wing state of mind will remain because it comes from a force in human nature which is a force we should try to understand. My own view is that it is a type of residue of religious feelings surviving into a secular age. But these are feelings which all of us share to some extent. The socialist way of conscripting them will always be with us. But what are the lessons which must be learned from the collapse of Leninism? The first, and the most important, I think is this.

What Lenin did in Russia was to destroy all the Russian institutions which made it possible to recognise their mistakes and to correct them. He destroyed parliaments, he destroyed law, he destroyed open discussion and opposition. This process was initiated by Lenin and brought to fruition by Stalin. But it is only through these sort of things that people can come to see that they have made a mistake and take measures to correct it. In my view the greatest mistake that humanity can make is to destroy the means to rectify mistakes. That is the mistake which was made. Therefore we must remember that we need institutions which enable us, collectively, to come to see where we have gone wrong. That means we need parliaments, above all, legal opposition and free opinions.

Another point, and Mr Matgamna agreed, the rule of law really matters. Lenin in November 1918 issued a decree on courts which abolished the entire legal system of the Soviet Union. All the consequences which we see flowing from that are too horrendous to relate. We know that, whatever else we do, we must maintain the rule of law — a continuous structure of legal authority and impartial courts, insofar as we can achieve them. All human institutions are imperfect, and there will always be mistakes, nevertheless, just to abolish law is one of the primary errors of revolutionary socialism in the Leninist mould.

Another lesson we should learn, although I think Mr Matgamna would disagree with this, is that private property is a primary right of the individual. I do not know the Soviet Union very well, but I do know Eastern Europe. I know from the experience of my friends there that the one thing that would have helped them more than anything else was the right to be able to shut their door in someone's face, particularly the face of the secret police. The right to have that piece of territory of your own. Without private property it seems to me there is no such right. Private property is the thing that gives someone control over his own life. What-ever else we think about the revolutions of 1989 the demand for private property was at the heart of them. And anyone who knows Poland and Czechoslovakia will recognise this. You might think people were wrong to demand that right, that there is some ideal socialist world where it would not be necessary, but in the actually existing situation private property is one of the best institutions which has ever evolved, to protect us from the bullying of others.

Another lesson which you should draw from the collapse of Leninism is slightly more philosophical. It is: human institutions are more easy to destroy than to create. In destroying them you do not always know what you are losing. It was very easy for Lenin to destroy the rule of law in Russia, to destroy the principles of a free economy, to destroy all the old academic institutions, the Orthodox church and so on. All these things crumbled immediately. You only had to breathe on them. But what came in their place? In my view, nothing, organised nihilism. A moral, political and spiritual vacuum in which only power could reside. I believe we should learn that lesson. We should remember that, even if we want to reform things — and reform is very different from destruction. Until we understand the function of an institution — be it parliament, a school, a university, or whatever — we should not arrogate to ourselves the right to cast it down. We should try to find what it does and try to reform it in the direction we want.

Finally, the last lesson from the collapse of Leninism is that they ought to inform themselves a little bit better about the history of our century and what has actually happened. Many, many millions of people have paid with their lives, freedom and happiness to the Great Socialist Ex-periment. It is not good enough to wash your hands of it, you must un-derstand what went wrong. Mr Matgamna talked about bourgeois democracy which, apparently, we all live in, as a system of lies. But I sug-gest that if you really want to know what it is like to live in a system of lies you do a bit of reading about the systems that actually obtained in

Eastern Europe. I am not talking about the Soviet Union, but about Eastern Europe. These were capitalist economies which should have developed into socialism, and which the Communists were only giving a helping hand to, after all. Read Vaclav Havel's essays and come to see just what it means when truth is completely marginalised in everyday life. We can have this discussion. At least it helps us to clear the air of unnecessary lies lying too long in our opponent's conscience. In that part of the world, until 1989, such a discussion would have led to the arrest of all the people in this room.

I think that when history is examined it is much more complex than the simplified schemes that appeal to you because they seem to make sense of it. One of these schemes was given to us by Mr Matgamna. A Marxist scheme where history proceeds from feudalism through to capitalism, on to socialism by necessary and logical steps. In which, until the final stage, there is always a ruling class against which the rest are struggling. I think this is all myth. If you look at our country and the rule of law which he says the workers struggled to institute, often against great resistance. The rule of law existed in this country since the reign of Edward II, in one form or another. It was not introduced by workers' struggle. Nor was it anything to do with capitalism. It was part of feudal England.

England, even then, was not really feudal. It had a money economy and so on. If you look at the facts all these simplifications become unacceptable. Along with them comes the unacceptable idea of "the workers". Is Mr Matgamna a worker? Am I a worker? Are any of you workers? What does it mean to say that workers are going to rise up once again and take possession of their birthright? This language belongs to the 19th century, and was even wrong when applied then. You should revise your rhetoric to something more appropriate to the days in which you live.

Roger Scruton sums up

I WILL ADDRESS THE POINTS made in the discussion one by one. Firstly: has socialism come to an end? I don't believe socialism has come to an end, because I believe that the moral and emotional roots of socialism will always be there. Socialism will take a different form, and I entirely agree with the point made from the floor that the rhetoric of socialism in our day is outmoded. It must be amended, but once amended it will channel once again the emotion which Rousseau called "compassionating zeal". I think this is what we have heard from several people here today.

One of the pieces of rhetoric which should be amended is that of socialism versus capitalism. One gentleman, on behalf of social democracy, said absolutely rightly that this is an anachronistic debate. Nothing in the modern world is recognisably capitalist if you mean by capitalist that system that was described in *Das Kapital*. Certainly the opposition which exists is no longer socialism as then defined. For a start, capitalism has never been a system of beliefs. It was mainly used to describe an economic system. The Marxist assumption is that economic systems determine the whole social superstructure. I believe that assumption is wrong. I would never use the word capitalism to describe the conditions of any actually existing order. Let us just remember that this language comes from 19th-century debate.

Several people have said: why have I not explained what is good about "the rotten corrupt system". Someone said it has been cheeky of me to avoid what capitalism has done to the world and asked why I did not defend "my system"? Well, I was here to debate the future for socialism after Stalinism, not to defend what I believe. If asked to do so, I would have done so. As I said in the course of my talk, I do recognise the imperfections of human institutions, and I will defend nothing as an idea. I will defend certain established historical compromises as the best that we have got. One gentleman has said that this is just a cop-out, and that I am just taking Burke's line that because of human imperfections all we can do is to sustain the given things. He said that this is not going to appeal to anyone. If this is what the Right believe, then the Right has no future.

Well, I would say that it is true that the Right's future will always be precarious so long as it believes something as unexciting as the truth. That is the problem for us. You on the left have this great advantage that you can propagate exciting myths which appeal directly to emotions and which we will never see, but nevertheless will always inspire a following. I am not in that happy position. I will only be able to rely on decency, common sense and scepticism. l agree with you that perhaps on those grounds the Right does not have much of a future. We have had a lucky run, but maybe we will have to go under. But I am a philosopher. I am only interested in the truth, not what the future may bring.

Someone said: why do I talk only about individuals whereas Mr O'Mahony was talking about social groups and classes? Do I not believe that there are classes? Are they not economically determined? Do they have contradictions? If so, how are they resolved? This is straight from the heart of Marxist theory. I do not believe that classes are the most important form of association between people. I believe that there are other forms of association that come about in completely different ways —

such as this, a debating club, a corporation, a church, a school, a university. All these bring people together and establish their collective and social nature a lot more firmly than classes do. I do not know what class I belong to. But I do know something about clubs and discussion groups and other things I belong to — not all of which some of the people in this room would approve of. And the same is true of most of you. Many people here have spoken loudly of their situation as workers, but l wonder how many here are really confident that you as opposed to me are the genuine item when it comes to being a worker or not? Perhaps we are all workers. Perhaps none of us are. I sit in front of a VDU, just like the lady here, for quite a bit of the day too.

This question also belongs to the 19th century. It has a dusty air to it. The most important question for us today is not the question of what we are as individuals, but what groups, clubs, social units, we would like to belong to. My only point is this: whatever we belong to, we ought to be free to belong to it, or not. We should not be blamed for belonging to things which it was never our choice to belong to in the first place. Perhaps I am, objectively speaking, as the Marxists used to say, a member of the bourgeoisie. But that does not mean I am a fat spiv as one gentleman referred to that class. I know a lot of people who you could classify as owners of the means of production who are neither fat nor spivs. Put on one side all this myth-making about class and talk about real social entities!

I agree that if conservatism as a philosophy confines itself to advocating the rights of individuals, as Mrs Thatcher and her ideologues used to do, it dissolves into another kind of 19th-century nonsense, a John Stuart Mill-type of individualism which also, today, has no credibility. All of us are anxious for some type of social belonging. This goes as much for people on the Right as those on the Left. This is what we must try to define and identify. All this talk about classes is a myth and an illusion.

Now, the lady here accused me of believing that sympathy for the underdog was misguided, recommending me to read Hume. I do not think it is misguided. I think it is a natural human instinct. Again, one person said this feeling made him into a socialist. It made me into a socialist too, for a short while, admittedly under some fairly severe tuition. If I had confessed something else, I would have been out on my ear. Nevertheless, I also believe it is quite possible to be like me and think there has to be an underdog, because there has to be an overdog, and yet also feel sympathy for the underdog. I am just sceptical about the socialist plans that have been propagated for rectifying the situation of the underdog.

Someone said, quite rightly, that Marxist sympathy for the underdog was irrelevant to the argument. Marx was presenting an objective, scientific description of the material basis of society, its basis in human labour. From that description certain things followed. I agree that this is what he said he was doing. But I disagree that it was objective and scientific. The proof of its wrongness comes from the disasters of the attempts to implement it. I know that this is a deep question, and that we were not assembled to discuss it, but all that I would say is that for me the division between material base and social superstructure is untenable, the labour theory of value is untenable. The idea that certain social forms succeed each other according to the laws of motion declared in *Das Kapital* is also untenable. I reject all these three crucial theses. So I do not accept that there is anything remaining of an objective theory to replace what I described as the instinctive feeling we have for the underdog, which will always remain.

Someone went on to say that democracy takes priority over socialism. She said it is what people want that matters. You rebutted my suggestion that socialists are in a quandary as to whether they should have democracy or socialism. I think her very language went on to reveal exactly why I am worried. "The majority of the working class will take power for themselves. That will show that socialism is achieved by democracy". Firstly, you use a violent language of "taking power", not the language of constitutional process, where people vote and display their wants. You talk about a particular class, the working class. What about the rest? They have no say. What if it turns out that the majority are middle class, as in my view they may well be? Do you say they have no rights?

You go on to defend Leninism, saying the invention of the Cheka was a tactical, short-term measure designed to protect the workers' revolution against people like me. I was specifically cited as the type of person who does need to be dealt with quite severely in these transitional periods. I fully agree. If you go in that direction you will have to deal severely with people like me. But I think there are a lot more people like me than you think. I think you may find that there are 20 million of them. You have to make the moral choice: what to do with them? This is a choice that Lenin made, and we are living with the consequences.

Someone said I should look at Eastern Europe — the gentleman from Pakistan, or somewhere like that; oh, I am not allowed to say things like that — before the Communist take-over. Well, I agree. But we should look at what was possible in Eastern Europe. Eastern Europe is very important. They have been through what we have not been through. They suffered Nazism and Communism in rapid succession. It is a big question why that happened, and what went wrong with the settlement after the First World War. Maybe that settlement was in itself wrong. But everyone knows that at least the Austrian part of the Austro-Hungarian empire had introduced some kind of democracy, at least universal adult male suffrage, in 1903. That was working quite well. Something went wrong. What went wrong is something, fortunately, we have escaped in this country. So we do not know all the forces that went first of all to make Nazism and then Communism in that part of the world. We must concentrate on the actual history of these events and try to see whether they are relevant to us at all. Maybe they went through this tragic succession of events because of the peculiar circumstances they were in after the First World War. Maybe we don't have to think about this in the same way. Maybe we don't have to worry about whether Marxism contains anything relevant to our condition at all.

Why did I say so many positive things about private property? Someone mentioned Chile under Pinochet. Surely, private property does not guarantee democracy, it was said. It is not sufficient for introducing an ideal order. But it is a necessary protection for the individual against the state. It is one thing which defines for the individual some sphere of sovereignty of his own, something he can give away if he wants, something he can exchange. Marx himself said that the condition of the proletariat was miserable because the proletarian has nothing to exchange but his own labour power. Surely you would want the proletarians to have something more than that to exchange if you want to liberate them. That "more" must be their own property.

Sean Matgamna sums up

THE LAST SPEECH BY MR SCRUTON was hypocritical. Only if Stalinism in the Soviet Union really was socialist and working class can you reasonably go on about the Stalinist massacres as discrediting socialism. The issue is not properly posed in terms of the massacre of the ruling class or of the Roger Scrutons. It is posed in terms of the fact of history: they massacred us. It is not a matter of whether we are willing, if we had the chance, to murder 20 million Roger Scrutons. The massacres have largely been massacres of our people. The history of capitalism has been a history of massacres of our people. In Paris in 1871, something in the region of 10,000 to 15,000 of our people were murdered in cold blood after they had been captured. There are many, many other examples.

No Marxist socialist would seriously argue you can get socialism without the majority of the population wanting it. The whole idea that socialism can be imposed by a minority is absurd! The attempt would lead to all sorts of convulsions. The important issue is whether or not, if socialists have a majority, the ruling class will submit to that majority.

The evidence of history is that if we came anywhere near to a majority the ruling class would disrupt bourgeois democratic procedures. Take Chile in 1970-73, for example. A left-wing government — not particularly leftwing, in fact — but a left government was elected; and then it was smashed by a military regime backed by the CIA. This military regime had many of the features of fascism.

What do I mean by "democracy"? I mean real, collective self-rule of the essential features of the lives of the people making the decisions. In reality you do not have this under capitalism. For example, much of what happens in Britain is determined by a stable civil service. Most of what happens in the lives of ordinary people is determined by capitalist monopolies who are not subject to any sort of democracy at all. They are like the petty kings of the Dark Ages, the big capitalists now, ruling their economic kingdoms as autocrats! I would not say that democracy for shareholders is any type of democracy where a company employs a vast number of people who have absolutely no say in what happens. So present-day bourgeois democracy is not real democracy, except within certain narrow, formal, political limits. It is not what it promises to be. In America, for example, less than half the people vote. A vast number of things are decided by the Supreme Court. In reality, democracy in America or in Britain is very, very shallow. We want to deepen democracy. We want to give political, social, and economic substance to the bourgeois shadow of democracy.

I do not know about whether human nature is evil or not. If you look at what the Nazis did, when normal family men — some of whom were vegetarians for altruistic reasons! — went home to their kids after organising the gassings of other kids and adults, then you know that human nature is capable of awful, awful things when the internal and social inhibitions break down. What socialists want to do is to create a set of social institutions and conditions where human beings — who begin as animals with all the possibilities of animals, and who are capable of relapsing into bestiality — can rise, and rise on a stable basis, and continue to rise above that level.

It is irrelevant how you define basic human nature. It seems to me you can define it very negatively; but that I take as an argument for better social institutions. After all, the good family men who murdered people in the Nazi concentration camps only did these things in conditions where German capitalism licensed a legion of savages to take control of society. These savages took control to such an extent that when the German bourgeoisie wanted to stop what they were doing, in the early '40s, they could not stop them. They brought Germany down to complete disaster. We want to change the conditions where the bestiality which sometimes emerges in people cannot emerge in that way or to that extent.

Now, should we drop being called socialist? Well, in a way, yes. But that is the desire to escape from a whole series of associations which really are very difficult to escape from. What do we call ourselves? The best thing I can think of is "democratic collectivists". But then people would not know what we were talking about, or where we came from politically. We have to fight our way out of the situation we are in. So I agree, socialist is a lousy word, so is communism; but therefore let us try to define the ideas we are talking about.

Social Democracy, has it vanquished Leninism? Well, it depends on how you evaluate what Social Democracy has achieved. Nowhere has Social Democracy achieved anything better than a welfare state. It may have alleviated, over time, the conditions of rampant red-in-tooth-and-claw capitalism. That is good. It did not achieve the socialist goals of eliminating capitalism and going on to something higher. Therefore it is not vindicated.

Classes don't exist? Again, you can take every given thing, break it down to all its particulars and its components, and deny that any whole greater than those components exists. Does society exist? You know the old argument: is a river the same river as it was five minutes ago? It is not, it is flowing. Yet we work normally on the assumption that the river exists. If you de-structure everything around you, it becomes impossible to make sense of anything. When you do this ideologically, as Roger Scruton is doing, you do it to avoid facing the fact that there are classes. Fundamentally, there are groups of people, whatever the differences between them as individuals — and there are many — with a similar relationship to the means of production. For example, there are a vast number of people in this country who can only live by selling their labour power.

According to Roger Scruton, private property is a good thing. Well, on a certain level that is true. But if workers have houses as well as labour power, they can not live on the sale of their houses. They have to continue to sell their labour power.

Classes do exist. Some people live by selling their labour power; other people own the means of production and buy labour-power — the active lives of workers. Again, there are divisions within this categorisation, but the categorisation tries to make sense of society. Breaking things down to atoms is simply an ideological evasion of thinking about the composite reality. What about Roger Scruton's own identity, his "upwards" migration from class to class? It's become relatively easier to do this in Britain in the last 40 years. Other countries have a less structured class system — Australia and America, for instance. Individuals can change their place. But at any given time there is a vast and stable number of people who have to sell their labour power and who can not and will not escape from that condition. There is an inherent limit to the number of individuals who can migrate as Roger Scruton says he has. People can change their classes, but that does not tell you anything. In ancient Rome people could go from slaves to being very rich. One even went on to become emperor. But it did not alter the system of slavery. Most slaves remained slaves.

Lenin did found the Cheka. I agree with the comrade who argued that the Russian revolution was right to defend itself by whatever means it found necessary. In a calm, friendly discussion you could discuss whether the setting up of a lawless Cheka, which on a day to day basis was out of political control, was the right thing to do. You could ask whether or not, in retrospect, it was not a serious mistake. But before I would discuss that in an argument with Roger Scruton, I would insist on discussing the reality in which the Cheka was created. The Bolsheviks did not begin by starting the terror; they began by abolishing the death penalty. Then they were faced by the revolt of the old ruling class. They were faced with the invasion of no less than 14 states, including Britain. One of the consequences of the destruction this wreaked was that a society which was backward to start with was driven much further back economically. A large part of the working class was destroyed. They were physically destroyed, and driven back into the countryside. You can not talk about the Cheka or condemn what Lenin and his comrades did to defend themselves without taking all this into account.

This is an example of what I started out with: the ruling class resists. Lenin did not decree that there would be civil war. The first thing the Bolsheviks did when they took power — on 8 November 1917 — was to produce an appeal for peace. It was a sane, sensible, reasonable document in a world gone mad, where millions of people were being slaughtered in a mad capitalist war. The Bolsheviks did not begin as people who recklessly killed Roger Scruton's adopted class in Russia. They began as people who wanted a peaceful revolution. They were stopped, not by their own ill-will or their own evil natures, but by the nature of the resistance to them, and by the nature of serious political struggle in class society.

Are elites necessary? Much of what Roger Scruton said here about elites and private property is sophism. What are we talking about in terms of elites? Well, of course, there are and always will be differences among human beings. You will almost certainly get elites in particular fields. You will get people who are an elite in terms of knowledge, for example. I am prepared to accept that this is so and that it should be so,

160

and I am prepared to pay due respect to someone who has a great deal of knowledge. There are all sorts of ways people can be elites. No-one with any sense is going to tell you that you can equalise people on that level. What we want to do in terms of equality is to get rid of a system whereby there is inbuilt inequality, grotesque inequality, rooted not in the special human qualities some people may have, but in their ownership of the means of life, and where others have to work to live, submitting to the exploitation of the owners.

I don't have any objection to people owning houses. If Mrs Thatcher's selling of council houses had not meant the destruction of the social housing stock, there would not have been a particular problem from a socialist point of view. Under a socialist system perhaps people would not want to own houses, but if they did, then that would have little bearing on the socialist project.

But socialists are not arguing with you on this level about property. Socialists argue against the right to own, and exploit, other people's labour power. That is what is wrong here. Yes, and the prohibition of such property rights — in the means of production and in the buying and exploiting of labour power — is the limit we would put on "freedom" in order to achieve equality — equality as I have defined it, not as Roger Scruton has defined it. There are constraints on robbery. I think a society could exist in a condition of liberty which placed all sorts of basic legal, constitutional restraints on the right to exploit other people and the right to own the means of production. I mean large-scale production, I am not talking here about artisan workshops or the corner shop.

No Marxist advocated the sort of wholesale, cauterising economic collectivisation that Stalin carried out. Trotsky criticised it. This was no Marxist programme. It served the drive of the Stalinist bureaucracy to become the sole master of the surplus product. This was the way Trotsky described it. No Marxist is in favour of barrack-room equality. On the contrary, the whole point we make about bourgeois society is that bourgeois society, having created the possibility of a high degree of individualisation of people, actually limits the realisation of that possibility to a very small number. We are the individualists here, in the proper sense of the word. If you like, we want mass individualism! We want to create a whole, stable social system in which there will be a vast increase in individualism in that sense. The whole argument here, in terms of what Marxists say, is skewed by Stalinism, and utterly confused.

Marxists never advocated the sort of things the Maoists or the Khmer Rouge did. That is not and never has been our programme. It was not the programme of Marx, nor the programme of Lenin either. If someone who has read Marx and Lenin pretends to believe that Marxism and bar-

161

rack-room Maoism are the same thing, I take that as proof that he can not deal with the arguments of the real Marxists. He hides behind Stalinism from real Marxism.

So we are against private ownership of the means of production and against the right to exploit people. Beyond that there are all sorts of possibilities for the ownership of property. We are not against people owning property — the whole idea is absurd. Lenin at various times tried to organise planning, for instance, during the civil war, under "War Communism". Lenin in 1921 created a system whereby they allowed a limited but quite extensive revival of capitalism and the bourgeoisie, under the control of the state. The whole notion that Lenin created what has become known as totalitarian planning is not true to history. All of that was carried through by Stalin after 1928, when he broke with the reviving bourgeoisie, and the bureaucracy became the sole master of the surplus product. It was then that you got the whole absurd notion of totalitarian planning, with all initiative concentrated in the state. It would have been pretty absurd in a highly advanced country with an advanced state and a developed civilisation. It was utterly harmful to the USSR, and was said to be so by Marxist critics of Stalinism at the time, many of whom were in Stalin's jails and camps.

What about the rule of law? I did not claim, did not mean to claim, that the workers created the rule of law. But, if you look at the evolution of the rule of law in England you can't just locate it in the Middle Ages and present it thereafter as a continuous, flowing, evolutionary development — and forget about the 17th-century bourgeois revolutions! You cannot talk about a stable evolution of the rule of law, without revolutionary disruption. It would not be true. What I claimed was that the workers, by their struggles, expanded the possibilities of democracy. They forced acceptance of this on the ruling class.

The rule of law is a good thing, other things being equal. But the rule of law is frequently developed through disruptions of the rule of law. The question is: whose law? Right now the law of this country is very different from the law at the time of Cromwell, not to speak of the time which Roger Scruton mentioned. We are in favour of the rule of law. But the rule of better law — law which, for example, outlaws exploitation — must be established. We are in favour of breaking the law of the bourgeoisie, if necessary, to achieve that. For example, Yeltsin and the Russian parliament went against the legalities of the system when they opposed the coup. Yeltsin broke the rule of law when, for instance, he banned the Communist Party. Was it right to do that? Of course, it was right. Yeltsin did not act as someone who represented the naturally evolving, growing, expanding parliament-based rule of law. He acted as a revolutionary.

162

And he was right to act as a revolutionary.

Finally, I repeat: between Roger Scruton and Stalinism there is a great common bond, a common acceptance of elites. He wants a civilised elite but he wants an elite. We do not want elites; we want self-ruling democracy. And you cannot get self-ruling democracy unless you have some form of collective ownership of the basic means of production, otherwise you get gross inequality under formal equality. Roger Scruton, in terms of where he stands in history, has more in common with Stalinism — I make all the necessary qualifications here — than we socialists have. Much more!

The debate between Roger Scruton and Sean Matgamna took place at the Socialist Organiser London Forum on 4 November 1991.

Capitalism versus human life

1Martin Thomas

CAPITALISM HAS CREATED life-enhancing possibilities. It has even realised some of them. My older daughter has epilepsy. In pre-capitalist times, if she'd had medication at all, it would have had no, or harmful, effects, and the seizures would probably have become more severe until they disabled and killed her. Today, she has been able to end the seizures with just a few pills, without side-effects.

Not only in Britain, but in many poorer countries too, almost everyone learns to read and write, almost everyone has easy access to music and visual arts, a sizeable proportion can study at university. Most jobs are cleaner, quieter, and require less physical strength than they or their equivalents used to. Food, clothing, and housing sufficient for all can be produced by maybe 20% of the total labour-time of society, while previous societies required almost all society's labour-time to produce a scantier minimum.

At the same time that capitalism, by advancing technology, creates those possibilities, it also stunts and warps them. It diminishes and threatens human life. And in some respects the stunting, warping, diminishing, threatening increases. Capitalism threatens human life through global warming. Capitalism has given rise to technologies which, with judicious development and use, could reduce carbon emissions and save the environment. Yet in recent years most energy investment has gone not into improving and cheapening renewables or nuclear power, but into "extreme", high-carbon-emission, extraction of oil and gas: oil sands, shale oil, hydraulic fracturing. That offers the best profits in the short term. And capitalism puts profit before life. Other industrial emissions into the atmosphere threaten life. In the UK, 60,000 people die early each year because of such pollutants as nitrogen dioxide; world-wide, 3.3 million. London went above its safe limit for that air pollution over the whole of 2016 as early as 8 January. Corporations like Volkswagen, in pursuit of profit, have the technology to limit the emissions, but also have also used technology so that vehicles observe the limits only in test conditions and spew out 70 times as much pollution in actual use.

Emissions into the atmosphere threaten everyone, rich as well as poor. But capitalism also works to diminish and shorten the lives of the worse-off and favour the lives of the rich. In Britain, people in well-off areas can expect to live much longer than people in poor areas. And they can expect to live in good general health, free of permanent limiting ailments, 20 years longer. In the poorest areas, on average you live to 52 without permanent limiting ailments. 52! Remember, the government wants to raise the state pension age to 70. In well-off areas, on average you live to 71 without permanent limiting ailments.

Defenders of capitalism say that its inequalities are necessary to make it dynamic — by way of the striving generated by the competitive "rat race" — and benefit even the poorest, because we get pulled up along with, although behind, the rich. Yet, once economic life has reached the level that basic necessities can be produced by a small proportion of the available labour-time, and so almost no-one starves or freezes to death through sheer shortage, the evidence is that inequality, or relative poverty, is the major stunting factor.

Richard Wilkinson and Kate Pickett, in their book *The Spirit Level*, show that among the more prosperous capitalist countries, a composite index of health and social problems shows much worse levels in the most unequal countries (USA, Portugal, UK) and better levels in the less unequal (Scandinavia, Japan). The correlation with the country's inequality of incomes is high. The correlation with the country's absolute level of average income is low or zero. The same pattern — high correlation with inequality, little or no correlation with absolute income level (within the relevant range) — is shown by comparisons between states in the USA.

Children's well-being is better in less unequal countries, worse in more unequal countries, largely uncorrelated with absolute income

164

level. People's levels of confidence that they can trust neighbours and workmates are higher in less unequal countries, lower in more unequal, but by no means necessarily higher in countries with higher average incomes. Rates of mental illness are much higher in more unequal countries; so are murder rates, and rates of imprisonment.

In the abstract, a highly unequal society could still give better chances for an individual from a worse-off family background to rise high, and a less unequal society could rate low for that "social mobility". In fact, the more unequal countries also have less social mobility. Exactly why being much worse-off than the other side of the tracks is more blighting than low income as such (above a certain minimum level), we don't know. The fact is a fact. It is also a fact, documented in detail by Thomas Piketty in his book *Capital in the 21st Century*, that inequality, and the dominance of incomes from property, has been and is rising steadily across the most developed capitalist countries.

Despite crashes like 2008, on the whole capitalism tends to increase production. On the whole people get more smartphones, iPads, PCs, etc. than they used to. But simultaneously capitalism increases inequality and its blight on life. Some of the elements of inequality's blight we know. Being overstressed; frustrated; isolated; "alienated" in the sense that your creative abilities are appropriated, manipulated, and abused by others for alien purposes, diminishes your resilience, and eventually your health.

Not all stress is unhealthy. Complete languor is not the ideal. Hard work is not necessarily unhealthy. Marx, while strenuously avoiding detailed blueprints of the future cooperative commonwealth, described the expansion of free time, as against enforced drudgery, as its cardinal feature. Yet by "free time" he didn't just mean idling. "Really free activity, e.g. composing music, is at the same time precisely the most damned seriousness, the most intense exertion".

While the demands on physical strength of many jobs have been eased, they have been made more harmfully stressful by the way they are organised. Sometimes this involves long and arbitrarily-imposed hours. Generally, as Michael Marmot, a researcher in this field, notes: "Stress at work is not simply a matter of having too much to do, but also results from too little control over the work, and from insufficient reward for the effort expended". ("Insufficient reward" means not just low wages, but lack of satisfaction in having done something useful, lack of appreciation from others). "The way work is organised is crucial. The way to address the problem of stress at work is to look hard at the organisation of the workplace".

Capitalists look hard at the organisation of the workplace — but with the priority of exerting more control and squeezing out more profits, thus increasing unhealthy stress. School teachers are rated by the Health and Safety Executive as the most overstressed trade, with a suicide rate 40% above the average. Most of that is due to arbitrary, often educationally counterproductive, impositions by school management. Those impositions are constantly increasing, and driven not by direct profit-seeking but by an imperative to imitate competitive profit-seeking norms. There is much talk about "executive stress". Some managers, especially middle managers, are overstressed. Usually the highest levels of stress are not at the top of the heap but at the bottom. The trades with the highest levels of suicides are teachers, cleaners, construction workers, health workers, not top managers. In schools, students may well be more unhealthily stressed than the teachers — not because they are working hard at learning, which may be healthy, but because of petty school discipline and irrational impositions from a competitive exam system.

In 2015, I spent a lot of time on a 24/7 picket line run by Brisbane dockworkers fighting sackings. New technologies have created the basis for making dock work much less life-sapping. Dock work now involves little heavy manual labour. Container terminals are quiet and clean. Yet the dockworkers smoke much more than Australia's average (low by world standards). A doctor told me why: shift workers, especially shift workers with shifts that change constantly, smoke more than others. Although nurses know the dangers of smoking better than others, they smoke more because of the shifts they work. Those dockworkers are unhealthily stressed, despite the technical advances, because of the capitalist way the work is organised, with round-the-clock and unpredictable shifts, and arbitrary sackings.

In one of the most technically-advanced capitalist economies, Japan, since the 1970s "karoshi", death through overwork, has become an officially recognised condition. Each year, hundreds of families, on an increasing trend, win compensation because a family member is officially certified to have died from overwork. Yet the compensation is from the government, not the employer! Since the late 1980s, "karojisatsu", suicide from overwork, has also been officially recognised, with similar compensation. Overwork, in this context, means not just long hours, but "frustration", "psychological burdens", "lack of job control", etc. The difference in other capitalist countries is only that "karoshi" and "karojisatsu" are not officially recognised.

A poignant finding from research in 2002 shows that people who become convinced that they will end up lonely suffer damage to their complex-reasoning abilities. Their simple information-processing capacities are not damaged. Expectation of future physical injuries does not damage their complex-reasoning abilities. But the conviction that they will end up lonely does. And for many it is a well-grounded conviction. In Britain, 11% of all elderly people say that they talk with a neighbour, a friend, or a relative — someone they are connected with in a human way, rather than through market transactions or official procedures — less than once a month. Once a month! Millions of less extreme cases are achingly lonely. In an 1845 book, Engels wrote about how capitalism had atomised people in a way unknown to all previous societies. In the big capitalist cities, people "crowd by one another as though they had nothing in common, nothing to do with one another... [with] brutal indifference... unfeeling isolation of each in his private interest... This isolation of the individual, this narrow self-seeking, is the fundamental principle of our society everywhere, [and] it is nowhere so shamelessly barefaced, so self-conscious as just here in the crowding of the great city".

Capitalism has generated the possibilities of privacy, of "a room of one's own", of having "time to oneself", of choosing a path in life radically different from one's parents and neighbours. Those possibilities are progress compared to the conformity and narrow horizons imposed by many pre-capitalist communities. But capitalism also perverts those possibilities into enforced isolation and loneliness, and not only for the elderly. At the same time, the atomised nuclear-family households of modern capitalism create an imposed "togetherness" for young children, frequently over-supervised by their parents.

Capitalism is creating grand possibilities, but simultaneously stifling, blighting, and threatening human life. The choice for each one of us is passively to accept the stifling and blighting, and try to create a niche of relative contentment within it; or actively to take part in the collective struggle for collective democratic control over our economic life.

The Only Road

October 1917: the workers' revolution

An eyewitness account of the October Revolution

Hal Draper

THE FOLLOWING DISCUSSION by the American Marxist scholar Hal Draper is of a book written by a non-Bolshevik member of the government that took power in October 1917, I N Steinberg. Steinberg was a leader of the Socialist Revolutionary Party, of the faction known as the Left S-Rs, who were in coalition with the Bolsheviks for a few months after November 1917, from soon after the establishment of the Soviet Government.

Steinberg's book, *In the Workshop of the Revolution*, was published in 1954 long after he left Russia. Despite the Left S-Rs' split from the Bolshevik-led Soviet Government, Steinberg tells the truth about the Bolshevik seizure of power and about the early months of Soviet Government.

In his book, Steinberg presents the 1917 upheaval not as a conspiracy but as a real people's revolution. And he is very inconsiderate of the myths about the "democratic" Kerensky regime which the bad Bolsheviks overthrew, as well as the Menshevik and Right Socialist Revolutionary allies of Kerensky. Actually Steinberg's language about the "moderate socialist parties" (Menshevik and Right SRs) is very mild, but the outline of the picture he paints is damning enough. That picture is of an elemental revolutionary upsurge of the masses from blow, determined to throw off all oppression and equally determined to end the war, which the rights and moderates tried to oppose, and which the Bolsheviks (and Left SRs) supported. This was the simple difference between the historic reality and the anti-Bolshevik myth of a "conspiracy".

Of the right wing socialists, Steinberg writes that they believed "that the necessary conditions were not yet in evidence to realise the programme of the people. They conceived it impossible to end the war without the co-operation of the Allied powers. They thought it utopian to

169

transfer political power to the working classes since, in their view the capitalist order in Russia was inevitable. Their interpretation of the revolution as only a democratic bourgeois succession to Tsarism, demanded, of course, a corresponding strategy — the strategy of class compromise and political compliance. This strategy put the moderate parties (Mensheviks and Right Socialist-Revolutionaries) halfway between the bourgeois and the working-class programmes, gave their activities an air of vacillation and, in fact, fortified the position of the bourgeois camp."

Now to be sure, the anti-Bolsheviks argue strenuously that anything beyond a bourgeois revolution was indeed impossible, but what Steinberg point up sharply is that this line meant that the right-wingers had to set themselves against and get ready to suppress the revolutionary dynamism of the people. It is because the anti-Bolsheviks have to get around this inconvenient fact that the myth of a "conspiracy" was born.

By the time of the new Kerensky government of 10 July, Steinberg relates, "Kerensky had lost hold of the ties of confidence which once had bound him to the people." Discreditment rebounded not only against Kerensky but also against the Menshevik and Right SR ministers who joined his cabinet.

"The main speaker for and exponent of this rootless coalition", writes Steinberg "was the Social-Democrat (Menshevik) Tseretelli. As minister of the interior, he dispatched a circular to the whole country designed to redouble the power of the government commissars against the active local soviets. He ordered these commissars to block the 'illegal distribution of landed properties,' the 'appropriation, ploughing and sowing of other people's lands.' He thus sustained the policy of his predecessor, Prince Lvov. Every circular of this kind was like a match thrown into the powder keg of the revolution."

Being highly concerned with the democratic forms of the revolution, Steinberg especially emphasises the transformation of the Kerensky regime into a "quasi-dictatorship" — with the consent and support of the very democratic Mensheviks and S-Rs who were later to issue howling blasts of anguish at every step the Soviet government took even to defend itself against armed insurrection. Steinberg's general sketch of the whole development, of course, contributes nothing new to historical knowledge, its main interest lying the character of the narrator. There are vignette touches here and there.

• In August, at the State Conference organised by Kerensky, we see the scene where Bublikov, a leading industrial capitalist, steps up to shake Tseretelli's hand before the assemblage, an impressive piece of symbolism while at the same moment a general strike of workers in Moscow was going on.

• While we all know that Kerensky and a few die-hard slanderers still preserve the chestnut about the Bolsheviks being "German agents", we can read in Steinberg that the Kerensky government itself was thus accused. In the manifesto of the Kornilov revolt, the reaction declared "The Provisional Government standing as it does under the pressure of the Bolsheviks in the soviets, works in full agreement with the German General Staff..."

With regard to the seizure of power itself, Steinberg is typically ambivalent. "The Left Social-Revolutionaries" he relates "did not think it advisable to precipitate such a rebellion. In their opinion it would be sufficient for the [Soviet] Congress to maintain the positions of the people and lead the revolution to the Constituent Assembly. But they felt that, if the masses were to rebel, they would not stand against them."

No initiative toward revolution — and no opposition to it: you just go along with the surge of the people. The Left S-Rs could never have been leaders of the revolution, the role that had to be played by the Bolsheviks, and on the other hand they could never have been enemies of the revolution. They combined the fuzziest of ideologies with real revolutionary sentiments, a combination which doomed them to be simple fellow travellers of the revolution. They had no political compass of their own, but as sincere revolutionists they could feel which way the revolutionary aspirations of the people where blowing. When the wind stopped blowing in one clear direction, they were lost.

Steinberg does not link up his above-quoted reference to the Left SRs' coolish opinion on the seizure of power with what he describes later as the great result of the "inadvisable" rebellion. Left S-Rs like Steinberg never could orient themselves in the criss-cross of events and policies, but they could respond like sensitive barometers to revolutionary élan.

"The October Revolution brought tremendous exaltation to vast sections of the Russian people. After eight months of frustrated expectations, there was now a profound sense of relief. It is true that there was also great bitterness about the past, great anxiety for the future; but the deepest sensation which October aroused in the people was joy. In city, village and army, people rejoiced in the fullness of the their liberation, in the limitless freedom that now summoned their creative efforts. It was as if the walls of Jericho had crumbled before their eyes. A new life called to them with a thousand voices: from now on 'everything is possible to man'. Everything is possible' did not mean licence and wilful destruction, but full freedom to satisfy the constructive urges and the noblest ideals of man.

"All aspects of existence, social, economic, political, spiritual, moral, familial, were opened to purposeful fashioning by human hands. Ideas for social betterment and progress that had been gathering for generations in Russia and elsewhere seemed to wait on the threshold of the revolution ready to put forth and permeate the life of the Russian people. The issues were not only social and economic reforms and thoroughgoing political changes; with equal zeal the awakened people turned to the fields of justice and education, to art and literature. Everywhere the driving passion was to create something new, to effect a total difference with 'the old world' and its civilisation. It was one of those uncommon moments of self perception and self assertion. The storm passed nobody by: neither those who hailed it as a blessing nor those who spurned it as a curse."

It was this climate of a world reborn which in the first place doomed the Constituent Assembly as a vestigial remnant of the "old world". When the Constituent Assembly was swept away in the tide, it scarcely created even a ripple. It had ceased to have any significance.

What played a greater role at the time was a different question: coalition cabinet or one-party cabinet. And here, in Steinberg's account, we come to another reason why determined anti-Bolsheviks will not like this book. The reason is this: even when Steinberg is doing his best to be as "anti-Bolshevik" as they come, he just can't seem to squeeze out any facts to give colour to his strictures. The trouble it would seem, is that he had old-fashioned prejudices against simply inventing suitable "facts" to fit anti-Bolshevik specifications.

Steinberg and the Left S-Rs were enthusiastically in favour of constituting the first Soviet government as a coalition of all the socialist parties, including the Mensheviks and Right S-Rs. But the latter made it impossible, for a simple and straightforward reason: they were against the revolution and would enter its government only to behead it. Steinberg uses some language blaming "extremists" on both sides (Bolsheviks as well as the rightists, presumably) but every fact in his account speaks one way only: "Protesting violently, the Mensheviks and Right Socialist-Revolutionaries quit the Second Soviet Congress when it proclaimed the Soviet Republic. Thus, the moderates caused the final split in the camp of the working classes and facilitated the establishment eventually of a purely Bolshevik government..."

So the Left S-Rs set out to be the honest brokers who would bring the right-wing socialists back into the coalition. After all, these right-wing socialists had lived more or less happily in a coalition government dominated by imperialists and capitalists; why should they be so intransigent about entering a coalition with revolutionary socialists? It disconcerted the honest brokers no end.

On the day the first cabinet was established, the Bolsheviks formally invited the Left S-Rs to name three representatives. At this point the Left S-Rs refused, on the ground that they wanted an all-around coalition. So the Bolsheviks had to set up the cabinet themselves. Negotiations for the inclusion of the rightists continued, but uselessly; for the condition which the Mensheviks and Right S-Rs set for their participation was breathtaking: nothing more than that Lenin and Trotsky (by name) should be kicked out of the government! Fantastic as it seemed, they were not even clever enough to try to undermine the revolution by stealth: they openly demanded just as if they had not been defeated and discredited, that the revolution behead itself in order to obtain, as a reward their own worthy personages, now a little shopworn from being kicked around by Kerensky but still willing to "save" the revolution for capitalism and war.

"It was amazing" writes Steinberg. "During the February period, the Mensheviks and the Right Socialist-Revolutionaries had countenanced all possible coalitions with bourgeois parties, even when they were opening reactionary. But the same leaders now rejected indignantly the idea of a socialist coalition, that is, co-operation with the Bolshevik Party, which at that time was still weak and still sought support in other related elements. Lenin's face for them seemed to eclipse all of the revolution. And again they unwittingly helped prepare the ground for his future dictatorship."

So Steinberg complains that "Lenin's secret political purpose" was a "dictatorship" all the while, but whereas Steinberg was clever enough to mind-read Lenin's secret thoughts, no one else in the country had to be half so clever in order to see that it was in fact the right wing socialists who were torpedoing any unity. The Left S-Rs finally joined the coalition themselves, and their course afterwards is another story.

Steinberg's account of the Constituent Assembly adds nothing new to the question. What he choose to emphasise, however, is that it was the right wing socialists (again) who excluded any possible compromise. When the Constituent Assembly met, Chernov (Right S-R leader) was elected president and: "Of all possible attitudes toward the Soviets, Chernov (and the Right Socialist Revolutionary Party that stood behind him) chose the most dangerous, if not the most foolish tactic: he simply ignored the Soviets as if they did not exist at all. His major speech, which naturally encompassed all cardinal issues of the revolution, was delivered with the incredible pretence that the Constituent Assembly had convened in a social vacuum. He announced that negotiations for peace would be started with the Allied powers, that the socialisation of land would be carried through; that the federative rights of all nationalities would be proclaimed. Not with a single word did he mention that all these vital tasks were already being realised in the country and followed with intense interest in the whole world. What did all this mean? By implication it was a challenge to the Soviets and the masses that stood by them. For the Constituent Assembly, the only chance of survival lay in some compromise with the revolutionary forces that had already struck roots. It would have been easy to find some legal, constitutional and political form for such understanding. But this one way of averting civil war within the camp of the working people was ignored by the majority [of the assembly]. Did it then hope that the Soviets would simply capitulate?"

Like all the others in the mainstream of the revolution the Left SRs now looked on the Constituent Assembly as an obsolete reminder of pre-October Russia...

In chapter 13 of Steinberg's book we find him in jail! What has happened? For a whole chapter our honest author goes through description of some local prison colour, ponderings about the French Revolution, tales about prisoners etc... and not a word about why he and a whole group of Left S-R's have been imprisoned. He barely manages to mention casually even that the Left S-Rs had left the government: why? Not a word. At one point, he pictures himself as wondering "What this the final break-up of the once common front?" The reader naturally must suppose that this break up has taken place because of the Bolsheviks' action in jailing their ex-partners. It is well-nigh incredible but Steinberg drags the reader through three more whole chapters before he even discusses his own version of what had happened to the coalition. The reason for this peculiar structure is no mystery or personal idiosyncrasy.

Steinberg is deliberately engaged in recreating the impression — without deliberately lying at all — that he and his Left S-R party broke with the Bolsheviks over questions of democracy and terrorism, that is, over questions which today are "respectable" ones for anti-Bolsheviks. And of course, the indisputable historic fact is that his party broke with the Bolsheviks over an entirely different issue... because of their intransigent and violent opposition to the Brest-Litovsk peace with Germany and for no other reason.

The Tsarist army had disintegrated, the whole land in revolution was in turmoil, the German army was threatening on the borders, whole regiments were deserting the lines, the front could not be held; better yield to the Germans' robber demands for a peace than have the revolution crushed: a revolutionary war against the German invasion could not be sustained; there was no choice... So Lenin argued, not only against the Steinbergian phrasemongers but also against a strong minority of the Bolsheviks themselves, a minority which publicly campaigned for its position outside of the party and against its majority.

The Left S-Rs advocated war, not peace; but this position was defeated at the Congress of Soviets which met to ratify the Brest Treaty. Thereupon, right there, Steinberg announced for the Left S-Rs that they were withdrawing from the government — "to the consternation of all present" he adds.

One searches the six meagre pages which he devotes to the whole issue... for Steinberg's statement of reasons in favour of his position of continuing the war rather than accepting the forced peace. This is what one finds. Continuing the war by partisan warfare "might encourage the German people to resistance against their own masters. But 'peace' would automatically strengthen the German imperialist forces both at home and abroad."

Now, as a matter of record it was the Brest peace which did play an important part in stimulating revolutionary discontent in Germany; but the 1917 general strike wave in Germany and Austria proved that the revolution there was not yet ripe; and it was not at all necessary for the Left S-Rs to agitate Lenin about the quintessential need for the German revolution to come to the aid of the Soviets; and... But all this is really beside the point.

Steinberg and the Left S-Rs did not adopt their position out of overweaning anxiety for the German revolution. It is transparent rationalisation. If not, the Left S-R position would have been merely tactical opposition to the Brest treaty, as indeed was the case with the dissident Bolsheviks. On the contrary, as Steinberg makes clear, for the Left S-Rs the surrender of Russian territory to the German robbers was a principled "capitulation" of the revolution.

Steinberg quotes himself from an 1918 article: If we sign, "no trace will remain of the meaning and content of the [Soviet] republic." At the end of this chapter we also find that the Brest treaty "broke the moral backbone of the coalition."

Why? Why were the Left S-Rs so frenetically and principledly outraged by this peace signed at the point of Germany's guns? Was it perhaps, the infusion of sheer national-chauvinism in their fuzzy ideology which prevented them from accepting the loss of Russian territory, even in order to save the revolution? Yes.

Well, then... had the Bolsheviks thrown the [Steinberg] in jail just because he and his Left S-Rs had left the government? Of course, no...

The Left S-R party decided to make up for their defeat in the Soviet Changer by embroiling Russia in war with Germany by their own organised provocation.

On 6 July, two Left S-R agents assassinated the German ambassador, count von Mirbach. Steinberg does not boggle over the question of the party Central Committee's responsibility for this move. The party's leaders, Spiridonova, proudly claimed full responsibility for the act, in the traditions of S-R individual terrorism. The last thing the party wanted was to have the assassination treated as merely involving two individual murderers. It was the party that had ordered Mirbach's assassination in order to provoke Germany into renewing its assault on Russia.

Steinberg writes that "In actuality the Left S-Rs *at that time* had had no intentions of staging a revolt." [Italics added]. That is at that time they were "merely" trying to get a war started against the country so as to bring about the "revolutionary war" which the majority of the country had rejected. (Democrats they are, you see.)

Perhaps some readers will not believe that a man can be so naïve as to tell this story on himself and still continue to write as if his party was engaged in nothing out of the ordinary from the point of view of its democratic rights. But the fact is that Steinberg actually writes the following fantastic and almost unbelievable words: "but Lenin and Trotsky could not forgive another party for acting independently and thus challenging their dictatorship."

He actually writes this after himself recounting his party's war plot! The Left S-Rs were just "acting independently" of the government, is that a crime? Doesn't a party have the democratic right to assassinate an ambassador in order to get a war started against its own country! You call this a revolt? And so what if our "revolutionary war" program has been voted down by the Soviet Congress? So what if I, Steinberg, nowhere in my own book even claim that a majority of the country was really for it? Is it not another proof of Lenin's "dictatorship" that he could not "forgive" this little innocent plan to start a war? Are we not great democrats and he a dictator?

Like a character straight out of Wonderland, Steinberg continues to write about the Left S-Rs' "deep shock" when the Bolshevik government reacted sharply. But this was July 1918. It was not until seven months later that Steinberg found himself wondering about things in prison. What had happened in this interval?

Specifically we have already seen that Steinberg had written that "the Left S-Rs at that time [July 1918] had had no intentions of staging a revolt" How did their intentions develop? This brings us to the question of the Left S-Rs going over to the programme of armed struggle against the Soviet government.

This party, which had broken with the Bolsheviks over the issue of war rather than peace, which proclaimed that it regarded this issue as involving the whole content of the revolution, which was so frantically anxious to blow up the Brest peace that it reverted to its terrorist-assassination methods in order to embroil the country in a war on the vote of its own narrow Central Committee as against the vote of the Soviet Congress — was it true or wasn't it true that this party then moved to a programme of armed insurrection against the government?

Steinberg not only states but documents the party position.

Steinberg first summarise the thinking of the party on attitude to the government. "Almost unwittingly, a policy of 'war on two fronts' evolved," he writes — one war against the White interventionists and simultaneous war against the Soviet government. "They might have said We shall fight the bourgeois counter-revolution as if the Bolshevik state did not exist, and we shall fight Bolshevism as if social reaction did not stand poised to stab us in the back."

But — Steinberg continues in summary of his comrades' thinking — could such a two-front war succeed? Perhaps we should table our quarrel with Bolshevik policy in order to defend the revolution's future?

"Should the Left S-Rs then inform the regime of their decision, so that they might be released and take part in the battle? The conclusion seemed logical, but — "it did not satisfy the moral conscience of the prisoners." (Note that Steinberg implicitly demonstrates that he has no doubt that the Left S-Rs would have been freed from jail if they had been willing to adopt this position, against armed insurrection.)

How did the party divide on the question? It was debated among the Left S-R prisoners and "argued in the secret correspondence with the illegal Central Committee of the Left S-Rs outside."

One faction (the "moderates") declared "We... reject for the time being any armed struggle against the Bolshevik government because it might play into the hands of forces hostile to the revolution." (Italics added.) The other faction ("intransigents") argued for the two-front war: "you cannot destroy one without the other." They were for armed struggle now and against calling for a "fight against the Denikins under Bolshevik leadership."

Who won? All Steinberg reports is that the "moderates" were "restrained" and their will "paralysed" by their fear that they might be regarded by the others as selling out to the Bolsheviks. Is it fair to conclude then that the "intransigents" dominated the party councils? At this point Steinberg simply ignores the obvious question. And of course it should be remembered the "moderates" were those who did not favour *immediate* organisation of armed struggle.

In any case, Steinberg next presents the text of a document hitherto unknown to me, which is decisive by itself.

It proves to the hilt without any possibility of doubt whatsoever that the Bolshevik government asked only, as the condition for releasing the

Left S-Rs that they state publicly that they were against "armed action" to overthrow the government. This the S-Rs refused to do. Hence there is no possibility of dispute over why they were in prison. All this emerges from the text of the document itself. Steinberg does not point it up one way or the other. One can even wonder whether he realised the meaning of the document which he quotes!

In August 1919 the Left S-R Central Committee with the agreement of "all party circles" decided on negotiations with the Bolsheviks for an agreement which would legalise their party and free their prisoners. Kamenev, Beloborodoff and Stassova represented the Bolsheviks, the Left S-R delegation of three included Steinberg. There are six pages of direct quotations from the discussion, as selected by Steinberg himself.

The Left S-Rs proposed to "transfer the centre of our political operations to the provinces occupied by the Whites." In exchange for this they demanded: legality in these provinces after liberation and immediate release of all jailed party members. Immediately what Kamenev wanted to know was: "Will you give up your tactics of armed struggle against us!"

Of course, the Bolsheviks also kept pointing out that it was impossible and absurd to have a situation where a party was illegal in (say) Moscow because of its programme of armed insurrection while it was legal in a recently liberated province, insecurely held, with the same programme.

The Bolsheviks kept hammering away at the main point. In his very first speech Kamenev said "Can we ever come to an agreement with you, as clear and decisive as our split has been? Back in October (1917) we had differences of opinion too, yet we were able to work together." And in this framework he posed the decisive question of "armed action".

Turning and twisting the Left S-Rs refused to say yes or no. One of them evaded by merely saying that "You have no proofs whatsoever of our participation in any plots." But the Bolsheviks were not asking for proof one way or the other. They were merely asking for a public statement of party policy against armed action.

The second S-R evaded with the following phrase: "And anyway we have been refraining from armed action against you for some time" — apparently not even realising what he was admitting with this formulation. Steinberg didn't even refer to Kamenev's insistent question (according to the text of the first conference as given in his book).

The second and last negotiation conference took place in September. Here the Bolsheviks were even more insistent in narrowing the issue down to insurrection.

It is not enough for you S-Rs, the Bolsheviks explained quite patiently, to say that you reject armed insurrection because at the present time you don't actually have the means for it. That only convinces us that as soon as you can gather your forces, locally or nationally, you will act as before. What we are asking for is a statement of party policy against it…

Steinberg replied: "Our party has not, so far, officially proclaimed any armed struggle against the Bolsheviks. You will not be able to find a single such decision in our party conferences. That is why we do not need a paragraph about it."

Of course the party had not yet proclaimed any armed struggle. That was in question at no point. As to a statement of party policy not a word could be elicited from the Left S-R delegation other than what we have quoted above.

And that settles that.

Labor Action, 14 and 21 June 1954 (abridged)

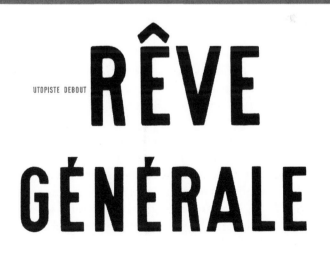

1917 was a democratic revolution!

Max Shachtman

LESS THAN THREE MONTHS after the victory of the Bolshevik revolution, Lenin remarked at a meeting that the Soviet power of the Russian workers had already lasted longer than the Paris Commune of 1871 which lived for only 10 weeks. The statement was made with pride, but no doubt with some wonderment. It reflected the conditions, incredibly complicated and difficult, under which the Russian proletariat took power into its own hands so that, for the first time in history, it could proceed to translate into reality the oldest dream of man: a society of free and equal brothers.

Thirty-one years have passed since the attempt was begun. It is not a very long time as history is measured. But we live in an age when change is rapid, frequent and profound. The thirty-one years since the Russian Revolution have seen epochal changes. None is so deepgoing, so unexpected and so confounding as the change in the direction of that Revolution. The attempt made in 1917 failed. The hideous reality of Stalinism is nothing like the noble purpose of socialism which the Bolsheviks set out to achieve. In almost every respect, the former is the gruesome caricature of the latter; in many respects it is diametrically opposite. In the great initiative of the Bolsheviks, millions throughout the world saw the beginnings of the new freedom. In the present-day outcome in Russia, millions see the new slavery and millions more suffer in silenced anguish under it. No great enterprise in history ever started under brighter auspices or ended under gloomier ones. When it began, there began also a stormy and confident offensive of revolutionary socialism, of Marxism, whose principles and programmes were embodied in the Bolshevik movement. With the triumph of the Stalinist counterrevolution, Marxism is today everywhere on the defensive.

The ideas of Bolshevism were summed up in this: the road to freedom lies through the establishment of socialism; the road to socialism lies through the overturn of capitalism by the revolutionary power of the working class. The offensive against Marxism is directed against these ideas, as tested in the Russian Revolution. It is an offensive on an unparalleled scale. It is sponsored by the highest government authorities. Dutifully and enthusiastically, it is carried out in virtually every number of every daily, weekly and monthly periodical...

The theme of this offensive is quite familiar: "Bolshevism leads to

180

Stalinism. The Stalinist totalitarianism was inherent in Bolshevism itself. The Russian Revolution could have produced nothing else than what we have in Russia today". At the right wing of the stage, you hear: "Stalinist despotism is socialism, it is the only thing you can get if you fight for socialism". At the left wing of the stage, you hear a variation on the same theme: "Stalinist despotism is not socialism, to be sure, but it is the only thing you can get if you fight for socialism which is now proved to be unattainable. In any case, it is true that Stalinism is the inevitable product of Bolshevism".

The aim of this offensive is a political one; its effects certainly are. And its political aim is a reactionary one.

The whole capitalist world, including that part of the working class world whose ideas and activities are decisively influenced by it, is now mobilised for preparations for the third world war, the war between the US and Russia. War preparations are inconceivable nowadays without ideological preparation of the people to accept the war or at least without a campaign to prevent the people from fighting during and after the war to put an end to the social system and the regime which breed war.

Because they are worried about the popular opposition to the war and the war preparations, the warmongers try to present their course to the people as a crusade for democracy against totalitarianism.

Because they are worried about the people bringing an end to the war the way the Russians did in 1917, they cry out in every imaginable key: "Don't even think of it! Whatever else you do, don't even dream of such a thing! Look what happened in Russia when the people took power into their own hands! All they got and all they could get and all you would be able to get is the monstrosity of Stalinist despotism! And if you don't believe us, who have such a miserable reputation, why, here are some experts whom you can believe — people right out of the socialist and even the Bolshevik movement itself. . . "

That is the political meaning of the contemporary offensive against the Russian Revolution. The abysmal degeneration of Stalinist Russia and of the Stalinist movement everywhere has provided the enemies of socialism with all the basic materials for the weapons in their offensive, with materials of such a kind and in such quantity as they never dreamed of having in their century long struggle against socialism.

With the weapons they have thus forged, they have slashed and mutilated the true portrait of the Bolshevik revolution so that it can no longer be recognised. We know a good deal already, thanks above all to Leon Trotsky, of the Stalinist school of falsification. We do not realise, however, that there is another school of falsification about the Russian Revolution that is actively at work. It is the school run by the social-democrats, zealously assisted by turncoats from the revolutionary movement. It is at once the complement of the Stalin school and of the reactionary imperialist campaign against socialism. Like all falsifiers of history, it operates with outright lies, with snapshots of events ripped away from the attending circumstances, and in the best of cases with an utter failure to understand what a revolution is or with criteria applied to a revolution which belong at best in a drawing room discussion or a game of cricket...

The fact which enemies of socialism are most anxious to keep in the dark is that the Bolsheviks represented not only the most revolutionary socialist movement of their time but also the most consistently vigorous democratic movement.

There is no other intelligent or intelligible explanation for the big fact that the Bolsheviks, starting as a tiny party even after the overturn of the rule of the Czar, took power and were able to maintain it for years with the support of the decisive sections of the people of Russia.

Whatever the forms it may take, democracy must express the will of the people. In 1917, the people of Russia were completely exhausted by the war, tired of the horrible bloodletting, tired of fighting for the imperialist aims not only of Russian Czarism but of British and French bankers and monopolists. They wanted peace above all other things. They wanted it so passionately that they overthrew the regime of the Czars which they and their ancestors had endured for centuries.

What they got in place of Czarism was a government of the Russian capitalists which wanted to continue the war, which wanted to maintain the reactionary landlordism of Russia, which feared and hated the aroused masses and sought to circumvent the will of the people and to thwart their aspirations by all the vicious devices of modern governments. This government, the provisional government of Kerensky, was supported by the two non-Bolshevik parties which enjoyed popular support, the Mensheviks and the Social Revolutionaries, or S.R.s...

The Bolsheviks gathered millions and ever more millions of workers, soldiers and peasants around them by militantly supporting the demands of the people. They did not talk about them but fought for them. They were for immediate peace, for land to the peasants, for workers' control of the factories, for immediate convocation of a Constituent Assembly, for a truly democratic republic. And that is the fundamental reason why the Soviets rallied, in one locality after another, to the support of the Bolsheviks — in the cities, in the trenches and in the villages...

The taking over of power by the Soviets was the greatest victory in history for democracy, and this victory was made possible by the Bolshevik leadership and no other. The Bolsheviks had not invented the Soviets in some cellar or house of dogma. The Soviets were first brought into existence in 1905 by the Mensheviks. In the 1917 revolution, they were constituted and for a long time led by the Mensheviks and S.R.s, not by the Bolsheviks. But it was only the Bolsheviks who said that these most democratic organs and representatives of the people shall rule in the name of the people and in their interests.

Once in power, the Bolsheviks did everything in their power to bring peace to war-exhausted Russia. If Russia was to know very little peace within its own frontiers for the next few years, the responsibility was in no sense that of the Bolsheviks and the Soviet power. The Bolsheviks took Russia out of the imperialist war, even if it meant great sacrifices in the form of tribute to the armies of the German Kaiser. The Bolsheviks actually gave the land to the peasants, which no other political group in Russia was prepared to do except the allies of the Bolsheviks, the Left-wing S.R.s...

The Bolsheviks actually proceeded to suppress the counterrevolutionary forces and movements of the Czarists, the bankers, the clergy, the reactionary generals and the landlords. And as is befitting in a revolutionary upheaval. they proceeded by revolutionary means. When rifles were raised against the Soviet power, the Soviets replied with rifles. No revolutionary government in history worthy of the name has ever acted differently. The criticisms of the Bolsheviks in this case are made by people who never seem to have heard of the Great French Revolution or even the American Revolution and the Civil War. Every revolution has its traducers and its detractors — the dilettante detractor and the malicious detractor — who complain because it acted like a revolution and did not deal with its opponents the way you deal with them at a game of bridge. The Bolshevik revolution is no exception.

One of the greatest difficulties about a revolution is that those who oppose its victory seldom understand its purpose and its determination, seldom reconcile themselves to its working existence. Here too the Bolshevik revolution was no exception. The Bolsheviks, for example, did not even start with the idea of suppressing the capitalist parties or of disenfranchising the capitalist class. Lenin repeatedly insisted that depriving the capitalists of the right to vote was a specifically Russian phenomenon, that it might not be necessary in the revolution of other countries, and that in any case it was not a principle of Bolshevism.

Neither did the Bolsheviks start with the idea of confiscating all capitalist property and nationalising all industry. On the contrary, they opposed it. They knew the backwardness of Russia. They knew the lack of experience and culture, not only of the workers in general but of themselves as well. They not only wanted the capitalists to remain in the factories but even guaranteed a reasonable profit.

But the logic of the class struggle is inexorable. The Russian capitalist class could not reconcile itself with the idea of a Soviet state ruled by the workers and peasants. They sabotaged their own plants; they refused to co-operate in any way; they fled from the revolutionary centres and immediately launched a counterrevolutionary civil war to overturn the Soviet power. They outlawed themselves; they placed themselves, voluntarily and even eagerly, outside of Soviet legality, and nobody, least of all the Bolsheviks, did that for them. Confronted with this situation, with the fact that complete economic chaos threatened the already chaotic country, the Bolsheviks proceeded to take over industry, to nationalise it, or more accurately, to legalise the seizures of the industries which the workers themselves were spontaneously carrying out, on their own initiative.

What held for the Russian capitalist class, held in substantially the same way for the two big popular parties, the Mensheviks and the S.R.s. They could not reconcile themselves to the decisive fact that a great revolution had taken place which brought the Bolsheviks to power. They could not understand the decisive fact that the Soviets of workers, soldiers and peasants were the most democratic and the most widely supported organisations in existence, the ones through which the Russian people could rule the country in the most democratic way, the ones through which the economic reconstruction of the country could be undertaken, directed and controlled. Instead, these two parties championed the Constituent Assembly which finally convened two months after the Bolshevik revolution but which no longer represented the people of Russia. Not only the Bolsheviks withdrew from this Assembly but also the Left-wing S.R.s, who had split with the Right-wing but which represented the big majority of the peasants.

The Soviet government was not weakened, but strengthened thereby. The Constituent Assembly could only become a rallying centre, a war-cry, for the counterrevolution in Russia, and that is why it was dispersed by the revolutionary regime. That is what the Mensheviks and Right-wing S.R.s did not understand. But its truth was soon demonstrated.

The Assembly became the programme of every counterrevolutionary inside and outside of Russia — from the Cossack generals to Winston Churchill, who was soon to spend millions of pounds sterling in the attempt to overturn the workers' and peasants' power in Russia. Nowhere did the cry for the Constituent Assembly appeal successfully to the workers and peasants. They understood who championed it and why. The result was inevitable: the people rallied more firmly around the Soviets and the Soviet regime. All the efforts of the counterrevolution, organised with world-wide imperialist support, failed to overturn the new regime. Its contribution was solid, and even now it remains our permanent acquisition: for the first time in history a government of, for and by the toiling masses.

Labor Action, 15 November 1948

Stalinism and Bolshevism

Leon Trotsky

REACTIONARY EPOCHS LIKE OURS not only disintegrate and weaken the working class and isolate its vanguard but also lower the general ideological level of the movement and throw political thinking back to stages long since passed through. In these conditions the task of the vanguard is, above all, not to let itself be carried along by the backward flow: it must swim against the current. If an unfavourable relation of forces prevents it from holding political positions it has won, it must at least retain its ideological positions, because in them is expressed the dearly paid experience of the past. Fools will consider this policy "sectarian". Actually it is the only means of preparing for a new tremendous surge forward with the coming historical tide.

The Reaction Against Marxism and Bolshevism

Great political defeats provoke a reconsideration of values, generally occurring in two directions. On the one hand the true vanguard, enriched by the experience of defeat, defends with tooth and nail the heritage of revolutionary thought and on this basis strives to educate new cadres for the mass struggle to come. On the other hand the routinists, centrists and dilettantes, frightened by defeat, do their best to destroy the authority of the revolutionary tradition and go backwards in their search for a "New World".

One could indicate a great many examples of ideological reaction, most often taking the form of prostration. All the literature of the Second and Third Internationals, as well as of their satellites of the London Bureau, consists essentially of such examples. Not a suggestion of Marxist analysis. Not a single serious attempt to explain the causes of defeat, About the future, not one fresh word. Nothing but cliches, conformity, lies and above all solicitude for their own bureaucratic self-preservation. It is enough to smell ten words from some Hilferding or Otto Bauer to know this rottenness. The theoreticians of the Comintern are not even worth mentioning. The famous Dimitrov is as ignorant and commonplace as a shopkeeper over a mug of beer. The minds of these people are too lazy to renounce Marxism: they prostitute it. But it is not they that interest us now. Let us turn to the "innovators".

The former Austrian communist, Willi Schlamm, has devoted a small book to the Moscow trials, under the expressive title, *The Dictatorship of the Lie*. Schlamm is a gifted journalist, chiefly interested in current affairs. His criticism of the Moscow frame-up, and his exposure of the psychological mechanism of the "voluntary confessions", are excellent. However, he does not confine himself to this: he wants to create a new theory of socialism that would insure us against defeats and frame-ups in the future. But since Schlamm is by no means a theoretician and is apparently not well acquainted with the history of the development of socialism, he returns entirely to pre-Marxist socialism, and notably to its German, that is to its most backward, sentimental and mawkish variety. Schlamm denounces dialectics and the class struggle, not to mention the dictatorship of the proletariat. The problem of transforming society is reduced for him to the realisation of certain "eternal" moral truths with which he would imbue mankind, even under capitalism. Willi Schlamm's attempts to save socialism by the insertion of the moral gland is greeted with joy and pride in Kerensky's review, *Novaya Rossia* (an old provincial Russian review now published in Paris); as the editors justifiably conclude, Schlamm has arrived at the principles of true Russian socialism, which a long time ago opposed the holy precepts of faith, hope and charity to the austerity and harshness of the class struggle. The "novel" doctrine of the Russian "Social Revolutionaries" represents, in its "theoretical" premises, only a return to the pre-March (1848!) Germany. However, it would be unfair to demand a more intimate knowledge of the history of ideas from Kerensky than from Schlamm. Far more important is the fact that Kerensky, who is in solidarity with Schlamm, was, while head of the government, the instigator of persecutions against the Bolsheviks as agents of the German general staff: organised, that is, the same frame-ups against which Schlamm now mobilises his moth-eaten metaphysical absolutes.

The psychological mechanism of the ideological reaction of Schlamm and his like, is not at all complicated. For a while these people took part in a political movement that swore by the class struggle and appealed, in word if not in thought, to dialectical materialism. In both Austria and Germany the affair ended in a catastrophe. Schlamm draws the wholesale conclusion: this is the result of dialectics and the class struggle! And since the choice of revelations is limited by historical experience and... by personal knowledge, our reformer in his search for the word falls on a bundle of old rags which he valiantly opposes not only to Bolshevism but to Marxism as well.

At first glance Schlamm's brand of ideological reaction seems too primitive (from Marx ... to Kerensky!) to pause over. But actually it is very instructive: precisely in its primitiveness it represents the common denominator of all other forms of reaction, particularly of those expressed by wholesale denunciation of Bolshevism.

"Back to Marxism"?

Marxism found its highest historical expression in Bolshevism. Under the banner of Bolshevism the first victory of the proletariat was achieved and the first workers' state established. No force can now erase these facts from history. But since the October Revolution has led to the present stage of the triumph of the bureaucracy, with its system of repression, plunder and falsification — the "dictatorship of the lie", to use Schlamm's happy expression — many formalistic and superficial minds jump to a summary conclusion: one cannot struggle against Stalinism without renouncing Bolshevism. Schlamm, as we already know, goes further: Bolshevism, which degenerated into Stalinism, itself grew out of Marxism; consequently one cannot fight Stalinism while remaining on the foundation of Marxism. There are others, less consistent but more numerous, who say on the contrary: "We must return Bolshevism to Marxism." How? To what Marxism? Before Marxism became "bankrupt" in the form of Bolshevism it has already broken down in the form of social democracy. Does the slogan "Back to Marxism" then mean a leap over the periods of the Second and Third Internationals... to the First International? But it too broke down in its time. Thus in the last analysis it is a question of returning to the collected works of Marx and Engels. One can accomplish this historic leap without leaving one's study and even without taking off one's slippers. But how are we going to go from our classics (Marx died in 1883, Engels in 1895) to the tasks of a new epoch, omitting several decades of theoretical and political struggles, among them Bolshevism and the October revolution? None of those who propose to renounce Bolshevism as an historically bankrupt tendency has indicated any other course. So the question is reduced to the simple advice to study *Capital*. We can hardly object. But the Bolsheviks, too, studied *Capital*, and not badly either. This did not however prevent the degeneration of the Soviet state and the staging of the Moscow trials. So what is to be done?

Is Bolshevism Responsible for Stalinism?

Is it true that Stalinism represents the legitimate product of Bolshevism, as all reactionaries maintain, as Stalin himself avows, as the Mensheviks, the anarchists, and certain left doctrinaires considering themselves Marxist believe? "We have always predicted this" they say, "Having started with the prohibition of other socialist parties, the repression of the anarchists, and the setting up of the Bolshevik dictatorship in the Soviets, the October Revolution could only end in the dictatorship of the bureaucracy. Stalin is the continuation and also the bankruptcy of Leninism."

The flaw in this reasoning begins in the tacit identification of Bolshevism, October Revolution and Soviet Union. The historical process of the struggle of hostile forces is replaced by the evolution of Bolshevism in a vacuum. Bolshevism, however, is only a political tendency closely fused with the working class but not identical with it. And aside from the working class there exist in the Soviet Union a hundred million peasants, diverse nationalities, and a heritage of oppression, misery and ignorance. The state built up by the Bolsheviks reflects not only the thought and will of Bolshevism but also the cultural level of the country, the social composition of the population, the pressure of a barbaric past and no less barbaric world imperialism. To represent the process of degeneration of the Soviet state as the evolution of pure Bolshevism is to ignore social reality in the name of only one of its elements, isolated by pure logic. One has only to call this elementary mistake by its true name to do away with every trace of it.

Bolshevism, in any case, never identified itself either with the October Revolution or with the Soviet state that issued from it. Bolshevism considered itself as one of the factors of history, its "conscious" factor — a very important but not decisive one. We never sinned on historical subjectivism. We saw the decisive factor — on the existing basis of productive forces — in the class struggle, not only on a national scale but on an international scale.

When the Bolsheviks made concessions to the peasant tendency, to private ownership, set up strict rules for membership of the party, purged the party of alien elements, prohibited other parties, introduced the NEP, granted enterprises as concessions, or concluded diplomatic agreements with imperialist governments, they were drawing partial conclusions from the basic fact that had been theoretically clear to them from the beginning; that the conquest of power, however important it may be in itself, by no means transforms the party into a sovereign ruler of the historical process. Having taken over the state, the party is able, certainly, to influence the development of society with a power inaccessible to it before; but in return it submits itself to a ten times greater influence from all other elements in society. It can, by the direct attack by hostile forces, be thrown out of power. Given a more drawn out tempo of development, it can degenerate internally while holding on to power. It is precisely this dialectic of the historical process that is not understood by those sectarian logicians who try to find in the decay of the Stalinist

190

bureaucracy a crushing argument against Bolshevism.

In essence these gentlemen say: the revolutionary party that contains in itself no guarantee against its own degeneration is bad. By such a criterion Bolshevism is naturally condemned: it has no talisman. But the criterion itself is wrong. Scientific thinking demands a concrete analysis: how and why did the party degenerate? No one but the Bolsheviks themselves have, up to the present time, given such an analysis. To do this they had no need to break with Bolshevism. On the contrary, they found in its arsenal all they needed for the explanation of its fate. They drew this conclusion: certainly Stalinism "grew out " of Bolshevism, not logically, however, but dialectically; not as a revolutionary affirmation but as a Thermidorian negation. It is by no means the same.

Bolshevism's Basic Prognosis

The Bolsheviks, however, did not have to wait for the Moscow trials to explain the reasons for the disintegration of the governing party of the USSR. Long ago they foresaw and spoke of the theoretical possibility of this development. Let us remember the prognosis of the Bolsheviks, not only on the eve of the October Revolution but years before. The specific alignment of forces in the national and international field can enable the proletariat to seize power first in a backward country such as Russia. But the same alignment of forces proves beforehand that without a more or less rapid victory of the proletariat in the advanced countries the workers' government in Russia will not survive. Left to itself the Soviet regime must either fall or degenerate. More exactly; it will first degenerate and then fall. I myself have written about this more than once, beginning in 1905. In my *History of the Russian Revolution* (cf. Appendix to the last volume: Socialism in One Country) are collected all the statements on the question made by the Bolshevik leaders from 1917 until 1923. They all amount to the following: without a revolution in the West, Bolshevism will be liquidated either by internal counter-revolution or by external intervention, or by a combination of both. Lenin stressed again and again that the bureaucratisation of the Soviet regime was not a technical question, but the potential beginning of the degeneration of the workers' state.

At the eleventh party congress in March, 1922, Lenin spoke of the support offered to Soviet Russia at the time of the NEP by certain bourgeois politicians, particularly the liberal professor Ustrialov. "I am for the support of the Soviet power in Russia" said Ustrialov, although he was a Cadet, a bourgeois, a supporter of intervention — "because it has taken the road that will lead it back to an ordinary bourgeois state". Lenin prefers the cynical voice of the enemy to "sugary communistic

191

nonsense". Soberly and harshly he warns the party of danger: "We must say frankly that the things Ustrialov speaks about are possible. History knows all sorts of metamorphoses. Relying on firmness of convictions, loyalty and other splendid moral qualities is anything but a serious attitude in politics. A few people may be endowed with splendid moral qualities, but historical issues are decided by vast masses, which, if the few don't suit them, may at times, treat them none too politely." In a word, the party is not the only factor of development and on a larger historical scale is not the decisive one.

"One nation conquers another" continued Lenin at the same congress, the last in which he participated ... "this is simple and intelligible to all. But what happens to the culture of these nations? Here things are not so simple. If the conquering nation is more cultured than the vanquished nation, the former imposes its culture on the latter, but if the opposite is the case, the vanquished nation imposes its culture on the conqueror. Has not something like this happened in the capital of the RSFSR? Have the 4700 Communists (nearly a whole army division, and all of them the very best) come under the influence of an alien culture?". This was said in 1922, and not for the first time. History is not made by a few people, even "the best"; and not only that: these "best" can degenerate in the spirit of an alien, that is, a bourgeois culture. Not only can the Soviet state abandon the way of socialism, but the Bolshevik party can, under unfavourable historic conditions, lose its Bolshevism.

From the clear understanding of this danger issued the Left Opposition, definitely formed in 1923. Recording day by day the symptoms of degeneration, it tried to oppose to the growing Thermidor the conscious will of the proletarian vanguard. However, this subjective factor proved to be insufficient. The "gigantic masses" which, according to Lenin, decide the outcome of the struggle, become tired of internal privations and of waiting too long for the world revolution. The mood of the masses declined. The bureaucracy won the upper hand. It cowed the revolutionary vanguard, trampled upon Marxism, prostituted the Bolshevik party. Stalinism conquered. In the form of the Left Opposition, Bolshevism broke with the Soviet bureaucracy and its Comintern. This was the real course of development.

To be sure, in a formal sense Stalinism did issue from Bolshevism. Even today the Moscow bureaucracy continues to call itself the Bolshevik party. It is simply using the old label of Bolshevism the better to fool the masses. So much the more pitiful are those theoreticians who take the shell for the kernel and appearance for reality. In the identification of Bolshevism and Stalinism they render the best possible service to the Thermidorians and precisely thereby play a clearly reactionary role.

In view of the elimination of all other parties from the political field the antagonistic interests and tendencies of the various strata of the population, to a greater or less degree, had to find their expression in the governing party, To the extent that the political centre of gravity has shifted from the proletarian vanguard to the bureaucracy, the party has changed its social structure as well as its ideology. Owing to the tempestuous course of development, it has suffered in the last 15 years a far more radical degeneration than did the social democracy in half a century. The present purge draws between Bolshevism and Stalinism not simply a bloody line but a whole river of blood. The annihilation of all the older generation of Bolsheviks, an important part of the middle generation which participated in the civil war, and that part of the youth that took up most seriously the Bolshevik traditions, shows not only a political but a thoroughly physical incompatibility between Bolshevism and Stalinism. How can this not be seen?

Stalinism and "State Socialism"

The anarchists, for their part, try to see in Stalinism the organic product, not only of Bolshevism and Marxism but of "state socialism" in general. They are willing to replace Bakunin's patriarchal "federation of free communes" by the modern federation of free Soviets. But, as formerly, they are against centralised state power. Indeed, one branch of "state" Marxism, social democracy, after coming to power became an open agent of capitalism. The other gave birth to a new privileged caste. It is obvious that the source of evil lies in the state. From a wide historical viewpoint, there is a grain of truth in this reasoning. The state as an apparatus of coercion is an undoubted source of political and moral infection. This also applies, as experience has shown, to the workers' state. Consequently it can be said that Stalinism is a product of a condition of society in which society was still unable to tear itself out of the strait-jacket of the state. But this position, contributing nothing to the elevation of Bolshevism and Marxism, characterises only the general level of mankind, and above all — the relation of forces between the proletariat and the bourgeoisie. Having agreed with the anarchists that the state, even the workers' state, is the offspring of class barbarism and that real human history will begin with the abolition of the state, we have still before us in full force the question: what ways and methods will lead, ultimately, to the abolition of the state? Recent experience bears witness that they are anyway not the methods of anarchism.

The leaders of the Spanish Federation of Labour (CNT), the only important anarchist organisation in the world, became, in the critical hour, bourgeois ministers. They explained their open betrayal of the theory of anarchism by the pressure of "exceptional circumstances". But did not the leaders of German social democracy produce, in their time, the same excuse? Naturally, civil war is not peaceful and ordinary but an "exceptional circumstance". Every serious revolutionary organisation, however, prepares precisely for "exceptional circumstances". The experience of Spain has shown once again that the state can be "denied" in booklets published in "normal circumstances" by permission of the bourgeois state, but the conditions of revolution leave no room for the denial of the state: they demand, on the contrary, the conquest of the state. We have not the slightest intention of blaming the anarchists for not having liquidated the state with the mere stroke of a pen. A revolutionary party, even having seized power (of which the anarchist leaders were incapable in spite of the heroism of the anarchist workers), is still by no means the sovereign ruler of society. But all the more severely do we blame the anarchist theory, which seemed to be wholly suitable for times of peace, but which had to be dropped rapidly as soon as the "exceptional circumstances" of the ... revolution had begun. In the old days there were certain generals — and probably are now — who considered that the most harmful thing for an army was war. Little better are those revolutionaries who complain that revolution destroys their doctrine.

Marxists are wholly in agreement with the anarchists in regard to the final goal: the liquidation of the state. Marxists are "state-ist" only to the extent that one cannot achieve the liquidation of the state simply by ignoring it. The experience of Stalinism does not refute the teaching of Marxism but confirms it by inversion. The revolutionary doctrine, which teaches the proletariat to orient itself correctly in situations and to profit actively by them, contains of course no automatic guarantee of victory. But victory is possible only through the application of this doctrine. Moreover, the victory must not be thought of as a single event. It must be considered in the perspective of an historical epoch. The workers' state — on a lower economic basis and surrounded by imperialism — was transformed into the gendarmerie of Stalinism. But genuine Bolshevism launched a life and death struggle against the gendarmerie. To maintain itself Stalinism is now forced to conduct a direct civil war against Bolshevism under the name of "Trotskyism", not only in the USSR but also in Spain. The old Bolshevik party is dead but Bolshevism is raising its head everywhere.

To deduce Stalinism from Bolshevism or from Marxism is the same as to deduce, in a larger sense, counter-revolution from revolution. Liberal-conservative and later reformist thinking has always been characterised by this cliche. Due to the class structure of society, revolutions have always produced counter-revolutions. Does not this indicate, asks the logician, that there is some inner flaw in the revolutionary method? However, neither the liberals nor reformists have succeeded, as yet, in inventing a more "economical" method. But if it is not easy to rationalise the living historic process, it is not at all difficult to give a rational interpretation of the alternation of its waves, and thus by pure logic to deduce Stalinism from "state socialism", fascism from Marxism, reaction from revolution, in a word, the antithesis from the thesis. In this domain as in many others anarchist thought is the prisoner of liberal rationalism. Real revolutionary thinking is not possible without dialectics.

The Political "Sins" of Bolshevism as the Source of Stalinism

The arguments of the rationalists assume at times, at least in their outer form, a more concrete character. They do not deduce Stalinism from Bolshevism as a whole but from its political sins. The Bolsheviks — according to Gorter, Pannekoek, certain German "Spartacists" and others — replaced the dictatorship of the proletariat with the dictatorship of the party; Stalin replaced the dictatorship of the party with the dictatorship of the bureaucracy, the Bolsheviks destroyed all parties except their own; Stalin strangled the Bolshevik party in the interests of a Bonapartist clique. The Bolsheviks compromised with the bourgeoisie; Stalin became its ally and support. The Bolsheviks recognised the necessity of participation in the old trade unions and in the bourgeois parliament; Stalin made friends with the trade union bureaucracy and bourgeois democracy. One can make such comparisons at will. For all their apparent effectiveness they are entirely empty.

The proletariat can take power only through its vanguard. In itself the necessity for state power arises from the insufficient cultural level of the masses and their heterogeneity. In the revolutionary vanguard, organised in a party, is crystallised the aspiration of the masses to obtain their freedom. Without the confidence of the class in the vanguard, without support of the vanguard by the class, there can be no talk of the conquest of power. In this sense the proletarian revolution and dictatorship are the work of the whole class, but only under the leadership of the vanguard. The Soviets are the only organised form of the tie between the vanguard and the class. A revolutionary content can be given this form only by the party. This is proved by the positive experience of the October Revolution and by the negative experience of other countries (Germany, Austria, finally, Spain). No one has either shown in practice or tried to explain articulately on paper how the proletariat can seize power without the political leadership of a party that knows what it wants. The fact that this party subordinates the Soviets politically to its leaders has, in itself, abolished the Soviet system no more than the domination of the conservative majority has abolished the British parliamentary system.

As far as the prohibition of other Soviet parties is concerned, it did not flow from any "theory" of Bolshevism but was a measure of defence of the dictatorship on a backward and devastated country, surrounded by enemies on all sides. For the Bolsheviks it was clear from the beginning that this measure, later completed by the prohibition of factions inside the governing party itself, signalised a tremendous danger. However, the root of the danger lay not in the doctrine or the tactics but in the material weakness of the dictatorship, in the difficulties of its internal and international situation. If the revolution had triumphed, even if only in Germany, the need of prohibiting the other Soviet parties would have immediately fallen away. It is absolutely indisputable that the domination of a single party served as the juridical point of departure for the Stalinist totalitarian regime. The reason for this development lies neither in Bolshevism nor in the prohibition of other parties as a temporary war measure, but in the number of defeats of the proletariat in Europe and Asia.

The same applies to the struggle with anarchism. In the heroic epoch of the revolution the Bolsheviks went hand in hand with genuinely revolutionary anarchists. Many of them were drawn into the ranks of the party. The author of these lines discussed with Lenin more then once the possibility of allotting the anarchists certain territories where, with the consent of the local population, they would carry out their stateless experiment. But civil war, blockade and hunger left no room for such plans. The Kronstadt insurrection? But the revolutionary government could naturally not "present" to the insurrectionary sailors the fortress which protected the capital only because the reactionary peasant-soldier rebellion was joined by a few doubtful anarchists. The concrete historical analysis of the events leaves not the slightest room for legends, built up on ignorance and sentimentality, concerning Kronstadt, Makhno and other episodes of the revolution.

There remains only the fact that the Bolsheviks from the beginning applied not only conviction but also compulsion, often to a most severe degree. It is also indisputable that later the bureaucracy which grew out of the revolution monopolised the system of compulsions in its own hands. Every stage of development, even such catastrophic stages as revolution and counter-revolution, flows from the preceding stage, is rooted in it and carries over some of its features. Liberals, including the Webbs, have always maintained that the Bolshevik dictatorship represented only a new edition of Tsarism. They close their eyes to such "details" as the abolition of the monarchy and the nobility, the handing over of the land to the peasants, the expropriation of capital, the introduction of the

196

planned economy, atheist education, and so on. In exactly the same way liberal- anarchist thought closes its eyes to the fact that the Bolshevik revolution, with all its repressions, meant an upheaval of social relations in the interests of the masses, whereas Stalin's Thermidorian upheaval accompanies the reconstruction of Soviet society in the interest of a privileged minority. It is clear that in the identification of Stalinism with Bolshevism there is not a trace of socialist criteria.

Questions of Theory

One of the most outstanding features of Bolshevism has been its severe, exacting, even quarrelsome attitude towards the question of doctrine. The 26 volumes of Lenin's works will remain forever a model of the highest theoretical conscientiousness. Without this fundamental quality Bolshevism would never have fulfilled its historic role. In this regard Stalinism, coarse, ignorant and thoroughly empirical, is its complete opposite.

The Opposition declared more than 10 years ago in its programme: "Since Lenin's death a whole set of new theories has been created, whose only purpose is to justify the Stalin group's sliding off the path of the international proletarian revolution." Only a few days ago an American writer, Liston M. Oak, who has participated in the Spanish revolution, wrote: "The Stalinists are in fact today the foremost revisionists of Marx and Lenin — Bernstein did not dare go half as far as Stalin in revising Marx." This is absolutely true. One must add only that Bernstein actually felt certain theoretical needs: he tried conscientiously to establish a correspondence between the reformist practices of social democracy and its programme. The Stalinist bureaucracy, however, not only had nothing in common with Marxism but is in general foreign to any doctrine or system whatsoever. Its "ideology" is thoroughly permeated with police subjectivism, its practice is the empiricism of crude violence. In keeping with its essential interests the caste of usurpers is hostile to any theory: it can give an account of its social role neither to itself nor to anyone else. Stalin revises Marx and Lenin not with the theoretician's pen but with the heel of the GPU.

Questions of Morals

Complaints of the "immorality" of Bolshevism come particularly from those boastful nonentities whose cheap masks were torn away by Bolshevism. In petit-bourgeois, intellectual, democratic, "socialist", literary, parliamentary and other circles, conventional values prevail, or a conventional language to cover their lack of values. This large and motley society for mutual protection — "live and let live" — cannot bear the touch of the Marxist lancet on its sensitive skin. The theoreticians, writers and moralists, hesitating between different camps, thought and continue to think that the Bolsheviks maliciously exaggerate differences, are incapable of "loyal" collaboration and by their "intrigues" disrupt the unity of the workers' movement. Moreover, the sensitive and touchy centrist has always thought that the Bolsheviks were "calumniating" him — simply because they carried through to the end for him his half-developed thoughts: he himself was never able to. But the fact remains that only that precious quality, an uncompromising attitude towards all quibbling and evasion, can educate a revolutionary party which will not be taken unawares by "exceptional circumstances".

The moral qualities of every party flow, in the last analysis, from the historical interests that it represents. The moral qualities of Bolshevism self-renunciation, disinterestedness, audacity and contempt for every kind of tinsel and falsehood — the highest qualities of human nature! — flow from revolutionary intransigence in the service of the oppressed. The Stalinist bureaucracy imitates also in this domain the words and gestures of Bolshevism. But when "intransigence" and "flexibility" are applied by a police apparatus in the service of a privileged minority they become a force of demoralisation and gangsterism. One can feel only contempt for these gentlemen who identify the revolutionary heroism of the Bolsheviks with the bureaucratic cynicism of the Thermidorians.

Even now, in spite of the dramatic events in the recent period, the average philistine prefers to believe that the struggle between Bolshevism ("Trotskyism") and Stalinism concerns a clash of personal ambitions, or, at best, a conflict between two "shades " of Bolshevism. The crudest expression of this opinion is given by Norman Thomas, leader of the American Socialist Party: "There is little reason to believe". he writes (*Socialist Review*, September 1937, p.6), "that if Trotsky had won (!) instead of Stalin, there would be an end of intrigue, plots, and a reign of fear in Russia". And this man considers himself ... a Marxist. One would have the same right to say: "There is little reason to believe that if instead of Pius XI, the Holy See were occupied by Norman I, the Catholic Church would have been transformed into a bulwark of socialism". Thomas fails to understand that it is not a question of antagonism between Stalin and Trotsky, but of an antagonism between the bureaucracy and the proletariat. To be sure, the governing stratum of the USSR is forced even now to adapt itself to the still not wholly liquidated heritage of revolution, while preparing at the same time through direct civil war (bloody "purge" — mass annihilation of the discontented) a change of the social regime. But in Spain the Stalinist clique is already acting openly as a bulwark of the bourgeois order against socialism. The struggle against the

Bonapartist bureaucracy is turning before our eyes into class struggle: two worlds, two programmes, two moralities. If Thomas thinks that the victory of the socialist proletariat over the infamous caste of oppressors would not politically and morally regenerate the Soviet regime, he proves only that for all his reservations, shufflings and pious sighs he is far nearer to the Stalinist bureaucracy than to the workers. Like other exposers of Bolshevik "immorality", Thomas has simply not grown to the level of revolutionary morality.

The Traditions of Bolshevism and the Fourth International

The "lefts" who tried to skip Bolshevism in their return to Marxism generally confined themselves to isolated panaceas: boycott of parliament, creation of "genuine" Soviets. All this could still seem extremely profound in the heat of the first days after the war. But now, in the light of most recent experience, such "infantile diseases" have no longer even the interest of a curiosity. The Dutchmen Gorter and Pannekoek, the German "Spartakists", the Italian Bordigists, showed their independence from Bolshevism only by artificially inflating one of its features and opposing it to the rest. But nothing has remained either in practice or in theory of these "left" tendencies: an indirect but important proof that Bolshevism is the only possible form of Marxism for this epoch.

The Bolshevik party has shown in action a combination of the highest revolutionary audacity and political realism. It established for the first time the correspondence between the vanguard and the class which alone is capable of securing victory. It has proved by experience that the alliance between the proletariat and the oppressed masses of the rural and urban petty bourgeoisie is possible only through the political overthrow of the traditional petit-bourgeois parties. The Bolshevik party has shown the entire world how to carry out armed insurrection and the seizure of power. Those who propose the abstraction of the Soviets from the party dictatorship should understand that only thanks to the party dictatorship were the Soviets able to lift themselves out of the mud of reformism and attain the state form of the proletariat. The Bolshevik party achieved in the civil war the correct combination of military art and Marxist politics. Even if the Stalinist bureaucracy should succeed in destroying the economic foundations of the new society, the experience of planned economy under the leadership of the Bolshevik party will have entered history for all time as one of the greatest teachings of mankind. This can be ignored only by sectarians who, offended by the bruises they have received, turn their backs on the process of history.

But this is not all. The Bolshevik party was able to carry on its magnificent "practical" work only because it illuminated all its steps with theory. Bolshevism did not create this theory: it was furnished by Marxism. But Marxism is a theory of movement, not of stagnation. Only events on such a tremendous historical scale could enrich the theory itself. Bolshevism brought an invaluable contribution to Marxism in its analysis of the imperialist epoch as an epoch of wars and revolutions; of bourgeois democracy in the era of decaying capitalism; of the correlation between the general strike and the insurrection; of the role of the party, Soviets and trade unions in the period of proletarian revolution; in its theory of the Soviet state, of the economy of transition, of fascism and Bonapartism in the epoch of capitalist decline; finally in its analysis of the degeneration of the Bolshevik party itself and of the Soviet state. Let any other tendency be named that has added anything essential to the conclusions and generalisations of Bolshevism. Theoretically and politically Vandervelde, De Brouckere, Hilferding, Otto Bauer, Leon Blum, Zyromski, not to mention Major Attlee and Norman Thomas, live on the tattered leftovers of the past. The degeneration of the Comintern is most crudely expressed by the fact that it has dropped to the theoretical level of the Second International. All the varieties of intermediary groups (Independent Labour Party of Great Britain, POUM and their like) adapt every week new haphazard fragments of Marx and Lenin to their current needs. Workers can learn nothing from these people.

Only the founders of the Fourth International, who have made their own the whole tradition of Marx and Lenin, take a serious attitude towards theory. Philistines may jeer that 20 years after the October victory the revolutionaries are again thrown back to modest propagandist preparation. The big capitalists are, in this question as in many others, far more penetrating than the petty bourgeois who imagine themselves "socialists" or "communists". It is no accident that the subject of the Fourth International does not leave the columns of the world press. The burning historical need for revolutionary leadership promises to the Fourth International an exceptionally rapid tempo of growth. The greatest guarantee of its further success lies in the fact that it has not arisen away from the great historical road, but has organically grown out of Bolshevism.

1937

Their morals and ours

Leon Trotsky

Moral Effluvia

During an epoch of triumphant reaction, Messrs. democrats, social-democrats, anarchists, and other representatives of the "left" camp begin to exude double their usual amount of moral effluvia, similar to persons who perspire doubly in fear. Paraphrasing the Ten Commandments or the Sermon on the Mount, these moralists address themselves not so much to triumphant reaction as to those revolutionists suffering under its persecution, who with their "excesses" and "amoral" principles "provoke" reaction and give it moral justification. Moreover they prescribe a simple but certain means of avoiding reaction: it is necessary only to strive and morally to regenerate oneself. Free samples of moral perfection for those desirous are furnished by all the interested editorial offices. The class basis of this false and pompous sermon is the intellectual petty bourgeoisie. The political basis — their impotence and confusion in the face of approaching reaction. Psychological basis — their effort at overcoming the feeling of their own inferiority through masquerading in the beard of a prophet.

A moralising Philistine's favourite method is the lumping of reaction's conduct with that of revolution. He achieves success in this device through recourse to formal analogies. To him czarism and Bolshevism are twins. Twins are likewise discovered in fascism and communism. An inventory is compiled of the common features in Catholicism — or more specifically, Jesuitism — and Bolshevism. Hitler and Mussolini, utilising from their side exactly the same method, disclose that liberalism, democracy, and Bolshevism represent merely different manifestations of one and the same evil. The conception that Stalinism and Trotskyism are "essentially" one and the same now enjoys the joint approval of liberals, democrats, devout Catholics, idealists, pragmatists, and anarchists. If the Stalinists are unable to adhere to this "People's Front", then it is only because they are accidentally occupied with the extermination of Trotskyists.

The fundamental feature of these approchements and similitudes lies in their completely ignoring the material foundation of the various currents, that is, their class nature and by that token their objective historical role. Instead they evaluate and classify different currents according to some external and secondary manifestation, most often according to their relation to one or another abstract principle which for the given classifier has a special professional value. Thus to the Roman pope Freemasons and Darwinists, Marxists and anarchists are twins because all of them sacrilegiously deny the immaculate conception. To Hitler, liberalism and Marxism are twins because they ignore "blood and honour". To a democrat, fascism and Bolshevism are twins because they do not bow before universal suffrage. And so forth.

Undoubtedly the currents grouped above have certain common features. But the gist of the matter lies in the fact that the evolution of mankind exhausts itself neither by universal suffrage, not by "blood and honour," nor by the dogma of the immaculate conception. The historical process signifies primarily the class struggle; moreover, different classes in the name of different aims may in certain instances utilise similar means. Essentially it cannot be otherwise. Armies in combat are always more or less symmetrical; were there nothing in common in their methods of struggle they could not inflict blows upon each other.

If an ignorant peasant or shopkeeper, understanding neither the origin nor the sense of the struggle between the proletariat and the bourgeoisie, discovers himself between the two fires, he will consider both belligerent camps with equal hatred. And who are all these democratic moralists? Ideologists of intermediary layers who have fallen, or are in fear of falling between the two fires. The chief traits of the prophets of this type are alienism to great historical movements, a hardened conservative mentality, smug narrowness, and a most primitive political cowardice. More than anything moralists wish that history should leave them in peace with their petty books, little magazines, subscribers, common sense, and moral copy books. But history does not leave them in peace. It cuffs them now from the left, now from the right. Clearly — revolution and reaction, Czarism and Bolshevism, communism and fascism, Stalinism and Trotskyism — are all twins. Whoever doubts this may feel the symmetrical skull bumps upon both the right and left sides of these very moralists.

Marxist Amoralism and Eternal Truths

The most popular and most imposing accusation directed against Bolshevik "amoralism" bases itself on the so-called Jesuitical maxim of Bolshevism: "The end justifies the means." From this it is not difficult to reach the further conclusion: since the Trotskyists, like all Bolsheviks (or Marxists) do not recognise the principles of morality, there is, consequently, no "principled" difference between Trotskyism and Stalinism Q.E.D.

One completely vulgar and cynical American monthly conducted a questionnaire on the moral philosophy of Bolshevism. The questionnaire, as is customary, was to have simultaneously served the ends of ethics and advertisement. The inimitable H.G. Wells, whose high fancy is surpassed only by his Homeric self-satisfaction, was not slow in solidarising himself with the reactionary snobs of *Common Sense*. Here everything fell into order. But even those participants who considered it necessary to defend Bolshevism did so, in the majority of cases, not without timid evasions (Eastman): the principles of Marxism are, of course, bad, but among the Bolsheviks there are, nevertheless, worthy people. Truly, such "friends" are more dangerous than enemies.

Should we care to take Messrs. Unmaskers seriously, then first of all we would ask them: what are your own moral principles? Here is a question which will scarcely receive an answer. Let us admit for the moment that neither personal nor social ends can justify the means. Then it is evidently necessary to seek criteria outside of historical society and those ends which arise in its development. But where? If not on earth, then in the heavens. In divine revelation popes long ago discovered faultless moral criteria. Petty secular popes speak about eternal moral truths without naming their original source. However, we are justified in concluding: since these truths are eternal, they should have existed not only before the appearance of half-monkey-half-man upon the earth but before the evolution of the solar system. Whence then did they arise? The theory of eternal morals can in nowise survive without god.

Moralists of the Anglo-Saxon type, in so far as they do not confine themselves to rationalist utilitarianism, the ethics of bourgeois bookkeeping, appear conscious or unconscious students of Viscount Shaftesbury, who at the beginning of the 18th century deduced moral judgments from a special "moral sense" supposedly once and for all given to man. Supra-class morality inevitably leads to the acknowledgment of a special substance, of a "moral sense", "conscience", some kind of absolute which is nothing more than the philosophic-cowardly pseudonym for god. Independent of "ends", that is, of society, morality, whether we deduce it from eternal truths or from the "nature of man", proves in the end to be a form of "natural theology". Heaven remains the only fortified position for military operations against dialectic materialism.

At the end of the last century in Russia there arose a whole school of "Marxists" (Struve, Berdyaev, Bulgakov, and others) who wished to supplement the teachings of Marx with a self-sufficient, that is, supra-class moral principle. These people began, of course, with Kant and the categorical imperative. But how did they end? Struve is now a retired minister of the Crimean baron Wrangel, and a faithful son of the church; Bulgakov is an orthodox priest; Berdyaev expounds the Apocalypse in sundry languages. These metamorphoses which seem so unexpected at first glance are not at all explained by the "Slavic soul" — Struve has a German soul — but by the sweep of the social struggle in Russia. The fundamental trend of this metamorphosis is essentially international.

Classical philosophic idealism, in so far as it aimed in its time to secularise morality, that is, to free it from religious sanction, represented a tremendous step forward (Hegel). But having torn from heaven, moral philosophy had to find earthly roots. To discover these roots was one of the tasks of materialism. After Shaftesbury came Darwin, after Hegel-Marx. To appeal now to eternal moral truths" signifies attempting to turn the wheels backward. Philosophic idealism is only a stage: from religion to materialism, or, contrariwise, from materialism to religion.

"The End Justifies the Means"

The Jesuit order, organised in the first half of the 16th century for combating Protestantism, never taught, let it be said, that any means, even though it be criminal from the point of view of the Catholic morals, was permissible if only it led to the "end,", that is, to the triumph of Catholicism. Such an internally contradictory and psychologically absurd doctrine was maliciously attributed to the Jesuits by their Protestant and partly Catholic opponents who were not shy in choosing the means for achieving their ends. Jesuit theologians who, like the theologians of other schools, were occupied with the question of personal responsibility, actually taught that the means in itself can be a matter of indifference but that the moral justification or judgment of the given means flows from the end. Thus shooting in itself is a matter of indifference; shooting a mad dog that threatens a child — a virtue; shooting with the aim of violation or murder — a crime. Outside of these commonplaces the theologians of this order made no promulgations.

In so far as their practical moral philosophy is concerned the Jesuits were not at all worse than other monks or Catholic priests, on the contrary, they were superior to them; in any case, more consistent, bolder, and perspicacious. The Jesuits represented a militant organisation, strictly centralised, aggressive, and dangerous not only to enemies but also to allies. In his psychology and method of action the Jesuit of the "heroic" period distinguished himself from an average priest as the warrior of a church from its shopkeeper. We have no reason to idealize either one or the other. But it is altogether unworthy to look upon a fanatic warrior with the eyes of an obtuse and slothful shopkeeper.

If we are to remain in the field of purely formal or psychological similitudes, then it can, if you like, be said that the Bolsheviks appear in relation to the democrats and social-democrats of all hues as did the Jesuits

— in relation to the peaceful ecclesiastical hierarchy. Compared to revolutionary Marxists, the social-democrats and centrists appear like morons, or a quack beside a physician: they do not think one problem through to the end, believe in the power of conjuration and cravenly avoid every difficulty, hoping for a miracle. Opportunists are peaceful shop-keepers in socialist ideas while Bolsheviks are its inveterate warriors. From this comes the hatred and slander against Bolsheviks from those who have an abundance of their historically conditioned faults but not one of their merits.

However, the juxtaposition of Bolshevism and Jesuitism still remains completely one-sided and superficial, rather of a literary than historical kind. In accordance with the character and interests of those classes upon which they based themselves, the Jesuits represented reaction, the Protestants — progress. The limitedness of this "progress" in its turn found direct expression in the morality of the Protestants. Thus the teachings of Christ "purified" by them did not at all hinder the city bourgeois, Luther, from calling for the execution of revolting peasants as "mad dogs". Dr. Martin evidently considered that the "end justifies the means" even before that maxim was attributed to the Jesuits. In turn the Jesuits, competing with Protestantism, adapted themselves ever more to the spirit of bourgeois society, and of the three vows: poverty, chastity, and obedience, preserved only the third, and at that in an extremely attenuated form. From the point of view of the Christian ideal, the morality of the Jesuits degenerated the more they ceased to be Jesuits. The warriors of the church became its bureaucrats and, like all bureaucrats, passable swindlers.

Jesuitism and Utilitarianism

This brief discussion is sufficient, perhaps, to show what ignorance and narrowness are necessary to consider seriously the contraposition of the "Jesuit" principle, "the end justifies the means", to another seemingly higher moral, in which each "means" carries its own moral tag like merchandise with fixed prices in a department store. It is remarkable that the common sense of the Anglo-Saxon Philistine has managed to wax indignant at the "Jesuit" principle and simultaneously to find inspiration in the utilitarian morality, so characteristic of British philosophy. Moreover, the criterion of Bentham-John Mill, "the greatest possible happiness for the greatest possible number", signifies that those means are moral which lead to the common welfare as the higher end. In its general philosophical formulations Anglo-Saxon utilitarianism thus fully coincides with the "Jesuit" principle, "the end justifies the means". Empiricism, we see, exists in the world only to free us from the necessity of making both ends meet.

Herbert Spencer, into whose empiricism Darwin inculcated the idea of "evolution", as a special vaccine, taught that in the moral sphere evolution proceeds from "sensations" to "ideas". Sensations conform to the criterion of immediate pleasure, while ideas permit one to be guided by the criterion of future, lasting and higher pleasure. Thus the moral criterion here too is "pleasure" and "happiness". But the content of this criterion acquires breadth and depth depending upon the level of "evolution". In this way Herbert Spencer too, through the methods of his own "evolutionary" utilitarianism, showed that the principle, "the end justifies the means", does not embrace anything immoral.

It is naive, however, to expect from this abstract "principle" an answer to the practical question: what may we, and what may we not do? Moreover, the principle, the end justifies the means, naturally raises the question: and what justifies the end? In practical life as in the historical movement the end and the means constantly change places. A machine under construction is an "end" of production only that upon entering the factory it may become the "means". Democracy in certain periods is the "end" of the class struggle only that later it may be transformed into its "means". Not embracing anything immoral, the so-called "Jesuit" principle fails, however, to resolve the moral problem.

The "evolutionary" utilitarianism of Spencer likewise abandons us half-way without an answer, since, following Darwin, it tries to dissolve the concrete historical morality in the biological needs or in the "social instincts" characteristic of a gregarious animal, and this at a time when the very understanding of morality arises only in an antagonistic milieu, that is, in a society torn by classes.

Bourgeois evolutionism halts impotently at the threshold of historical society because it does not wish to acknowledge the driving force in the evolution of social forms: the class struggle. Morality is one of the ideological functions in this struggle. The ruling class forces its ends upon society and habituates it into considering all those means which contradict its ends as immoral. That is the chief function of official morality. It pursues the idea of the "greatest possible happiness" not for the majority but for a small and ever diminishing minority. Such a regime could not have endured for even a week through force alone. It needs the cement of morality. The mixing of this cement constitutes the profession of the petty-bourgeois theoreticians, and moralists. They dabble in all colours of the rainbow but in the final instance remain apostles of slavery and submission.

"Moral Precepts Obligatory Upon All"

Whoever does not care to return to Moses, Christ or Mohammed; whoever is not satisfied with eclectic hodge-podges, must acknowledge that morality is a product of social development; that there is nothing invariable about it; that it serves social interests; that these interests are contradictory; that morality more than any other form of ideology has a class character.

But do not elementary moral precepts exist, worked out in the development of mankind as an integral element necessary for the life of every collective body? Undoubtedly such precepts exist but the extent of their action is extremely limited and unstable. Norms "obligatory upon all" become the less forceful the sharper the character assumed by the class struggle. The highest pitch of the class struggle is civil war which explodes into mid-air all moral ties between the hostile classes.

Under "normal" conditions a "normal" man observes the commandment: "Thou shalt not kill!" But if he murders under exceptional conditions for self-defence, the judge condones his action. If he falls victim to a murderer, the court will kill the murderer. The necessity of the court's action, as that of the self-defence, flows from antagonistic interests. In so far as the state is concerned, in peaceful times it limits itself to individual cases of legalised murder so that in time of war it may transform the "obligatory" commandment, "Thou shalt not kill!" into its opposite. The most "humane" governments, which in peaceful times "detest" war, proclaim during war that the highest duty of their armies is the extermination of the greatest possible number of people.

The so-called "generally recognised" moral precepts in essence preserve an algebraic, that is, an indeterminate character. They merely express the fact that man, in his individual conduct, is bound by certain common norms that flow from his being a member of society. The highest generalisation of these norms is the "categorical imperative" of Kant. But in spite of the fact that it occupies a high position upon the philosophic Olympus this imperative does not embody anything categoric because it embodies nothing concrete. It is a shell without content.

This vacuity in the norms obligatory upon all arises from the fact that in all decisive questions people feel their class membership considerably more profoundly and more directly than their membership in "society". The norms of "obligatory" morality are in reality charged with class, that is, antagonistic content. The moral norm becomes the more categoric the less it is "obligatory" upon all. The solidarity of workers, especially of strikers or barricade fighters, is incomparably more "categoric" than human solidarity in general.

The bourgeoisie, which far surpasses the proletariat in the completeness and irreconcilability of its class consciousness, is vitally interested in imposing its moral philosophy upon the exploited masses. It is exactly for this purpose that the concrete norms of the bourgeois catechism are concealed under moral abstractions patronised by religion, philosophy, or that hybrid which is called "common sense". The appeal to abstract norms is not a disinterested philosophic mistake but a necessary element in the mechanics of class deception. The exposure of this deceit which retains the tradition of thousands of years is the first duty of a proletarian revolutionist.

The Crisis in Democratic Morality

In order to guarantee the triumph of their interests in big questions, the ruling classes are constrained to make concessions on secondary questions, naturally only so long as these concessions are reconciled in the bookkeeping. During the epoch of capitalistic upsurge especially in the last few decades before the World War these concessions, at least in relation to the top layers of the proletariat, were of a completely genuine nature. Industry at that time expanded almost uninterruptedly. The prosperity of the civilised nations, partially, too, that of the toiling masses, increased. Democracy appeared solid. Workers' organisations grew. At the same time reformist tendencies deepened. The relations between the classes softened, at least outwardly. Thus certain elementary moral precepts in social relations were established along with the norms of democracy and the habits of class collaboration. The impression was created of an ever more free, more just, and more humane society. The rising line of progress seemed infinite to "common sense."

Instead, however, war broke out with a train of convulsions, crises, catastrophes, epidemics, and bestiality. The economic life of mankind landed in an impasse. The class antagonisms became sharp and naked. The safety valves of democracy began to explode one after the other. The elementary moral precepts seemed even more fragile than the democratic institutions and reformist illusions. Mendacity, slander, bribery, venality, coercion, murder grew to unprecedented dimensions. To a stunned simpleton all these vexations seem a temporary result of war. Actually they are manifestations of imperialist decline. The decay of capitalism denotes the decay of contemporary society with its right and its morals.

The "synthesis" of imperialist turpitude is fascism directly begotten of the bankruptcy of bourgeois democracy before the problems of the imperialist epoch. Remnants of democracy continue still to exist only in the rich capitalist aristocracies: for each "democrat" in England, France, Holland, Belgium there is a certain number of colonial slaves; "60 Families" dominate the democracy of the United States, and so forth. Moreover, shoots of fascism grow rapidly in all democracies. Stalinism in its turn is the product of imperialist pressure upon a backward and isolated workers' state, a symmetrical complement in its own genre to fascism.

While idealistic Philistines — anarchists of course occupy first place tirelessly unmask Marxist "amoralism" in their press, the American trusts, according to John L. Lewis (CIO), are spending not less than $80,000,000 a year on the practical struggle against revolutionary "demoralisation", that is, espionage, bribery of workers, frame-ups, and dark-alley murders. The categorical imperative sometimes chooses circuitous ways for its triumph!

Let us note in justice that the most sincere and at the same time the most limited petty bourgeois moralists still live even today in the idealised memories of yesterday and hope for its return. They do not understand that morality is a function of the class struggle; that democratic morality corresponds to the epoch of liberal and progressive capitalism; that the sharpening of the class struggle in passing through its latest phase definitively and irrevocably destroyed this morality; that in its place came the morality of fascism on one side, on the other the morality of proletarian revolution.

"Common Sense"

Democracy and "generally recognised" morality are not the only victims of imperialism. The third suffering martyr is "universal" common sense. This lowest form of the intellect is not only necessary under all conditions but under certain conditions is also adequate. Common sense's basic capital consists of the elementary conclusions of universal experience: not to put one's fingers in fire, whenever possible to proceed along a straight line, not to tease vicious dogs ... and so forth and so on. Under a stable social milieu common sense is adequate for bargaining, healing, writing articles, leading trade unions, voting in parliament, marrying and reproducing the race. But when that same common sense attempts to go beyond its valid limits into the arena of more complex generalisations, it is exposed as just a clot of prejudices of a definite class and a definite epoch. No more than a simple capitalist crisis brings common sense to an impasse; and before such catastrophes as revolution, counter-revolution and war, common sense proves a perfect fool. In order to realise the catastrophic transgressions against the "normal" course of events higher qualities of intellect are necessary, philosophically expressed as yet only by dialectic materialism.

Max Eastman, who successfully attempts to endow "common sense" with a most attractive literary style, has fashioned out of the struggle against dialectics nothing less than a profession for himself. Eastman seriously takes the conservative banalities of common sense wedded to good style as "the science of revolution". Supporting the reactionary snobs of *Common Sense*, he expounds to mankind with inimitable assurance that if Trotsky had been guided not by Marxist doctrine but by common sense then he would not have lost power. That inner dialectic which until now has appeared in the inevitable succession of determined stages in all revolutions does not exist for Eastman. Reaction's displacing revolution, to him, is determined through insufficient respect for common sense. Eastman does not understand that it is Stalin who in a historical sense fell victim to common sense, that is, its inadequacy, since that power which he possesses serves ends hostile to Bolshevism. Marxist doctrine, on the other hand, permitted us to tear away in time from the Thermidorian bureaucracy and to continue to serve the ends of international socialism.

Every science, and in that sense also the "science of revolution" is controlled by experience. Since Eastman well knows how to maintain revolutionary power under the condition of world counter revolution, then he also knows, we may hope, how to conquer power. It would be very desirable that he finally disclose his secrets. Best of all that it be done in the form of a draft program for a revolutionary party under the title: How to Conquer and Hold Power. We fear, however, that it is precisely common sense which will urge Eastman to refrain from such a risky undertaking. And this time common sense will be right.

Marxist doctrine, which Eastman, alas, never understood, permitted us to foresee the inevitability under certain historic conditions of the Soviet Thermidor with all its coil of crimes. That same doctrine long ago predicted the inevitability of the downfall of bourgeois democracy and its morality. However the doctrinaires of "common sense" were caught unaware by fascism and Stalinism. Common sense operates on invariable magnitudes in a world where only change is invariable. Dialectics, on the contrary, takes all phenomena, institutions, and norms in their rise, development and decay. The dialectical consideration of morals as a subservient and transient product of the class struggle seems to common sense an "amoralism". But there is nothing more flat, stale, self-satisfied and cynical than the moral rules of common sense!

Moralists and the G.P.U.

The Moscow trials provided the occasion for a crusade against Bolshevik "amoralism." However, the crusade was not opened at once. The truth is that in their majority the moralists, directly or indirectly, were friends of the Kremlin. As such they long attempted to hide their amaze-

210

ment and even feigned that nothing unusual had occurred.

But the Moscow trials were not at all an accident. Servile obedience, hypocrisy, the official cult of mendacity, bribery, and other forms of corruption had already begun to blossom ostentatiously in Moscow by 1924-1925. The future judicial frame-ups were being prepared openly before the eyes of the whole world. There was no lack of warning. The "friends", however, did not wish to notice anything. No wonder: the majority of these gentlemen, in their time irreconcilably hostile to the October Revolution, became friends of the Soviet Union merely at the rate of its Thermidorian degeneration — the petty bourgeois democrats of the West recognised in the petty bourgeois bureaucracy of the East a kindred soul.

Did these people really believe the Moscow accusations? Only the most obtuse. The others did not wish to alarm themselves by verification. Is it reasonable to infringe upon the flattering, comfortable, and often well-paying friendship with the Soviet embassies? Moreover they did not forget this indiscreet truth can injure the prestige of the U.S.S.R. These people screened the crimes by utilitarian considerations, that is, frankly applied the principle, "the end justifies the means."

The King's Counsellor, Pritt, who succeeded with timeliness in peering under the chiton of the Stalinist Themis and there discovered everything in order, took upon himself the shameless initiative. Romain Rolland, whose moral authority is highly evaluated by the Soviet publishing house bookkeepers, hastened to proclaim one of his manifestos where melancholy lyricism unites with senile cynicism. The French League for the Rights of Man, which thundered about the "amoralism of Lenin and Trotsky" in 1917 when they broke the military alliance with France, hastened to screen Stalin's crimes in 1936 in the interests of the Franco-Soviet pact. A patriotic end justifies, as is known, any means. *The Nation* and *The New Republic* closed their eyes to Yagoda's exploits since their "friendship" with the U.S.S.R. guaranteed their own authority. Yet only a year ago these gentlemen did not at all declare Stalinism and Trotskyism to be one and the same. They openly stood for Stalin, for his realism, for his justice and for his Yagoda. They clung to this position as long as they could.

Until the moment of the execution of Tukhachevsky, Yakir, and the others, the big bourgeoisie of the democratic countries, not without pleasure, though blanketed with fastidiousness, watched the execution of the revolutionists in the U.S.S.R. In this sense *The Nation* and *The New Republic,* not to speak of Duranty, Louis Fischer, and their kindred prostitutes of the pen, fully responded to the interests of "democratic" imperialism. The execution of the generals alarmed the bourgeoisie, compelling them to understand that the advanced disintegration of the Stalinist apparatus lightened the tasks of Hitler, Mussolini and the Mikado. The *New York Times* cautiously but insistently began to correct its own Duranty. The Paris *Le Temps* opened its columns slightly to shedding light upon the actual situation in the U.S.S.R. As for the petty bourgeois moralists and sycophants, they were never anything but servile echoes of the capitalist class. Moreover, after the International Commission of Inquiry, headed by John Dewey, brought out its verdict it became clear to every person who thought even a trifle that further open defence of the GPU signified peril of political and moral death. Only at this moment did the "friends" decide to bring the eternal moral truths into god's world, that is, to fall back to the second line trench.

Frightened Stalinists and semi-Stalinists occupy not the last place among moralists. Eugene Lyons during several years cohabited nicely with the Thermidorian clique, considering himself almost a Bolshevik. Withdrawing from the Kremlin — for a reason that is to us a matter of indifference — he rose, of course, immediately into the clouds of idealism. Liston Oak until recently enjoyed such confidence from the Comintern that it entrusted him with conducting the English propaganda for republican Spain. This did not, naturally, hinder him, once he had relinquished his post, from likewise relinquishing the Marxist alphabet. Expatriate Walter Krivitsky, having broken with the GPU, immediately joined the bourgeois democracy. Evidently this too is the metamorphosis of the very aged Charles Rappoport. Having tossed Stalinism overboard, people of such ilk — they are many — cannot help seeking indemnification in the postulates of abstract morality for the disillusionment and abasement of ideals they have experienced. Ask them: "Why have you switched from the Comintern or GPU ranks to the camp of the bourgeoisie?" They have a ready answer: "Trotskyism is no better than Stalinism."

The Disposition of Political Chessmen

"Trotskyism is revolutionary romanticism; Stalinism — practical politics." Of this banal contraposition with which the average Philistine until yesterday justified his friendship with Thermidor against the revolution, there remains not a trace today. Trotskyism and Stalinism are in general no longer counterposed but identified. They are identified, however, only in form not in essence. Having recoiled to the meridian of the "categorical imperative", the democrats actually continue to defend the G.P.U. except with greater camouflage and perfidy. He who slanders the victim aids the executioner. In this case, as in others, morality serves politics.

The democratic Philistine and Stalinist bureaucrat are, if not twins, brothers in spirit. In any case they belong politically to the same camp. The present governmental system of France and, if we add the anarchists, of republican Spain is based on the collaboration of Stalinists, social-democrats, and liberals. If the British Independent labour Party appears roughed up it is because for a number of years it has not withdrawn from the embrace of the Comintern. The French Socialist Party expelled the Trotskyists from their ranks exactly when it prepared to fuse with the Stalinists. If the fusion did not materialise, it was not because of principled divergences — what remains of them ? — but only because of the fear of the social-democratic careerists over their posts. Having returned from Spain, Norman Thomas declared that "objectively" the Trotskyists help Franco, and with this subjective absurdity he gave "objective" service to the GPU executioners. This righteous man expelled the American "Trotskyists" from his party precisely as the GPU shot down their co-thinkers in the U.S.S.R. and in Spain. In many democratic countries, the Stalinists in spite of their "amoralism" have penetrated into the government apparatus not without success. In the trade unions they cohabit nicely with bureaucrats of other hues. True, the Stalinists have an extremely lightminded attitude toward the criminal code and in that way frighten away their "democratic" friends in peaceful times; but in exceptional circumstances, as indicated by the example of Spain, they more surely become the leaders of the petty bourgeoisie against the proletariat.

The Second and Amsterdam Internationals naturally did not take upon themselves the responsibility for the frame-ups; this work they left to the Comintern. They themselves kept quiet. Privately they explained that from a "moral" point of view they were against Stalin, but from a political point of view, for him. Only when the People's Front in France cracked irreparably and forced the socialists to think about tomorrow did Leon Blum find at the bottom of his inkwell the necessary formulas for moral abhorrence.

If Otto Bauer mildly condemned Vyshinsky's justice, it was only in order to support Stalin's politics with greater "impartiality". The fate of socialism, according to Bauer's recent declaration, is tied with the fate of the Soviet Union. "And the fate of the Soviet Union", he continues, "is the fate of Stalinism so long as [!] the inner development of the Soviet Union itself does not overcome the Stalinist phase of development." All of Bauer is contained in this remarkable sentence, all of Austro-Marxism, the whole mendacity and rot of the social-democracy! "So long as" the Stalinist bureaucracy is sufficiently strong to murder the progressive representatives of the "inner development", until then Bauer sticks with

Stalin. When in spite of Bauer the revolutionary forces overthrow Stalin, then Bauer will generously recognise the "inner development" — with not more than ten years delay.

Behind the old Internationals, the London Bureau of the centrists trails along, happily combining in itself the characteristics of a kindergarten, a school for mentally arrested adolescents, and a home for invalids. The secretary of the Bureau, Fenner Brockway, began with the declaration that an inquiry into the Moscow trials could "harm the U.S.S.R." and proposed instead an investigation into ... the political activity of Trotsky through an "impartial" Commission of five irreconcilable enemies of Trotsky. Brandler and Lovestone publicly solidarised with Yagoda; they retreated only from Yezhov. Jacob Walcher, upon an obviously false pretext, refused to give testimony which was unfavourable to Stalin before the International Commission headed by John Dewey. The putrid morals of these people is only a product of their putrid politics.

But perhaps the most lamentable role is that played by the anarchists. If Stalinism and Trotskyism are one and the same, as they affirm in every sentence, then why do the Spanish anarchists assist the Stalinists in revenging themselves upon the Trotskyists and at the same time upon the revolutionary anarchists? The more frank anarchist theoreticians respond: this is payment for armaments. In other words: the end justifies the means. But what is their end? Anarchism? Socialism? No, merely the salvaging of this very same bourgeois democracy which prepared fascism's success. To base ends correspond base means.

That is the real disposition of the figures on the world political board!

Stalinism — A Product of the Old Society

Russia took the greatest leap in history, a leap in which the most progressive forces of the country found their expression. Now in the current reaction, the sweep of which is proportionate to the sweep of the revolution, backwardness is taking its revenge. Stalinism embodies this reaction. The barbarism of old Russian history upon new social bases seems yet more disgusting since it is constrained to conceal itself in hypocrisy unprecedented in history.

The liberals and the social-democrats of the West, who were constrained by the Russian Revolution into doubt about their rotted ideas, now experienced a fresh influx of courage. The moral gangrene of the Soviet bureaucracy seemed to them the rehabilitation of liberalism. Stereotyped copybooks are drawn out into the light: "every dictatorship contains the seeds of its own degeneration"; "only democracy guarantees the development of personality"; and so forth. The contrasting of democracy and dictatorship, including in the given case a condemnation of socialism in favour of the bourgeois regime, stuns one from the point of view of theory by its illiterateness and unscrupulousness. The Stalinist pollution, a historical reality, is counterpoised to democracy — a suprahistorical abstraction. But democracy also possesses a history in which there is no lack of pollution. In order to characterise Soviet bureaucracy we have borrowed the names of "Thermidor" and "Bonapartism" from the history of bourgeois democracy because — let this be known to the retarded liberal doctrinaires — democracy came into the world not at all through the democratic road. Only a vulgar mentality can satisfy itself by chewing on the theme that Bonapartism was the "natural offspring" of Jacobinism, the historical punishment for infringing upon democracy, and so on. Without the Jacobin retribution upon feudalism, bourgeois democracy would have been absolutely unthinkable. Contrasting to the concrete historical stages of Jacobinism, Thermidor, Bonapartism, the idealised abstraction of "democracy", is as vicious as contrasting the pains of childbirth to a living infant.

Stalinism in turn is not an abstraction of "dictatorship", but an immense bureaucratic reaction against the proletarian dictatorship in a backward and isolated country. The October Revolution abolished privileges, waged war against social inequality, replaced the bureaucracy with self-government of the toilers, abolished secret diplomacy, strove to render all social relationship completely transparent. Stalinism reestablished the most offensive forms of privileges, imbued inequality with a provocative character, strangled mass self-activity under police absolutism, transformed administration into a monopoly of the Kremlin oligarchy and regenerated the fetishism of power in forms that absolute monarchy dared not dream of.

Social reaction in all forms is constrained to mask its real aims. The sharper the transition from revolution to reaction; the more the reaction is dependent upon the traditions of revolution, that is, the greater its fear of the masses — the more is it forced to resort to mendacity and frameup in the struggle against the representatives of the revolution. Stalinist frame-ups are not a fruit of Bolshevik "amoralism"; no, like all important events in history, they are a product of the concrete social struggle, and the most perfidious and severest of all at that: the struggle of a new aristocracy against the masses that raised it to power.

Verily boundless intellectual and moral obtuseness is required to identify the reactionary police morality of Stalinism with the revolutionary morality of the Bolsheviks. Lenin's party has long ceased to exist — it was shattered between inner difficulties and world imperialism. In its place rose the Stalinist bureaucracy, transmissive mechanism of imperi-

alism. The bureaucracy substituted class collaboration for the class struggle on the world arena, social-patriotism for internationalism. In order
to adapt the ruling party to the tasks of reaction, the bureaucracy "renewed" its composition through executing revolutionists and recruiting
careerists.

Every reaction regenerates, nourishes and strengthens those elements
of the historic past which the revolution struck but which it could not
vanquish. The methods of Stalinism bring to the highest tension, to a cul-
mination and at the same time to an absurdity, all those methods of untruth, brutality and baseness which constitute the mechanics of control
in every class society including also that of democracy. Stalinism is a single clot of all monstrosities of the historical State, its most malicious caricature and disgusting grimace. When the representatives of old society
puritanically counterpoise a sterilised democratic abstraction to the gangrene of Stalinism, we can with full justice recommend to them, as to all
of old society, that they fall enamored of themselves in the warped mirror
of Soviet Thermidor. True, the GPU far surpasses all other regimes in the
nakedness of its crimes. But this flows from the immense amplitude of
events shaking Russia under the influence of world imperialist demoralisation.

Among the liberals and radicals there are not a few individuals who
have assimilated the methods of the materialist interpretation of events
and who consider themselves Marxists. This does not hinder them, however, from remaining bourgeois journalists, professors or politicians. A
Bolshevik is inconceivable, of course, without the materialist method, in
the sphere of morality too. But this method serves him not solely for the
interpretation of events but rather for the creation of a revolutionary
party of the proletariat. It is impossible to accomplish this task without
complete independence from the bourgeoisie and their morality. Yet
bourgeois public opinion actually now reigns in full sway over the official workers' movement from William Green in the United States, Leon
Blum and Maurice Thorez in France, to Garcia Oliver in Spain. In this
fact the reactionary character of the present period reaches its sharpest
expression.

A revolutionary Marxist cannot begin to approach his historical mission without having broken morally from bourgeois public opinion and
its agencies in the proletariat. For this, moral courage of a different calibre
is required than that of opening wide one's mouth at meetings and
yelling, "Down with Hitler!" "Down with Franco!" It is precisely this
resolute, completely thought-out, inflexible rupture of the Bolsheviks
from conservative moral philosophy, not only of the big but of the petty
bourgeoisie, which mortally terrorises democratic phrase-mongers,

216

drawing room prophets and lobbying heroes. From this is derived their complaints about the "amoralism" of the Bolsheviks.

Their identification of bourgeois morals with morals "in general" can best of all, perhaps, be verified at the extreme left wing of the petty bourgeoisie, precisely in the centrist parties of the so-called London Bureau. Since this organisation "recognises" the program of proletarian revolution, our disagreements with it seem, at first glance, secondary. Actually their "recognition" is valueless because it does not bind them to anything. They "recognise" the proletarian revolution as the Kantians recognised the categorical imperative, that is, as a holy principle but not applicable to daily life. In the sphere of practical politics they unite with the worst enemies of the revolution (reformists and Stalinists) for the struggle against us. All their thinking is permeated with duplicity and falsehood. If the centrists, according to a general rule, do not raise themselves to imposing crimes it is only because they forever remain in the byways of politics: they are, so to speak, petty pick-pockets of history. For this reason they consider themselves called upon to regenerate the workers' movement with a new morality.

At the extreme left wing of this "left" fraternity stands a small and politically completely insignificant grouping of German emigrés who publish the paper *Neuer Weg* (The New Road). Let us bend down lower and listen to these "revolutionary" indicters of Bolshevik amoralism. In a tone of ambiguous pseudo-praise the *Neuer Weg* proclaims that the Bolsheviks are distinguished advantageously from other parties by their absence of hypocrisy — they openly declare what others quietly apply in fact, that is, the principle: "the end justifies the means". But according to the convictions of *Neuer Weg* such a "bourgeois" precept is incompatible with a "healthy socialist movement". "Lying and worse are not permissible means of struggle, as Lenin still considered." The word "still" evidently signifies that Lenin did not succeed in overcoming his delusions only because he failed to live until the discovery of The New Road.

In the formula, "lying and worse", "worse" evidently signifies violence, murder, and so on, since under equal conditions violence is worse than lying; and murder — the most extreme form of violence. We thus come to the conclusion that lying, violence, murder are incompatible with a "healthy socialist movement". What, however, is our relation to revolution? Civil war is the most severe of all forms of war. It is unthinkable not only without violence against tertiary figures but, under contemporary technique, without murdering old men, old women and children. Must one be reminded of Spain? The only possible answer of the "friends" of republican Spain sounds like this: civil war is better than fascist slavery. But this completely correct answer merely signifies that

217

the end (democracy or socialism) justifies, under certain conditions, such means as violence and murder. Not to speak about lies! Without lies war would be as unimaginable as a machine without oil. In order to safeguard even the session of the Cortes (February 1, 1938) from Fascist bombs the Barcelona government several times deliberately deceived journalists and their own population. Could it have acted in any other way? Whoever accepts the end: victory over Franco, must accept the means: civil war with its wake of horrors and crimes.

Nevertheless, lying and violence "in themselves" warrant condemnation? Of course, even as does the class society which generates them. A society without social contradictions will naturally be a society without lies and violence. However there is no way of building a bridge to that society save by revolutionary, that is, violent means. The revolution itself is a product of class society and of necessity bears its traits. From the point of view of "eternal truths" revolution is of course "anti-moral". But this merely means that idealist morality is counter-revolutionary, that is, in the service of the exploiters.

"Civil war", will perhaps respond the philosopher caught unawares, "is however a sad exception. But in peaceful times a healthy socialist movement should manage without violence and lying." Such an answer however represents nothing less than a pathetic evasion. There is no impervious demarcation between "peaceful" class struggle and revolution. Every strike embodies in an unexpanded form all the elements of civil war. Each side strives to impress the opponent with an exaggerated representation of its resoluteness to struggle and its material resources. Through their press, agents, and spies the capitalists labour to frighten and demoralise the strikers. From their side, the workers' pickets, where persuasion does not avail, are compelled to resort to force. Thus "lie and worse" are an inseparable part of the class struggle even in its most elementary form. It remains to be added that the very conception of truth and lie was born of social contradictions.

Revolution and the Institution of Hostages

Stalin arrests and shoots the children of his opponents after these opponents have been themselves executed under false accusations. With the help of the institution of family hostages Stalin compels those Soviet diplomats to return from abroad who permitted themselves an expression of doubt upon the infallibility of Yagoda or Yezhov. The moralists of *Neuer Weg* consider it necessary and timely to remind us on this occasion of the fact that Trotsky in 1919 "also" introduced a law upon hostages. But here it becomes necessary to quote literally: "The detention of innocent relatives by Stalin is disgusting barbarism. But it remains a barbarism as well when it was dictated by Trotsky (1919)." Here is the idealistic moralist in all his beauty! His criteria are as false as the norms of bourgeois democracy — in both cases parity is supposed where in actuality there is not even a trace of it.

We will not insist here upon the fact that the Decree of 1919 led scarcely to even one execution of relatives of those commanders whose perfidy not only caused the loss of innumerable human lives but threatened the revolution itself with direct annihilation. The question in the end does not concern that. If the revolution had displayed less superfluous generosity from the very beginning, hundreds of thousands of lives would have been saved. Thus or otherwise I carry full responsibility for the Decree of 1919. It was a necessary measure in the struggle against the oppressors. Only in the historical content of the struggle lies the justification of the decree as in general the justification of the whole civil war which, too, can be called, not without foundation, "disgusting barbarism".

We leave to some Emil Ludwig or his ilk the drawing of Abraham Lincoln's portrait with rosy little wings. Lincoln's significance lies in his not hesitating before the most severe means once they were found to be necessary in achieving a great historic aim posed by the development of a young nation. The question lies not even in which of the warring camps caused or itself suffered the greatest number of victims. History has different yardsticks for the cruelty of the Northerners and the cruelty of the Southerners in the Civil War. A slave-owner who through cunning and violence shackles a slave in chains, and a slave who through cunning or violence breaks the chains — let not the contemptible eunuchs tell us that they are equals before a court of morality!

After the Paris Commune had been drowned in blood and the reactionary knaves of the whole world dragged its banner in the filth of vilification and slander, there were not a few democratic Philistines who, adapting themselves to reaction, slandered the Communards for shooting 64 hostages headed by the Paris archbishop. Marx did not hesitate a moment in defending this bloody act of the Commune. In a circular issued by the General Council of the First International, in which seethes the fiery eruption of lava, Marx first reminds us of the bourgeoisie adopting the institution of hostages in the struggle against both colonial peoples and their own toiling masses and afterwards refers to the systematic execution of the Commune captives by the frenzied reactionaries, continuing: "...the Commune, to protect their [the captives'] lives, was obliged to resort to the Prussian practice of securing hostages. The lives of the hostages had been forfeited over and over again by the continued shooting of prisoners on the part of the Versaillais. How could they be spared any longer after the carnage with which MacMahon's Praetorians celebrated their entry into Paris? Was even the last check upon the unscrupulous ferocity of bourgeois governments — the taking of hostages — to be made a mere sham of?" Thus Marx defended the execution of hostages although behind his back in the General Council sat not a few Fenner Brockways, Norman Thomases and other Otto Bauers. But so fresh was the indignation of the world proletariat against the ferocity of the Versaillais that the reactionary moralistic bunglers preferred to keep silent in expectation of times more favourable to them which, alas, were not slow in appearing. Only after the definite triumph of reaction did the petty-bourgeois moralists, together with the trade union bureaucrats and the anarchist phrase-mongers, destroy the First International.

When the October Revolution was defending itself against the united forces of imperialism on a 5,000 mile front, the workers of the whole world followed the course of the struggle with such ardent sympathy that in their forums it was extremely risky to indict the "disgusting barbarism" of the institution of hostages. Complete degeneration of the Soviet State and the triumph of reaction in a number of countries was necessary before the moralists crawled out of their crevices... to aid Stalin. If it is true that the reparations safeguarding the privileges of the new aristocracy have the same moral value as the revolutionary measures of the liberating struggle, then Stalin is completely justified, if — if the proletarian revolution is not completely condemned.

Seeking examples of immorality in the events of the Russian Civil War, Messrs. Moralists find themselves at the same time constrained to close their eyes to the fact that the Spanish revolution also produced an institution of hostages, at least during that period when it was a genuine revolution of the masses. If the indicters dare not attack the Spanish workers for their "disgusting barbarism", it is only because the ground of the Pyrennean peninsula is still too hot for them. It is considerably more convenient to return to 1919. This is already history, the old men have forgotten and the young ones have not yet learned. For the same reason Pharisees of various hues return to Kronstadt and Makhno with such obstinacy — here exists a free outlet for moral effluvia!

"Morality of the Kaffirs"

It is impossible not to agree with the moralists that history chooses grievous pathways. But what type of conclusion for practical activity is to be drawn from this? Leo Tolstoy recommended that we ignore the social conventions and perfect ourselves. Mahatma Gandhi advises that we drink goat's milk. Alas, the "revolutionary" moralists of *Neuer Weg* did not drift far from these recipes. "We should free ourselves," they preach, "from those morals of the Kaffirs to whom only what the enemy does is wrong." Excellent advice! "We should free ourselves". Tolstoy recommended in addition that we free ourselves from the sins of the flesh. However, statistics fail to confirm the success of his recommendation. Our centrist mannequins have succeeded in elevating themselves to supra-class morality in a class society. But almost 2,000 years have passed since it was stated: "Love your enemies", "Offer also the other cheek ..." However, even the holy Roman father so far has not "freed himself" from hatred against his enemies. Truly, Satan, the enemy of mankind, is powerful!

To apply different criteria to the actions of the exploiters and the exploited signifies, according to these pitiful mannequins, standing on the level of the "morals of the Kaffirs". First of all such a contemptuous reference to the Kaffirs is hardly proper from the pen of "socialists". Are the morals of the Kaffirs really so bad? Here is what the Encyclopedia Britannica says upon the subject:

"In their social and political relations they display great tact and intelligence; they are remarkably brave, warlike, and hospitable, and were honest and truthful until through contact with the whites they became suspicious, revengeful and thievish, besides acquiring most European vices." It is impossible not to arrive at the conclusion that white missionaries, preachers of eternal morals, participated in the corruption of the Kaffirs.

If we should tell the toiler-Kaffir how the workers arose in a part of our planet and caught their exploiters unawares, he would be very pleased. On the other hand, he would be chagrined to discover that the oppressors had succeeded in deceiving the oppressed. A Kaffir who has not been demoralised by missionaries to the marrow of his bones will never apply one and the same abstract moral norms to the oppressors and the oppressed. Yet he will easily comprehend an explanation that it is the function of these abstract norms to prevent the oppressed from arising against their oppressors.

What an instructive coincidence: in order to slander the Bolsheviks, the missionaries of *Neuer Weg* were compelled at the same time to slander the Kaffirs; moreover in both cases the slander follows the line of the official bourgeois lie: against revolutionists and against the coloured races. No, we prefer the Kaffirs to all missionaries, both spiritual and secular!

It is not necessary in any case, however, to overestimate the conscientiousness of the moralists of *Neuer Weg* and other cul-de-sacs. The intentions of these people are not so bad. But despite these intentions they serve as levers in the mechanics of reaction. In such a period as the present when the petty bourgeois parties who cling to the liberal bourgeoisie or its shadow (the politics of the "Peoples' Front") paralyse the proletariat and pave the road for Fascism (Spain, France ...), the Bolsheviks, that is, revolutionary Marxists, become especially odious figures in the eyes of bourgeois public opinion. The fundamental political pressure of our time shifts from right to left. In the final analysis the whole weight of reaction bears down upon the shoulders of a tiny revolutionary minority. This minority is called the Fourth International. Voila l'ennemi! There is the enemy!

In the mechanics of reaction Stalinism occupies many leading positions. All groupings of bourgeois society, including the anarchists, utilise its aid in the struggle against the proletarian revolution. At the same time the petty bourgeois democrats attempt, at least to the extent of fifty percent, to cast the repulsiveness of the crimes of its Moscow ally upon the indomitable revolutionary minority. Herein lies the sense of the now stylish dictum: "Trotskyism and Stalinism are one and the same." The adversaries of the Bolsheviks and the Kaffirs thus aid reaction in slandering the party of revolution.

The "Amoralism" of Lenin

The Russian "Socialist Revolutionaries" were always the most moral individuals: essentially they were composed of ethics alone. This did not prevent them, however, at the time of revolution from deceiving the Russian peasants. In the Parisian organ of Kerensky, that very ethical socialist who was the forerunner of Stalin in manufacturing spurious accusations against the Bolsheviks, another old "Socialist Revolutionary" Zenzinov writes:

"Lenin, as is known, taught that for the sake of gaining the desired ends communists can, and sometimes must 'resort to all sorts of devices, manoeuvres and subterfuge...'" (*New Russia*, February 17, 1938, p.3)

From this they draw the ritualistic conclusion: Stalinism is the natural offspring of Leninism. Unfortunately, the ethical indicter is not even capable of quoting honestly. Lenin said:

"It is necessary to be able ... to resort to all sorts of devices, manoeuvres, and illegal methods, to evasion and subterfuge, in order to penetrate into the trade unions, to remain in them, and to carry on communist work in then at all costs."

The necessity for evasion and manoeuvres, according to Lenin's explanation, is called forth by the fact that the reformist bureaucracy, betraying the workers to capital, baits revolutionists, persecutes them, and even resorts to turning the bourgeois police upon them. "Manoeuvres and subterfuge" are in this case only methods of valid self-defence against the perfidious reformist bureaucracy. The party of this very Zenzinov once carried on illegal work against Czarism, and later — against the Bolsheviks. In both cases it resorted to craftiness, evasion, false passports and other forms of "subterfuge". All these means were considered not only "ethical" but also heroic because they corresponded to political aims of the petty bourgeoisie. But the situation changes at once when proletarian revolutionists are forced to resort to conspirative measures against the petty bourgeois democracy. The key to the morality of these gentlemen has, as we see, a class character!

The "amoralist" Lenin openly, in the press, gives advice concerning military craftiness against perfidious leaders. And the moralist Zenzinov maliciously chops both ends from the quotation in order to deceive the reader: the ethical indicter is proved as usual a petty swindler. Not for nothing was Lenin fond of repeating: it is very difficult to meet a conscientious adversary!

A worker who does not conceal the "truth" about the strikers' plans from the capitalists is simply a betrayer deserving contempt and boycott. The soldier who discloses the "truth" to the enemy is punished as a spy. Kerensky tried to lay at the Bolsheviks' door the accusation of having disclosed the "truth" to Ludendorff's staff. It appears that even the "holy truth" is not an end in itself. More imperious criteria which, as analysis demonstrates, carry a class character, rule over it.

The life and death struggle is unthinkable without military craftiness, in other words, without lying and deceit. May the German proletariat then not deceive Hitler's police? Or perhaps Soviet Bolsheviks have an "immoral" attitude when they deceive the GPU? Every pious bourgeois applauds the cleverness of police who succeed through craftiness in seizing a dangerous gangster. Is military craftiness really permissible when the question concerns the overthrow of the gangsters of imperialism?

Norman Thomas speaks about "that strange communist amorality in which nothing matters but the party and its power" (*Socialist Call*, March 12, 1938, p.5). Moreover, Thomas throws into one heap the present Comintern, that is, the conspiracy of the Kremlin bureaucracy against the working class, with the Bolshevik party which represented a conspiracy of the advanced workers against the bourgeoisie. This thoroughly dishonest juxtaposition has already been sufficiently exposed above. Stalinism merely screens itself under the cult of the party; actually it destroys and tramples the party in filth. It is true, however, that to a Bolshevik the party is everything. The drawing-room socialist, Thomas, is surprised by and rejects a similar relationship between a revolutionist and revolution because he himself is only a bourgeois with a socialist "ideal". In the eyes of Thomas and his kind the party is only a secondary instrument for electoral combinations and other similar uses, not more. His personal life, interests, ties, moral criteria exist outside the party. With hostile astonishment he looks down upon the Bolshevik to whom the party is a weapon for the revolutionary reconstruction of society, including also its morality. To a revolutionary Marxist there can be no contradiction between personal morality and the interests of the party, since the party embodies in his consciousness the very highest tasks and aims of mankind. It is naive to imagine that Thomas has a higher understanding of morality than the Marxists. He merely has a base conception of the party.

"All that arises is worthy of perishing," says the dialectician, Goethe. The destruction of the Bolshevik party — an episode in world reaction — does not, however, disparage its world-wide historic significance. In the period of its revolutionary ascendance, that is, when it actually represented the proletarian vanguard, it was the most honest party in history. Wherever it could, it, of course, deceived the class enemies; on the other hand it told the toilers the truth, the whole truth, and nothing but the truth. Only thanks to this did it succeed in winning their trust to a degree never before achieved by any other party in the world.

The clerks of the ruling classes call the organisers of this party "amoralists". In the eyes of conscious workers this accusation carries a complimentary character. It signifies: Lenin refused to recognise moral norms established by slave-owners for their slaves and never observed by the slave-owners themselves; he called upon the proletariat to extend the class struggle into the moral sphere too. Whoever fawns before precepts established by the enemy will never vanquish that enemy!

The "amoralism" of Lenin, that is, his rejection of supra-class morals, did not hinder him from remaining faithful to one and the same ideal throughout his whole life; from devoting his whole being to the cause of the oppressed; from displaying the highest conscientiousness in the sphere of ideas and the highest fearlessness in the sphere of action, from maintaining an attitude untainted by the least superiority to an "ordinary" worker, to a defenceless woman, to a child. Does it not seem that "amoralism" in the given case is only a pseudonym for higher human morality?

An Instructive Episode

Here it is proper to relate an episode which, in spite of its modest dimensions, does not badly illustrate the difference between their morals and ours. In 1935, through a letter to my Belgian friends, I developed the conception that the attempt of a young revolutionary party to organise "its own" trade unions is equivalent to suicide. It is necessary to find the workers where they are. But this means paying dues in order to sustain an opportunist apparatus? "Of course," I replied, "for the right to undermine the reformists it is necessary temporarily to pay them a contribution." But reformists will not permit us to undermine them? "True," I answered, "undermining demands conspirative measures. Reformists are the political police of the bourgeoisie within the working class. We must act without their permission, and against their interdiction". Through an accidental raid on comrade D.'s home in connection, if I am not mistaken, with the matter of supplying arms for the Spanish workers, the Belgian police seized my letter. Within several days it was published. The press of Vandervelde, De Man, and Spaak did not of course spare lightning against my "Machiavellianism" and "Jesuitism". And who are these accusers? Vandervelde, president for many years of the Second International, long ago became a trusted servant of Belgian capital. De Man, who in a series of ponderous tomes ennobled socialism with idealistic morals, making overtures to religion, seized the first suitable occasion in which to betray the workers and became a common bourgeois minister. Even more lovely is Spaak's case. A year and a half previously this gentleman belonged to the left-socialist opposition and came to me in France for advice upon the methods of struggle against Vandervelde's bureaucracy. I set forth the same conceptions which later constituted my letter. But within a year after his visit, Spaak rejected the thorns for the roses. Betraying his comrades of the opposition, he became one of the most cynical ministers of Belgian capital. In the trade unions and in their own party these gentlemen stifle every critical voice, systematically corrupt and bribe the most advanced workers and just as systematically expel the refractory ones. They are distinguished from the GPU only by the fact that they have not yet resorted to spilling blood — as good patriots they husband the workers' blood for the next imperialist war. Obviously — one must be a most hellish abomination, a moral deformation, a "Kaffir", a Bolshevik, in order to advise the revolutionary workers to observe the precepts of conspiracy in the struggle against these gentlemen!

From the point of view of the Belgian laws, my letter did not of course contain anything criminal. The duty of the "democratic" police was to return the letter to the addressee with an apology. The duty of the socialist party was to protest against the raid which had been dictated by concern over General Franco's interests. But Messrs. Socialists were not at all shy at utilising the indecent police service — without this they could not have enjoyed the happy occasion of once more exposing the superiority of their morals over the amoralism of the Bolsheviks.

Everything is symbolical in this episode. The Belgian social-democrats dumped the buckets of their indignation upon me exactly while their Norwegian co-thinkers held me and my wife under lock and key in order to prevent us from defending ourselves against the accusations of the GPU. The Norwegian government well knew that the Moscow accusations were spurious — the social-democratic semi-official newspaper affirmed this openly during the first days. But Moscow touched the Norwegian ship-owners and fish merchants on the pocketbook — and Messrs. Social-Democrats immediately flopped down on all fours. The leader of the party, Martin Tranmel, is not only an authority in the moral sphere but openly a righteous person: he does not drink, does not smoke, does not indulge in meat, and in winter bathes in an ice hole. This did not hinder him, after he had arrested us upon the order of the GPU, from especially inviting a Norwegian agent of the GPU, one Jacob Fries — a bourgeois without honour or conscience — to calumniate me. But enough...

The morals of these gentlemen consists of conventional precepts and turns of speech which are supposed to screen their interests, appetites and fears. In the majority they are ready for any baseness — rejection of convictions, perfidy, betrayal — in the name of ambition or cupidity. In the holy sphere of personal interests the end to them justifies any means. But it is precisely because of this that they require special codes of morals, durable, and at the same time elastic, like good suspenders. They detest anyone who exposes their professional secrets to the masses. In "peaceful" times their hatred is expressed in slander — in Billingsgate or "philosophical" language. In times of sharp social conflicts, as in Spain, these moralists, hand in hand with the GPU, murder revolutionists. In order to justify themselves, they repeat: "Trotskyism and Stalinism are one and the same."

Dialectic Interdependence of End and Means

A means can be justified only by its end. But the end in its turn needs to be justified. From the Marxist point of view, which expresses the historical interests of the proletariat, the end is justified if it leads to increasing the power of man over nature and to the abolition of the power of man over man.

"We are to understand then that in achieving this end anything is permissible?" sarcastically demands the Philistine, demonstrating that he understood nothing. That is permissible, we answer, which really leads to the liberation of mankind. Since this end can be achieved only through revolution, the liberating morality of the proletariat of necessity is endowed with a revolutionary character. It irreconcilably counteracts not only religious dogma but every kind of idealistic fetish, these philosophic

226

gendarmes of the ruling class. It deduces a rule for conduct from the laws of the development of society, thus primarily from the class struggle, this law of all laws.

"Just the same," the moralist continues to insist, "does it mean that in the class struggle against capitalists all means are permissible: lying, frame-up, betrayal, murder, and so on?" Permissible and obligatory are those and only those means, we answer, which unite the revolutionary proletariat, fill their hearts with irreconcilable hostility to oppression, teach them contempt for official morality and its democratic echoers, imbue them with consciousness of their own historic mission, raise their courage and spirit of self-sacrifice in the struggle. Precisely from this it flows that not all means are permissible. When we say that the end justifies the means, then for us the conclusion follows that the great revolutionary end spurns those base means and ways which set one part of the working class against other parts, or attempt to make the masses happy without their participation; or lower the faith of the masses in themselves and their organisation, replacing it by worship for the "leaders". Primarily and irreconcilably, revolutionary morality rejects servility in relation to the bourgeoisie and haughtiness in relation to the toilers, that is, those characteristics in which petty bourgeois pedants and moralists are thoroughly steeped.

These criteria do not, of course, give a ready answer to the question as to what is permissible and what is not permissible in each separate case. There can be no such automatic answers. Problems of revolutionary morality are fused with the problems of revolutionary strategy and tactics. The living experience of the movement under the clarification of theory provides the correct answer to these problems.

Dialectic materialism does not know dualism between means and end. The end flows naturally from the historical movement. Organically the means are subordinated to the end. The immediate end becomes the means for a further end. In his play, *Franz von Sickingen*, Ferdinand Lassalle puts the following words into the mouth of one of the heroes:

... "Show not the goal
But show also the path. So closely interwoven
Are path and goal that each with other
Ever changes, and other paths forthwith
Another goal set up."

Lassalle's lines are not at all perfect. Still worse is the fact that in practical politics Lassalle himself diverged from the above expressed precept — it is sufficient to recall that he went as far as secret agreements with Bismark! But the dialectic interdependence between means and end is expressed entirely correctly in the above-quoted sentences. Seeds of wheat must be sown in order to yield an ear of wheat.

Is individual terror, for example, permissible or impermissible from the point of view of "pure morals"? In this abstract form the question does not exist at all for us. Conservative Swiss bourgeois even now render official praise to the terrorist William Tell. Our sympathies are fully on the side of Irish, Russian, Polish or Hindu terrorists in their struggle against national and political oppression. The assassinated Kirov, a rude satrap, does not call forth any sympathy. Our relation to the assassin remains neutral only because we know not what motives guided him. If it became known that Nikolayev acted as a conscious avenger for workers' rights trampled upon by Kirov, our sympathies would be fully on the side of the assassin. However, not the question of subjective motives but that of objective expediency has for us the decisive significance. Are the given means really capable of leading to the goal? In relation to individual terror, both theory and experience bear witness that such is not the case. To the terrorist we say: it is impossible to replace the masses; only in the mass movement can you find expedient expression for your heroism. However, under conditions of civil war, the assassination of individual oppressors ceases to be an act of individual terror. If, we shall say, a revolutionist bombed General Franco and his staff into the air, it would hardly evoke moral indignation even from the democratic eunuchs Under the conditions of civil war a similar act would be politically completely expedient. Thus, even in the sharpest question — murder of man by man — moral absolutes prove futile. Moral evaluations, together with those political, flow from the inner needs of struggle.

The liberation of the workers can come only through the workers themselves. There is, therefore, no greater crime than deceiving the masses, palming off defeats as victories, friends as enemies, bribing workers' leaders, fabricating legends, staging false trials, in a word, doing what the Stalinists do. These means can serve only one end: lengthening the domination of a clique already condemned by history. But they cannot serve to liberate the masses. That is why the Fourth International leads against Stalinism a life and death struggle.

The masses, of course, are not at all impeccable. Idealisation of the masses is foreign to us. We have seen them under different conditions, at different stages and in addition in the biggest political shocks. We have observed their strong and weak sides. Their strong side — resoluteness, self-sacrifice, heroism — has always found its clearest expression in times of revolutionary upsurge. During this period the Bolsheviks headed the masses. Afterward a different historical chapter loomed when the weak side of the oppressed came to the forefront: heterogeneity, insufficiency of culture, narrowness of world outlook. The masses tired of the tension, became disillusioned, lost faith in themselves — and cleared the road for the new aristocracy. In this epoch the Bolsheviks ("Trotskyists") found themselves isolated from the masses. Practically we went through two such big historic cycles: 1897-1905, years of flood tide; 1907-1913, years of the ebb; 1917-1923, a period of upsurge unprecedented in history; finally, a new period of reaction which has not ended even today. In these immense events the "Trotskyists" learned the rhythm of history, that is, the dialectics of the class struggle. They also learned, it seems, and to a certain degree successfully, how to subordinate their subjective plans and programs to this objective rhythm. They learned not to fall into despair over the fact that the laws of history do not depend upon their individual tastes and are not subordinated to their own moral criteria. They learned to subordinate their individual desires to the laws of history. They learned not to become frightened by the most powerful enemies if their power is in contradiction to the needs of historical development. They know how to swim against the stream in the deep conviction that the new historic flood will carry them to the other shore. Not all will reach that shore, many will drown. But to participate in this movement with open eyes and with an intense will — only this can give the highest moral satisfaction to a thinking being!

P.S. — I wrote these line during those days when my son struggled, unknown to me, with death. I dedicate to his memory this small work which, I hope, would have met with his approval — Leon Sedoff was a genuine revolutionist and despised the Pharisees. — L.T.

1938

What is Leninism?

Leon Trotsky

LENINISM CANNOT be conceived of without theoretical breadth, without a critical analysis of the material bases of the political process. The weapon of Marxian investigation must be constantly sharpened and applied. It is precisely in this that tradition consists, and not in the substitution of a formal reference or of an accidental quotation.

Least of all can Leninism be reconciled with ideological superficiality and theoretical slovenliness. Lenin cannot be chopped up into quotations suited for every possible case, because for Lenin the formula never stands higher than the reality; it is always the tool that makes it possible to grasp the reality and to dominate it. It would not be hard to find in Lenin dozens and hundreds of passages which, formally speaking, seem to be contradictory. But what must be seen is not the formal relationship of one passage to another, but the real relationship of each of them to the concrete reality in which the formula was introduced as a lever. The Leninist truth is always concrete!

As a system of revolutionary action, Leninism presupposes a revolutionary sense sharpened by reflection and experience which, in the social realm, is equivalent to the muscular sensation in physical labour. But revolutionary sense cannot be confused with demagogical flair. The latter may yield ephemeral successes, sometimes even sensational ones. But it is a political instinct of an inferior type.

It always leans toward the line of least resistance. Leninism, on the other hand, seeks to pose and resolve the fundamental revolutionary problems.

Leninism is, first of all, realism, the highest qualitative and quantitative appreciation of reality, from the standpoint of revolutionary action. Precisely because of this it is irreconcilable with the flight from reality behind the screen of hollow agitationalism, with the passive loss of time, with the haughty justification of yesterday's mistakes on the pretext of saving the tradition of the party.

Leninism is genuine freedom from formalistic prejudices, from moralising doctrinalism, from all forms of intellectual conservatism attempting to bind the will to revolutionary action. But to believe that Leninism signifies that "anything goes" would be an irremediable mistake. Leninism includes the morality, not formal but genuinely revolutionary, of mass action and the mass party. Nothing is so alien to it as functionary-arrogance and bureaucratic cynicism.

A mass party has its own morality, which is the bond of fighters in and for action. Demagogy is irreconcilable with the spirit of a revolutionary party because it is deceitful: by presenting one or another simplified solution of the difficulties of the hour it inevitably undermines the next future, weakens the party's self-confidence.

Swept by the wind and gripped by a serious danger, demagogy easily dissolves into panic. It is hard to juxtapose, even on paper, panic and Leninism.

Leninism is warlike from head to foot. War is impossible without cunning, without subterfuge, without deception of the enemy. Victorious war cunning is a constituent element of Leninist politics.

But, at the same time, Leninism is supreme revolutionary honesty toward the party and the working class. It admits of no fiction, no bubble-blowing, no pseudo-grandeur.

Leninism is orthodox, obdurate, irreducible, but it does not contain so much as a hint of formalism, canon, nor bureaucratism. In the struggle, it takes the bull by the horns. To make out of the traditions of Leninism a supra-theoretical guarantee of infallibility of all the words and thoughts of the interpreters of these traditions is to scoff at genuine revolutionary tradition and transform it into social bureaucratism. It is ridiculous and pathetic to try to hypnotise a great revolutionary party by the repetition of the same formulae, according to which the right line should be sought not in the essence of each question, not in the methods of posing and solving this question, but in information of a biographical character.

This character of the revolutionary tradition is bound up with the peculiar character of revolutionary discipline. Where tradition is conservative, discipline is passive and is violated at the first moment of crisis. Where, as in our party, tradition consists in the highest revolutionary activity, discipline attains its maximum point, for its decisive importance is constantly checked in action. Thence, the indestructible alliance of revolutionary initiative, of critical, bold elaboration of questions, with iron discipline in action. And it is only by this superior activity that the youth can receive from the old this tradition of discipline and carry it on.

We cherish the tradition of Bolshevism as much as anybody. But let no one dare identify bureaucratism with Bolshevism, tradition with vacuous routine.

From *The New Course*, 1923

What is Trotskyism?

Max Shachtman

OUR CRITICISM OF Trotsky's later theory of the "workers' state" introduces into it an indispensable correction. Far from "demolishing" Trotskyism, it eliminates from it a distorting element of contradiction and restores its essential inner harmony and continuity. The writer considers himself a follower of Trotsky, as of Lenin before him, and of Marx and Engels in the earlier generation.

Such has been the intellectual havoc wrought in the revolutionary movement by the manners and standards of Stalinism, that "follower" has come to mean serf, worshipper, or parrot. We have no desire to be this kind of "follower." Trotsky was not, and we learned much of what we know from him. In *The New Course* he wrote these jewelled words, which are worth repeating a hundred times:

"If there is one thing likely to strike a mortal blow to the spiritual life of the party and to the doctrinal training of the youth, it is certainly the transformation of Leninism from a method demanding for its application initiative, critical thinking and ideological courage into a canon which demands nothing more than interpreters appointed for good and aye. Leninism cannot be conceived of without theoretical breadth, without a critical analysis of the material bases of the political process. The weapon of Marxian investigation must he constantly sharpened and applied. It is precisely in this that tradition consists, and not in the substitution of a formal reference or of an accidental quotation. Least of all can Leninism be reconciled with ideological superficiality and theoretical slovenliness.

"Lenin cannot be chopped up into quotations suited for every possible case, because for Lenin the formula never stands higher than the reality; it is always the tool that makes it possible to grasp the reality and to dominate it. It would not be hard to find in Lenin dozens and hundreds of passages which, formally speaking, seem to be contradictory. But what must be seen is not the formal relationship of one passage to another, but the real relationship of each of them to the concrete reality in which the formula was introduced as a lever. The Leninist truth is always concrete! ...

"Leninism is orthodox, obdurate, irreducible, but it does not contain so much as a hint of formalism, canon, nor bureaucratism. In the struggle it takes the bull by the horns. To make out of the traditions of Leninism a supra-theoretical guarantee of the infallibility of all the words and thoughts of the interpreters of these traditions, is to scoff at genuine revolutionary tradition and transform it into official bureaucratism. It is ridiculous and pathetic to try to hypnotise a great revolutionary party by the repetition of the same formula, according to which the right line should be sought not in the essence of each question, not in the methods of posing, and solving this question, but in information ... of a biographical character."

There are "followers" who seem to think that the whole of Trotskyism (that is, the revolutionary Marxism of our time) is contained in the theory that Russia is still a workers' state and in the slogan of "unconditional defence of the Soviet Union." They merely prove that they have retired from a life of active and critical thought, and from the realities of life in general, and confine themselves to memorising by heart two pages of an otherwise uncut and unread book. They would be the first to deny, by the way, that the whole of Leninism is contained in Lenin's theory of the "democratic dictatorship of the proletariat and peasantry" or in his strictures against Trotsky and the theory of the permanent revolution.

The whole of Trotsky, for the new generation of Marxists that must be trained up and organised, does not lie in his contradictory theory of the class character of Russia; it is not even a decisively important part of the whole. Trotskyism is all of Marx, Engels and Lenin that has withstood the test of time and struggle — and that is a good deal! Trotskyism is its leader's magnificent development and amplification of the theory of the permanent revolution. Trotskyism is the defence of the great and fundamental principles of the Russian Bolshevik revolution and the Communist International, which it brought into existence. Trotskyism is the principle of workers' democracy, of the struggle for democracy and socialism.

In this sense — and it is the only one worth talking about — *The New Course* is a Trotskyist classic. It was not only a weapon hitting at the very heart of decaying bureaucratism in revolutionary Russia. It was and is a guide for the struggle against the vices of bureaucratism throughout the labour and revolutionary movements.

Bureaucratism is not simply a direct product of certain economic privileges acquired by the officialdom of the labour movement. It is also an ideology, a concept of leadership and of its relationship to the masses, which is absorbed even by labour and revolutionary officialdoms who enjoy no economic privileges at all. It is an ideology that reeks of its bourgeois origin. Boiled down to its most vicious essence, it is the kind of thinking and living and leading which says to the rank and file, in the words Trotsky once used to describe the language of Stalinism: "No thinking! Those at the top have more brains than you."

We see this ideology reflected in the every-day conduct of our own American trade union bureaucracy: "We will handle everything. Leave things to us. You stay where you are, and keep still." We see it reflected throughout the big social-democratic (to say nothing of the Stalinist) parties: "We will negotiate things. We will arrange everything. We will manoeuvre cleverly with the enemy, and get what you want without struggle. You sit still until further orders. That is all you are fit for." We even see it in those smaller revolutionary groups which are outside the reformist and Stalinist movements and which consider that this fact alone immunises them from bureaucratism. We repeat, it is a bourgeois ideology through and through. It is part of the ideas that the bourgeoisie, through all its agencies for moulding the mind of the masses, seeks to have prevail: "Whatever criticism you may have to make of us, remember this: The masses are stupid. It is no accident that they are at the bottom of the social ladder. They are incapable of rising to the top. They need a ruler over them; they cannot rule themselves. For their own good, they must be kept where they are."

The New Course does more than dismiss this odious ideology that fertilises the mind of the labour bureaucracy. It analyses its source and its nature. It diagnoses the evil to perfection. It indicates the operation needed to remove it, and the tools with which to perform the operation. It is the same tool needed by the proletariat for its emancipation everywhere. Its name is the democratically organised and controlled, self-acting, dynamic, critical, revolutionary political party of the working class.

The counter-revolution in Russia was made possible only because Stalinism blunted, then wore down, then smashed to bits this indispensable tool of the proletariat. The bureaucracy won. "If Trotsky had been right," says the official iconographer of Stalin, Henri Barbusse, "he would have won." How simple! What a flattering compliment to ... Hitler. The bureaucracy not only won, but consolidated its power on a scale unknown in any country of the world throughout all history. Stalin himself is now the Pope-Czar of the Russian Empire.

But that is only how it seems on the surface; that is how it is only for a very short while, as history counts. "Any imbecile can rule with a state of siege," said Rochefort. Only the really powerful and confident can rule by establishing peaceful relations in the country. That, the new bureaucracy, without a past and without a future, cannot do. The combined efforts of world capitalism cannot do that nowadays, still less the efforts of the Stalinist nobility. The latter has succeeded in establishing "socialism," for itself and "in a single country." It will not live long to enjoy it. Together with all modern rulers, it is doomed to perish in the unrelenting world crisis that it cannot solve, or to perish at the hands of an avenging socialist proletariat.

Cromwell's Roundheads marched with Bibles in their hands. The militant proletariat needs no divine revelations or scriptural injunctions, no Bibles or saviours. But it will march to victory only if its conscious vanguard has assimilated the rich and now-more-timely-than-ever lessons to be learned from the classic work of the organiser of the first great proletarian revolution.

From *The Struggle for the New Course,* preface to an edition of
Trotsky's *The New Course,* 1943

"EQUAL SACRIFICE"

Bedrock socialism

From *Socialism, Utopian and Scientific*

Frederick Engels

I

WHEN EUROPE EMERGED from the Middle Ages, the rising middle-class of the towns constituted its revolutionary element. It had conquered a recognised position within mediaeval feudal organisation, but this position, also, had become too narrow for its expansive power. The development of the middle-class, the bourgeoisie, became incompatible with the maintenance of the feudal system; the feudal system, therefore, had to fall.

But the great international centre of feudalism was the Roman Catholic Church. It united the whole of feudalised Western Europe, in spite of all internal wars, into one grand political system, opposed as much to the schismatic Greeks as to the Mohammedan countries. It had organised its own hierarchy on the feudal model, and, lastly, it was itself by far the most powerful feudal lord, holding, as it did, fully one-third of the soil of the Catholic world. Before profane feudalism could be successfully attacked in each country and in detail, this, its sacred central organisation, had to be destroyed.

Moreover, parallel with the rise of the middle-class went on the great revival of science; astronomy, mechanics, physics, anatomy, physiology were again cultivated. And the bourgeoisie, for the development of its industrial production, required a science which ascertained the physical properties of natural objects and the modes of action of the forces of Nature. Now up to then science had but been the humble handmaid of the Church, had not been allowed to overlap the limits set by faith, and for that reason had been no science at all. Science rebelled against the Church; the bourgeoisie could not do without science, and, therefore, had to join in the rebellion.

The above, though touching but two of the points where the rising middle-class was bound to come into collision with the established religion, will be sufficient to show, first, that the class most directly interested in the struggle against the pretensions of the Roman Church was the bourgeoisie; and second, that every struggle against feudalism, at that time, had to take on a religious disguise, had to be directed against the Church in the first instance. But if the universities and the traders of the cities started the cry, it was sure to find, and did find, a strong echo in the masses of the country people, the peasants, who everywhere had to struggle for their very existence with their feudal lords, spiritual and temporal.

The long fight of the bourgeoisie against feudalism culminated in three great, decisive battles.

The first was what is called the Protestant Reformation in Germany. The war cry raised against the Church, by Luther, was responded to by two insurrections of a political nature; first, that of the lower nobility under Franz von Sickingen (1523), then the great Peasants' War, 1525. Both were defeated, chiefly in consequence of the indecision of the parties most interested, the burghers of the towns — an indecision into the causes of which we cannot here enter. From that moment, the struggle degenerated into a fight between the local princes and the central power, and ended by blotting out Germany, for 200 years, from the politically active nations of Europe. The Lutheran Reformation produced a new creed indeed, a religion adapted to absolute monarchy. No sooner were the peasant of North-east Germany converted to Lutheranism than they were from freemen reduced to serfs.

But where Luther failed, Calvin won the day. Calvin's creed was one fit for the boldest of the bourgeoisie of his time. His predestination doctrine was the religious expression of the fact that, in the commercial world of competition, success or failure does not depend upon a man's activity or cleverness, but upon circumstances uncontrollable by him. It is not of him that willeth or of him that runneth, but of the mercy of unknown superior economic powers; and this was especially true at a period of economic revolution, when all old commercial routes and centres were replaced by new ones, when India and America were opened to the world, and when even the most sacred economic articles of faith — the value of gold and silver — began to totter and to break down. Calvin's church constitution of God was thoroughly democratic and republican; and where the kingdom of God was republicanised, could the kingdoms of this world remains subject to monarchs, bishops, and lords? While German Lutheranism became a willing tool in the hands of princes, Calvinism founded a republic in Holland, and active republican parties in England, and, above all, Scotland.

In Calvinism, the second great bourgeois upheaval found its doctrine ready cut and dried. This upheaval took place in England. The middle-class of the towns brought it on, and the yeomanry of the country districts fought it out. Curiously enough, in all the three great bourgeois risings, the peasantry furnishes the army that has to do the fighting; and the peasantry is just the class that, the victory once gained, is most surely ruined by the economic consequences of that victory. A hundred years after Cromwell, the yeomanry of england had almost disappeared. Anyhow, had it not been for that yeomanry and for the plebian element in the towns, the bourgeoisie alone would never have fought the matter out to the bitter end, and would never have brought Charles I to the scaffold. In order to secure even those conquests of the bourgeoisie that were ripe for gathering at the time, the revolution had to be carried considerably further — exactly as in 1793 in France and 1848 in Germany. This seems, in fact, to be one of the laws of evolution of bourgeois society.

Well, upon this excess of revolutionary activity there necessarily followed the inevitable reaction which, in its turn, went beyond the point where it might have maintained itself. After a series of oscillations, the new centre of gravity was at last attained and became a new starting-point. The grand period of English history, known to respectability under the name of "the Great Rebellion", and the struggles succeeding it, were brought to a close by the comparatively puny events entitled by Liberal historians "the Glorious Revolution".

The new starting-point was a compromise between the rising middle-class and the ex-feudal landowners. The latter, though called, as now, the aristocracy, had been long since on the way which led them to become what Louis Philippe in France became at a much later period: "The first bourgeois of the kingdom". Fortunately for England, the old feudal barons had killed one another during the War of the Roses. Their successors, though mostly scions of the old families, had been so much out of the direct line of descent that they constituted quite a new body, with habits and tendencies far more bourgeois than feudal. They fully understood the value of money, and at once began to increase their rents by turning hundreds of small farmers out and replacing them with sheep. Henry VIII, while squandering the Church lands, created fresh bourgeois landlords by wholesale; the innumerable confiscation of estates, re-granted to absolute or relative upstarts, and continued during the whole of the 17th century, had the same result. Consequently, ever since Henry VII, the English "aristocracy", far from counteracting the development of industrial production, had, on the contrary, sought to indirectly profit thereby; and there had always been a section of the great landowners willing, from economical or political reasons, to cooperate with the leading men of the financial and industrial bourgeoisie. The compromise of 1689 was, therefore, easily accomplished. The political spoils of "pelf and place" were left to the great landowning families, provided the economic interests of the financial, manufacturing, and commercial middle-class were sufficiently attended to. And these economic interests were at that time powerful enough to determine the general policy of the nation.

There might be squabbles about matters of detail, but, on the whole, the aristocratic oligarchy knew too well that its own economic prosperity was irretrievably bound up with that of the industrial and commercial middle-class.

From that time, the bourgeoisie was a humble, but still a recognised, component of the ruling classes of England. With the rest of them, it had a common interest in keeping in subjection the great working mass of the nation. The merchant or manufacturer himself stood in the position of master, or, as it was until lately called, of "natural superior" to his clerks, his work-people, his domestic servants. His interest was to get as much and as good work out of them as he could; for this end, they had to be trained to proper submission. He was himself religious; his religion had supplied the standard under which he had fought the king and the lords; he was not long in discovering the opportunities this same religion offered him for working upon the minds of his natural inferiors, and making them submissive to the behests of the masters it had pleased God to place over them. In short, the English bourgeoisie now had to take a part in keeping down the "lower orders", the great producing mass of the nation, and one of the means employed for that purpose was the influence of religion.

There was another factor that contributed to strengthen the religious leanings of the bourgeoisie. That was the rise of materialism in England. This new doctrine not only shocked the pious feelings of the middle-class; it announced itself as a philosophy only fit for scholars and cultivated men of the world, in contrast to religion, which was good enough for the uneducated masses, including the bourgeoisie. With Hobbes, it stepped on the stage as a defender of royal prerogative and omnipotence; it called upon absolute monarchy to keep down that puer robustus sed malitiosus ["robust but malicious boy"] — to wit, the people. Similarly, with the successors of Hobbes, with Bolingbroke, Shaftesbury, etc., the new deistic form of materialism remained an aristocratic, esoteric doctrine, and, therefore, hateful to the middle-class both for its religious heresy and for its anti-bourgeois political connections. Accordingly, in opposition to the materialism and deism of the aristocracy, those Protestant sects which had furnished the flag and the fighting contingent against the Stuarts continued to furnish the main strength of the progressive middle-class, and form even today the backbone of "the Great Liberal Party".

In the meantime, materialism passed from England to France, where it met and coalesced with another materialistic school of philosophers, a branch of Cartesianism. In France, too, it remained at first an exclusively aristocratic doctrine. But, soon, its revolutionary character asserted itself.

240

The French materialists did not limit their criticism to matters of religious belief; they extended it to whatever scientific tradition or political institution they met with; and to prove the claim of their doctrine to universal application, they took the shortest cut, and boldly applied it to all subjects of knowledge in the giant work after which they were named — the Encyclopaedia. Thus, in one or the other of its two forms — avowed materialism or deism — it became the creed of the whole cultured youth of France; so much so that, when the Great Revolution broke out, the doctrine hatched by English Royalists gave a theoretical flag to French Republicans and Terrorists, and furnished the text for the Declaration of the Rights of Man. The Great French Revolution was the third uprising of the bourgeoisie, but the first that had entirely cast off the religious cloak, and was fought out on undisguised political lines; it was the first, too, that was really fought out up to the destruction of one of the combatants, the aristocracy, and the complete triumph of the other, the bourgeoisie. In England, the continuity of pre-revolutionary and post-revolutionary institutions, and the compromise between landlords and capitalists, found its expression in the continuity of judicial precedents and in the religious preservation of the feudal forms of the law. In France, the Revolution constituted a complete breach with the traditions of the past; it cleared out the very last vestiges of feudalism, and created in the Code Civil a masterly adaptation of the old Roman law — that almost perfect expression of the juridical relations corresponding to the economic stage called by Marx the production of commodities — to modern capitalist conditions; so masterly that this French revolutionary code still serves as a model for reforms of the law of property in all other countries, not excepting England. Let us, however, not forget that if English law continues to express the economic relations of capitalist society in that barbarous feudal language which corresponds to the thing expressed just as English spelling corresponds to English pronunciation — vous ecrivez Londres et vous prononcez Constantinople, said a Frenchman — that same English law is the only one which has preserved through ages, and transmitted to America and the Colonies, the best part of that old Germanic personal freedom, local self-government, and independence from all interference (but that of the law courts), which on the Continent has been lost during the period of absolute monarchy, and has nowhere been as yet fully recovered.

To return to our British bourgeois. The French Revolution gave him a splendid opportunity, with the help of the Continental monarchies, to destroy French maritime commerce, to annex French colonies, and to crush the last French pretensions to maritime rivalry. That was one reason why he fought it. Another was that the ways of this revolution went very much against his grain. Not only its "execrable" terrorism, but the very attempt to carry bourgeois rule to extremes. What should the British bourgeois do without his aristocracy, that taught him manners, such as they were, and invented fashions for him — that furnished officers for the army, which kept order at home, and the navy, which conquered colonial possessions and new markets aboard? There was, indeed, a progressive minority of the bourgeoisie, that minority whose interests were not so well attended to under the compromise; this section, composed chiefly of the less wealthy middle-class, did sympathise with the Revolution, but it was powerless in Parliament.

Thus, if materialism became the creed of the French Revolution, the God-fearing English bourgeois held all the faster to his religion. Had not the reign of terror in Paris proved what was the upshot, if the religious instincts of the masses were lost? The more materialism spread from France to neighbouring countries, and was reinforced by similar doctrinal currents, notably by German philosophy, the more, in fact, materialism and free thought generally became, on the Continent, the necessary qualifications of a cultivated man, the more stubbornly the English middle-class stuck to its manifold religious creeds. These creeds might differ from one another, but they were, all of them, distinctly religious, Christian creeds.

While the Revolution ensured the political triumph of the bourgeoisie in France, in England Watt, Arkwright, Cartwright, and others, initiated an industrial revolution, which completely shifted the centre of gravity of economic power. The wealth of the bourgeoisie increased considerably faster than that of the landed aristocracy. Within the bourgeoisie itself, the financial aristocracy, the bankers, etc., were more and more pushed into the background by the manufacturers. The compromise of 1689, even after the gradual changes it had undergone in favour of the bourgeoisie, no longer corresponded to the relative position of the parties to it. The character of these parties, too, had changed; the bourgeoisie of 1830 was very different from that of the preceding century. The political power still left to the aristocracy, and used by them to resist the pretensions of the new industrial bourgeoisie, became incompatible with the new economic interests. A fresh struggle with the aristocracy was necessary; it could end only in a victory of the new economic power. First, the Reform Act was pushed through, in spite of all resistance, under the impulse of the French Revolution of 1830. It gave to the bourgeoisie a recognised and powerful place in Parliament. Then the Repeal of the Corn Laws [a move toward free-trade], which settled, once and for all, the supremacy of the bourgeoisie, and especially of its most active portion, the manufacturers, over the landed aristocracy. This was the greatest victory of the bourgeoisie; it was, however, also the last it gained in its own exclusive interest. Whatever triumphs it obtained later on, it had to share with a new social power — first its ally, but soon its rival.

The industrial revolution had created a class of large manufacturing capitalists, but also a class — and a far more numerous one — of manufacturing work-people. This class gradually increased in numbers, in proportion as the industrial revolution seized upon one branch of manufacture after another, and in the same proportion it increased its power. This power it proved as early as 1824, by forcing a reluctant Parliament to repeal the acts forbidding combinations of workmen. During the Reform agitation, the workingmen constituted the Radical wing of the Reform party; the Act of 1832 having excluded them from the suffrage, the formulated their demands in the People's Charter, and constituted themselves, in opposition to the great bourgeois Anti-Corn Law party, into an independent party, the Chartists, the first working-men's party of modern times.

Then came the Continental revolutions of February and March 1848, in which the working people played such a prominent part, and, at least in Paris, put forward demands which were certainly inadmissible from the point of view of capitalist society. And then came the general reaction. First, the defeat of the Chartists on April 10, 1848; then the crushing of the Paris workingmen's insurrection in June of the same year; then the disasters of 1849 in Italy, Hungary, South Germany, and at last the victory of Louis Bonaparte over Paris, December 2, 1851. For a time, at least, the bugbear of working-class pretensions was put down, but at what cost! If the British bourgeois had been convinced before of the necessity of maintaining the common people in a religious mood, how much more must he feel that necessity after all these experiences? Regardless of the sneers of his Continental compeers, he continued to spend thousands and tens of thousands, year after year, upon the evangelisation of the lower orders; not content with his own native religious machinery, he appealed to Brother Jonathan, the greatest organiser in existence of religion as a trade, and imported from America revivalism, Moody and Sankey, and the like; and, finally, he accepted the dangerous aid of the Salvation Army, which revives the propaganda of early Christianity, appeals to the poor as the elect, fights capitalism in a religious way, and thus fosters an element of early Christian class antagonism, which one day may become troublesome to the well-to-do people who now find the ready money for it.

It seems a law of historical development that the bourgeoisie can in no European country get hold of political power — at least for any length of time — in the same exclusive way in which the feudal aristocracy kept hold of it during the Middle Ages. Even in France, where feudalism was completely extinguished, the bourgeoisie as a whole has held full possession of the Government for very short periods only. During Louis Philippe's reign, 1830-48, a very small portion of the bourgeoisie ruled the kingdom; by far the larger part were excluded from the suffrage by the high qualification. Under the Second Republic, 1848-51, the whole bourgeoisie ruled but for three years only; their incapacity brought on the Second Empire. It is only now, in the Third Republic, that the bourgeoisie as a whole have kept possession of the helm for more than 20 years; and they are already showing lively signs of decadence. A durable reign of the bourgeoisie has been possible only in countries like America, where feudalism was unknown, and society at the very beginning started from a bourgeois basis. And even in France and America, the successors of the bourgeoisie, the working people, are already knocking at the door.

In England, the bourgeoisie never held undivided sway. Even the victory of 1832 left the landed aristocracy in almost exclusive possession of all the leading Government offices. The meekness with which the middle-class submitted to this remained inconceivable to me until the great Liberal manufacturer, Mr. W. A. Forster, in a public speech, implored the young men of Bradford to learn French, as a means to get on in the world, and quoted from his own experience how sheepish he looked when, as a Cabinet Minister, he had to move in society where French was, at least, as necessary as English! The fact was, the English middle-class of that time were, as a rule, quite uneducated upstarts, and could not help leaving to the aristocracy those superior Government places where other qualifications were required than mere insular narrowness and insular conceit, seasoned by business sharpness. Even now the endless newspaper debates about middle-class education show that the English middle-class does not yet consider itself good enough for the best education, and looks to something more modest. Thus, even after the repeal of the Corn Laws, it appeared a matter of course that the men who had carried the day — the Cobdens, Brights, Forsters, etc. — should remain excluded from a share in the official government of the country, until 20 years afterwards a new Reform Act opened to them the door of the Cabinet. The English bourgeoisie are, up to the present day, so deeply penetrated by a sense of their social inferiority that they keep up, at their own expense and that of the nation, an ornamental caste of drones to represent the nation worthily at all State functions; and they consider themselves highly honoured whenever one of themselves is found worthy of admission into this select and privileged body, manufactured, after all, by themselves.

244

The industrial and commercial middle-class had, therefore, not yet succeeded in driving the landed aristocracy completely from political power when another competitor, the working-class, appeared on the stage. The reaction after the Chartist movement and the Continental revolutions, as well as the unparalleled extension of English trade from 1848-66 (ascribed vulgarly to Free Trade alone, but due far more to the colossal development of railways, ocean steamers, and means of intercourse generally), had again driven the working-class into the dependency of the Liberal party, of which they formed, as in pre-Chartist times, the Radical wing. Their claims to the franchise, however, gradually became irresistible; while the Whig leaders of the Liberals "funked", Disraeli showed his superiority by making the Tories seize the favourable moment and introduce household suffrage in the boroughs, along with a redistribution of seats. Then followed the ballot; then, in 1884, the extension of household suffrage to the counties and a fresh redistribution of seats, by which electoral districts were, to some extent, equalised. All these measures considerably increased the electoral power of the working-class, so much so that in at least 150 to 200 constituencies that class now furnished the majority of the voters. But parliamentary government is a capital school for teaching respect for tradition; if the middle-class look with awe and veneration upon what Lord John Manners playfully called "our old nobility", the mass of the working-people then looked up with respect and deference to what used to be designated as "their betters", the middle-class. Indeed, the British workman, some 15 years ago, was the model workman, whose respectful regard for the position of his master, and whose self-restraining modesty in claiming rights for himself, consoled our German economists of the Katheder-Socialist school for the incurable communistic and revolutionary tendencies of their own working-men at home.

But the English middle-class — good men of business as they are — saw farther than the German professors. They had shared their powers but reluctantly with the working-class. They had learnt, during the Chartist years, what that puer robustus sed malitiosus, the people, is capable of. And since that time, they had been compelled to incorporate the better part of the People's Charter in the Statutes of the United Kingdom. Now, if ever, the people must be kept in order by moral means, and the first and foremost of all moral means of action upon the masses is and remains — religion. Hence the parsons' majorities on the School Boards, hence the increasing self-taxation of the bourgeoisie for the support of all sorts of revivalism, from ritualism to the Salvation Army.

And now came the triumph of British respectability over the free thought and religious laxity of the Continental bourgeois. The workmen

245

of France and Germany had become rebellious. They were thoroughly infected with Socialism, and, for very good reasons, were not at all particular as to the legality of the means by which to secure their own ascendancy. The puer robustus, here, turned from day-to-day more malitiosus. Nothing remained to the French and German bourgeoisie as a last resource but to silently drop their free thought, as a youngster, when sea-sickness creeps upon him, quietly drops the burning cigar he brought swaggeringly on board; one-by-one, the scoffers turned pious in outward behaviour, spoke with respect of the Church, its dogmas and rites, and even conformed with the latter as far as could not be helped. French bourgeois dined maigre on Fridays, and German ones sat out long Protestant sermons in their pews on Sundays. They had come to grief with materialism. "Die Religion muss dem Volk erhalten werden" — religion must be kept alive for the people — that was the only and the last means to save society from utter ruin. Unfortunately for themselves, they did not find this out until they had done their level best to break up religion for ever. And now it was the turn of the British bourgeoisie to sneer and to say: "Why, you fools, I could have told you that 200 years ago!"

However, I am afraid neither the religious stolidity of the British, nor the post festum conversion of the Continental bourgeois will stem the rising proletarian tide. Tradition is a great retarding force, is the vis inertiae of history, but, being merely passive, is sure to be broken down; and thus religion will be no lasting safeguard to capitalist society. If our juridical, philosophical, and religious ideas are the more or less remote offshoots of the economical relations prevailing in a given society, such ideas cannot, in the long run, withstand the effects of a complete change in these relations. And, unless we believe in supernatural revelation, we must admit that no religious tenets will ever suffice to prop up a tottering society.

In fact, in England too, the working-people have begun to move again. They are, no doubt, shackled by traditions of various kinds. Bourgeois traditions, such as the widespread belief that there can be but two parties, Conservatives and Liberals, and that the working-class must work out its salvation by and through the great Liberal Party. Working-men's traditions, inherited from their first tentative efforts at independent action, such as the exclusion, from ever so many old Trade Unions, of all applicants who have not gone through a regular apprenticeship; which means the breeding, by every such union, of its own blacklegs. But, for all that, the English working-class is moving, as even Professor Brentano has sorrowfully had to report to his brother Katheder-Socialists. It moves, like all things in England, with a slow and measured step, with hesitation here, with more or less unfruitful, tentative attempts there; it moves now and then with an over-cautious mistrust of the name of Socialism, while it gradually absorbs the substance; and the movement spreads and seizes one layer of the workers after another. It has now shaken out of their torpor the unskilled labourers of the East End of London, and we all know what a splendid impulse these fresh forces have given it in return. And if the pace of the movement is not up to the impatience of some people, let them not forget that it is the working-class which keeps alive the finest qualities of the English character, and that, if a step in advance is once gained in England, it is, as a rule, never lost afterwards. If the sons of the old Chartists, for reasons unexplained above, were not quite up to the mark, the grandsons bid fair to be worthy of their forefathers.

But the triumph of the European working-class does not depend upon England alone. It can only be secured by the cooperation of, at least, England, France, and Germany. In both the latter countries, the working-class movement is well ahead of England. In Germany, it is even within measurable distance of success. The progress it has there made during the last 25 years is unparalleled. It advances with ever-increasing velocity. If the German middle-class have shown themselves lamentably deficient in political capacity, discipline, courage, energy, and perseverance, the German working-class have given ample proof of all these qualities. Four hundred years ago, Germany was the starting-point of the first upheaval of the European middle-class; as things are now, is it outside the limits of possibility that Germany will be the scene, too, of the first great victory of the European proletariat?

II

Modern Socialism is, in its essence, the direct product of the recognition, on the one hand, of the class antagonisms existing in the society of today between proprietors and non-proprietors, between capitalists and wage-workers; on the other hand, of the anarchy existing in production. But, in its theoretical form, modern Socialism originally appears ostensibly as a more logical extension of the principles laid down by the great French philosophers of the 18th century. Like every new theory, modern Socialism had, at first, to connect itself with the intellectual stock-in-trade ready to its hand, however deeply its roots lay in material economic facts.

The great men, who in France prepared men's minds for the coming revolution, were themselves extreme revolutionists. They recognised no external authority of any kind whatever. Religion, natural science, society, political institutions — everything was subjected to the most unsparing criticism: everything must justify its existence before the judgment-seat of reason or give up existence. Reason became the sole measure of everything. It was the time when, as Hegel says, the world stood upon its head; first in the sense that the human head, and the principles arrived at by its thought, claimed to be the basis of all human action and association; but by and by, also, in the wider sense that the reality which was in contradiction to these principles had, in fact, to be turned upside down. Every form of society and government then existing, every old traditional notion, was flung into the lumber-room as irrational; the world had hitherto allowed itself to be led solely by prejudices; everything in the past deserved only pity and contempt. Now, for the first time, appeared the light of day, the kingdom of reason; henceforth superstition, injustice, privilege, oppression, were to be superseded by eternal truth, eternal Right, equality based on Nature and the inalienable rights of man.

We know today that this kingdom of reason was nothing more than the idealised kingdom of the bourgeoisie; that this eternal Right found its realisation in bourgeois justice; that this equality reduced itself to bourgeois equality before the law; that bourgeois property was proclaimed as one of the essential rights of man; and that the government of reason, the Contrat Social of Rousseau, came into being, and only could come into being, as a democratic bourgeois republic. The great thinkers of the 18th century could, no more than their predecessors, go beyond the limits imposed upon them by their epoch.

But, side by side with the antagonisms of the feudal nobility and the burghers, who claimed to represent all the rest of society, was the general antagonism of exploiters and exploited, of rich idlers and poor workers. It was this very circumstance that made it possible for the representatives of the bourgeoisie to put themselves forward as representing not one special class, but the whole of suffering humanity. Still further. From its origin the bourgeoisie was saddled with its antithesis: capitalists cannot exist without wage-workers, and, in the same proportion as the mediaeval burgher of the guild developed into the modern bourgeois, the guild journeyman and the day-labourer, outside the guilds, developed into the proletarian. And although, upon the whole, the bourgeoisie, in their struggle with the nobility, could claim to represent at the same time the interests of the different working-classes of that period, yet in every great bourgeois movement there were independent outbursts of that class which was the forerunner, more or less developed, of the modern proletariat. For example, at the time of the German Reformation and the Peasants' War, the Anabaptists and Thomas Münzer; in the great English Revolution, the Levellers; in the great French Revolution, Babeuf.

These were theoretical enunciations, corresponding with these revolutionary uprisings of a class not yet developed; in the 16th and 17th centuries, Utopian pictures of ideal social conditions; in the 18th century, actual communistic theories (Morelly and Mably). The demand for equality was no longer limited to political rights; it was extended also to the social conditions of individuals. It was not simply class privileges that were to be abolished, but class distinctions themselves. A Communism, ascetic, denouncing all the pleasures of life, Spartan, was the first form of the new teaching. Then came the three great Utopians: Saint-Simon, to whom the middle-class movement, side by side with the proletarian, still had a certain significance; Fourier; and Owen, who in the country where capitalist production was most developed, and under the influence of the antagonisms begotten of this, worked out his proposals for the removal of class distinction systematically and in direct relation to French materialism.

One thing is common to all three. Not one of them appears as a representative of the interests of that proletariat which historical development had, in the meantime, produced. Like the French philosophers, they do not claim to emancipate a particular class to begin with, but all humanity at once. Like them, they wish to bring in the kingdom of reason and eternal justice, but this kingdom, as they see it, is as far as Heaven from Earth, from that of the French philosophers.

For, to our three social reformers, the bourgeois world, based upon the principles of these philosophers, is quite as irrational and unjust, and, therefore, finds its way to the dust-hole quite as readily as feudalism and all the earlier stages of society. If pure reason and justice have not, hitherto, ruled the world, this has been the case only because men have not rightly understood them. What was wanted was the individual man of genius, who has now arisen and who understands the truth. That he has now arisen, that the truth has now been clearly understood, is not an inevitable event, following of necessity in the chains of historical development, but a mere happy accident. He might just as well have been born 500 years earlier, and might then have spared humanity 500 years of error, strife, and suffering.

We saw how the French philosophers of the 18th century, the forerunners of the Revolution, appealed to reason as the sole judge of all that is. A rational government, rational society, were to be founded; everything that ran counter to eternal reason was to be remorselessly done away with. We saw also that this eternal reason was in reality nothing but the idealised understanding of the 18th century citizen, just then evolving into the bourgeois. The French Revolution had realised this rational society and government.

But the new order of things, rational enough as compared with earlier conditions, turned out to be by no means absolutely rational. The state based upon reason completely collapsed. Rousseau's Contrat Social had found its realisation in the Reign of Terror, from which the bourgeoisie, who had lost confidence in their own political capacity, had taken refuge first in the corruption of the Directorate, and, finally, under the wing of the Napoleonic despotism. The promised eternal peace was turned into an endless war of conquest. The society based upon reason had fared no better. The antagonism between rich and poor, instead of dissolving into general prosperity, had become intensified by the removal of the guild and other privileges, which had to some extent bridged it over, and by the removal of the charitable institutions of the Church. The "freedom of property" from feudal fetters, now veritably accomplished, turned out to be, for the small capitalists and small proprietors, the freedom to sell their small property, crushed under the overmastering competition of the large capitalists and landlords, to these great lords, and thus, as far as the small capitalists and peasant proprietors were concerned, became "freedom from property". The development of industry upon a capitalistic basis made poverty and misery of the working masses conditions of existence of society. Cash payment became more and more, in Carlyle's phrase, the sole nexus between man and man. The number of crimes increased from year to year. Formerly, the feudal vices had openly stalked about in broad daylight; though not eradicated, they were now at any rate thrust into the background. In their stead, the bourgeois vices, hitherto practiced in secret, began to blossom all the more luxuriantly. Trade became to a greater and greater extent cheating. The "fraternity" of the revolutionary motto was realised in the chicanery and rivalries of the battle of competition. Oppression by force was replaced by corruption; the sword, as the first social lever, by gold. The right of the first night was transferred from the feudal lords to the bourgeois manufacturers. Prostitution increased to an extent never heard of. Marriage itself remained, as before, the legally recognised form, the official cloak of prostitution, and, moreover, was supplemented by rich crops of adultery.

In a word, compared with the splendid promises of the philosophers, the social and political institutions born of the "triumph of reason" were bitterly disappointing caricatures. All that was wanting was the men to formulate this disappointment, and they came with the turn of the century. In 1802, Saint-Simon's Geneva letters appeared; in 1808 appeared Fourier's first work, although the groundwork of his theory dated from 1799; on January 1, 1800, Robert Owen undertook the direction of New Lanark.

At this time, however, the capitalist mode of production, and with it the antagonism between the bourgeoisie and the proletariat, was still very incompletely developed. Modern Industry, which had just arisen in England, was still unknown in France. But Modern Industry develops, on the one hand, the conflicts which make absolutely necessary a revolution in the mode of production, and the doing away with its capitalistic character — conflicts not only between the classes begotten of it, but also between the very productive forces and the forms of exchange created by it. And, on the other hand, it develops, in these very gigantic productive forces, the means of ending these conflicts. If, therefore, about the year 1800, the conflicts arising from the new social order were only just beginning to take shape, this holds still more fully as to the means of ending them. The "have-nothing" masses of Paris, during the Reign of Terror, were able for a moment to gain the mastery, and thus to lead the bourgeois revolution to victory in spite of the bourgeoisie themselves. But, in doing so, they only proved how impossible it was for their domination to last under the conditions then obtaining. The proletariat, which then for the first time evolved itself from these "have-nothing" masses as the nucleus of a new class, as yet quite incapable of independent political action, appeared as an oppressed, suffering order, to whom, in its incapacity to help itself, help could, at best, be brought in from without or down from above.

This historical situation also dominated the founders of Socialism. To the crude conditions of capitalistic production and the crude class conditions correspond crude theories. The solution of the social problems, which as yet lay hidden in undeveloped economic conditions, the Utopians attempted to evolve out of the human brain. Society presented nothing but wrongs; to remove these was the task of reason. It was necessary, then, to discover a new and more perfect system of social order and to impose this upon society from without by propaganda, and, wherever it was possible, by the example of model experiments. These new social systems were foredoomed as Utopian; the more completely they were worked out in detail, the more they could not avoid drifting off into pure phantasies.

These facts once established, we need not dwell a moment longer upon this side of the question, now wholly belonging to the past. We can leave it to the literary small fry to solemnly quibble over these phantasies, which today only make us smile, and to crow over the superiority of their own bald reasoning, as compared with such "insanity". For ourselves, we delight in the stupendously grand thoughts and germs of thought that everywhere break out through their phantastic covering, and to which these Philistines are blind.

Saint-Simon was a son of the great French Revolution, at the outbreak of which he was not yet 30. The Revolution was the victory of the Third Estate — i.e., of the great masses of the nation, working in production and in trade, over the privileged idle classes, the nobles and the priests. But the victory of the Third Estate soon revealed itself as exclusively the victory of a smaller part of this "estate", as the conquest of political power by the socially privileged section of it — i.e., the propertied bourgeoisie. And the bourgeoisie had certainly developed rapidly during the Revolution, partly by speculation in the lands of the nobility and of the Church, confiscated and afterwards put up for sale, and partly by frauds upon the nation by means of army contracts. It was the domination of these swindlers that, under the Directorate, brought France to the verge of ruin, and thus gave Napoleon the pretext for his coup d'état.

Hence, to Saint-Simon the antagonism between the Third Estate and the privileged classes took the form of an antagonism between "workers" and "idlers". The idlers were not merely the old privileged classes, but also all who, without taking any part in production or distribution, lived on their incomes. And the workers were not only the wage-workers, but also the manufacturers, the merchants, the bankers. That the idlers had lost the capacity for intellectual leadership and political supremacy had been proved, and was by the Revolution finally settled. That the non-possessing classes had not this capacity seemed to Saint-Simon proved by the experiences of the Reign of Terror. Then, who was to lead and command? According to Saint-Simon, science and industry, both united by a new religious bond, destined to restore that unity of religious ideas which had been lost since the time of the Reformation — a necessarily mystic and rigidly hierarchic "new Christianity". But science, that was the scholars; and industry, that was, in the first place, the working bourgeois, manufacturers, merchants, bankers. These bourgeois were, certainly, intended by Saint-Simon to transform themselves into a kind of public officials, of social trustees; but they were still to hold, vis-à-vis of the workers, a commanding and economically privileged position. The bankers especially were to be called upon to direct the whole of social production by the regulation of credit. This conception was in exact keeping with a time in which Modern Industry in France and, with it, the chasm between bourgeoisie and proletariat was only just coming into existence. But what Saint-Simon especially lays stress upon is this: what interests him first, and above all other things, is the lot of the class that is the most numerous and the most poor ("la classe la plus nombreuse et la plus pauvre").

Already in his Geneva letters, Saint-Simon lays down the proposition that "all men ought to work". In the same work he recognises also that the Reign of Terror was the reign of the non-possessing masses.

"See," says he to them, "what happened in France at the time when your comrades held sway there; they brought about a famine." [Lettres d'un habitant de Genève à ses contemporains, Saint-Simon, 1803]

But to recognise the French Revolution as a class war, and not simply one between nobility and bourgeoisie, but between nobility, bourgeoisie, and the non-possessors, was, in the year 1802, a most pregnant discovery. In 1816, he declares that politics is the science of production, and foretells the complete absorption of politics by economics. The knowledge that economic conditions are the basis of political institutions appears here only in embryo. Yet what is here already very plainly expressed is the idea of the future conversion of political rule over men into an administration of things and a direction of processes of production — that is to say, the "abolition of the state", about which recently there has been so much noise.

Saint-Simon shows the same superiority over his contemporaries, when in 1814, immediately after the entry of the allies into Paris, and again in 1815, during the Hundred Days' War, he proclaims the alliance of France and England, and then of both of these countries, with Germany, as the only guarantee for the prosperous development and peace of Europe. To preach to the French in 1815 an alliance with the victors of Waterloo required as much courage as historical foresight.

If in Saint-Simon we find a comprehensive breadth of view, by virtue of which almost all the ideas of later Socialists that are not strictly economic are found in him in embryo, we find in Fourier a criticism of the existing conditions of society, genuinely French and witty, but not upon that account any the less thorough. Fourier takes the bourgeoisie, their inspired prophets before the Revolution, and their interested eulogists after it, at their own word. He lays bare remorselessly the material and moral misery of the bourgeois world. He confronts it with the earlier philosophers' dazzling promises of a society in which reason alone should reign, of a civilisation in which happiness should be universal, of an illimitable human perfectibility, and with the rose-coloured phraseology of the bourgeois ideologists of his time. He points out how everywhere the most pitiful reality corresponds with the most high-sounding phrases, and he overwhelms this hopeless fiasco of phrases with his mordant sarcasm.

Fourier is not only a critic; his imperturbably serene nature makes him a satirist, and assuredly one of the greatest satirists of all time. He depicts, with equal power and charm, the swindling speculations that blossomed out upon the downfall of the Revolution, and the shopkeeping spirit prevalent in, and characteristic of, French commerce at that time. Still more masterly is his criticism of the bourgeois form of the re-

253

lations between sexes, and the position of woman in bourgeois society. He was the first to declare that in any given society the degree of woman's emancipation is the natural measure of the general emancipation.

But Fourier is at his greatest in his conception of the history of society. He divides its whole course, thus far, into four stages of evolution — savagery, barbarism, the patriarchate, civilisation. This last is identical with the so-called civil, or bourgeois, society of today — i.e., with the social order that came in with the 16th century. He proves "that the civilised stage raises every vice practiced by barbarism in a simple fashion into a form of existence, complex, ambiguous, equivocal, hypocritical" — that civilisation moves "in a vicious circle", in contradictions which it constantly reproduces without being able to solve them; hence it constantly arrives at the very opposite to that which it wants to attain, or pretends to want to attain, so that, e.g., "under civilisation poverty is born of superabundance itself".

Fourier, as we see, uses the dialectic method in the same masterly way as his contemporary, Hegel. Using these same dialectics, he argues against talk about illimitable human perfectibility, that every historical phase has its period of ascent and also its period of descent, and he applies this observation to the future of the whole human race. As Kant introduced into natural science the idea of the ultimate destruction of the Earth, Fourier introduced into historical science that of the ultimate destruction of the human race.

Whilst in France the hurricane of the Revolution swept over the land, in England a quieter, but not on that account less tremendous, revolution was going on. Steam and the new tool-making machinery were transforming manufacture into modern industry, and thus revolutionising the whole foundation of bourgeois society. The sluggish march of development of the manufacturing period changed into a veritable storm and stress period of production. With constantly increasing swiftness the splitting-up into large capitalists and non-possessing proletarians went on. Between these, instead of the former stable middle-class, an unstable mass of artisans and small shopkeepers, the most fluctuating portion of the population, now led a precarious existence.

The new mode of production was, as yet, only at the beginning of its period of ascent; as yet it was the normal, regular method of production — the only one possible under existing conditions. Nevertheless, even then it was producing crying social abuses — the herding together of a homeless population in the worst quarters of the large towns; the loosening of all traditional moral bonds, of patriarchal subordination, of family relations; overwork, especially of women and children, to a frightful

254

extent; complete demoralisation of the working-class, suddenly flung into altogether new conditions, from the country into the town, from agriculture into modern industry, from stable conditions of existence into insecure ones that change from day to day.

At this juncture, there came forward as a reformer a manufacturer 29-years-old — a man of almost sublime, childlike simplicity of character, and at the same time one of the few born leaders of men. Robert Owen had adopted the teaching of the materialistic philosophers: that man's character is the product, on the one hand, of heredity; on the other, of the environment of the individual during his lifetime, and especially during his period of development. In the industrial revolution most of his class saw only chaos and confusion, and the opportunity of fishing in these troubled waters and making large fortunes quickly. He saw in it the opportunity of putting into practice his favourite theory, and so of bringing order out of chaos. He had already tried it with success, as superintendent of more than 500 men in a Manchester factory. From 1800 to 1829, he directed the great cotton mill at New Lanark, in Scotland, as managing partner, along the same lines, but with greater freedom of action and with a success that made him a European reputation. A population, originally consisting of the most diverse and, for the most part, very demoralised elements, a population that gradually grew to 2,500, he turned into a model colony, in which drunkenness, police, magistrates, lawsuits, poor laws, charity, were unknown. And all this simply by placing the people in conditions worthy of human beings, and especially by carefully bringing up the rising generation. He was the founder of infant schools, and introduced them first at New Lanark. At the age of two, the children came to school, where they enjoyed themselves so much that they could scarely be got home again. Whilst his competitors worked their people 13 or 14 hours a day, in New Lanark the working-day was only 10 and a half hours. When a crisis in cotton stopped work for four months, his workers received their full wages all the time. And with all this the business more than doubled in value, and to the last yielded large profits to its proprietors.

In spite of all this, Owen was not content. The existence which he secured for his workers was, in his eyes, still far from being worthy of human beings. "The people were slaves at my mercy." The relatively favourable conditions in which he had placed them were still far from allowing a rational development of the character and of the intellect in all directions, much less of the free exercise of all their faculties.

"And yet, the working part of this population of 2,500 persons was daily producing as much real wealth for society as, less than half a century before, it would have required the working part of a population of

600,000 to create. I asked myself, what became of the difference between the wealth consumed by 2,500 persons and that which would have been consumed by 600,000?"

The answer was clear. It had been used to pay the proprietors of the establishment 5 per cent on the capital they had laid out, in addition to over £300,000 clear profit. And that which held for New Lanark held to a still greater extent for all the factories in England.

"If this new wealth had not been created by machinery, imperfectly as it has been applied, the wars of Europe, in opposition to Napoleon, and to support the aristocratic principles of society, could not have been maintained. And yet this new power was the creation of the working-classes." To them, therefore, the fruits of this new power belonged. The newly-created gigantic productive forces, hitherto used only to enrich individuals and to enslave the masses, offered to Owen the foundations for a reconstruction of society; they were destined, as the common property of all, to be worked for the common good of all.

Owen's communism was based upon this purely business foundation, the outcome, so to say, of commercial calculation. Throughout, it maintained this practical character. Thus, in 1823, Owen proposed the relief of the distress in Ireland by Communist colonies, and drew up complete estimates of costs of founding them, yearly expenditure, and probable revenue. And in his definite plan for the future, the technical working out of details is managed with such practical knowledge — ground plan, front and side and bird's-eye views all included — that the Owen method of social reform once accepted, there is from the practical point of view little to be said against the actual arrangement of details.

His advance in the direction of Communism was the turning-point in Owen's life. As long as he was simply a philanthropist, he was rewarded with nothing but wealth, applause, honour, and glory. He was the most popular man in Europe. Not only men of his own class, but statesmen and princes listened to him approvingly. But when he came out with his Communist theories that was quite another thing. Three great obstacles seemed to him especially to block the path to social reform: private property, religion, the present form of marriage.

He knew what confronted him if he attacked these — outlawry, excommunication from official society, the loss of his whole social position. But nothing of this prevented him from attacking them without fear of consequences, and what he had foreseen happened. Banished from official society, with a conspiracy of silence against him in the press, ruined by his unsuccessful Communist experiments in America, in which he sacrificed all his fortune, he turned directly to the working-class and continued working in their midst for 30 years. Every social movement, every

256

real advance in England on behalf of the workers links itself on to the name of Robert Owen. He forced through in 1819, after five years' fighting, the first law limiting the hours of labour of women and children in factories. He was president of the first Congress at which all the Trade Unions of England united in a single great trade association. He introduced as transition measures to the complete communistic organisation of society, on the one hand, cooperative societies for retail trade and production. These have since that time, at least, given practical proof that the merchant and the manufacturer are socially quite unnecessary. On the other hand, he introduced labour bazaars for the exchange of the products of labour through the medium of labour-notes, whose unit was a single hour of work; institutions necessarily doomed to failure, but completely anticipating Proudhon's bank of exchange of a much later period, and differing entirely from this in that it did not claim to be the panacea for all social ills, but only a first step towards a much more radical revolution of society.

The Utopians' mode of thought has for a long time governed the Socialist ideas of the 19th century, and still governs some of them. Until very recently, all French and English Socialists did homage to it. The earlier German Communism, including that of Weitling, was of the same school. To all these, Socialism is the expression of absolute truth, reason and justice, and has only to be discovered to conquer all the world by virtue of its own power. And as an absolute truth is independent of time, space, and of the historical development of man, it is a mere accident when and where it is discovered. With all this, absolute truth, reason, and justice are different with the founder of each different school. And as each one's special kind of absolute truth, reason, and justice is again conditioned by his subjective understanding, his conditions of existence, the measure of his knowledge and his intellectual training, there is no other ending possible in this conflict of absolute truths than that they shall be mutually exclusive of one another. Hence, from this nothing could come but a kind of eclectic, average Socialism, which, as a matter of fact, has up to the present time dominated the minds of most of the socialist workers in France and England. Hence, a mish-mash allowing of the most manifold shades of opinion: a mish-mash of such critical statements, economic theories, pictures of future society by the founders of different sects, as excite a minimum of opposition; a mish-mash which is the more easily brewed the more definite sharp edges of the individual constituents are rubbed down in the stream of debate, like rounded pebbles in a brook.

To make a science of Socialism, it had first to be placed upon a real basis.

III

The materialist conception of history starts from the proposition that the production of the means to support human life and, next to production, the exchange of things produced, is the basis of all social structure; that in every society that has appeared in history, the manner in which wealth is distributed and society divided into classes or orders is dependent upon what is produced, how it is produced, and how the products are exchanged. From this point of view, the final causes of all social changes and political revolutions are to be sought, not in men's brains, not in men's better insights into eternal truth and justice, but in changes in the modes of production and exchange. They are to be sought, not in the philosophy, but in the economics of each particular epoch. The growing perception that existing social institutions are unreasonable and unjust, that reason has become unreason, and right wrong, is only proof that in the modes of production and exchange changes have silently taken place with which the social order, adapted to earlier economic conditions, is no longer in keeping. From this it also follows that the means of getting rid of the incongruities that have been brought to light must also be present, in a more or less developed condition, within the changed modes of production themselves. These means are not to be invented by deduction from fundamental principles, but are to be discovered in the stubborn facts of the existing system of production.

What is, then, the position of modern Socialism in this connection?

The present situation of society — this is now pretty generally conceded — is the creation of the ruling class of today, of the bourgeoisie. The mode of production peculiar to the bourgeoisie, known, since Marx, as the capitalist mode of production, was incompatible with the feudal system, with the privileges it conferred upon individuals, entire social ranks and local corporations, as well as with the hereditary ties of subordination which constituted the framework of its social organisation. The bourgeoisie broke up the feudal system and built upon its ruins the capitalist order of society, the kingdom of free competition, of personal liberty, of the equality, before the law, of all commodity owners, of all the rest of the capitalist blessings. Thenceforward, the capitalist mode of production could develop in freedom. Since steam, machinery, and the making of machines by machinery transformed the older manufacture into modern industry, the productive forces, evolved under the guidance of the bourgeoisie, developed with a rapidity and in a degree unheard of before. But just as the older manufacture, in its time, and handicraft, becoming more developed under its influence, had come into collision with the feudal trammels of the guilds, so now modern industry, in its complete development, comes into collision with the bounds within which

258

the capitalist mode of production holds it confined. The new productive forces have already outgrown the capitalistic mode of using them. And this conflict between productive forces and modes of production is not a conflict engendered in the mind of man, like that between original sin and divine justice. It exists, in fact, objectively, outside us, independently of the will and actions even of the men that have brought it on. Modern Socialism is nothing but the reflex, in thought, of this conflict in fact; its ideal reflection in the minds, first, of the class directly suffering under it, the working class.

Now, in what does this conflict consist?

Before capitalist production — i.e., in the Middle Ages — the system of petty industry obtained generally, based upon the private property of the labourers in their means of production; in the country, the agriculture of the small peasant, freeman, or serf; in the towns, the handicrafts organised in guilds. The instruments of labour — land, agricultural implements, the workshop, the tool — were the instruments of labour of single individuals, adapted for the use of one worker, and, therefore, of necessity, small, dwarfish, circumscribed. But, for this very reason, they belonged as a rule to the producer himself. To concentrate these scattered, limited means of production, to enlarge them, to turn them into the powerful levers of production of the present day — this was precisely the historic role of capitalist production and of its upholder, the bourgeoisie. In the fourth section of *Capital*, Marx has explained in detail how since the 15th century this has been historically worked out through the three phases of simple co-operation, manufacture, and modern industry. But the bourgeoisie, as is shown there, could not transform these puny means of production into mighty productive forces without transforming them, at the same time, from means of production of the individual into social means of production only workable by a collectivity of men. The spinning wheel, the hand-loom, the blacksmith's hammer, were replaced by the spinning-machine, the power-loom, the steam-hammer; the individual workshop, by the factory implying the co-operation of hundreds and thousands of workmen. In like manner, production itself changed from a series of individual into a series of social acts, and the production from individual to social products. The yarn, the cloth, the metal articles that now come out of the factory were the joint product of many workers, through whose hands they had successively to pass before they were ready. No one person could say of them: "I made that; this is my product."

But where, in a given society, the fundamental form of production is that spontaneous division of labour which creeps in gradually and not upon any preconceived plan, there the products take on the form of commodities, whose mutual exchange, buying and selling, enable the individual producers to satisfy their manifold wants. And this was the case in the Middle Ages. The peasant, e.g., sold to the artisan agricultural products and bought from him the products of handicraft. Into this society of individual producers, of commodity producers, the new mode of production thrust itself. In the midst of the old division of labour, grown up spontaneously and upon no definite plan, which had governed the whole of society, now arose division of labour upon a definite plan, as organised in the factory; side by side with individual production appeared social production. The products of both were sold in the same market, and, therefore, at prices at least approximately equal. But organisation upon a definite plan was stronger than spontaneous division of labour. The factories working with the combined social forces of a collectivity of individuals produced their commodities far more cheaply than the individual small producers. Individual producers succumbed in one department after another. Socialised production revolutionised all the old methods of production. But its revolutionary character was, at the same time, so little recognised that it was, on the contrary, introduced as a means of increasing and developing the production of commodities. When it arose, it found ready-made, and made liberal use of, certain machinery for the production and exchange of commodities: merchants' capital, handicraft, wage-labor. Socialised production thus introducing itself as a new form of the production of commodities, it was a matter of course that under it the old forms of appropriation remained in full swing, and were applied to its products as well.

In the medieval stage of evolution of the production of commodities, the question as to the owner of the product of labour could not arise. The individual producer, as a rule, had, from raw material belonging to himself, and generally his own handiwork, produced it with his own tools, by the labour of his own hands or of his family. There was no need for him to appropriate the new product. It belonged wholly to him, as a matter of course. His property in the product was, therefore, based upon his own labour. Even where external help was used, this was, as a rule, of little importance, and very generally was compensated by something other than wages. The apprentices and journeymen of the guilds worked less for board and wages than for education, in order that they might become master craftsmen themselves.

Then came the concentration of the means of production and of the producers in large workshops and manufactories, their transformation into actual socialised means of production and socialised producers. But the socialised producers and means of production and their products were still treated, after this change, just as they had been before — i.e., as the means of production and the products of individuals. Hitherto, the owner of the instruments of labour had himself appropriated the product, because, as a rule, it was his own product and the assistance of others was the exception. Now, the owner of the instruments of labour always appropriated to himself the product, although it was no longer his product but exclusively the product of the labour of others. Thus, the products now produced socially were not appropriated by those who had actually set in motion the means of production and actually produced the commodities, but by the capitalists. The means of production, and production itself, had become in essence socialised. But they were subjected to a form of appropriation which presupposes the private production of individuals, under which, therefore, every one owns his own product and brings it to market. The mode of production is subjected to this form of appropriation, although it abolishes the conditions upon which the latter rests.

This contradiction, which gives to the new mode of production its capitalistic character, contains the germ of the whole of the social antagonisms of today. The greater the mastery obtained by the new mode of production over all important fields of production and in all manufacturing countries, the more it reduced individual production to an insignificant residuum, the more clearly was brought out the incompatibility of socialised production with capitalistic appropriation.

The first capitalists found, as we have said, alongside of other forms of labour, wage-labor ready-made for them on the market. But it was exceptional, complementary, accessory, transitory wage-labor. The agricultural labourer, though, upon occasion, he hired himself out by the day, had a few acres of his own land on which he could at all events live at a pinch. The guilds were so organised that the journeyman to today became the master of tomorrow. But all this changed, as soon as the means of production became socialised and concentrated in the hands of capitalists. The means of production, as well as the product, of the individual producer became more and more worthless; there was nothing left for him but to turn wage-worker under the capitalist. Wage-labor, aforetime the exception and accessory, now became the rule and basis of all production; aforetime complementary, it now became the sole remaining function of the worker. The wage-worker for a time became a wage-worker for life. The number of these permanent was further enormously increased by the breaking-up of the feudal system that occurred at the same time, by the disbanding of the retainers of the feudal lords, the eviction of the peasants from their homesteads, etc. The separation was made complete between the means of production concentrated in the hands of the capitalists, on the one side, and the producers, possessing nothing but their labour-power, on the other. The contradiction between socialised production and capitalistic appropriation manifested itself as the antagonism of proletariat and bourgeoisie.

We have seen that the capitalistic mode of production thrust its way into a society of commodity-producers, of individual producers, whose social bond was the exchange of their products. But every society based upon the production of commodities has this peculiarity: that the producers have lost control over their own social inter-relations. Each man produces for himself with such means of production as he may happen to have, and for such exchange as he may require to satisfy his remaining wants. No one knows how much of his particular article is coming on the market, nor how much of it will be wanted. No one knows whether his individual product will meet an actual demand, whether he will be able to make good his costs of production or even to sell his commodity at all. Anarchy reigns in socialised production.

But the production of commodities, like every other form of production, has it peculiar, inherent laws inseparable from it; and these laws work, despite anarchy, in and through anarchy. They reveal themselves in the only persistent form of social inter-relations — i.e., in exchange — and here they affect the individual producers as compulsory laws of competition. They are, at first, unknown to these producers themselves, and have to be discovered by them gradually and as the result of experience. They work themselves out, therefore, independently of the producers, and in antagonism to them, as inexorable natural laws of their particular form of production. The product governs the producers.

In mediaeval society, especially in the earlier centuries, production was essentially directed toward satisfying the wants of the individual. It satisfied, in the main, only the wants of the producer and his family. Where relations of personal dependence existed, as in the country, it also helped to satisfy the wants of the feudal lord. In all this there was, therefore, no exchange; the products, consequently, did not assume the character of commodities. The family of the peasant produced almost everything they wanted: clothes and furniture, as well as the means of subsistence. Only when it began to produce more than was sufficient to supply its own wants and the payments in kind to the feudal lords, only then did it also produce commodities. This surplus, thrown into socialised exchange and offered for sale, became commodities.

The artisan in the towns, it is true, had from the first to produce for exchange. But they, also, themselves supplied the greatest part of their individual wants. They had gardens and plots of land. They turned their cattle out into the communal forest, which, also, yielded them timber and firing. The women spun flax, wool, and so forth. Production for the purpose of exchange, production of commodities, was only in its infancy. Hence, exchange was restricted, the market narrow, the methods of production stable; there was local exclusiveness without, local unity within; the mark in the country; in the town, the guild.

But with the extension of the production of commodities, and especially with the introduction of the capitalist mode of production, the laws of commodity-production, hitherto latent, came into action more openly and with greater force. The old bonds were loosened, the old exclusive limits broken through, the producers were more and more turned into independent, isolated producers of commodities. It became apparent that the production of society at large was ruled by absence of plan, by accident, by anarchy; and this anarchy grew to greater and greater height. But the chief means by aid of which the capitalist mode of production intensified this anarchy of socialised production was the exact opposite of anarchy. It was the increasing organisation of production, upon a social basis, in every individual productive establishment. By this, the old, peaceful, stable condition of things was ended. Wherever this organisation of production was introduced into a branch of industry, it brooked no other method of production by its side. The field of labour became a battle-ground. The great geographical discoveries, and the colonisation following them, multiplied markets and quickened the transformation of handicraft into manufacture. The war did not simply break out between the individual producers of particular localities. The local struggles begat, in their turn, national conflicts, the commercial wars of the 17th and 18th centuries.

Finally, modern industry and the opening of the world-market made the struggle universal, and at the same time gave it an unheard-of virulence. Advantages in natural or artificial conditions of production now decide the existence or non-existence of individual capitalists, as well as of whole industries and countries. He that falls is remorselessly cast aside. It is the Darwinian struggle of the individual for existence transferred from Nature to society with intensified violence. The conditions of existence natural to the animal appear as the final term of human development. The contradiction between socialised production and capitalistic appropriation now presents itself as an antagonism between the organisation of production in the individual workshop and the anarchy of production in society generally.

The capitalistic mode of production moves in these two forms of the antagonism immanent to it from its very origin. It is never able to get out of that "vicious circle" which Fourier had already discovered. What Fourier could not, indeed, see in his time is that this circle is gradually narrowing; that the movement becomes more and more a spiral, and must come to an end, like the movement of planets, by collision with the centre. It is the compelling force of anarchy in the production of society at large that more and more completely turns the great majority of men into proletarians; and it is the masses of the proletariat again who will finally put an end to anarchy in production. It is the compelling force of anarchy in social production that turns the limitless perfectibility of machinery under modern industry into a compulsory law by which every individual industrial capitalist must perfect his machinery more and more, under penalty of ruin.

But the perfecting of machinery is making human labour superfluous. If the introduction and increase of machinery means the displacement of millions of manual by a few machine-workers, improvement in machinery means the displacement of more and more of the machine-workers themselves. It means, in the last instance, the production of a number of available wage workers in excess of the average needs of capital, the formation of a complete industrial reserve army, as I called it in 1845, available at the times when industry is working at high pressure, to be cast out upon the street when the inevitable crash comes, a constant dead weight upon the limbs of the working-class in its struggle for existence with capital, a regulator for keeping of wages down to the low level that suits the interests of capital.

Thus it comes about, to quote Marx, that machinery becomes the most powerful weapon in the war of capital against the working-class; that the instruments of labour constantly tear the means of subsistence out of the hands of the labourer; that they very product of the worker is turned into an instrument for his subjugation.

Thus it comes about that the economising of the instruments of labour becomes at the same time, from the outset, the most reckless waste of labour-power, and robbery based upon the normal conditions under which labour functions; that machinery, "the most powerful instrument for shortening labour time, becomes the most unfailing means for placing every moment of the labourer time and that of his family at the disposal of the capitalist for the purpose of expanding the value of his capital." (*Capital*)

Thus it comes about that the overwork of some becomes the preliminary condition for the idleness of others, and that modern industry, which hunts after new consumers over the whole world, forces the consumption of the masses at home down to a starvation minimum, and in doing thus destroys its own home market.

"The law that always equilibrates the relative surplus-population, or industrial reserve army, to the extent and energy of accumulation, this law rivets the labourer to capital more firmly than the wedges of Vulcan

264

did Prometheus to the rock. It establishes an accumulation of misery, corresponding with the accumulation of capital. Accumulation of wealth at one pole is, therefore, at the same time accumulation of misery, agony of toil, slavery, ignorance, brutality, mental degradation, at the opposite pole, i.e., on the side of the class that produces its own product in the form of capital" (Marx's *Capital*).

And to expect any other division of the products from the capitalist mode of production is the same as expecting the electrodes of a battery not to decompose acidulated water, not to liberate oxygen at the positive, hydrogen at the negative pole, so long as they are connected with the battery.

We have seen that the ever-increasing perfectibility of modern machinery is, by the anarchy of social production, turned into a compulsory law that forces the individual industrial capitalist always to improve his machinery, always to increase its productive force. The bare possibility of extending the field of production is transformed for him into a similarly compulsory law. The enormous expansive force of modern industry, compared with which that of gases is mere child's play, appears to us now as a necessity for expansion, both qualitative and quantitative, that laughs at all resistance. Such resistance is offered by consumption, by sales, by the markets for the products of modern industry. But the capacity for extension, extensive and intensive, of the markets is primarily governed by quite different laws that work much less energetically. The extension of the markets cannot keep pace with the extension of production. The collision becomes inevitable, and as this cannot produce any real solution so long as it does not break in pieces the capitalist mode of production, the collisions become periodic. Capitalist production has begotten another "vicious circle".

As a matter of fact, since 1825, when the first general crisis broke out, the whole industrial and commercial world, production and exchange among all civilised peoples and their more or less barbaric hangers-on, are thrown out of joint about once every ten years. Commerce is at a stand-still, the markets are glutted, products accumulate, as multitudinous as they are unsaleable, hard cash disappears, credit vanishes, factories are closed, the mass of the workers are in want of the means of subsistence, because they have produced too much of the means of subsistence; bankruptcy follows upon bankruptcy, execution upon execution. The stagnation lasts for years; productive forces and products are wasted and destroyed wholesale, until the accumulated mass of commodities finally filter off, more or less depreciated in value, until production and exchange gradually begin to move again. Little by little, the pace quickens. It becomes a trot. The industrial trot breaks into a canter, the canter in turn grows into the headlong gallop of a perfect steeple-chase of industry, commercial credit, and speculation, which finally, after breakneck leaps, ends where it began — in the ditch of a crisis. And so over and over again. We have now, since the year 1825, gone through this five times, and at the present moment (1877), we are going through it for the sixth time. And the character of these crises is so clearly defined that Fourier hit all of them off when he described the first "crise plethorique", a crisis from plethora.

In these crises, the contradiction between socialised production and capitalist appropriation ends in a violent explosion. The circulation of commodities is, for the time being, stopped. Money, the means of circulation, becomes a hindrance to circulation. All the laws of production and circulation of commodities are turned upside down. The economic collision has reached its apogee. The mode of production is in rebellion against the mode of exchange.

The fact that the socialised organisation of production within the factory has developed so far that it has become incompatible with the anarchy of production in society, which exists side by side with and dominates it, is brought home to the capitalist themselves by the violent concentration of capital that occurs during crises, through the ruin of many large, and a still greater number of small, capitalists. The whole mechanism of the capitalist mode of production breaks down under the pressure of the productive forces, its own creations. It is no longer able to turn all this mass of means of production into capital. They lie fallow, and for that very reason the industrial reserve army must also lie fallow. Means of production, means of subsistence, available labourers, all the elements of production and of general wealth, are present in abundance. But "abundance becomes the source of distress and want" (Fourier), because it is the very thing that prevents the transformation of the means of production and subsistence into capital. For in capitalistic society, the means of production can only function when they have undergone a preliminary transformation into capital, into the means of exploiting human labour-power. The necessity of this transformation into capital of the means of production and subsistence stands like a ghost between these and the workers. It alone prevents the coming together of the material and personal levers of production; it alone forbids the means of production to function, the workers to work and live. On the one hand, therefore, the capitalistic mode of production stands convicted of its own incapacity to further direct these productive forces. On the other, these productive forces themselves, with increasing energy, press forward to the removal of the existing contradiction, to the abolition of their quality as capital, to the practical recognition of their character as social production forces. This rebellion of the productive forces, as they grow more and more powerful, against their quality as capital, this stronger and stronger command that their social character shall be recognised, forces the capital class itself to treat them more and more as social productive forces, so far as this is possible under capitalist conditions. The period of industrial high pressure, with its unbounded inflation of credit, not less than the crash itself, by the collapse of great capitalist establishments, tends to bring about that form of the socialisation of great masses of the means of production which we meet with in the different kinds of joint-stock companies. Many of these means of production and of distribution are, from the outset, so colossal that, like the railways, they exclude all other forms of capitalistic expansion. At a further stage of evolution, this form also becomes insufficient. The producers on a large scale in a particular branch of an industry in a particular country unite in a "trust", a union for the purpose of regulating production. They determine the total amount to be produced, parcel it out among themselves, and thus enforce the selling price fixed beforehand.

But trusts of this kind, as soon as business becomes bad, are generally liable to break up, and on this very account compel a yet greater concentration of association. The whole of a particular industry is turned into one gigantic joint-stock company; internal competition gives place to the internal monopoly of this one company. This has happened in 1890 with the English alkali production, which is now, after the fusion of 48 large works, in the hands of one company, conducted upon a single plan, and with a capital of 6,000,000 pounds.

In the trusts, freedom of competition changes into its very opposite — into monopoly; and the production without any definite plan of capitalistic society capitulates to the production upon a definite plan of the invading socialistic society. Certainly, this is so far still to the benefit and advantage of the capitalists. But, in this case, the exploitation is so palpable, that it must break down. No nation will put up with production conducted by trusts, with so barefaced an exploitation of the community by a small band of dividend-mongers.

In any case, with trusts or without, the official representative of capitalist society — the state — will ultimately have to undertake the direction of production. This necessity for conversion into State property is felt first in the great institutions for intercourse and communication — the post office, the telegraphs, the railways.

If the crises demonstrate the incapacity of the bourgeoisie for managing any longer modern productive forces, the transformation of the great establishments for production and distribution into joint-stock companies, trusts, and State property, show how unnecessary the bourgeoisie are for that purpose. All the social functions of the capitalist has no further social function than that of pocketing dividends, tearing off coupons, and gambling on the Stock Exchange, where the different capitalists despoil one another of their capital. At first, the capitalistic mode of production forces out the workers. Now, it forces out the capitalists, and reduces them, just as it reduced the workers, to the ranks of the surplus-population, although not immediately into those of the industrial reserve army.

But, the transformation — either into joint-stock companies and trusts, or into State-ownership — does not do away with the capitalistic nature of the productive forces. In the joint-stock companies and trusts, this is obvious. And the modern State, again, is only the organisation that bourgeois society takes on in order to support the external conditions of the capitalist mode of production against the encroachments as well of the workers as of individual capitalists. The modern state, no matter what its form, is essentially a capitalist machine — the state of the capitalists, the ideal personification of the total national capital. The more it proceeds to the taking over of productive forces, the more does it actually become the national capitalist, the more citizens does it exploit. The workers remain wage-workers — proletarians. The capitalist relation is not done away with. It is, rather, brought to a head. But, brought to a head, it topples over. State-ownership of the productive forces is not the solution of the conflict, but concealed within it are the technical conditions that form the elements of that solution.

This solution can only consist in the practical recognition of the social nature of the modern forces of production, and therefore in the harmonising with the socialised character of the means of production. And this can only come about by society openly and directly taking possession of the productive forces which have outgrown all control, except that of society as a whole. The social character of the means of production and of the products today reacts against the producers, periodically disrupts all production and exchange, acts only like a law of Nature working blindly, forcibly, destructively. But,with the taking over by society of the productive forces, the social character of the means of production and of the products will be utilised by the producers with a perfect understanding of its nature, and instead of being a source of disturbance and periodical collapse, will become the most powerful lever of production itself.

Active social forces work exactly like natural forces: blindly, forcibly, destructively, so long as we do not understand, and reckon with, them. But, when once we understand them, when once we grasp their action, their direction, their effects, it depends only upon ourselves to subject them more and more to our own will, and, by means of them, to reach our own ends. And this holds quite especially of the mighty productive forces of today. As long as we obstinately refuse to understand the nature and the character of these social means of action — and this understanding goes against the grain of the capitalist mode of production, and its defenders — so long these forces are at work in spite of us, in opposition to us, so long they master us, as we have shown above in detail.

But when once their nature is understood, they can, in the hand working together, be transformed from master demons into willing servants. The difference is as that between the destructive force of electricity in the lightning in the storm, and electricity under command in the telegraph and the voltaic arc; the difference between a conflagration, and fire working in the service of man. With this recognition, at last, of the real nature of the productive forces of today, the social anarchy of production gives place to a social regulation of production upon a definite plan, according to the needs of the community and of each individual. Then the capitalist mode of appropriation, in which the product enslaves first the producer, and then the appropriator, is replaced by the mode of appropriation of the products that is based upon the nature of the modern means of production; upon the one hand, direct social appropriation, as means to the maintenance and extension of production — on the other, direct individual appropriation, as means of subsistence and of enjoyment.

Whilst the capitalist mode of production more and more completely transforms the great majority of the population into proletarians, it creates the power which, under penalty of its own destruction, is forced to accomplish this revolution. Whilst it forces on more and more of the transformation of the vast means of production, already socialised, into State property, it shows itself the way to accomplishing this revolution. The proletariat seizes political power and turns the means of production into State property.

But, in doing this, it abolishes itself as proletariat, abolishes all class distinction and class antagonisms, abolishes also the State as State. Society, thus far, based upon class antagonisms, had need of the State. That is, of an organisation of the particular class which was, pro tempore, the exploiting class, an organisation for the purpose of preventing any interference from without with the existing conditions of production, and, therefore, especially, for the purpose of forcibly keeping the exploited classes in the condition of oppression corresponding with the given mode of production (slavery, serfdom, wage-labor). The State was the official representative of society as a whole; the gathering of it together into a visible embodiment. But, it was this only in so far as it was the State of that class which itself represented, for the time being, society as a whole: in ancient times, the State of slave-owning citizens; in the Middle Ages, the feudal lords; in our own times, the bourgeoisie.

When, at last, it becomes the real representative of the whole of society, it renders itself unnecessary. As soon as there is no longer any social class to be held in subjection; as soon as class rule, and the individual struggle for existence based upon our present anarchy in production, with the collisions and excesses arising from these, are removed, nothing more remains to be repressed, and a special repressive force, a State, is no longer necessary. The first act by virtue of which the State really constitutes itself the representative of the whole of society — the taking possession of the means of production in the name of society — this is, at the same time, its last independent act as a State. State interference in social relations becomes, in one domain after another, superfluous, and then dies out of itself; the government of persons is replaced by the administration of things, and by the conduct of processes of production. The State is not "abolished". It dies out. This gives the measure of the value of the phrase: "a free State", both as to its justifiable use at times by agitators, and as to its ultimate scientific inefficiency; and also of the demands of the so-called anarchists for the abolition of the State out of hand.

Since the historical appearance of the capitalist mode of production, the appropriation by society of all the means of production has often been dreamed of, more or less vaguely, by individuals, as well as by sects, as the ideal of the future. But it could become possible, could become a historical necessity, only when the actual conditions for its realisation were there. Like every other social advance, it becomes practicable, not by men understanding that the existence of classes is in contradiction to justice, equality, etc., not by the mere willingness to abolish these classes, but by virtue of certain new economic conditions. The separation of society into an exploiting and an exploited class, a ruling and an oppressed class, was the necessary consequences of the deficient and restricted development of production in former times. So long as the total social labour only yields a produce which but slightly exceeds that barely necessary for the existence of all; so long, therefore, as labour engages all or almost all the time of the great majority of the members of society — so long, of necessity, this society is divided into classes. Side by side with the great majority, exclusively bond slaves to labour, arises a class freed from directly productive labour, which looks after the general affairs of society: the direction of labour, State business, law, science, art, etc. It is, therefore, the law of division of labour that lies at the basis of the division into classes. But this does not prevent this division into classes from being carried out by means of violence and robbery, trickery and fraud. it does not prevent the ruling class, once having the upper hand, from consolidating its power at the expense of the working-class, from turning its social leadership into an intensified exploitation of the masses.

But if, upon this showing, division into classes has a certain historical justification, it has this only for a given period, only under given social conditions. It was based upon the insufficiency of production. It will be swept away by the complete development of modern productive forces. And, in fact, the abolition of classes in society presupposes a degree of historical evolution at which the existence, not simply of this or that particular ruling class, but of any ruling class at all, and, therefore, the existence of class distinction itself, has become a obsolete anachronism. It presupposes, therefore, the development of production carried out to a degree at which appropriation of the means of production and of the products, and, with this, of political domination, of the monopoly of culture, and of intellectual leadership by a particular class of society, has become not only superfluous but economically, politically, intellectually, a hindrance to development.

This point is now reached. Their political and intellectual bankruptcy is scarcely any longer a secret to the bourgeoisie themselves. Their economic bankruptcy recurs regularly every 10 years. In every crisis, society is suffocated beneath the weight of its own productive forces and products, which it cannot use, and stands helpless, face-to-face with the absurd contradiction that the producers have nothing to consume, because consumers are wanting. The expansive force of the means of production burst the bonds that the capitalist mode of production had imposed upon them. Their deliverance from these bonds is the one precondition for an unbroken, constantly-accelerated development of the productive forces, and therewith for a practically unlimited increase of production itself. Nor is this all. The socialised appropriation of the means of production does away, not only with the present artificial restrictions upon production, but also with the positive waste and devastation of productive forces and products that are at the present time the inevitable concomitants of production, and that reach their height in the crises. Further, it sets free for the community at large a mass of means of production and of products, by doing away with the senseless extravagance of the ruling classes of today, and their political representatives. The possibility of securing for every member of society, by means of socialised production, an existence not only fully sufficient materially, and becoming day-by-day more full, but an existence guaranteeing to all the free development and exercise of their physical and mental faculties — this possibility is now, for the first time, here, but it is here.

With the seizing of the means of production by society, production of commodities is done away with, and, simultaneously, the mastery of the product over the producer. Anarchy in social production is replaced by systematic, definite organisation. The struggle for individual existence disappears. Then, for the first time, man, in a certain sense, is finally marked off from the rest of the animal kingdom, and emerges from mere animal conditions of existence into really human ones. The whole sphere of the conditions of life which environ man, and which have hitherto ruled man, now comes under the dominion and control of man, who for the first time becomes the real, conscious lord of nature, because he has now become master of his own social organisation. The laws of his own social action, hitherto standing face-to-face with man as laws of Nature foreign to, and dominating him, will then be used with full understanding, and so mastered by him. Man's own social organisation, hitherto confronting him as a necessity imposed by Nature and history, now becomes the result of his own free action. The extraneous objective forces that have, hitherto, governed history, pass under the control of man himself. Only from that time will man himself, more and more consciously, make his own history — only from that time will the social causes set in movement by him have, in the main and in a constantly growing measure, the results intended by him. It is the ascent of man from the kingdom of necessity to the kingdom of freedom.

Let us briefly sum up our sketch of historical evolution.

I. Mediaeval Society — Individual production on a small scale. Means of production adapted for individual use; hence primitive, ungainly, petty, dwarfed in action. Production for immediate consumption, either of the producer himself or his feudal lord. Only where an excess of production over this consumption occurs is such excess offered for sale, enters into exchange. Production of commodities, therefore, only in its infancy. But already it contains within itself, in embryo, anarchy in the production of society at large.

II. Capitalist Revolution — transformation of industry, at first be means of simple cooperation and manufacture. Concentration of the means of production, hitherto scattered, into great workshops. As a consequence, their transformation from individual to social means of production — a transformation which does not, on the whole, affect the form of exchange. The old forms of appropriation remain in force. The capitalist appears. In his capacity as owner of the means of production, he also appropriates the products and turns them into commodities. Production has become a social act. Exchange and appropriation continue to be individual acts, the acts of individuals. The social product is appropriated by the individual capitalist. Fundamental contradiction, whence arise all the contradictions in which our present-day society moves, and which modern industry brings to light.

A. Severance of the producer from the means of production. Condemnation of the worker to wage-labor for life. Antagonism between the proletariat and the bourgeoisie.

B. Growing predominance and increasing effectiveness of the laws governing the production of commodities. Unbridled competition. Contradiction between socialised organisation in the individual factory and social anarchy in the production as a whole.

C. On the one hand, perfecting of machinery, made by competition compulsory for each individual manufacturer, and complemented by a constantly growing displacement of labourers. Industrial reserve-army. On the other hand, unlimited extension of production, also compulsory under competition, for every manufacturer. On both sides, unheard-of development of productive forces, excess of supply over demand, overproduction, glutting of the markets, crises every ten years, the vicious circle: excess here of means of production and products — excess there, of labourers, without employment and without means of existence. But these two levers of production and of social well-being are unable to work together, because the capitalist form of production prevents the productive forces from working and the products from circulating, unless they are first turned into capital — which their very superabundance prevents. The contradiction has grown into an absurdity. The mode of production rises in rebellion against the form of exchange.

D. Partial recognition of the social character of the productive forces forced upon the capitalists themselves. Taking over of the great institutions for production and communication, first by joint-stock companies, later in by trusts, then by the State. The bourgeoisie demonstrated to be a superfluous class. All its social functions are now performed by salaried employees.

III. Proletarian Revolution — Solution of the contradictions. The proletariat seizes the public power, and by means of this transforms the socialised means of production, slipping from the hands of the bourgeoisie, into public property. By this act, the proletariat frees the means of production from the character of capital they have thus far borne, and gives their socialised character complete freedom to work itself out. Socialised production upon a predetermined plan becomes henceforth possible. The development of production makes the existence of different classes of society thenceforth an anachronism. In proportion as anarchy in social production vanishes, the political authority of the State dies out. Man, at last the master of his own form of social organisation, becomes at the same time the lord over Nature, his own master — free.

To accomplish this act of universal emancipation is the historical mission of the modern proletariat. To thoroughly comprehend the historical conditions and this the very nature of this act, to impart to the now oppressed proletarian class a full knowledge of the conditions and of the meaning of the momentous act it is called upon to accomplish, this is the task of the theoretical expression of the proletarian movement, scientific Socialism.

NOTES

1. It is hardly necessary in this connection to point out that, even if the form of appropriation remains the same, the character of the appropriation is just as much revolutionised as production is by the changes described above. It is, of course, a very different matter whether I appropriate to myself my own product or that of another. Note in passing that wage-labor, which contains the whole capitalist mode of production in embryo, is very ancient; in a sporadic, scattered form, it existed for centuries alongside slave-labor. But the embryo could duly develop into the capitalistic mode of production only when the necessary historical pre-conditions had been furnished.

2. I say "have to". For only when the means of production and distribution have actually outgrown the form of management by joint-stock companies, and when, therefore, the taking them over by the State has become economically inevitable, only then — even if it is the State of today that effects this — is there an economic advance, the attainment of another step preliminary to the taking over of all productive forces by society itself. But of late, since Bismarck went in for State-ownership of industrial establishments, a kind of spurious Socialism has arisen, degenerating, now and again, into something of flunkeyism, that without more ado declares all State-ownership, even of the Bismarckian sort, to be socialistic. Certainly, if the taking over by the State of the tobacco industry is socialistic, then Napoleon and Metternich must be numbered among the founders of Socialism. If the Belgian State, for quite ordinary political and financial reasons, itself constructed its chief railway lines; if Bismarck, not under any economic compulsion, took over for the State the chief Prussian lines, simply to be the better able to have them in hand in case of war, to bring up the railway employees as voting cattle for the Government, and especially to create for himself a new source of income independent of parliamentary votes — this was, in no sense, a socialistic measure, directly or indirectly, consciously or unconsciously. Otherwise, the Royal Maritime Company, the Royal porcelain manufacture, and even the regimental tailor of the army would also be socialistic institutions, or even, as was seriously proposed by a sly dog in Frederick William III's reign, the taking over by the State of the brothels.

1880

Manifesto of the Socialist League

Ernest Belfort Bax and William Morris

FELLOW CITIZENS: WE COME BEFORE YOU as a body advocating the principles of Revolutionary International Socialism; that is, we seek a change in the basis of society — a change which would destroy the distinctions of classes and nationalities.

As the civilised world is at present constituted, there are two classes of society — the one possessing wealth and the instruments of its production, the other producing wealth by means of those instruments but only by the leave and for the use of the possessing classes.

These two classes are necessarily in antagonism to one another. The possessing class, or non-producers, can only live as a class on the unpaid labour of the producers — the more unpaid labour they can wring out of them, the richer they will be; therefore the producing class — the workers — are driven to strive to better themselves at the expense of the possessing class, and the conflict between the two is ceaseless. Sometimes it takes the form of open rebellion, sometimes of strikes, sometimes of mere widespread mendicancy and crime; but it is always going on in one form or other, though it may not always be obvious to the thoughtless looker-on.

We have spoken of unpaid labour: it is necessary to explain what that means. The sole possession of the producing class is the power of labour inherent in their bodies; but since, as we have already said, the richer classes possess all the instruments of labour, that is, the land, capital, and machinery, the producers or workers are forced to sell their sole possession, the power of labour, on such terms as the possessing class will grant them. These terms are, that after they have produced enough to keep them in working order, and enable them to beget children to take their places when they are worn out, the surplus of their products shall belong to the possessors of property, which bargain is based on the fact that every man working in a civilised community can produce more than he needs for his own sustenance.

This relation of the possessing class to the working class is the essential basis of the system of producing for a profit, on which our modern society is founded. The way in which it works is as follows. The manufacturer produces to sell at a profit to the broker or factor, who in his turn makes a profit out of his dealings with the merchant, who again sells for a profit to the retailer, who must make his profit out of the general public, aided by various degrees of fraud and adulteration and the ignorance of the value and quality of goods to which this system has reduced the consumer.

The profit-grinding system is maintained by competition, or veiled war, not only between the conflicting classes, but also within the classes themselves: there is always war among the workers for bare subsistence, and among their masters, the employers and middle-men, for the share of the profit wrung out of the workers; lastly, there is competition always, and sometimes open war, among the nations of the civilised world for their share of the world-market. For now, indeed, all the rivalries of nations have been reduced to this one — a degraded struggle for their share of the spoils of barbarous countries to be used at home for the purpose of increasing the riches of the rich and the poverty of the poor.

For, owing to the fact that goods are made primarily to sell, and only secondarily for use, labour is wasted on all hands; since the pursuit of profit compels the manufacturer competing with his fellows to force his wares on the markets by means of their cheapness, whether there is any real demand for them or not. In the words of the Communist Manifesto of 1847: "Cheap goods are the artillery for battering down Chinese walls and for overcoming the obstinate hatred entertained against foreigners by semi-civilised nations: under penalty of ruin the bourgeoisie compel by competition the universal adoption of their system of production; they force all nations to accept what is called civilisation — to become bourgeois — and thus the middle-class shapes the world after its own image."

Moreover, the whole method of distribution under this system is full of waste; for it employs whole armies of clerks, travellers, shopmen, advertisers, and what not, merely for the sake of shifting money from one person's pocket to another's; and this waste in production and waste in distribution, added to the maintenance of the useless lives of the possessing and non-producing class, must all be paid for out of the products of the workers, and is a ceaseless burden on their lives.

Therefore the necessary results of this so-called civilisation are only too obvious in the lives of its slaves, the working-class — in the anxiety and want of leisure amidst which they toil, in the squalor and wretchedness of those parts of our great towns where they dwell; in the degradation of their bodies, their wretched health, and the shortness of their lives; in the terrible brutality so common among them, and which is indeed but the reflection of the cynical selfishness found among the well-to-do classes, a brutality as hideous as the other; and lastly, in the crowd of criminals who are as much manufactures of our commercial system as the cheap and nasty wares which are made at once for the consumption and the enslavement of the poor.

What remedy, then, do we propose for this failure of our civilisation, which is now admitted by almost all thoughtful people?

We have already shown that the workers, although they produce all the wealth of society, have no control over its production or distribution: the people, who are the only really organic part of society, are treated as a mere appendage to capital — as a part of its machinery. This must be altered from the foundation: the land, the capital, the machinery, factories, workshops, stores, means of transit, mines, banking, all means of production and distribution of wealth, must be declared and treated as the common property of all. Every man will then receive the full value of his labour, without deduction for the profit of a master, and as all will have to work, and the waste now incurred by the pursuit of profit will be at an end, the amount of labour necessary for every individual to perform in order to carry on the essential work of the world will be reduced to something like two or three hours daily; so that every one will have abundant leisure for following intellectual or other pursuits congenial to his nature.

This change in the method of production and distribution would enable every one to live decently, and free from the sordid anxieties for daily livelihood which at present weigh so heavily on the greatest part of mankind. But, moreover, men's social and moral relations would be seriously modified by this gain of economical freedom, and by the collapse of the superstitions, moral and other, which necessarily accompany a state of economical slavery: the test of duty would now rest on the fulfilment of clear and well-defined obligations to the community rather than on the moulding of the individual character and actions to some preconceived standard outside social responsibilities.

Our modern bourgeois property-marriage, maintained as it is by its necessary complement, universal venal prostitution, would give place to kindly and human relations between the sexes.

Education freed from the trammels of commercialism on the one hand and superstition on the other, would become a reasonable drawing out of men's varied faculties in order to fit them for a life of social intercourse and happiness; for mere work would no longer be proposed as the end of life, but happiness for each and all.

Only by such fundamental changes in the life of man, only by the transformation of Civilisation into Socialism, can those miseries of the world before mentioned be amended.

As to mere politics, Absolutism, Constitutionalism, Republicanism, have all been tried in our day and under our present social system, and all have alike failed in dealing with the real evils of life.

Nor, on the other hand, will certain incomplete schemes of social reform now before the public solve the question. Co-operation so-called — that is, competitive co-operation for profit — would merely increase the number of small joint-stock capitalists, under the mask of creating an aristocracy of labour, while it would intensify the severity of labour by its temptations to overwork. Nationalisation of the land alone, which many earnest and sincere persons are now preaching, would be useless so long as labour was subject to the fleecing of surplus value inevitable under the Capitalist system.

No better solution would be that of State Socialism, by whatever name it may be called, whose aim it would be to make concessions to the working class while leaving the present system of capital and wages still in operation: no number of merely administrative changes, until the workers are in possession of all political power, would make any real approach to Socialism.

The Socialist League therefore aims at the realisation of complete Revolutionary Socialism, and well knows that this can never happen in any one country without the help of the workers of all civilisation. For us neither geographical boundaries, political history, race, nor creed makes rivals or enemies; for us there are no nations, but only varied masses of workers and friends, whose mutual sympathies are checked or perverted by groups of masters and fleecers whose interest it is to stir up rivalries and hatreds between the dwellers in different lands.

It is clear that for all these oppressed and cheated masses of workers and their masters a great change is preparing: the dominant classes are uneasy, anxious, touched in conscience even, as to the condition of those they govern; the markets of the world are being competed for with an eagerness never before known; everything points to the fact that the great commercial system is becoming unmanageable, and is slipping from the grasp of its present rulers.

The one change possible out of all this is Socialism. As chattel-slavery passed into serfdom, and serfdom into the so-called free-labour system, so most surely will this latter pass into social order.

To the realisation of this change the Socialist League addresses itself with all earnestness. As a means thereto it will do all in its power towards the education of the people in the principles of this great cause, and will strive to organise those who will accept this education, so that when the crisis comes, which the march of events is preparing, there may be a body of men ready to step into their due places and deal with and direct the irresistible movement.

Close fellowship with each other, and steady purpose for the advancement of the cause, will naturally bring about the organisation and discipline amongst ourselves absolutely necessary to success; but we shall look to it that there shall be no distinctions of rank or dignity amongst us to give opportunities for the selfish ambition of leadership which has so often injured the cause of the workers. We are working for equality and brotherhood for all the world, and it is only through equality and brotherhood that we can make our work effective.

Let us all strive, then, towards this end of realising the change towards social order, the only cause worthy the attention of the workers of all that are proffered to them: let us work in that cause patiently, yet hopefully, and not shrink from making sacrifices to it. Industry in learning its principles, industry in teaching them, are most necessary to our progress; but to these we must add, if we wish to avoid speedy failure, frankness and fraternal trust in each other, and single-hearted devotion to the religion of socialism, the only religion which the Socialist League professes.

1885

State socialists and social democrats

Henry Hyndman

A FEW DAYS AGO one of the oldest and most active members of the Social Democratic Federation opened an interesting discussion at that home of interesting discussions, the Central Branch of our organisation, upon the question whether we should repudiate the designation of State Socialists. He was in favour of our not doing so. His reasons, briefly, were that we are constantly appealing to the State, as the organised force of the whole nation, to remedy evils engendered by our economic system. When we are calling upon the State to feed our children, to organise the labour of the unemployed, to provide better education for all, to distribute our letters and telegrams cheaply and effectively, to take control of our railroads, to set on foot a thorough scheme for the housing of the people, etc., it is a contradiction in terms to say we are not in favour of State action, and that therefore it weakens our position to disclaim being State Socialists. Furthermore, we run no risk by accepting that designation. For what, after all, is the State? The State is the representative of the whole people, as distinguished from the various sections into which it is divided. It holds the balance between any conflicting interests; or, if it does not, this is its proper duty, and we ought not to assume it will decline to accept and fulfil this great trust. We have to look to the State as a collectivity to restrain tendencies to anarchy and to organise the forces of the nation for the increasing advantage of all. This idea of the State has been accepted by many great men in ancient and modern times, and the Greeks more particularly understood the function of the State as the ordering power of the entire people. The State, in fact, is what we choose to make it, and there is no inherent antagonism between the State and democracy. Therefore, Social Democrats need not be squeamish about being called State Socialists. Such was the argument.

Now it is worth while to deal seriously with points of this sort when they are raised. Socialism is no cut-and-dried collection of dogmas, which are to be taken without investigation. If each successive generation of Socialists considers itself bound to argue out over again all the bedrock principles of their creed, so much the better. The process will, as we believe, give them only a firmer grip of their entire soundness. And this of State Socialism and State Socialists is not a mere question of words. Much lies behind it, both in the abstract and in the concrete, in theory and in practice.

To begin with practice. No Social-Democrat who works for the attainment of our "stepping stones" through the State, regards those palliatives of existing capitalist anarchy as anything more than temporary ameliorations of unendurable conditions. The State is used for this purpose, not because we admire or even tolerate the State, but because, with all its innumerable drawbacks, it is the only machinery available for such partial improvement. We have no illusions whatever in the matter. We know and have frequently pointed out that if we realised them all as set forth above, they would, except in so far as they helped forward the breakdown of the whole capitalist system, and therefore the State, merely furnish forth better wage-slaves and better organisation for the profit-takers. That is indisputable. State departments maintain competition wage-earning and the whole of the forms of wage-slavery. Even if State employees are well-paid, and are assured of continuous employment, they are still only privileged menials, so long as they are unable conjointly with their fellows to control the entire management of the industrial community. State control of this sort may be better or it may be worse than private control, but brings with it no complete change from competition to cooperation such as we are striving for.

Moreover, there is an ever-present danger of fostering Caesarism and crystallising a bureaucracy, and the admission that we Democratic Socialists can be in any sense State-Socialists cannot fail greatly to increase this danger. Words still count largely in the formation of ideas. If we, as Social-Democrats, do not force into men's minds the truth that we are working and fighting for a complete social revolution, which shall abolish the present State and establish a Society in its place, we mislead our readers and hearers, and induce them to think we, too, are merely tinkerers with present forms of social development. That in itself is a great practical drawback to our allowing it to be thought for a moment that we are in any sense State-Socialists, or men and women who look to the State as a definite entity through which, without entire transformation, we can achieve our ultimate ends. The State means to the infinite majority of people a government dependent nominally upon the people, but imposing its authority from above. But that is precisely what we are endeavouring to overturn. To permit ourselves to be called State-Socialists without demur is to convey a false impression to the public mind. And all false impressions cause confusion and delay, and hamper the cause to which we have devoted ourselves.

So much for the practical and the concrete. Now for the abstract and the theoretical. We English, as a people, are terribly behindhand in all that relates to abstract thought or theoretical investigation. Yet it is impossible in many cases to arrive at the truth by direct concrete illustration that has no theoretical basis. Now the State, or the Civitas, as opposed to the Community, or the Societas, has always been based upon property and class interest and privilege, as opposed to kinship and common enjoyment and social equality. State rule always has meant class rule, and has involved a whole series of class antagonisms, at present in course of simplification into one great and final antagonism. The ordering of a State is through departments dominated by bureaucrats, who therefore dominate the people. The arrangement of a Society or Co-operative Commonwealth is by a series of citizens dominated by the community, who act as functions of the society, not as controllers of the society. Private property in the powers of producing and distributing wealth having been abrogated, the State, in any intelligible sense, ceases to exist. It is no longer, that is to say, a State constituted to restrain and "hold the balance" between conflicting interests; but a co-operative Social-Democracy, instituted to produce and distribute, and to increase the general health, wealth, and enjoyment by common consent for the advantage of all. There is then no State to handle and control, as the trusts virtually handle and control it in the nominal democracy of America, or as the aristocracy and plutocracy virtually handle and control it in the nominal democracy of the United Kingdom.

During the transition period, no doubt, we shall try, as we are trying today, to use the State against both landlords and capitalists; but we shall do so with the deliberate intention of putting an end to the State, just as we shall abolish Capital, altogether. Consequently, we are no more State-Socialists than we are Capital-Socialists. We recognise that the State and Capital are inevitable stages in social evolution, which will endure a longer or a shorter time as circumstances or experience may determine. But both will have to go. So I, for one, refuse to let myself be called a State-Socialist when I am doing my best to sweep away the State.

Justice, 15 July 1905

Industrial unionism

Eugene V Debs

THE UNITY OF LABOUR, economic and political, upon the basis of the class struggle, is at this time the supreme need of the working class. The prevailing lack of unity implies lack of class consciousness; that is to say, enlightened self-interest; and this can, must and will be overcome by revolutionary education and organisation. Experience, long, painful and dearly bought, has taught some of us that craft division is fatal to class unity. To accomplish its mission the working class must be united. They must act together; they must assert their combined power, and when they do this upon the basis of the class struggle, then and then only will they break the fetters of wage slavery.

We are engaged today in a class war; and why? For the simple reason that in the evolution of the capitalist system in which we live, society has been mainly divided into two economic classes — a small class of capitalists who own the tools with which work is done and wealth is produced, and a great mass of workers who are compelled to use those tools. Between these two classes there is an irrepressible economic conflict. Unfortunately for himself, the workingman does not yet understand the nature of the conflict, and for this reason has hitherto failed to accomplish any effective unity of his class.

It is true that workers in the various departments of industrial activity have organised trade unions. It is also true that in this capacity they have from time to time asserted such power as this form of organisation has conferred upon them. It is equally true that mere craft unionism, no matter how well it may be organised, is in the present highly developed capitalist system utterly unable to successfully cope with the capitalist class. The old craft union has done its work and belongs to the past. labour unionism, like everything else, must recognise and bow to the inexorable law of evolution.

The craft union says that the worker shall receive a fair day's pay for a fair day's work. What is a fair day's pay for a fair day' work? Ask the capitalist and he will give you his idea about it. Ask the worker and, if he is intelligent, he will tell you that a fair day's pay for a fair day's work is all the workingman produces.

While the craft unionist still talks about a fair day's pay for a fair day's work, implying that the economic interests of the capitalist and the worker can be harmonised upon a basis of equal justice to both, the Industrial Worker says, "I want all I produce by my labour.'

If the worker is not entitled to all he produces, then what share is anybody else entitled to? Does the worker today receive all he produces? Does he receive anything like a fair (?) share of the product of his labour? Will any trade-unionist of the old school make any such claim, and if he is bold enough to make it, can he verify it?

The student of this question knows that, as a matter of fact, in the capitalist system in which we live today the worker who produces all wealth receives but enough of his product to keep him in working and producing order. His wage, in the aggregate, is fixed by his living necessities. It suffices, upon the average, to maintain him according to the prevailing standard of living and to enable him to reproduce himself in the form of labour power. He receives, as a matter of fact, but about 17 per cent of what his labour produces.

The worker produces a certain thing. It goes from the manufacturer to the jobber, from the jobber to the wholesaler, and from the wholesaler to the retailer — each of these adding a profit, and when it completes the circle and comes back to the worker who produced it and he stands face to face with the product of his own labour, he can buy back, upon the average, with his paltry wage but about 17 per cent of it. In other words, he is exploited, robbed, of about 83 per cent of what his labour produces. And why? For the simple reason that in modern industry, the tool, in the form of a great machine with which he works and produces, is the private property of the capitalist, who didn't make it, and could not, if his life depended upon it, use it.

The evolution is not yet complete.

By virtue of his private ownership of the social tool — made and used by the co-operative labour of the working class — the employer has the economic power to appropriate to himself, as a capitalist, what is produced by the social labour of the working class. This accounts for the fact that the capitalist becomes fabulously rich, lives in a palace where there is music and singing and dancing, and where there is the luxury of all climes, while the workingmen who do the work and produce the wealth and endure the privations and make the sacrifices of health and limb and life, remain in a wretched state of poverty and dependence.

The exploiting capitalist is the economic master and the political ruler in capitalist society, and as such holds the exploited wage worker in utter contempt. No master ever had any respect for his slave, and no slave ever had, or ever could have, any real love for his master.

I must beg you to indulge the hoarseness of my voice, which has been somewhat strained addressing meetings of the Industrial Workers held in and about Chicago during the last two or three evenings; but, fortunately, my eyesight has not been strained reading the accounts of these meetings in the capitalist papers of Chicago. Alert, vigilant, argus-eyed as the capitalist dailies of Chicago are, there is not one of them that knows of this meeting of the Industrial Workers. But if this were a meeting of the American Federation of labour and an old trade union leader were here, you would read tomorrow morning a full account of it and him in every capitalist paper in the city. There is a reason for this that explains itself.

The capitalist papers know that there is such an organisation as the Industrial Workers, because they have lied about it. Just now they are ignoring it. Let me serve notice on them through you and the thousands of other who flock to our meetings everywhere, that they will reckon with the Industrial Workers before six months have rolled around.

There are those wage workers who feel their economic dependence, who know that the capitalist for whom they work is the owner of their job, and therefore the master of their fate, who are still vainly seeking by individual effort and through waning craft unions to harmonise the conflicting interests of the exploiting capitalist and the exploited wage slave. They are engaged in a vain and hopeless task. They are wasting time and energy worthy of a better cause. These interests never can and never will be harmonised permanently, and when they are adjusted even temporarily it is always at the expense of the working class.

It is no part of the mission of this revolutionary working class union to conciliate the capitalist class. We are organised to fight that class, and we want that class to distinctly understand it. And they do understand it, and in time the working class will also understand it; and then the capitalist class will have reason to understand it better still. Their newspapers understand it so well even now that they have not a single favourable comment to make upon it.

When the convention of delegates was in session here in June last for the purpose of organising the Industrial Workers, every report that appeared in a Chicago paper — capitalist paper I mean — every single report was a tissue of perversion, misstatement and downright falsehood. They knew that we had met for a purpose, and that purpose was to fight the class of which they are the official mouthpieces. Now, it seems to me that this uniform hostility of the capitalist press ought to be significant to even the unthinking workingman.

Capitalist papers are, as a rule, quite friendly to the craft unions. They do not misrepresent them; do no lie about them; do not traduce their representatives. They are exceedingly fond of them, because they know enough about their own interests to know that the craft unions are not only not a menace to them, but are in fact bulwarks of defence to them.

And why? Because, chiefly, craft unions divide and do not unite the working class. And I challenge contradiction. There was a time when the craft union expressed in terms of unionism the prevailing mode of industry. That was long ago when production was still mainly carried on by handicraftsmen with hand tools; when one man worked for another to learn his trade that he might become its master. The various trades involved skill and cunning; considerable time was required to master them. This was in the early stages of the capitalist system. Even at that early day the antagonism between employer and employed found expression, although the employer was not at that time the capitalist as he is today. The men who followed these trades found it necessary in order to protect themselves in their trade interests to band together, form a union, so that they might act together in resisting the encroachments of the "boss". So the trade union came into existence.

The mode of production since that time has been practically revolutionised. The hand tool has all but disappeared. The mammoth machine has taken its place. The hand tool was made and used by the individual worker and was largely within his own control. Today the machine that has supplanted the old tool is not owned nor controlled by the man, or rather the men, who use it. As I have already said, it is the private property of some capitalist who may live at a remote point and never have seen the machine or the wage slaves who operate it.

In other words, the production of wealth, in the evolution of industry, from being an individual act a half century ago has become a social act. The tool, from being an individual tool, has become a social instrument. So that the tool has been socialised and production has also been socialised. But the evolution is yet to complete its work. This social tool, made socially and used socially, must be socially owned.

In the evolution of industry the trade has been largely undermined. The old trade union expresses the old form of industry, the old mode of individual production based upon the use of the individual tool. That tool has about disappeared; that mode of production has also about disappeared, but the trade union built upon that mode of production, springing from the use of the hand tool, remains essentially the same.

The pure and simple trade union, in seeking to preserve its autonomy, is forced into conflict with other trade unions by the unceasing operation of the laws of industrial evolution. How many of the skilled trades that were in operation half a century ago are still practised?

At the town where I live there used to be quite a number of cooper shops. Barrels were made by hand and a cooper shop consisted wholly of coopers. The coopers' union was organised and served fairly well the purposes of the coopers of that day, but it does not serve the purposes of the workers who make barrels today. They do not make barrels in the

287

way they used to be made. Today we want a union that expresses the economic interests of all the workers in the cooperage plant engaged in making and handling barrels. But a few coopers still remain, a very few. It is no longer necessary to be a cooper to make a barrel. The machine is the cooper today. The machine makes the barrel, and almost anyone can operate the machine that makes the barrel.

You will observe that labour has been subdivided and specialised and that the trade has been dissipated; and now a body of men and boys work together co-operatively in the making of a barrel, each making a small part of a barrel. Now we want a union which embraces all the workers engaged in making barrels. We lose sight of the cooper trade as evolution has practically disposed of that. We say that since the trade has completely changed, the union which expressed that trade must also change accordingly. In the new union we shall include not only the men who are actually engaged in the making of barrels directly, but also those who are placing them upon the market. There are the typewriters, the bookkeepers, the teamsters, and all other classes of labour that are involved in the making and delivering of the barrels. We insist that all the workers in the whole of any given plant shall belong to one and the same union.

This is the very thing the workers need and the capitalist who owns the establishment does not want. He believes in labour unionism if it is the "right kind". And if it is the right kind for him it is the wrong kind for you. He is more than willing that his employers shall join the craft union. He has not the slightest objection. On the contrary, it is easily proven that capitalists are among the most active upholders of the old craft unions.

The capitalists are perfectly willing that you shall organise, as long as you don't do a thing against them; as long as you don't do a thing for yourselves. You cannot do a thing for yourselves without antagonising them; and you don't antagonise them through your craft unions nearly as much as you buttress their interests and prolong their mastery.

The average workingman imagines that he must have a leader to look to; a guide to follow, right or wrong. He has been taught in the craft union that he is a very dependent creature; that without a leader the goblins would get him without a doubt, and he therefore instinctively looks to his leader. And even while he is looking at his leader there is someone else looking at the same leader from the other side.

You have depended too much on that leader and not enough on yourself. I don't want you to follow me. I want you to cultivate self-reliance. If I have the slightest capacity for leadership I can only give evidence of it by leading you to rely upon yourselves.

As long as you can be led by an individual you will be betrayed by an individual. That does not mean that all leaders are dishonest or corrupt. I make no such sweeping indictment. I know that many of them are honest. I know also that many of them are in darkness themselves, blind leaders of the blind. That is the worst that can be said of them. And let me say to you that the most dangerous leader is not the corrupt leader, but the honest, ignorant leader. That leader is just as fatal to your interests as the one who deliberately sells you out for a paltry consideration.

You are a workingman! Now, at your earliest leisure look yourself over and take an inventory of your resources. Invoice your mental stock; see what you have on hand.

You may be of limited mentality; and that is all you require in the capitalist system. You need only small brains, but huge hands.

Most of your hands are calloused and you are taught by the capitalist politician, who is the political mercenary of the capitalist who fleeces you, you are taught by him to be proud of your horny hands. If that is true he ought to be ashamed of his. He doesn't have any horns on his hands. He has them on his brain. He is as busy with his brain as you are with your hands, and because he is busy with his brain and you neglect yours, he gets a goodly share of what you produce with your hands. He is the gentleman who calls you the horny handed sons of toil. That fetches you every time. I tell you that the time has come for you to use your brains in your own interest, and until you do that you will have to use your hands in the interest of your masters.

Now, after you have looked yourself over; after you have satisfied yourself what you are, or rather, what you are not, you will arrive at the conclusion that as a wage worker in capitalist society you are not a man at all. You are simply a thing. And that thing is bought in the labour market, just as hair, hides and other forms of merchandise are bought.

When the capitalist requires the use of your hands, does he call for men? Why, certainly not. He doesn't want men, he only wants hands. And when he calls for hands, that is what he wants. Have you ever seen a placard posted: "Fifty hands wanted"? Did you ever know of a capitalist to respond to that kind of an invitation?

President [Theodore] Roosevelt would have you believe that there are no classes in the United States. He was made president by the votes of the working class. Did you ever know of his stopping over night in the home of a workingman? Is it by mere chance that he is always sheltered beneath the hospitable roof of some plutocrat? Not long ago he made a visit here and he gave a committee representing the workers about fifteen minutes of his precious time, just time enough to rebuke them with the intimation that organised labour consisted of a set of lawbreakers, and then he gave fifteen hours to the plutocrats of Chicago, being wined and dined by them to prove that there are no classes in the United States, and that you, horny handed veteran, with your wage of $1.50 a day, with six children to support on that, are in the same class with John D. Rockefeller! Your misfortune is that you do not know you are in the same class. But on election day it dawns upon you and you prove it by voting the same ticket.

Since you have looked yourself over thoroughly, you realise by this time that, as a workingman, you have been supporting, through your craft unions and through your ballots, a social system that is the negation of your manhood.

The capitalist for whom you work doesn't have to go out and look for you; you have to look for him, and you belong to him just as completely as if he had a title to your body; as if you were his chattel slave.

He doesn't own you under law, but he does under the fact.

Why? Because he owns the tool with which you work, and you have got to have access to that tool if you work; and if you want to live you have got to work. If you don't work you don't eat; and so, scourged by hunger pangs, you look about for that tool and you locate it, and you soon discover that between yourself, a workingman, and that tool that is an essential part of yourself in industry, there stands the capitalist who owns it. He is your boss; he owns your job, takes your product and controls your destiny. Before you can touch that tool to earn a dime you must petition the owner of it to allow you to use it, in consideration of your giving to him all you produce with it, except just enough to keep you alive and in working order.

Observe that you are displaced by the surplus product of your own labour; that what you produce is of more value under capitalism than you who produce it; that the commodity which is the result of your labour is of greater value under capitalism than your own life. You consist of palpitating flesh; you have wants. You have necessities. You cannot satisfy them, and you suffer. But the product of your labour, the property of the capitalist, that is sacred; that must be protected at all hazards. After you have been displaced by the surplus product of your labour and you have been idle long enough, you become restive and you begin to speak out, and you become a menace. The unrest culminates in trouble. The capitalist presses a button and the police are called into action. Then the capitalist presses button No. 2 and injunctions are issued by the judges, the judicial allies and servants of the capitalist class. Then button No. 3 is pressed and the state troops fall into line; and if this is not sufficient button No. 4 is pressed and the regular soldiers come marching to the scene. That is what President Roosevelt meant when he said that back of the mayor is the governor, back of the governor the President; or, to use his own words, back of the city, the state, and back of the state, the nation — the capitalist nation.

If you have been working in a steel mill and you have made more steel than your master can sell, and you are locked out and get hungry, and the soldiers are called out, it is to protect the steel and shoot you who made the steel — to guard the men who steal the steel and kill the men who made it.

I am not asking you to withdraw from the craft unions simply because the Industrial Workers has been formed. I am asking you to think about these matters for yourselves.

I belonged to a craft union from the time I was nineteen years of age. I can remember the very evening I first joined the Brotherhood of Locomotive Firemen. I can recall with what zeal I went to work to organise my craft, and it was the pride of my life to see that union expand. I did what I could to build it up. In time I was made to realise that that union was not sufficient unto itself. I next did what I could to organise other branches of the service and then establish a federation of the various unions of railroad employees, and finally succeeded; but soon after the federation was formed, on account of craft jealousies, it was disrupted. I then, along with a number of others who had had the same experience and had profited by it, undertook to organise the railway men within one organisation, known as the American Railway Union. The railroad corporations were the deadly enemies of that organisation. They understood that its purpose was to unify all the railroad employees. They knew that the unity of the working class meant their end, and so they set their faces like flint against the American Railway Union. And while they were using all their powers to crush and to stamp out the American Railway Union, they were bestowing all their favours upon the several craft brotherhoods, the engineers and the firemen, the conductors and the brakemen. They knew that so long as these craft unions existed there could be no unification of the men employed in the railway service.

Are the railroad men of this country organised today? No! Not nearly one-half of them are organised at all. And when the railroad corporations from motives of good policy make a concession to the engineers or the conductors, it is gouged out of the poor devils who work for a dollar a day and are compelled to submit.

There are a great many engineers who are perfectly willing to be tied up in a contract. They think they can save themselves at the expense of their fellow-workers. But they are going to reap, sooner or later, just what they have sown. In the next few years they will become motormen.

While we are upon this question, let us consult industrial history a moment. We will begin with the craft union railroad strike of 1888. The Brotherhood of Engineers and the Brotherhood of Firemen on the C., B. & Q. system went out on strike. Some 2,000 engineers and firemen vacated their posts and went out on one of the most bitterly contested railroad strikes, the rest of the employees, especially the conductors, who were organised in craft unions of their own, remained at their posts, and the union conductors piloted the scab engineers over the line. I know whereof I speak. I was there. I took an active part in that strike.

I saw craft union pitted against craft union, and I saw the Brotherhood of Engineers and the Brotherhood of Firemen completely wiped from the C.,B. & Q. system. And now you find these men, seventeen years later, scattered all over the United States. They had to pay the penalty of their ignorance in organising a craft instead of organising as a whole.

In 1892 a strike occurred on the Lehigh Valley; the same result. Another on the Toledo, Ann Arbor & North Michigan. Same result. The engineers have had no strike from that time to this. Every time they have had a strike they have been defeated.

The railroad corporations are shrewd enough to recognise the fact that if they can keep certain departments in their employ in a time of emergency they can defeat all the rest. A manager of a railroad who can keep control of 15 per cent of the old men can allow 85 per cent to go out on strike and defeat them every time. That is why they have made some concessions to the engineers and conductors and brakesmen, and now and then to the switchmen, the most militant labour union of them all.

A year and a half ago the telegraph operators on the Missouri, Kansas & Texas went out on strike. The engineer remained at his post; so did the fireman; the conductor at his; and the brakeman at his. And they hauled the scabs that flocked from all parts of the country to the several points along the line, and delivered them in good order to take the places vacated by the strikers; worked all round them and with them until they had mastered the details of their several duties; and having done this, the strike was at an end, and the 1,300 craft unionists out of jobs. You will find them scattered all over the country.

Now, were not these other craft unions scabbing on the telegraphers just as flagrantly as if they had stepped into their positions and discharged their duties? They were acting with the corporation against their union fellow workingmen, helping the corporation to defeat and crush them. Without their aid the corporation could not have succeeded. With their aid it was very easily done.

Is it possible that a craft unionist can see such an object lesson as this so plainly presented to him and still refuse to profit by it? Still close his eyes and, as it were, shut up his reason, and absolutely decline to see that this is suicidal policy and that its fruit must always be disruption and disaster?

This world only respects as it is compelled to respect; and if you workingmen would be respected you must begin by respecting yourselves. You have had enough of this sort of experience. You have had more than enough of it right here in Chicago.

Why didn't the steel trust annihilate the Amalgamated Steelworkers? Only two years ago they defeated them completely. The trust had its iron heel upon the neck of the Steelworkers' Union, and could have, had it chosen, completely crushed the life out of it. But Morgan was too wily. Schwab was too wise. They used to oppose trade unions. They don't oppose them any longer. They have discovered that a union can be turned the other way; that it can be made useful to them instead of being useful to the working class. Morgan now says he is in favour of trade unions, and Schwab agrees. They didn't crush out the Steelworkers' Union because they knew that another and a better one would spring from its ruins. They were perfectly willing that the old craft union should grow up again and block the way to real union.

You have had a machinists' strike here in Chicago. You are well aware of this without my telling you. There is something pathetic to me about every strike.

I have said and say again that no strike was ever lost; that it has always been worth all it cost. An essential part of a workingman's education is the defeats he encounters. The strikes he loses are after all the only ones he wins. I am heartily glad for myself that I lost the strike. It is the best thing that ever happened to me. I lost the strike of the past that I may win the strike of the future.

I am a discredited labour leader, but I have good staying qualities. The very moment the capitalist press credits me with being a wise labour leader, I will invite you to investigate me upon the charge of treason. I am discredited by the capitalist simply because I am true to his victim. I don't want his favours. I do not court his approbation. I would not have it. I can't afford it. If I had his respect it would be at the price of my own.

I don't care anything about what is called public opinion. I know precisely what that means. It is but the reflect of the interests of the capitalist class. As between the respect of the public and my own, I prefer my own; and I am going to keep it until I can have both.

When I pick up a capitalist newspaper and read a eulogy of some labour leader, I know that that leader has at least two afflictions; the one is mental weakness and the other is moral cowardice — and they go together. Put it down that when the capitalist who is exploiting you credits your leader with being safe and conservative and wise, that leader is not serving you. And if you take exception to that statement, just ask me to prove it.

The rank and file of all unions, barring their ignorance, are all right. The working class as a whole is all right. Many of them are misguided, and stand in the light of their own interest.

It is sometimes necessary that we offend you and even shock you, that you may understand that we are your friends and not your enemies. And if we are against your unions it is because we are for you. We know that you have paid your dues into them for years and that you are animated by a spirit of misdirected loyalty to those unions.

I can remember that it was not a very easy matter for me to give up the union in which I had spent my boyhood and all the years of my young manhood. I remember that I felt there was something in it in the nature of a sacrifice, and yet I had to make it in the nature of a sacrifice, and yet I had to make it in the interest of the larger duty that I owned myself and the working class.

Let me say to you, if you are a craft unionist, that infinitely greater than your loyalty to your craft is your loyalty to the working class as a whole. No craft union can fight this great battle successfully alone. The craft is a part, a part only, of the great body of the working class. And the time has come for his class, numerically overwhelming in the majority, to follow in one respect at least the example of its capitalist masters and unite as whole.

In this barbarous competitive struggle in which we are engaged, the workers, the millions, are fighting each other to sell themselves into slavery; the middle class are fighting each other to other to get enough trade to keep soul and body together, and the professional class are fighting each other like savages for practice. And this is called civilisation! What a mockery! What a sham! There is no real civilisation in the capitalist system.

Today there is nothing so easily produced as wealth. The whole earth consists of raw materials; and in every breath of nature, in sunshine, and in shower, hidden everywhere, are the subtle forces that may, by the touch of the hand of labour, be set into operation to transmute these raw materials into wealth, the finished products, in all their multiplied forms and in opulent abundance for all. The merest child can press a button that will set in operation a forest of machinery and produce wealth enough for a community.

Whatever may be said of the ignorant, barbarous past, there is no excuse for poverty today. And yet it is the scourge of the race. It is the Nemesis of capitalist civilisation. Ten millions, one-eighth of our whole population, are in a state of chronic poverty. Three millions of these have been sunk to unresisting pauperism. The whole working class is in a sadly dependent state, and even the most favoured wage-worker is left suspended by a single thread. He does not know what hour a machine may be invented to make his trade useless, displace him and throw him into the increasing army of the unemployed.

And how does labour live today? Here in Chicago you may walk along a certain boulevard, say 18th Street, and you will find it lined with magnificent palaces. Beyond that you will find a larger district where the still complacent middle class abide. Beyond that is a very much larger territory where the working class exist; and still beyond that, to complete the circle, you see the red lights flickering in the distance. Prostitution is a part, a necessary part, of capitalist society. The department store empties in the slums.

I have been here enough to know that when the daughter of a workingman is obliged to go up the street to look for employment, when she is fourteen or fifteen years of age, and ought to be in the care and keeping of a loving mother, and have all of the advantages that our civilisation makes possible for all — when she is forced to go to a department store, to one of those capitalist emporiums, and there find a place, if she can, and work for a wage of $3 a week, and have to obey a code of cast-iron regulations, appear tidy and neatly dressed and be subjected to a thousand temptations daily, and then takes a misstep, the first, as she is more than apt to do, especially if she has no home in any decent sense of that term — the very instant this is added to her poverty, she is doomed — damned. All the doors of capitalist society are closed in her face. The coals of contumely are poured upon her head. There is for her no redemption, and she takes the next step, and the next, until at last she ends a disgraceful career in a brothel hell.

This may be your child. And if you are a workingman, and this should fall to the lot of the innocent blue-eyed child that you love more than you do your own life — I want you to realise that if such a horror be written in the book of fate, that you are responsible for it, if you use or misuse your power to perpetuate the capitalist system and working class slavery.

You can change this condition — not tomorrow, not next week, nor next year; but in the meantime the next thing to changing it is making up your mind that it shall be changed. That is what we Industrial Unionists have done. And so there has come to us a new state of mind, and in our hearts there is the joy of service and the serenity of triumph.

We are united and we cannot be disunited. We cannot be stampeded. We know that we are confronted by ten thousand difficulties. We know that all the powers of capitalism are to be arrayed against us. But were these obstacles multiplied by a million, it would simply have the effect of multiplying our determination by a million, to overcome them all. And so we are organising and appealing to you.

The workingman today does not understand his industrial relation to his fellow-workers. He has never been correlated with others in the same industry. He has mechanically done his part. He has simply been a cog, with little reference to, or knowledge of, the rest of the cogs. Now, we teach him to hold up his head and look over the whole mechanism. If he is employed in a certain plant, as an Industrial Unionist, his eyes are opened. He takes a survey of the entire productive mechanism, and he understands his part in it, and his relation to every other worker in that industry. The very instant he does that he is buoyed by a fresh hope and thrilled with a new aspiration. He becomes a larger man. He begins to feel like a collective son of toil.

Then he and his fellows study to fit themselves to take control of this productive mechanism when it shall be transferred from the idle capitalist to the workers to whom it rightfully belongs.

In every mill and every factory, every mine and every quarry, every railroad and every shop, everywhere, the workers, enlightened, understanding their self-interest, are correlating themselves in the industrial and economic mechanism. They are developing their industrial consciousness, their economic and political power; and when the revolution comes, they will be prepared to take possession and assume control of every industry. With the education they will have received in the Industrial Workers they will be drilled and disciplined, trained and fitted for Industrial Mastery and Social Freedom.

Speech in Chicago, 25 November 1905

The socialist ideal

Paul Lafargue

OUR COMRADES IN GERMANY were discussing some time since the question whether Socialism is a science. Socialism is not and cannot be a science for the simple reason that it is a political party and must disappear when its work is accomplished after the abolition of the classes which gave birth to it; but the end which it pursues is scientific.

Guizot, who had a vague idea of the theory of the class struggle — himself a product of the Revolution, which was a dramatic struggle between classes — said with good reason that a class cannot emancipate itself until it possesses the qualities requisite for taking the leadership of society; now one of these qualities is to have a more or less definite conception of the social order which it proposes to substitute for that which is oppressing it. This conception cannot but be a social ideal, or, to employ a scientific word, a social hypothesis; but an hypothesis, as well in the natural sciences as in social science, may be utopian or scientific.

Socialism, because it is a political party of the oppressed class, has therefore an ideal. It groups and organises the efforts of the individuals who wish to build on the ruins of capitalist society, based upon individual property, an ideal or hypothetical society based upon common property in the means of production.

Only through the class struggle can modern socialism realise its social ideal, which possesses the dualities demanded of any hypothesis that claims a scientific character. The fact of choosing a scientific goal, and of trying to reach it only through the class struggle, distinguishes it from the Socialism of 1848, which was pursuing through the reconciliation of classes a social ideal which could not but be utopian considering the historic moment in which it was conceived. Socialism has thus evolved from Utopia into science. Engels has traced the main lines of this evolution in his memorable pamphlet, *Socialism, Utopian and Scientific*. It is the same with all sciences, which begin with Utopia to arrive at positive knowledge; this course is imposed by the very nature of the human mind.

Man progresses in social life as in intellectual life, only by starting from the known and travelling toward the unknown, and that unknown must be represented by the imagination; that imaginary conception of the unknown, which cannot but be hypothetical, is one of the most powerful incentives to action, it is the very condition of every forward step. It is natural that men like Bernstein in Germany and Jaurès in France should seek to domesticate Socialism and to put it in tow of liberalism, accusing it of hypnotising its soldiers with an ideal of the year 3000, which makes them live in the expectation of a Messianic "catastrophe" and reject the immediate advantages of an understanding and cooperation with bourgeois parties, and which blinds them to their shocking errors regarding the concentration of wealth, the disappearance of small industry and the middle class, the increase of class antagonisms, the spreading and intensification of the misery of the working class, etc. These errors may have been plausible hypotheses before 1848, but since then events have shown their falsity. This unfortunate ideal prevents them from descending from the revolutionary heights to accept the responsibilities of power and of setting aside the cause of labour to devote themselves entirely tongue and pen, to the rehabilitation of a millionaire leader; it obliges them to oppose all exterior policies and acts, to vote not a cent nor a soldier for colonial expeditions, which carry labour, Christianity, syphilis and the alcoholism of civilisation to the barbaric tribes. The neo-methodists of the ancient and outworn gospel of the brotherhood of classes advise the socialists to suppress their ideal, or, since it unfortunately captivates the masses of the people, to speak of it without caring for it, as Jaurès does, that they may consecrate themselves to practical necessities, to the vast plans of agricultural and industrial co-operation, to popular universities, etc.

The dilettantes of politics, these practical groundlings of opportunism, nevertheless hold themselves up for transcendent idealists and march with their eyes fixed upon the stars, because they substitute for ideas a brilliant orchestra of sonorous words and eternal principles.

These bourgeois idealists edge their way in everywhere; after the Revolution of 1789 they rebuked the scientists for their hypotheses and their theories; according to them science should have stopped with the study of facts in themselves without dreaming of uniting them into a general system. "What is the use of cutting stones without putting up a building", replied Geoffroy-Saint-Hilaire, the genial disciple of Lamarck, who lived to see the extinction of his theory on the continuity of species, which, only thirty years after his death, was to take on a new birth with Darwin. They are still reproaching the physiologists for wasting their time in elaborating hypotheses which last on an average only three years and which cannot explain what takes place in a muscle which contracts and in a brain which thinks. They grumble against the hypotheses of the physicists, who do not know the real nature of elasticity, of electrical conductivity, or even what happens when a particle of sugar is dissolved. They would like to prohibit scientists from any speculation because it is disastrous and may lead into error. But the latter protest and declare that imagination is one of the first and most indispensable faculties of the scientist, and that the hypotheses to which they give birth, even though they be erroneous and able to survive only three years are nevertheless the necessary condition of all scientific progress.

If the communist ideal were an hypothesis undemonstrable and false it would still be a propelling force of social progress, but such is not the case.

The hypothesis in science, as in the social field, is the more undemonstrable and susceptible of error in proportion as the data contributing to its elaboration are less numerous and more uncertain. Greek science, which had to furnish a conception of the world when the data regarding the phenomena of nature were of the most rudimentary, was obliged to resort to hypotheses which for boldness and intuitive accuracy are marvels of history and of thought; after having admitted, according to the vulgar opinion, that the earth was flat, and that the temple of Delphi was situated at its center, they put forth the hypothesis of its spherical form, then undemonstrable.

Socialism, which dates from the first years of the nineteenth century, started, like Greek science, from hypotheses the more erroneous, and from ideals the more utopian, in that the social world which it proposed to transform was less known; and at that epoch could not be known for the excellent reason that it was in course of formation.

The machine operated by steam was beginning to edge into industry where the tool, managed by the artisan, was moved by human power, and in some rare circumstances by animals, wind or waterfalls. The Socialist thinkers, as Engels observes, were then obliged to draw from their own brain the social ideal which they could not extract from the tumultuous economic environment in full course of transformation. They grasped again, infusing new life into it, the communist ideal which has slumbered in the mind of man since he emerged from the communism of primitive society which the poetic Greek mythology calls the golden age and which has awakened to shine here and there with a glorious splendour at great epochs of social upheaval. They sought, then, to establish communism, not because the economic environment was ready for its introduction, but because men were miserable, because the laws of justice and equality were violated, because the precepts of the Christ could not be followed in their purity. The communistic ideal, not springing from economic reality, was then but an unconscious reminiscence of a prehistoric past, and came only from idealistic notions upon a justice, an equality and a gospel law no less idealistic; it is then idealistic in the second degree, and consequently utopian.

The Socialists of the first half of the nineteenth century, who rekindled the communist ideal, had the rare merit of giving it a consistency less

299

idealistic. They spoke little of the Christian religion, of justice and of equality; Robert Owen laid the responsibilities of social evils upon the family, property and religion; Charles Fourier criticised the ideas of justice and morality introduced by the bourgeois Revolution of '89 with incomparable animation and irony. They did not weep over the misery of the poor, but left that to Victor Hugo and the charlatans of romanticism. They preached the social problem from its realistic side, the only side from which it can be solved. They used their talents to prove that a social organisation of production would succeed in satisfying the desires of all without reducing the share of any, not even that of the privileged capitalist class. Meanwhile the recent application of steam and machinery demanded also a new organisation of labour, and this was the constant concern of the industrial bourgeoisie. The socialists were thus pursuing the same end as the industrialists; bourgeois and socialists might consequently come to an understanding. We therefore find in the socialist sects of that epoch industrialists, engineers and financiers who in the second half of the century cast away their sympathy for the workers and occupied an important place in capitalist society.

The socialism of that epoch could not under these conditions be anything else than pacific; instead of entering on the struggle with the capitalists, the socialists thought only of converting them to their system of social reform from which they were to be the first to benefit. They proclaimed the association of capital, intelligence and labour, the interests of which according to them, were identical! They preached a mutual understanding between the employer and the employed, between the exploiter and the exploited; they know no class struggle: they condemned strikes and all political agitation, especially if it were revolutionary; they desired order in the street and harmony in the workshop. They demanded, finally, nothing more than was desired by the new industrial bourgeoisie.

They foresaw that industry, strengthened by the motive power of steam, machinery and the concentration of the instruments of labour, would have a colossal producing power, and they had the simplicity to believe that the capitalists would content themselves with taking only a reasonable part of the wealth thus created, and would leave to their co-operators, the manual and intellectual labourers, a portion sufficient to enable them to live in comfort. This socialism was marvellously agreeable to capital, since it promised an increase of wealth and advised an understanding between the labourer and the employer. It recruited the great majority of its adepts in the educational hotbeds of the bourgeoisie. It was utopian, therefore it was the socialism of the intellectuals.

But precisely because it was utopian, the labourers, in constant antagonism with their employers on questions of labour and hours, looked on it with suspicion. They could understand nothing of this socialism which condemned strikes and political action and which assumed to harmonise the interests of capital and labour, of the exploiter and exploited. They kept aloof from the socialists and gave all their sympathies to the bourgeois republicans, because they were revolutionary. They joined their secret societies and climbed with them upon the barricades to make riots and political revolutions.

Marx and Engels took socialism at the point to which the great utopians had brought it, but instead of torturing their brains to improvise the organisation of labour and of production, they studied that which was already created by the very necessities of the new mechanical industry which had arrived at a degree of development sufficient to permit its power and its tendency to be apparent. Its productivity was so enormous, as Fourier and Saint Simon had foreseen, that it was capable of providing abundantly for the normal needs of all the members of society. This was the first time in history that such a productive power had been observed, and it was because capitalist production could satisfy all needs, and for that reason alone, that it is possible to reintroduce communism, that is to say the equal participation of all in social wealth, and the free and complete development of the physical, intellectual and moral faculties. Communism is no longer a utopia but a possibility.

Machinery replaces the individualistic production of the small industry, by the communistic production of the capitalistic factory, but property in the means of labour has remained individual, as in the time of the small industry. There is then a contradiction between the individualistic mode of possession and the communist mode of production and this contradiction translates itself into the antagonism between the labourer and the capitalist employer. The producers, who form the immense majority of the nation, no longer possess the instruments of labour, the possession of which is centralised in the idle hands of a decreasing minority. The social problem imposed by mechanical production will be solved, as the social problems imposed by preceding modes of production have been solved, by precipitating the evolution begun by economic force, by, finishing the expropriation of the individual in the means of production, by giving to the communistic mode of possession which it demands.

The communism of contemporary socialists no longer proceeds, like that of former times, from the cerebral lucubrations of gifted thinkers; it proceeds from economic reality, it is the final goal of the economic forces which, without attracting the attention of the capitalists and their intellectuals, have fashioned the communistic mould of a new society, the coming of which we only have to hasten. Communism, then, is no longer a utopian hypothesis; it is a scientific ideal. It may be added that never has the economic structure of any society been better and more completely analysed than capitalist society, and that never was a social ideal conceived with such numerous and positive data as the communist idea of modern socialism.

Although it is the economic forces which fashion men at the pleasure and spur them to action, and although these constitute the mysterious force determining the great currents of history which the Christians attribute to God, and the free-thinking bourgeois assign to Progress, to Civilisation, to the Immortal Principles and other similar manitous, worthy of savage tribes, they are nevertheless the product of human activity. Man, who created them and brought them into the world, has thus far let himself be guided by them; yet now that he has understood their nature and grasped their tendency, he can act upon their evolution. The socialists who are accused of being stricken by Oriental fatalism and of relying upon the good pleasure of economic forces to bring to light the communist society instead of crossing their arms like the fakirs of official Economics, and of bending the knee before its fundamental dogma, laissez faire, laissez passer, propose on the contrary to subdue them, as the blind forces of nature have been subdued, and force them to do good to men instead of leaving them to work misery to the toilers of civilisation. They do not wait for their ideal to fall from heaven as the Christians hope for the grace of God, and the capitalists for wealth, they prepare, on the contrary, to realise it, not by appealing to the intelligence of the capitalist class and to its sentiments of justice and humanity, but by fighting it, by expropriating it from its political power, which protects its economic despotism.

Socialism, because it possesses a social ideal, has in consequence a criticism of its own. Every class which struggles for its enfranchisement seeks to realise a social ideal, in complete opposition with that of the ruling class. The struggle is waged at first in the ideological world before the physical shock of the revolutionary battle. It thus begins the criticism of the ideas of the society which must he revolted against, for "the ideas of the ruling class are the ideas of society", or these ideas are the intellectual reflection of its material interests.

Thus, the wealth of the ruling class is produced by slave labour; religion, ethics, philosophy and literature agree in authorising slavery. The ugly God of the Jews and Christianity strikes with his curse the progeny of Ham, that it may furnish slaves. Aristotle, the encyclopedic thinker of Greek philosophy, declares that slaves are predestined by nature and that no rights exist for them, for there can be no rights except between equals.

302

Euripides in his tragedies preaches the doctrine of servile morality; St. Paul, St. Augustine and the Church teach slaves submission to their earthly masters that they may deserve the favour of their heavenly master; Christian civilisation introduced slavery into America and maintains it there until economic phenomena proved that slave labour is a method of exploitation more costly, and less profitable than free labour.

At the epoch when the Greco-Roman civilisation was dissolving, when the labour of artisans and free workers began to be substituted for slave labour, pagan religion, philosophy and literature decided to accord them certain rights. The same Euripides who advised the slave to lose his personality in that of the master does not wish him to be despised. "There is nothing shameful in slavery but the name", says the pedagogue in *Ion*, "the slave, moreover, is not inferior to the free man when he has a noble heart".

The mysteries of Eleusis and of Orphism, like Christianity, which continues their work, admit slaves among their initiated and promise them liberty, equality and happiness after death.

The dominating class of the Middle Ages being military, the Christian religion and social ethics condemned lending money at interest, and covered the lender with infamy; to take interest for money loaned was then something so ignominious that the Jewish race, obliged to specialise itself in the trade of money, still bears the shame of it. But Today, now that the Christians have become Jews, and the ruling class lives on the interest of its capital, the trade of the lender at interest is the most honourable, the most desirable, the most exclusive.

The oppressed class, although the ideology of the oppressing class is imposed upon it, nevertheless elaborates religious, ethical and political ideas corresponding to its condition of life; vague and secret at first, the gain in precision and force in proportion as the oppressed class takes definite form and acquires the consciousness of its social utility and of its strength; and the hour of its emancipation is near when its conception of nature and of society opposes itself openly and boldly to that of the ruling class.

The economic conditions in which the bourgeois moves and evolves make of it a class essentially religious. Christianity is its work and will last as long as this class shall rule society. Seven or eight centuries before Christ, when the bourgeoisie had its birth in the commercial and industrial cities of the Mediterranean sea, we may observe the elaboration of a new religion; the gods of paganism created by warrior tribes could not be suited to a class consecrated to the production and sale of merchandise. Mysterious cults (the mysteries of the Cabiri, of Demeter, of Dionysus, etc.) revive the religious traditions of the prehistoric matriarchical period; the idea of a soul and its existence after death revive; the idea of posthumous punishments and rewards to compensate for acts of social injustice are introduced, etc. These religious elements, combined with the intellectual data of Greek philosophy, contribute to form Christianity, the religion, par excellence, of societies which have for their foundation property belonging to the individual and the class which enrich themselves by the exploitation of wage labour. For fifteen centuries all the movements of the bourgeoisie, either for organisation, or for self-emancipation, or for the acquisition of power have been accompanied and complicated by religious crises; but always Christianity more or less modified remains the religion of society. The revolutionists of 1789, who in the ardor of the struggle promised themselves to de-Christianise France, were eager when the bourgeoisie were victorious to raise again the altars they had overthrown and to reintroduce the cult that they had proscribed.

The economic environment which produces the proletariat relieves it on the contrary from every idea of sentiment. There is not seen either in Europe nor in America among the labouring masses of the great industries any anxiety to elaborate a religion to replace Christianity, nor any desire to reform it. The economic and political organisations of the working class are completely uninterested as to any doctrinal discussion of religious and spiritual dogmas, although they combat the priests of all cults because they are the lackeys of the capitalist class.

The victory of the proletariat will deliver humanity from the nightmare of religion. The belief in superior beings to explain the natural world and the social inequality, and to prolong the dominion of the ruling class, and the belief in the posthumous existence of the soul to recompense the inequality of fate will have no more justification once man, who has already grasped the general causes of the phenomena of nature, shall live in a communist society from whence shall have disappeared the inequality and the injustice of capitalistic society.

The militant socialists, following the example of the encyclopedists of the eighteenth century, have to make a merciless criticism of the economic, political, historical, philosophical, moral and religious ideas of the capitalist class in order to prepare in all spheres of thought the triumph of the new ideology which the proletariat introduces into the world.

From *The Right To Be Lazy and Other Studies*, 1900

Why socialism?

Albert Einstein

IS IT ADVISABLE for one who is not an expert on economic and social issues to express views on the subject of socialism? I believe for a number of reasons that it is. Let us first consider the question from the point of view of scientific knowledge. It might appear that there are no essential methodological differences between astronomy and economics: scientists in both fields attempt to discover laws of general acceptability for a circumscribed group of phenomena in order to make the interconnection of these phenomena as clearly understandable as possible. But in reality such methodological differences do exist. The discovery of general laws in the field of economics is made difficult by the circumstance that observed economic phenomena are often affected by many factors which are very hard to evaluate separately. In addition, the experience which has accumulated since the beginning of the so-called civilised period of human history has — as is well known — been largely influenced and limited by causes which are by no means exclusively economic in nature. For example, most of the major states of history owed their existence to conquest. The conquering peoples established themselves, legally and economically, as the privileged class of the conquered country. They seized for themselves a monopoly of the land ownership and appointed a priesthood from among their own ranks. The priests, in control of education, made the class division of society into a permanent institution and created a system of values by which the people were thenceforth, to a large extent unconsciously, guided in their social behaviour. But historic tradition is, so to speak, of yesterday; nowhere have we really overcome what Thorstein Veblen called "the predatory phase" of human development. The observable economic facts belong to that phase and even such laws as we can derive from them are not applicable to other phases. Since the real purpose of socialism is precisely to overcome and advance beyond the predatory phase of human development, economic science in its present state can throw little light on the socialist society of the future.

Second, socialism is directed towards a social-ethical end. Science, however, cannot create ends and, even less, instill them in human beings; science, at most, can supply the means by which to attain certain ends. But the ends themselves are conceived by personalities with lofty ethical ideals and — if these ends are not stillborn, but vital and vigorous — are adopted and carried forward by those many human beings who, half unconsciously, determine the slow evolution of society. For these reasons, we should be on our guard not to overestimate science and scientific methods when it is a question of human problems; and we should not assume that experts are the only ones who have a right to express themselves on questions affecting the organisation of society.

Man is, at one and the same time, a solitary being and a social being. As a solitary being, he attempts to protect his own existence and that of those who are closest to him, to satisfy his personal desires, and to develop his innate abilities. As a social being, he seeks to gain the recognition and affection of his fellow human beings, to share in their pleasures, to comfort them in their sorrows, and to improve their conditions of life. Only the existence of these varied, frequently conflicting, strivings accounts for the special character of a man, and their specific combination determines the extent to which an individual can achieve an inner equilibrium and can contribute to the well-being of society. It is quite possible that the relative strength of these two drives is, in the main, fixed by inheritance. But the personality that finally emerges is largely formed by the environment in which a man happens to find himself during his development, by the structure of the society in which he grows up, by the tradition of that society, and by its appraisal of particular types of behaviour. The abstract concept "society" means to the individual human being the sum total of his direct and indirect relations to his contemporaries and to all the people of earlier generations. The individual is able to think, feel, strive, and work by himself; but he depends so much upon society — in his physical, intellectual, and emotional existence — that it is impossible to think of him, or to understand him, outside the framework of society. It is "society" which provides man with food, clothing, a home, the tools of work, language, the forms of thought, and most of the content of thought; his life is made possible through the labour and the accomplishments of the many millions past and present who are all hidden behind the small word "society."

It is evident, therefore, that the dependence of the individual upon society is a fact of nature which cannot be abolished — just as in the case of ants and bees. However, while the whole life process of ants and bees is fixed down to the smallest detail by rigid, hereditary instincts, the social pattern and interrelationships of human beings are very variable and susceptible to change. Memory, the capacity to make new combinations, the gift of oral communication have made possible developments among human beings which are not dictated by biological necessities. Such developments manifest themselves in traditions, institutions, and organisations; in literature; in scientific and engineering accomplishments; in works of art. This explains how it happens that, in a certain sense, man

306

can influence his life through his own conduct, and that in this process conscious thinking and wanting can play a part.

Man acquires at birth, through heredity, a biological constitution which we must consider fixed and unalterable, including the natural urges which are characteristic of the human species. In addition, during his lifetime, he acquires a cultural constitution which he adopts from society through communication and through many other types of influences. It is this cultural constitution which, with the passage of time, is subject to change and which determines to a very large extent the relationship between the individual and society. Modern anthropology has taught us, through comparative investigation of so-called primitive cultures, that the social behaviour of human beings may differ greatly, depending upon prevailing cultural patterns and the types of organisation which predominate in society. It is on this that those who are striving to improve the lot of man may ground their hopes: human beings are not condemned, because of their biological constitution, to annihilate each other or to be at the mercy of a cruel, self-inflicted fate.

If we ask ourselves how the structure of society and the cultural attitude of man should be changed in order to make human life as satisfying as possible, we should constantly be conscious of the fact that there are certain conditions which we are unable to modify. As mentioned before, the biological nature of man is, for all practical purposes, not subject to change. Furthermore, technological and demographic developments of the last few centuries have created conditions which are here to stay. In relatively densely settled populations with the goods which are indispensable to their continued existence, an extreme division of labour and a highly-centralised productive apparatus are absolutely necessary. The time — which, looking back, seems so idyllic — is gone forever when individuals or relatively small groups could be completely self-sufficient. It is only a slight exaggeration to say that mankind constitutes even now a planetary community of production and consumption.

I have now reached the point where I may indicate briefly what to me constitutes the essence of the crisis of our time. It concerns the relationship of the individual to society. The individual has become more conscious than ever of his dependence upon society. But he does not experience this dependence as a positive asset, as an organic tie, as a protective force, but rather as a threat to his natural rights, or even to his economic existence. Moreover, his position in society is such that the egotistical drives of his make-up are constantly being accentuated, while his social drives, which are by nature weaker, progressively deteriorate. All human beings, whatever their position in society, are suffering from this process of deterioration. Unknowingly prisoners of their own egotism,

307

they feel insecure, lonely, and deprived of the naive, simple, and unso-
phisticated enjoyment of life. Man can find meaning in life, short and
perilous as it is, only through devoting himself to society.

The economic anarchy of capitalist society as it exists today is, in my
opinion, the real source of the evil. We see before us a huge community
of producers the members of which are unceasingly striving to deprive
each other of the fruits of their collective labour — not by force, but on
the whole in faithful compliance with legally established rules. In this
respect, it is important to realise that the means of production — that is
to say, the entire productive capacity that is needed for producing consumer goods as well as additional capital goods — may legally be, and
for the most part are, the private property of individuals.

For the sake of simplicity, in the discussion that follows I shall call
"workers" all those who do not share in the ownership of the means of
production — although this does not quite correspond to the customary
use of the term. The owner of the means of production is in a position to
purchase the labour power of the worker. By using the means of production, the worker produces new goods which become the property of the
capitalist. The essential point about this process is the relation between
what the worker produces and what he is paid, both measured in terms
of real value. Insofar as the labour contract is "free," what the worker receives is determined not by the real value of the goods he produces, but
by his minimum needs and by the capitalists' requirements for labour
power in relation to the number of workers competing for jobs. It is important to understand that even in theory the payment of the worker is
not determined by the value of his product.

Private capital tends to become concentrated in few hands, partly because of competition among the capitalists, and partly because technological development and the increasing division of labour encourage the
formation of larger units of production at the expense of smaller ones.
The result of these developments is an oligarchy of private capital the
enormous power of which cannot be effectively checked even by a democratically organised political society. This is true since the members of
legislative bodies are selected by political parties, largely financed or otherwise influenced by private capitalists who, for all practical purposes,
separate the electorate from the legislature. The consequence is that the
representatives of the people do not in fact sufficiently protect the interests of the underprivileged sections of the population. Moreover, under
existing conditions, private capitalists inevitably control, directly or indirectly, the main sources of information (press, radio, education). It is
thus extremely difficult, and indeed in most cases quite impossible, for
the individual citizen to come to objective conclusions and to make in-

telligent use of his political rights. The situation prevailing in an economy based on the private ownership of capital is thus characterised by two main principles: first, means of production (capital) are privately owned and the owners dispose of them as they see fit; second, the labour contract is free. Of course, there is no such thing as a pure capitalist society in this sense. In particular, it should be noted that the workers, through long and bitter political struggles, have succeeded in securing a somewhat improved form of the "free labour contract" for certain categories of workers. But taken as a whole, the present day economy does not differ much from "pure" capitalism

Production is carried on for profit, not for use. There is no provision that all those able and willing to work will always be in a position to find employment; an "army of unemployed" almost always exists. The worker is constantly in fear of losing his job. Since unemployed and poorly paid workers do not provide a profitable market, the production of consumers' goods is restricted, and great hardship is the consequence. Technological progress frequently results in more unemployment rather than in an easing of the burden of work for all. The profit motive, in conjunction with competition among capitalists, is responsible for an instability in the accumulation and utilisation of capital which leads to increasingly severe depressions. Unlimited competition leads to a huge waste of labour, and to that crippling of the social consciousness of individuals which I mentioned before.

This crippling of individuals I consider the worst evil of capitalism. Our whole educational system suffers from this evil. An exaggerated competitive attitude is inculcated into the student, who is trained to worship acquisitive success as a preparation for his future career.

I am convinced there is only one way to eliminate these grave evils, namely through the establishment of a socialist economy, accompanied by an educational system which would be oriented toward social goals. In such an economy, the means of production are owned by society itself and are utilised in a planned fashion. A planned economy, which adjusts production to the needs of the community, would distribute the work to be done among all those able to work and would guarantee a livelihood to every man, woman, and child. The education of the individual, in addition to promoting his own innate abilities, would attempt to develop in him a sense of responsibility for his fellow men in place of the glorification of power and success in our present society.

Nevertheless, it is necessary to remember that a planned economy is not yet socialism. A planned economy as such may be accompanied by the complete enslavement of the individual. The achievement of socialism requires the solution of some extremely difficult socio-political problems: how is it possible, in view of the far-reaching centralisation of political and economic power, to prevent bureaucracy from becoming all-powerful and overweening? How can the rights of the individual be protected and therewith a democratic counterweight to the power of bureaucracy be assured?

Monthly Review, May 1949

"Freedom is always the freedom of the one who thinks differently"

What is German Bolshevism?

Rosa Luxemburg

THE REVOLUTION THAT HAS JUST BEGUN can have but one outcome: the realisation of socialism! The working class, in order to accomplish its purpose, must, first of all, secure entire political control of the state. But to the socialist, political power is only a means to an end. It is the instrument with which labour will achieve the complete, fundamental reconstruction of our entire industrial system. Today all wealth, the largest and most fruitful tracts of land, the mines, the mills and the factories belong to a small group of Junkers and private capitalists. From them the great masses of the labouring class receive a scanty wage in return for long hours of arduous toil, hardly enough for a decent livelihood. The enrichment of a small class of idlers is the purpose and end of present-day society. To give to modern society and to modern production a new impulse and a new purpose — that is the foremost duty of the revolutionary working class.

To this end all social wealth, the land and all that it produces, the factories and the mills must be taken from their exploiting owners to become the common property of the entire people. It thus becomes the foremost duty of a. revolutionary government of the working class to issue a series of decrees making all important instruments of production national property and placing them under social control. But this is only the first step. The most difficult task, the creation of an industrial state upon an entirely new foundation, has only just begun.

Today production in every manufacturing unit is conducted by the individual capitalist independently of all others. What and where commodities are to be produced, where, when and how the finished product is to be sold, is decided by the individual capitalist owner. Nowhere does labour have the slightest influence upon these questions. It is simply the living machine that has its work to do. In a Socialist state of society all this will be changed. Private ownership of the means of production and subsistence must disappear. Production will be carried on not for the enrichment of the individual but solely for the creation of a supply of commodities sufficient to supply the wants and needs of the working class. Accordingly factories, mills and farms must be operated upon an entirely new basis, from a wholly different point of view.

In the first place, now that production is to be carried on for the sole purpose of securing to all a more humane existence, of providing for all plentiful food, clothing and other cultural means of subsistence, the productivity of labour must be materially increased. Farms must be made

311

to yield richer crops, the most advanced technical processes must be introduced into the factories, of the mines only the most productive, for the present, must be intensively exploited. It follows, therefore, that the process of socialisation will begin with the most highly developed industries and farm lands. We need not, and will not deprive the small farmer or artisan of the bit of land or the little workshop from which he ekes out a meagre existence by the work of his own hands. As time goes by he will realise the superiority of socialised production over private ownership and will come to us of his own accord.

In order that all members of society may enjoy prosperity, all must work. Only he who performs useful service to society, manual or mental, will be entitled to a share of products for the satisfaction of his needs and desires. Idleness must cease and in its stead will come universal compulsory labour for all who are physically capable. Obviously those who are unable to work, children, invalids and the aged, must be supported by society. But not as it is done today, by niggardly charity. Bountiful sustenance, socialised education for the children, comfortable care for the aged, public health service for the sick — -these must form an important part of our social structure.

For the same reason, i. e., in the interest of general welfare, society will be more economical, more rational in the utilisation of its commodities, its means of production and its labour power. Waste such as we find today on every hand, must cease. The production of munitions and other implements of warfare must pass out of existence, for a Socialist state of society needs no tools of murder. Instead the precious materials and the enormous labour power that were devoted to this purpose will be used for useful production. The manufacture of useless and costly foolishness for the edification of wealthy idlers will stop. Personal service will be prohibited, and the labour power thus released will find more useful and more worthy employment.

While we are thus creating a nation of workers where all must be productively employed for the general welfare, labour itself must be completely revolutionised. Today labour in industry, on the farm and in the office is usually a torture and a burden to the proletarian. Men and women work because they must in order to obtain the necessities of life. In a Socialist state of society, where all work together for their own well-being, the health of the individual worker, and his joy in his work must be conscientiously fostered and sustained. Short hours of labour not in excess of the normal human capacity must be established; recreation and rest periods must be introduced into the workday, so all may do their share, willingly and joyously.

But the success of such reforms depend upon the human beings who

312

will carry them out. Today the capitalist with his whip stands behind the workingman, in person or in the form of a manager-or overseer. Hunger drives the worker to the factory, to the Junker or the farm-owner, into the business office. Everywhere the employer sees to it that no time is wasted, no material squandered, that good, efficient work is done.

In a Socialist state of society the capitalist with his whip disappears. Here all workingmen are free and on an equal footing, working for benefit and enjoyment, tolerating no waste of social wealth, rendering honest and punctual service. To be sure, every Socialist plant needs its technical superintendents who understand its workings, who are able to supervise production so that everything runs smoothly, to assure an output commensurate with the labour power expended by organising the process of manufacture according to most efficient methods. To insure successful production the individual workingman must follow his instructions entirely and willingly, must maintain discipline and order, cause no friction or confusion. In a word: the workingman in a Socialist industrial state must show that he can work decently and diligently, without capitalists and slave-drivers behind his back; that of his own volition he can maintain discipline and "do his best". This demands mental discipline, moral stamina, it demands a feeling of self-respect and responsibility, a spiritual rebirth of the workingman.

Socialism cannot be realised with lazy, careless, egotistic, thoughtless and shiftless men and women. A Socialist state of society needs people everyone of whom is full of enthusiasm and fervour for the general welfare, full of a spirit of self-sacrifice and sympathy for his fellow men, full of courage and tenacity and the willingness to dare even against the greatest odds.

But we need not wait centuries or decades until such a race of human beings shall grow up. The struggle, the Revolution will teach the proletarian masses idealism, has given them mental ripeness, courage and perseverance, clearness of purpose and a self-sacrificing spirit, if it is to lead to victory. While we are enlisting fighters for the revolution, we are creating Socialist workers for the future, workers who can become the basis of a new social state. The young people of the proletariat are ordained to carry out this great work as the true foundation of the Socialist state. They must show, even now, that they are equal to the great task of bearing the future of the human race upon their shoulders. There is still an old world to be overthrown. A new world must be built!

What is German Bolshevism? by Rosa Luxemburg (December 1918). From *The Class Struggle*, New York, Aug 1919

Repealing the anti-homosexual laws

August Bebel

THE FOLLOWING IS THE FIRST POLITICAL SPEECH ever made for homosexual rights. On 13 January 1898, the leader of German Social Democracy, August Bebel, took the floor of the Reichstag [Parliament], during a discussion of penal code reform, to argue for a petition being circulated by the Scientific Humanitarian Committee calling for the repeal of Germany's sodomy statute, Paragraph 175. The Scientific Humanitarian Committee (wissenschaftlich-humanitäre Komitée), the world's first activist homosexual rights organisation, had been founded on 15 May 1897. Bebel's speech may seem tame today, but it was far in advance of the time. It is clear from commotions and interruptions indicated on the Reichstag record that Bebel's remarks were thoroughly shocking to the ears of his colleagues. Paragraph 175 was not repealed until 1994. In between times, the Nazis had tightened it up, hugely increased the number of prosecutions, and sent many thousands of gay people to concentration camps.

Gentlemen, the penal code exists to be enforced — that is to say, so that the authorities who have the primary responsibility for maintaining compliance with and respect for the law should be dutifully watchful for violations and act accordingly. But there are provisions of our penal code, some of them contained in the motion before us, where the authorities, although fully aware that these provisions are systematically violated by a great number of people, men as well as women, only in the rarest cases bother to call for action on the part of the prosecutor. Here I have particularly in mind the section with the provisions of Paragraph 175 — it has to do with "unnatural fornication".

I am informed by the best sources that the police of Berlin do not bring the names of men who commit offences which Paragraph 175 makes punishable by imprisonment to the attention of the district attorney as seen as they have become aware of the fact, but rather add the names of the persons involved to the list of those who for the same reasons are already in their files.

The number of these persons is so great and reaches so far into all levels of society, that if the police here scrupulously carried out their duty, the Prussian State would immediately be compelled to build two new penitentiaries just to take care of those offences against Paragraph

175 that are committed in Berlin alone.

That is not an exaggeration: it has to do with thousands of persons from all walks of life. But then it further raises the question of whether the provisions of Paragraph 175 should apply not only to men, but also to women who on their part commit the same offence. What is just in the case of one sex, is fair for the other. But gentlemen, I'll tell you this: if in this area the Berlin police did their duty all the way — I want to say a word about this — then there would be a scandal such as the world have never known, a scandal compared with which the Panama scandal, the Dreyfus scandal, the Lützow-Ledert and the Tausch-Normann scandals are pure child's play. Perhaps this is one of the reasons why the offence punishable under this Paragraph is treated with such extraordinary laxity on the part of the police. Gentlemen, Paragraph 175 is part of the penal code, and because it is there, it must be enforced. However, if for whatever reasons this part of the criminal law cannot be enforced, or can be enforced only selectively, then the question arises whether this provision of the penal code can equitably be retained.

In this very session we have before us a printed petition signed by me personally, among others, and by a number of colleagues from other parties, and further by people from literary and academic circles, by jurists of the most illustrious standing, by psychologists and pathologists, by experts of the highest rank in this field. The petition advocated a revision of the penal code so as to repeal the relevant provisions of Paragraph 175.

Abridged from Reichstag 16th Session Thursday, 13 January 1898

The women's struggle and socialism

Clara Zetkin

THE PERIOD OF THE RENAISSANCE is the storm and stress period of the awakening of modern individuality that was able to develop fully and completely in the most diverse directions. We encounter individuals who are giants in both good and evil, who spurn the commandments of both religion and morals and despise equally both heaven and hell. We discover women at the center of the social, artistic and political life. And yet there is not a trace of a women's movement. This is all the more characteristic because at that time the old family economic system began to crumble under the impact of the division of labour. Thousands upon thousands of women no longer found their livelihood and their lives' meaning within the family. But this women's question, as far as one can designate it as such, was solved at that time by convents, charitable institutions and religious orders.

The machines, the modern mode of production, slowly undermined domestic production and not just for thousands but for millions of women the question arose: Where do we now find our livelihood? Where do we find a meaningful life as well as a, job that gives us mental satisfaction? Millions were now forced to find their livelihood and their meaningful lives outside of their families and within society as a whole. At that moment they became aware of the fact that their social illegality stood in opposition to their most basic interests. It was from this moment on that there existed the modern women's question...

The women's question, however, is only present within those classes of society who are themselves the products of the capitalist mode of production. Thus it is that we find no women's question in peasant circles that possess a natural (although severely curtailed and punctured) economy. But we certainly find a women's question within those classes of society who are the very children of the modern mode of production. There is a women's question for the women of the proletariat, the bourgeoisie, the intelligentsia and the Upper Ten Thousand. It assumes a different form according to the class situation of each one of these strata.

How does the women's question shape up as far as the Upper Ten Thousand are concerned? The woman of the Upper Ten Thousand, thanks to her property, may freely develop her individuality and live as she pleases. In her role as wife, however, she is still dependent upon her husband. The guardianship of the weaker sex has survived in the family law which still states: And he shall be your master... If the women of these circles have the desire to give their lives a serious purpose, they must, first of all, raise the demand to dispose of their property in an independent and free manner. This demand, therefore, represents the core of the demands raised by the women's movement of the Upper Ten Thousand. These women, in their fight for the realisation of their demand vis-a-vis the masculine world of their class, fight exactly the same battle that the bourgeoisie fought against all of the privileged estates; i.e., a battle to remove all social differences based upon the possession of property.

How does the women's question appear in the circles of the petit-bourgeoisie, the middle class and the bourgeois intelligentsia? Here it is not property which dissolves the family, but mainly the concomitant symptoms of capitalist production... In these circles women are not equal to men in the form of possessors of private property as they are in the upper circles. The women of these circles have yet to achieve their economic equality with men and they can only do so by making two demands: The demand for equal professional training and the demand for equal job opportunities for both sexes. In economic terms, this means nothing less than the realisation of free access to all jobs and the untrammeled competition between men and women. The realisation of this demand unleashes a conflict of interest between the men and women of the bourgeoisie and the intelligentsia. The competition of the women in the professional world is the driving force for the resistance of men against the demands of bourgeois women's rights advocates. It is, pure and simple, the fear of competition. All other reasons which are listed against the mental work of women, such as the smaller brain of women or their allegedly natural avocation to be a mother, are only pretexts. This battle of competition pushes the women of these social strata towards demanding their political rights so that they may, by fighting politically, tear down all barriers which have been created against their economic activity.

So far I have addressed myself only to the basic and purely economic substructure. We would, however, perform an injustice to the bourgeois women's rights movement if we would regard it as solely motivated by economics. No, this movement also contains a more profound spiritual and moral aspect. The bourgeois woman not only demands her own bread but she also requests spiritual nourishment and wants to develop her individuality. It is exactly among these strata that we find these tragic, yet psychologically interesting Nora figures, women who are tired of living like dolls in doll houses and who want to share in the development of modern culture. The economic as well as the intellectual and moral endeavors of bourgeois women's rights advocates are completely justified.

As far as the proletarian woman is concerned, it is capitalism's need to exploit and to search incessantly for a cheap labour force that has created the women's question. It is for this reason, too, that the proletarian woman has become enmeshed in the mechanism of the economic life of our period and has been driven into the workshop and to the machines. She went out into the economic life in order to aid her husband in making a living, but the capitalist mode of production transformed her into on unfair competitor. She wanted to bring prosperity to her family, but instead misery descended upon it. The proletarian woman obtained her own employment because she wanted to create a more sunny and pleasant life for her children, but instead she became almost entirely separated from them. She became an equal of the man as a worker; the machine rendered muscular force superfluous and everywhere women's work showed the same results in production as men's work. And since women constitute a cheap labour force and above all a submissive one that only in the rarest of cases dares to kick against the thorns of capitalist exploitation, the capitalists multiply the possibilities of women's work in industry. As a result of all this, the proletarian woman has achieved her independence. But verily, the price was very high and for the moment they have gained very little. If during the Age of the Family, a man had the right to tame his wife occasionally with a whip, capitalism is now taming her with scorpions. In former times, the rule of a man over his wife was ameliorated by their personal relationship. Between an employer and his worker, however, exists only a cash nexus. The proletarian woman has gained her economic independence, but neither as a human being nor as a woman or wife has she had the possibility to develop her individuality. For her task as a wife and a mother, there remain only the breadcrumbs which the capitalist production drops from the table.

Therefore the liberation struggle of the proletarian woman cannot be similar to the struggle that the bourgeois woman wages against the male of her class. On the contrary, it must be a joint struggle with the male of her class against the entire class of capitalists. She does not need to fight against the men of her class in order to tear down the barriers which have been raised against her participation in the free competition of the market place. Capitalism's need to exploit and the development of the modern mode of production relieves her of having to fight such a struggle. On the contrary, new barriers need to be erected against the exploitation of the proletarian woman. Her rights as wife and mother need to be restored and permanently secured. Her final aim is not the free competition with the man, but the achievement of the political rule of the proletariat. The proletarian woman fights hand in hand with the man of her class against capitalist society. To be sure, she also agrees with the demands of the bourgeois women's movement, but she regards the fulfillment of these demands simply as a means to enable that movement to enter the battle, equipped with the same weapons, alongside the proletariat.

The less bourgeois democracy comprehends its task, the more important it is for Social-Democracy to advocate the political equality of women.

In the resolution which has been submitted to you, it is proposed to elect shop stewards among the women whose task it will be to stimulate the union and economic organisation of women and to consolidate it in a uniform and planned manner. This proposal is not new; it was adopted in principle at the Party Congress of Frankfurt, and in a few regions it has been enacted most successfully. Time will tell whether this proposal, when introduced on a larger scale, is suited to draw proletarian women to a greater extent into the proletarian movement.

The proletariat will be able to attain its liberation only if it fights together without the difference of nationality and profession. In the same way it can attain its liberation only if it stands together without the distinction of sex. The incorporation of the great masses of proletarian women in the liberation struggle of the proletariat is one of the prerequisites for the victory of the Socialist idea and for the construction of a Socialist society.

Only in Conjunction With the Proletarian Woman Will Socialism Be Victorious, 1896.

The Champions of Democracy at Work!

Socialism and democracy

The metaphysics of democracy

Leon Trotsky

FEELING THE HISTORICAL GROUND shaking under his feet on the question of democracy, Kautsky crosses to the ground of metaphysics. Instead of inquiring into what is, he deliberates about what ought to be.

The principles of democracy — the sovereignty of the people, universal and equal suffrage, personal liberties — appear, as presented to him, in a halo of moral duty. They are turned from their historical meaning and presented as unalterable and sacred things-in-themselves. This metaphysical fall from grace is not accidental. It is instructive that the late Plekhanov, a merciless enemy of Kantism at the best period of his activity, attempted at the end of his life, when the wave of patriotism had washed over him, to clutch at the straw of the categorical imperative. That real democracy with which the German people is now making practical acquaintance Kautsky confronts with a kind of ideal democracy, as he would confront a common phenomenon with the thing-in-itself. Kautsky indicates with certitude not one country in which democracy is really capable of guaranteeing a painless transition to Socialism. But he does know, and firmly, that such democracy ought to exist. The present German National Assembly, that organ of helplessness, reactionary malice, and degraded solicitations, is confronted by Kautsky with a different, real, true National Assembly, which possesses all virtues — excepting the small virtue of reality.

The doctrine of formal democracy is not scientific Socialism, but the theory of so-called natural law. The essence of the latter consists in the recognition of eternal and unchanging standards of law, which among different peoples and at different periods find a different, more or less limited and distorted expression. The natural law of modern history — i.e., as it emerged from the Middle Ages — included first of all a protest against class privileges, the abuse of despotic legislation, and the other "artificial" products of feudal positive law. The theoreticians of the, as yet, weak Third Estate expressed its class interests in a few ideal standards, which later on developed into the teaching of democracy, acquiring at the same time an individualist character. The individual is absolute; all persons have the right of expressing their thoughts in speech

321

and print; every man must enjoy equal electoral rights. As a battle cry against feudalism, the demand for democracy had a progressive character. As time went on, however, the metaphysics of natural law (the theory of formal democracy) began to show its reactionary side — the establishment of an ideal standard to control the real demands of the labouring masses and the revolutionary parties.

If we look back to the historical sequence of world concepts, the theory of natural law will prove to be a paraphrase of Christian spiritualism freed from its crude mysticism. The Gospels proclaimed to the slave that he had just the same soul as the slave-owner, and in this way established the equality of all men before the heavenly tribunal. In reality, the slave remained a slave, and obedience became for him a religious duty. In the teaching of Christianity, the slave found an expression for his own ignorant protest against his degraded condition. Side by side with the protest was also the consolation. Christianity told him: "You have an immortal soul, although you resemble a pack-horse." Here sounded the note of indignation. But the same Christianity said: "Although you are like a pack-horse, yet your immortal soul has in store for it an eternal reward." Here is the voice of consolation. These two notes were found in historical Christianity in different proportions at different periods and amongst different classes. But as a whole, Christianity, like all other religions, became a method of deadening the consciousness of the oppressed masses.

Natural law, which developed into the theory of democracy, said to the worker: "all men are equal before the law, independently of their origin, their property, and their position; every man has an equal right in determining the fate of the people." This ideal criterion revolutionised the consciousness of the masses in so far as it was a condemnation of absolutism, aristocratic privileges, and the property qualification. But the longer it went on, the more it sent the consciousness to sleep, legalising poverty, slavery and degradation: for how could one revolt against slavery when every man has an equal right in determining the fate of the nation? Rothschild, who has coined the blood and tears of the world into the gold napoleons of his income, has one vote at the parliamentary elections. The ignorant tiller of the soil who cannot sign his name, sleeps all his life without taking his clothes off, and wanders through society like an underground mole, plays his part, however, as a trustee of the nation's sovereignty, and is equal to Rothschild in the courts and at the elections. In the real conditions of life, in the economic process, in social relations, in their way of life, people became more and more unequal; dazzling luxury was accumulated at one pole, poverty and hopelessness at the other. But in the sphere of the legal edifice of the State, these glaring contradictions disappeared, and there penetrated thither only unsubstantial legal shadows. The landlord, the labourer, the capitalist, the proletarian, the minister, the bootblack — all are equal as "citizens" and as "legislators." The mystic equality of Christianity has taken one step down from the heavens in the shape of the "natural," "legal" equality of democracy. But it has not yet reached earth, where lie the economic foundations of society. For the ignorant day-labourer, who all his life remains a beast of burden in the service of the bourgeoisie, the ideal right to influence the fate of the nations by means of the parliamentary elections remained little more real than the palace which he was promised in the kingdom of heaven.

In the practical interests of the development of the working class, the Socialist Party took its stand at a certain period on the path of parliamentarism. But this did not mean in the slightest that it accepted in principle the metaphysical theory of democracy, based on extra-historical, super-class rights. The proletarian doctrines examined democracy as the instrument of bourgeois society entirely adapted to the problems and requirements of the ruling classes; but as bourgeois society lived by the labour of the proletariat and could not deny it the legalisation of a certain part of its class struggle without destroying itself, this gave the Socialist Party the possibility of utilising, at a certain period, and within certain limits, the mechanism of democracy, without taking an oath to do so as an unshakable principle. The root problem of the party, at all periods of its struggle, was to create the conditions for real, economic, living equality for mankind as members of a united human commonwealth. It was just for this reason that the theoreticians of the proletariat had to expose the metaphysics of democracy as a philosophic mask for political mystification. The democratic party at the period of its revolutionary enthusiasm, when exposing the enslaving and stupefying lie of church dogma, preached to the masses: "You are lulled to sleep by promises of eternal bliss at the end of your life, while here you have no rights and you are bound with the chains of tyranny." The Socialist Party, a few decades later, said to the same masses with no less right: "You are lulled to sleep with the fiction of civic equality and political rights, but you are deprived of the possibility of realising those rights. Conditional and shadowy legal equality has been transformed into the convicts' chain with which each of you is fastened to the chariot of capitalism."

In the name of its fundamental task, the Socialist Party mobilised the masses on the parliamentary ground as well as on others; but nowhere and at no time did any party bind itself to bring the masses to Socialism only through the gates of democracy. In adapting ourselves to the parliamentary regime, we stopped at a theoretical exposure of democracy, because we were still too weak to overcome it in practice. But the path of Socialist ideas which is visible through all deviations, and even betrayals, foreshadows no other outcome but this: to throw democracy aside and replace it by the mechanism of the proletariat, at the moment when the latter is strong enough to carry out such a task.

We shall bring one piece of evidence, albeit a sufficiently striking one. "Parliamentarism," wrote Paul Lafargue in the Russian review, *Sozialdemokrat*, in 1888, "is a system of government in which the people acquires the illusion that it is controlling the forces of the country itself, when, in reality, the actual power is concentrated in the hands of the bourgeoisie — and not even of the whole bourgeoisie, but only of certain sections of that class. In the first period of its supremacy the bourgeoisie does not understand, or, more correctly, does not feel, the necessity for making the people believe in the illusion of self-government. Hence it was that all the parliamentary countries of Europe began with a limited franchise. Everywhere the right of influencing the policy of the country by means of the election of deputies belonged at first only to more or less large property holders, and was only gradually extended to less substantial citizens, until finally in some countries it became from a privilege the universal right of all and sundry.

"In bourgeois society, the more considerable becomes the amount of social wealth, the smaller becomes the number of individuals by whom it is appropriated. The same takes place with power: in proportion as the mass of citizens who possess political rights increases, and the number of elected ruler's increases, the actual power is concentrated and becomes the monopoly of a smaller and smaller group of individuals." Such is the secret of the majority.

For the Marxist, Lafargue, parliamentarism remains as long as the supremacy of the bourgeoisie remains. "On the day," writes Lafargue, "when the proletariat of Europe and America seizes the State, it will have to organise a revolutionary government, and govern society as a dictatorship, until the bourgeoisie has disappeared as a class."

Kautsky in his time knew this Marxist estimate of parliamentarism, and more than once repeated it himself, although with no such Gallic sharpness and lucidity. The theoretical apostasy of Kautsky lies just in this point: having recognised the principle of democracy as absolute and eternal, he has stepped back from materialist dialectics to natural law. That which was exposed by Marxism as the passing mechanism of the bourgeoisie, and was subjected only to temporary utilisation with the object of preparing the proletarian revolution, has been newly sanctified by Kautsky as the supreme principle standing above classes, and unconditionally subordinating to itself the methods of the proletarian struggle. The counterrevolutionary degeneration of parliamentarism finds its most perfect expression in the deification of democracy by the decaying theoreticians of the Second International.

From *Terrorism and Communism.*

Democracy and class rule

Vladimir Ilyich Lenin

FACED WITH THE GROWTH of the revolutionary workers' movement in every country, the bourgeoisie and their agents in the workers' organisations are making desperate political arguments in defence of the rule of the exploiters. Condemnation of dictatorship and defence of democracy are particularly prominent among these arguments. The falsity and hypocrisy of this argument are obvious to all who refuse to betray the fundamental principles of socialism.

First, this argument employs the concepts of "democracy in general" and "dictatorship in general", without posing the question of the class concerned. This non-class or above class presentation, which supposedly is popular, is an outright travesty of the basic tenet of socialism, namely, its theory of class struggle. For in no civilised capitalist country does "democracy in general" exist. All that exists is bourgeois democracy, and it is not a question of "dictatorship in general", but of the dictatorship of the oppressed class, i.e. the proletariat, over its oppressors and exploiters, i.e. the bourgeoisie, in order to overcome the resistance offered by the exploiters in their fight to maintain their domination.

History teaches us that no oppressed class ever did, or could, achieve power without going through a period of dictatorship, i.e. the conquest of political power and forcible suppression of the resistance always offered by the exploiters — a resistance that is most desperate, most furious, and that stops at nothing. The bourgeoisie, whose domination is now defended by the Socialists who denounce "dictatorship in general" and extol "democracy in general", won power in the advanced countries through a series of insurrections, civil wars, and the forcible suppression of kings, feudal lords, slave owners, and their attempts at restoration.

In books, pamphlets, congress resolutions, and propaganda speeches socialists everywhere have thousands and millions of times explained to the people the class nature of the bourgeois revolution and this bourgeois dictatorship. The most democratic bourgeois republic is no more than a machine for the suppression of the working class by the bourgeoisie, for the suppression of the working people by a handful of capitalists. It was Marx who best appraised the historical significance of the [Paris] Commune [of 1871]. In his analysis, he revealed the exploiting nature of bourgeois democracy and the bourgeois parliamentary system under which the oppressed classes enjoy the right to decide once in several years which representative of the propertied classes shall "represent and suppress" the people in parliament.

The significance of the Commune, furthermore, lies in the fact that it endeavoured to crush, to smash to its very foundations, the bourgeois state apparatus, the bureaucratic, judicial, military, and police machine, and to replace it why a self-governing, mass workers' organisation in which there was no division between legislative and executive power. All contemporary bourgeois-democratic republics, including the German republic, which the traitors to socialism, in mockery of the truth, describe as a proletarian republic, retain this state apparatus. We therefore again get quite clear confirmation of the point that shouting in defence of "democracy in general" is actually defence of the bourgeoisie and their privileges as exploiters.

"Freedom of the press" is another of the principal slogans of "pure democracy". And here, too, the workers know — and socialists everywhere have explained it millions of times — that this freedom is a deception while the best printing presses and the biggest stocks of paper are appropriated by the capitalists and while capitalist rule over the press remains, a rule that is manifested throughout the world all the more strikingly, sharply, and cynically, the more democracy and the republican system are developed, as in America for example. The first thing to do to win real equality and genuine democracy for the working people, for the workers and peasants, is to deprive capital of the possibility of hiring writers, buying up publishing houses, and hiring newspapers. And to do that the capitalists and exploiters have to be overthrown and their resistance suppressed. The capitalists have always used the term "freedom" to mean freedom for the rich to get richer and for the workers to starve to death. In capitalist usage, freedom of the press means freedom of the rich to bribe the press, freedom to use their wealth to shape and fabricate so-called public opinion.

In this respect. too, the defenders of "pure democracy" prove to be defenders of an utterly foul and venal system that gives the rich control over the mass media. They prove to be deceivers of the people who, with the aid of plausible, fine-sounding, but thoroughly false phrases, divert them from the concrete historical task of liberating the press from capitalist enslavement.

Genuine freedom and equality will be embodied in the system which the communists are building and in which there will be no opportunity for amassing wealth at the expense of others, no objective opportunities for putting the press under the direct or indirect power of money, and no impediments in the way of any workingman (or groups of working-men, in any numbers) for enjoying and practising equal rights in the use of public printing presses and public stocks of paper.

The imperialist war of 1914-18 conclusively revealed even to back-ward workers the true nature of bourgeois democracy, even in the freest republics, as being a dictatorship of the bourgeoisie. Tens of millions were killed for the sake of enriching the German or the British group of millionaires and multimillionaires.

The main thing that [reformist] Socialists fail to understand and that constitutes their short-sightedness in matters of theory, their sub-servience to bourgeois prejudices, and their political betrayal of the pro-letariat, is that in capitalist society, whenever there is any serious aggravation of the class struggle intrinsic to that society, there can be no alternative but the dictatorship of the bourgeoisie or the dictatorship of the proletariat. Dreams of some third way are reactionary, petty-bour-geois lamentations. That is borne out by more than a century of devel-opment of bourgeois democracy and the working class movement in all the advanced countries and notably by the experience of the past five years. This is also borne out by the whole science of political economy, by the entire content of Marxism, which reveals the economic inevitabil-ity, wherever commodity economy prevails, of the dictatorship of the bourgeoisie that can be replaced only by the class which the very growth of capitalism develops, multiplies, welds together, and strengthens, that is, the proletarian class.

Proletarian dictatorship is similar to the dictatorship of other classes in that it arises out of the need, as every other dictatorship does, to sup-press forcibly the resistance of the class that is losing its political sway. The fundamental distinction between the dictatorship of the proletariat and the dictatorship of other classes — landlord dictatorship in the Mid-dle Ages and bourgeois dictatorship in all the civilised capitalist coun-tries — consists in the fact that the dictatorship of the landowners and bourgeoisie was the forcible suppression of the resistance offered by the vast majority of the population, namely, the working people. In contrast, proletarian dictatorship is the forcible suppression of the resistance of the exploiters, i.e. an insignificant minority of the population, the landowners and capitalists.

It follows that proletarian dictatorship must inevitably entail not only a change in democratic forms and institutions, generally speaking, but precisely such a change as provides an unparalleled extension of the actual enjoyment of democracy by those oppressed by capitalism the toiling classes.

The substance of Soviet government is that the permanent and only foundations of state power, the entire machinery of state. is the mass-scale organisation of the classes oppressed by capitalism, i.e. the workers and semi-proletarians (peasants who do not exploit the labour of others and regularly resort to the sale of at least part of their own labour power). It is the people, who even in the most democratic bourgeois republics, while possessing equal rights by law, have in fact been debarred by thousands of devices and subterfuges from participation in political life and enjoyment of democratic rights and liberties, that are now drawn into constant and unfailing, moreover, decisive participation in the democratic administration of the state.

The old, i.e. bourgeois democracy and the parliamentary system were so organised that it was the mass of working people who were kept furthest away from the machinery of government. Soviet power, i.e. the dictatorship of the proletariat' on the other hand, is so organised as to bring the working people close to the machinery of government. That, too, is the purpose of combining the legislative and executive authority under the soviet organisation of the state and to replacing territorial constituencies by production units — the factory.

The army was a machine of oppression under not only the monarchy. It remains as such in all bourgeois republics, even the most democratic ones. Only the soviets, the permanent organisations of government authority of the classes that were oppressed by capitalism, are in a position to destroy the army's subordination to bourgeois commanders and really merge the proletariat with the army; only the soviets can effectively arm the proletariat and disarm the bourgeoisie. Unless this is done, the victory of socialism is impossible.

Only the soviet organisation of the state can really effect the immediate break-up and total destruction of the old, i.e. bourgeois, bureaucratic and judicial machinery which has been, and has inevitably had to be, retained under capitalism even in the most democratic republics, and which is, in actual fact, the greatest obstacle to the practical implementation of democracy for the workers and the working people generally. The Paris Commune took the first epoch-making step along this path. The soviet system has taken the second.

Destruction of state power is the aim set by all socialists, including Marx above all. Genuine democracy, i.e. liberty and equality, is unrealisable unless this aim is achieved. But its practical achievement is possible only through soviet, or proletarian democracy, for by enlisting the mass organisations of the working people in constant and unfailing participation in the administration of the state, it immediately begins to prepare the complete withering away of any state.

The ludicrous attempt to combine the soviet system, i.e. proletarian dictatorship, with the National Assembly, i.e. bourgeois dictatorship, utterly exposes the paucity of thought of the Yellow Socialists and Social Democrats, their reactionary petty-bourgeois political outlook, and their cowardly concessions to the irresistibly growing strength of the new, proletarian democracy.

Theses on bourgeois democracy and the dictatorship of the proletariat, from the First Congress of the Communist International, March 1919 (abridged to remove long-forgotten examples and illustrations).

Fighting for a more generous democracy

By Leon Trotsky

AS LONG AS the majority of the working class continues on the basis of bourgeois democracy, we are ready to defend it with all our forces against violent attacks from the Bonapartist and fascist bourgeoisie. However, we demand from our class brothers who adhere to 'democratic' socialism that they be faithful to their ideas, that they draw inspiration from the ideas and methods not of the Third Republic but of the Convention of 1793.

Down with the Senate, which is elected by limited suffrage and which renders the power of universal suffrage a mere illusion! Down with the presidency of the republic, which serves as a hidden point of concentration for the forces of militarism and reaction! A single assembly must combine the legislative and executive powers. Members would be elected for two years, by universal suffrage at eighteen years of age, with no discrimination of sex or nationality. Deputies would be elected on the basis of local assemblies, constantly revocable by their constituents, and would receive the salary of a skilled worker.

This is the only measure that would lead the masses forward instead of pushing them backward. A more generous democracy would facilitate the struggle for workers' power.

From the Action Program for France, 1934

MAI 68

DEBUT D'UNE LUTTE PROLONGEE

What socialists do, and why they do it

Sean Matgamna

WHAT IS THE SOCIALIST REVOLUTION? How does it relate to the existing system? What makes the socialists' belief in their own cause rational, the product of a scientific view of history, despite the present weakness of socialism?

Capitals grow by the eating up of the smaller by the bigger capitals, in a progression that has led in our time to global companies richer than many governments. Today, world-wide, the capitalist classes are dominant in a way less than ever before alloyed by old customs and compromises, and they are more closely intermeshed across national frontiers. Simultaneously, the old measures of social provision implemented by Western welfare states and Third World bureaucratic regimes are being stripped away. Inequality between rich and poor is increasing worldwide, and within most individual countries.

Marx explained: "Hand in hand with centralisation, or this expropriation of many capitalists by few, develop, on an ever-extending scale, the co-operative form of the labour-process, the conscious technical application of science, the methodical cultivation of the soil, the transformation of the instruments of labour into instruments of labour only usable in common, the economising of all means of production by their use as means of production of combined, socialised labour, the entanglement of all peoples in the net of the world-market, and with this, the international character of the capitalistic regime.

"Along with the constantly diminishing number of the magnates of capital, who usurp and monopolise all advantages of this process of transformation, grows the mass of misery, oppression, slavery, degradation, exploitation; but with this too grows the revolt of the working-class, a class always increasing in numbers, and disciplined, united, organised by the very mechanism of the process of capitalist production itself.

"The monopoly of capital becomes a fetter upon the mode of production, which has sprung up and flourished along with, and under it. Centralisation of the means of production and socialisation of labour at last reach a point where they become incompatible with their capitalist integument. This integument is burst asunder. The knell of capitalist private property sounds. The expropriators are expropriated...

331

"This does not re-establish private property for the producer, but gives him individual property based on the acquisition of the capitalist era: i.e., on co-operation and the possession in common of the land and of the means of production...

"The transformation of capitalistic private property, already practically resting on socialised production, into socialised property... is the expropriation of a few usurpers by the mass of the people".

The revolutionary potential of the working class

Capitalism rests on the exploitation of wage workers, people with no property in the means of production and only their own labour power to sell — the proletariat. Capitalism creates the proletariat. What do we mean when we say that the proletariat is central to the socialist alternative to capitalism?

Marx again: "The first attempt of workers to associate among themselves always takes place in the form of combinations. Large-scale industry concentrates in one place a crowd of people unknown to one another. Competition divides their interests. But the maintenance of wages, this common interest which they have against their boss, unites them in a common thought of resistance — combination. Thus combination always has a double aim, that of stopping competition among the workers, so that they can carry on general competition with the capitalist.

"If the first aim of resistance was merely the maintenance of wages, combinations, at first isolated, constitute themselves into groups as the capitalists in their turn unite for the purpose of repression, and in the face of always united capital, the maintenance of the association becomes more necessary to them than that of wages. This is so true that English economists are amazed to see the workers sacrifice a good part of their wages in favour of associations, which, in the eyes of these economists, are established solely in favour of wages. In this struggle — a veritable civil war — all the elements necessary for a coming battle unite and develop. Once it has reached this point, association takes on a political character. Economic conditions had first transformed the mass of the people of the country into workers. The combination of capital has created for this mass a common situation, common interests. This mass is thus already a class as against capital, but not yet for itself. In the struggle, of which we have noted only a few phases, this mass becomes united, and constitutes itself as a class for itself. The interests it defends becomes class interests. But the struggle of class against class is a political struggle...

"When it is a question of making a precise study of strikes, combinations and other forms in which the proletarians carry out before our eyes their organisation as a class, some are seized with real fear and others display a transcendental disdain. An oppressed class is the vital condition for every society founded on the antagonism of classes. The emancipation of the oppressed class thus implies necessarily the creation of a new society. For the oppressed class to be able to emancipate itself, it is necessary that the productive powers already acquired and the existing social relations should no longer be capable of existing side by side. Of all the instruments of production, the greatest productive power is the revolutionary class itself. The organisation of revolutionary elements as a class supposes the existence of all the productive forces which could be engendered in the bosom of the old society.

"Does this mean that after the fall of the old society there will be a new class domination? No. The condition for the emancipation of the working class is the abolition of every class, just as the condition for the liberation of the third estate, of the bourgeois order, was the abolition of all estates and all orders. The working class, in the course of its development, will substitute for the old civil society an association which will exclude classes and their antagonism...

"Meanwhile the antagonism between the proletariat and the bourgeoisie is a struggle of class against class, a struggle which carried to its highest expression is a total revolution. Indeed, is it at all surprising that a society founded on the opposition of classes should culminate in brutal contradiction, the shock of body against body, as its final denouement?

"Do not say that social movement excludes political movement. There is never a political movement which is not at the same time social. It is only in an order of things in which there are no more classes and class antagonisms that social evolutions will cease to be political revolutions. Till then, on the eve of every general reshuffling of society, the last word of social science will always be: 'Le combat ou la mort; la lutte sanguinaire ou le néant. C'est ainsi que la question est invinciblement posée.'" [From the novel *Jean Siska* by George Sand: "Combat or Death: bloody struggle or extinction. It is thus that the question is inexorably put".]

Blockages and obstacles

Today the wage-working class is, for the first time in history, probably the largest social class on the planet. There are probably also more organised workers across the world than ever before, with maybe 200 million trade unionists today. Nominal trade union numbers were bigger before 1989, but were artificially inflated by including the members of the state-controlled fake unions of the USSR, Eastern Europe, etc.

But the idea that they exist to replace capitalism with a higher system, to take humankind to socialism, is not the guiding principle of these labour movements. Explosions recur, both in the older capitalist countries and the newer ones. But even when the working class struggles and organises on a large scale, it finds that capitalism has tremendous flexibility for accommodating such struggles and for seducing and pacifying the leaders of workers' organisations.

Earlier generations of socialists thought of the transition from capitalism to socialism as a much more simple business than it has proved to be, as something covering a shorter time span than it is taking. They thought of the self-preparation of the working class to lead humankind out of capitalist neo-barbarism as much more straightforward thing than it has been.

Labour movements experience not only phases of growth and political development, but also phases of destruction and defeat — such as that experienced by the revolutionary labour movement before World War Two — of decay, decline and political regression, and then, again, periods of new growth and political refocusing.

The bourgeoisie too spent ages as a class that needed to remake society in its own image. It took the bourgeoisie, living within feudalism and monarchist absolutist systems, hundreds of years to make itself fit to be the ruling class. It went through many phases, experienced false starts, defeats, was led into "historical compromises" with its class-antagonists.

Yet as a revolutionary class it had immense advantages compared to the proletariat in capitalist society. Its wealth, power, self-rule and historical self-awareness grew even within the old system; the growth of markets, the increasing role of money in the old society, cleared its way and made it socially a subordinate segment of the exploiters even before it ruled. By contrast, the working class in capitalism remains the basic exploited class: it can progress only by independent organisation and by way of its social and political awareness. It can progress only by building a labour and socialist movement.

The Russian labour movement which, led by the Bolshevik Party, took state power in October 1917 was, in the sharpness of its theory and the adequacy of the revolutionary practice guided by that theory, the highest point reached by the working class in world history so far. It remains the great model and guide for the socialists who have come after it.

The activists and the spontaneous struggle

George Plekhanov answered the question "What is the socialist movement"? "Shortly before the revolutionary year of 1848 there emerged among the Socialists men who looked at socialism in a completely new perspective. Seen in this new perspective the principal error of previous Socialists was precisely the fact that [for them] 'future history resolves itself, in their eyes, into propaganda and the practical implementation of their social plans'. The Socialists with the new outlook saw in the future history of the civilised world something else, something incomparably more promising. What precisely did the Socialists with the new outlook see in it? Above all class struggle, the struggle of the exploited with the exploiters, the proletariat with the bourgeoisie. In addition they saw in it the inevitability of the impending triumph of the proletariat, the fall of the present bourgeois social order, the socialist organisation of production and the corresponding alteration in the relationships between people, i.e. even the destruction of classes, among other things.

"Although they knew full well (better than their predecessors) that the socialist revolution involves a complete transformation in all social relationships, the Socialists of the new tendency did not concern themselves at all with working out a plan for the future organisation of society.

"If for the followers of scientific socialism the whole future history of bourgeois society resolves itself in the struggle of the proletariat with the bourgeoisie, all their practical tasks are prompted by precisely this class struggle. Standing resolutely on the side of the proletariat, the new Socialists do everything in their power to facilitate and hasten its victory. But what exactly can they do in this case? A necessary condition for the victory of the proletariat is its recognition of its own position, its relations with its exploiters, its historic role and its socio-political tasks.

"For this reason the new Socialists consider it their principal, perhaps even their only, duty to promote the growth of this consciousness among the proletariat, which for short they call its class consciousness. The whole success of the socialist movement is measured for them in terms of the growth in the class consciousness of the proletariat. Everything that helps this growth they see as useful to their cause: everything that slows it down as harmful. Anything that has no effect one way or the other is of no consequence for them, it is politically uninteresting.

"You will only be recognised as a Socialist if your activity has directly facilitated the growth of the class consciousness of the proletariat. If it does not exert this direct influence then you are not a Socialist at all, even though the more or less remote consequences of your non-socialist activity may bring some degree of advantage for the cause of socialism. My view, I hope, is sufficiently clear. It is expressed in its entirety in the epigram: *Without workers who are conscious of their class interests there can be no socialism.*

"If I assert that the promotion of the growth of the class consciousness of the proletariat is the sole purpose and the direct and sacred duty of

335

the Socialists, then this does not mean that the contemporary Socialists stand for propaganda, for propaganda alone, and for nothing but propaganda. In the broad sense of the word this is perhaps true, but only in the very broad sense. In general it is not easy to draw the line between agitation and what is usually called propaganda. Agitation is also propaganda, but propaganda that takes place in particular circumstances, that is in circumstances in which even those who would not normally pay any attention are forced to listen to the propagandist's words. Propaganda is agitation that is conducted in the normal everyday course of the life of a particular country. Agitation is propaganda occasioned by events that are not entirely ordinary and that provoke a certain upsurge in the public mood. Socialists would be very bad politicians if they were not to use such notable events for their own ends".

Side by side with the broad, elemental class struggle of the working class — and with some autonomy from it, not necessarily on the same rhythms and tempos — a certain proportion of each generation of young people growing up under capitalism become convinced that they must fight to replace this society of exploitation and competition by socialism, a society of solidarity. And some of them are consolidated as activists.

For working-class struggles to move towards revolutionary conclusions, what is needed is that those activists organise themselves; educate themselves; keep their theory and their revolutionary drive bright and sharp; and integrate themselves into the existing labour movement and win respect there, so that at critical moments of class battle they can directly challenge the old time-serving leaders and prevent the diversion of the "spontaneous socialist" impulses of the workers in struggle.

That way the activists can win wider influence, recruit new activists, refresh their own ideas by learning from the battles, and ultimately enlarge, improve, and sharpen their organisation so that at one of the inevitable points where large working-class struggle coincides with drastic internal crisis for capitalism they can lead the working class to revolutionary victory.

That is what the Russian Marxists did between the 1880s and 1917. In Russia the first revolutionary socialists — most of whom also considered themselves "Marxists" — were the populists. The development of the Russian Marxist movement involved a small section of activists separating themselves off from a populist movement which, though in crisis, was still large, active, and influential, in order to argue in theoretical pamphlets for a new approach.

That approach was summed up by Plekhanov in the idea that the Marxists were "convinced that not the workers are necessary for the revolution, but the revolution for the workers"

Later the Marxists became a mass movement in 1905, only to split definitively and be reduced to very small numbers of reliable activists in the years of reaction which followed. As Lenin put it, "Russia achieved Marxism... through the agony she experienced in half a century of unparalleled torment and sacrifice, of unparalleled revolutionary heroism, incredible energy, devoted searching, study, practical trial, disappointment, verification, and comparison with European experience".

The revolutionary party

The working class is unique among all revolutionary classes in that it remains a class of wage slaves until, by seizing political power and the means of production, it makes the decisive step towards emancipating itself. Contrast the classic bourgeois experience.

The bourgeoisie develops historically within feudalism and neo-feudalism as part of a division of labour within society which allows the bourgeoisie to own a segment of the means of production, and itself to be an exploiter, long before it takes political power in society. It thus builds up wealth, culture, systems of ideas to express its interests and view of the world. It, so to speak, ripens organically, and the taking of power, the sloughing off of the old system — even if accompanied by violence — represents the natural maturing and growth of a class already in possession of important means of production and a share of the surplus. The working class remains an exploited class — in more developed capitalist countries, the basic exploited class — up to the death knell of bourgeois social and political rule. It does not accumulate leisure, wealth or its own distinct culture. Its natural condition as a raw social category is to be dominated by the ideas of the ruling class. Its own natural and spontaneous self-defence and bargaining within the capitalist system — trade unionism — binds it ideologically to the ruling class, to bargaining within the system and in times of crisis taking responsibility for it. Its natural tribunes and intellectuals are the trade union bureaucracy.

On the face of it the proletariat might be doomed to go through history as a subordinate class. Marx and Engels themselves wrote: "The ruling ideology in every society is the ideology of the ruling class." In fact the working class becomes a revolutionary class, conscious of its own historic class interests and possibilities in the following way, according to the views of Marx, Engels, Lenin and Trotsky. A set of social theories is created and developed on the basis of bourgeois social science (economics, philosophy, history) which uncovers the necessary logic of the historic evolution of capitalism towards the completion of its organic tendency to become more and more social and monopolistic — by way of common ownership and the abolition of capitalism. The proletariat is located as the protagonist in this stage of history. A segment of the intellectuals of the bourgeoisie comes over to the proletarian wage slaves.

The proletariat itself evolves as a class through the stage of primitive elemental revolt at being driven into the capitalist industrial hell-holes to the stage of organising itself in combinations to get fair wages, and then to the stage of banding itself together for political objectives.

Instead of control of a portion of the means of production, the working class develops its own organisations. Within these organisations a struggle takes place between the ideas that represent the historic interests of the proletariat — Marxism — and the ideas of the bourgeoisie. This struggle occurs even where Marxists are the founders of the labour movement.

Antonio Gramsci summed up the threefold nature of the class struggle: "We know that the proletariat's struggle against capitalism is waged on three fronts: the economic, the political and the ideological. The economic struggle has three phases: resistance to capitalism, i.e. the elementary trade-union phase; the offensive against capitalism for workers' control of production; and the struggle to eliminate capitalism through socialisation.

"The political struggle too has three principal phases: the struggle to check the bourgeoisie's power in the parliamentary State, in other words to maintain or create a democratic situation, of equilibrium between the classes, which allows the proletariat to organise; the struggle to win power and create the workers' State, in other words a complex political activity through which the proletariat mobilises around it all the anti-capitalist social forces (first and foremost the peasant class) and leads them to victory; and the phase of dictatorship of the proletariat, organised as a ruling class to eliminate all the technical and social obstacles which prevent the realisation of communism.

"The economic struggle cannot be separated from the political struggle, nor can either of them be separated from the ideological struggle.

"In its first, trade-union phase, the economic struggle is spontaneous; in other words, it is born inevitably of the very situation in which the proletariat finds itself under the bourgeois order. But in itself, it is not revolutionary; in other words, it does not necessarily lead to the overthrow of capitalism...

"For the trade-union struggle to become a revolutionary factor, it is necessary for the proletariat to accompany it with political struggle: in other words, for the proletariat to be conscious of being the protagonist of a general struggle which touches all the most vital questions of social organisation; i.e. for it to be conscious that it is struggling for socialism...

"The element of consciousness is needed, the 'ideological' element:

in other words, an understanding of the conditions of the struggle, the social relations in which the worker lives, the fundamental tendencies at work in the system of those relations, and the process of development which society undergoes as a result of the existence within it of insoluble antagonisms, etc.

"The three fronts of proletarian struggle are reduced to a single one for the party of the working class, which is this precisely because it resumes and represents all the demands of the general struggle. One certainly cannot ask every worker from the masses to be completely aware of the whole complex function which his class is destined to perform in the process of development of humanity. But this must be asked of members of the party. One cannot aim, before the conquest of the State, to change completely the consciousness of the entire working class... But the party can and must, as a whole, represent this higher consciousness."

The blight of Stalinism

For more than 100 years, things other than working class defeat and the continuation of capitalism to this stage have been possible. Working class victory and the beginning of a rational socialist system were possible; but we have had defeats. Trotsky, who had helped the Russian workers in October 1917 demonstrate that the working class suffers from no inbuilt organic political incapacity, understood that the crux of the crisis of human civilisation in the mid-20th century was a crisis of the labour movement. Great labour movements had been created on the perspective of preparing the working class to suppress wage labour and capitalism — a working class that would make itself the ruling class, and freeing itself from capitalism, begin to free humankind from class society. The leaderships, bureaucracies and upper layers of the old socialist movement had, when the first imperialist World War broke out, delivered the labour movements into the hands of their bourgeois enemy as cannon fodder and butchers of the workers of other nations.

The Communist International had been created in 1919 and after to restore independent working class politics after the collapse of 1914. The Stalinist counter-revolution in the USSR in the 1920s tied the Communist International to the new bureaucratic ruling class in the USSR.

When, after 1929, capitalism reached the stage of convulsive semi-collapse, powerful labour movements existed that were strong enough to kick it into its historical grave. But they were everywhere tied to either the bourgeoisie, through the reform-socialist "labour movements", or to the Russian ruling class, through its Communist Parties. Trotsky wrote of their "perfidy" and "betrayal".

In the confusion created by the existence of big socialist parties that weren't socialist, and big Communist Parties that weren't communist, the working class suffered murderous accumulating defeat. Trotsky organised the tiny forces that could be organised to compete, with desperate urgency, for the leadership of the working class against the perfidious incumbent leaderships. But Trotsky and everything he represented were defeated and — as we have to recognise in retrospect — defeated for a whole historical period. Capitalism renewed itself on the mass graves, on the destroyed means of production and the ruined cities of the Second World War and began a long period of expansion. Stalinism survived, expanded, and then slowly asphyxiated in its own bureaucratic caul until, in Europe, it collapsed.

Big labour movements grew in Western Europe, especially, in the new Golden Age of capitalism between 1950 and the early 1970s. But they grew deeply imbued with reformism and, often, Stalinist ideas. When they exploded into big battles between 1968 and the early 80s, new revolutionary-minded groupings grew, but not sufficient, and not sufficiently clear, to reconstruct a mass revolutionary socialist culture in the time available.

Defeats in the early 1980s allowed a new, more aggressive, mode of capitalist rule to consolidate, and led to a slow ebbing of the old labour movements. New labour movements emerged in new industrial centres, but, again, not yet revolutionary in temper.

The collapse of the USSR in 1991 came at a time when the workers' movement in the West had been on the retreat for a decade. It fuelled a great surge of capitalist triumphalism, which continues to this day. In many countries it demoralised and dissipated large numbers of the men and women who considered themselves "communists" and "socialists" and who really were the people who provided the activist backbone of the labour movement, the trade union branches and the workplace committees. It created wider openings for the genuine communists, the Trotskyists. But the collapse also revealed how much, in the long years of its isolation, the Trotskyist milieu had become waterlogged with seepage from Stalinism. Today groupings like the SWP, nominally Trotskyist, actually operate more like a small replica of the 1960s Communist Parties, their politics dominated by the "popular front" approach both internationally and in domestic politics.

Who are we, the AWL? We are those who continue to fight for independent working-class politics and for working-class self-liberation against both capitalism and reactionary anti-capitalism (such as Islamic fundamentalism). We are those who continue, as best we can, the Trotskyism of Trotsky and his comrades in the 1930s, rather than extrapolating the cod "orthodox Trotskyism" shaped in the 1940s and early 1950s into a Stalinist-influenced neo-populism. We are the pioneers of the future mass revolutionary workers' parties which will be free of Stalinist seepage and sharp-edged in their drive for independent working-class struggle.

Marxists today

It is impossible to tell how long it will take the working class to make itself ready to suppress capitalism and take humankind forward. It is more easily definable in terms of things that must be accomplished.

The labour movements again need to learn by way of their own experience and by the enlightening work of socialists:

• that capitalism is neither natural nor eternal;

• that it is a historically finite system whose inner processes — the creation and recreation of a proletariat and the relentless socialisation of the means of production, of which "globalisation" is the latest manifestation — prepare its own end;

• that capitalism digs its own grave;

• that the working class, which finds no class in society "lower" than itself and which can only organise the economy collectively, that is, democratically, is the representative within capitalism of the post-capitalist future, and the only force that can suppress this neo-barbarism and replace it with something better.

Quick, seemingly miraculous, transformations in the thinking of labour movements have occurred and will occur. That worker who accepts capitalism is in a condition in which her objective interests as both worker and human being are at odds with the ideas about society and the world she has been taught to accept. Once that begins to change, everything can change.

Marxism is a necessary part of this process. Labour movements can arrive at vaguely "socialist" hopes and aspirations, just as young people can arrive at angry rebellion against capitalism. Scientific understanding of capitalism, of society, of the centrality of the working class and the politics of working class self-liberation — in short, understanding of how we can map the way from capitalism neo-barbarism to human liberation — does not arise "spontaneously". That is what Marxist theory is for. That is Marxism's irreplaceable contribution.

Writing about Russia 100 years ago, Lenin put it like this: "Social-Democracy [the revolutionary Marxist movement] is a combination of the labour movement with socialism. Its task is not passively to serve the labour movement at each of its separate stages, but to represent the interests of the movement as a whole, to point out to this movement its ultimate aims and its political tasks, and to protect its political and ideological independence. Isolated from Social-Democracy, the labour movement becomes petty and inevitably becomes bourgeois: in conducting only the economic struggle, the working class loses its political independence; it becomes the tail of other parties and runs counter to the great slogan: 'The emancipation of the workers must be the task of the workers themselves'.

"In every country there has been a period in which the labour movement existed separately from the socialist movement, each going its own road; and in every country this state of isolation weakened both the socialist movement and the labour movement. Only the combination of socialism with the labour movement in each country created a durable basis for both the one and the other. But in each country this combination of socialism with the labour movement took place historically, was brought about in a special way, in accordance with the conditions prevailing at the time in each country. The process of combining the two movements is an extremely difficult one, and there is therefore nothing surprising in the fact that it is accompanied by vacillations and doubts."

And again: "The strikes of the 1890s [in Russia] revealed far greater flashes of consciousness: definite demands were put forward, the time to strike was carefully chosen, known cases and examples in other places were discussed, etc. While the earlier riots were simply uprisings of the oppressed, the systematic strikes represented the class struggle in embryo, but only in embryo.

"Taken by themselves, these strikes were simply trade union struggles, but not yet Social-Democratic struggles. They testified to the awakening antagonisms between workers and employers, but the workers were not and could not be conscious of the irreconcilable antagonism of their interests to the whole of the modern political and social system, i.e., it was not yet Social-Democratic consciousness. In this sense, the strikes of the 1890s, in spite of the enormous progress they represented as compared with the 'riots', represented a purely spontaneous movement.

"We said that there could not yet be Social-Democratic consciousness among the workers. This consciousness could only be brought to them from without. The history of all countries shows that the working class, exclusively by its own efforts, is able to develop only trade union consciousness, i.e., it may itself realise the necessity for combining in unions, for fighting against the employers and for striving to compel the government to pass necessary labour legislation, etc. The theory of socialism, however, grew out of the philosophic, historical and economic theories that were elaborated by the educated representatives of the propertied classes, the intellectuals. According to their social status, the founders of modern scientific socialism, Marx and Engels, themselves belonged to the bourgeois intelligentsia. Similarly, in Russia, the theoretical doctrine of Social-Democracy arose quite independently of the spontaneous growth of the labour movement; it arose as a natural and inevitable outcome of the development of ideas among the revolutionary socialist intelligentsia."

Today, Marxism, scientific socialism — what in Lenin's time was called Social Democracy — is everywhere separate from the labour movement, greatly more so than when Lenin was writing. To unite Marxism with the labour movement is the task of revolutionary socialists and consistent democrats everywhere. The collapse of Stalinism gives us a better chance of doing that then we have had in 90 years.

But Marxism itself — the consciousness of the unconscious processes of society — Marxism as a guide to revolutionary action, has suffered tremendous blows in the last historical period. The supreme irony is that the collapse of Russian Stalinism, which had through much of the 20th century turned "Marxism" into the pidgin religion of a totalitarian state, should have as its first consequence the discrediting of "Marxism". That is only the first consequence. The collapse of the Russian state-fostered pidgin Marxism clears the way for the development of unfalsified Marxism. We have a considerable way to go yet to achieve that.

Renewing Marxism

The revolutionary Marxist tradition is "given", but Marxism is not. Marxism as a living force in socialist organisations and in the labour movement is not something given — it has to be fought for and won and then again fought for and won over again, and then yet again.

It has to be clarified and refined and augmented, again and again in a never-ending process. That process is, in a word, "the class struggle on the ideological front".

Lenin said it plainly and truly: "Without revolutionary theory there can be no revolutionary movement." He also said: "Practice without theory is blind: theory without practice is sterile." In a declaration of the Editorial Board of the revolutionary newspaper *Iskra*, Lenin wrote:

"The intellectual unity of Russian Social-Democrats has still be to established, and in order to achieve this it is necessary, in our opinion, to have an open and thorough discussion of the fundamental principles and tactical questions. Before we can unite, and in order that we may unite, we must first of all firmly and definitely draw the lines of demarcation. Otherwise, our unity will be merely a fictitious unity, which will conceal the prevailing confusion and prevent its complete elimination. Naturally, therefore, we do not intend to utilise our publication merely as a storehouse for various views. On the contrary, we shall conduct it along the lines of a strictly defined tendency. This tendency can be expressed by the word Marxism, and there is hardly need to add that we stand for the consistent development of the ideas of Marx and Engels, and utterly reject the half-way, vague and opportunistic emendations which have now become so fashionable".

Having rejected eclecticism and indifferentism, he went on:

"But while discussing all questions from our own definite point of view, we shall not rule out of our columns polemics between comrades. Open polemics within the sight and hearing of all Russian Social-Democrats and class conscious workers are necessary and desirable, in order to explain the profound differences that exist, to obtain a comprehensive discussion of disputed questions, and to combat the extremes into which the representatives, not only of various views, but also of various localities or various 'crafts' in the revolutionary movement inevitably fall. As has already been stated, we also consider one of the drawbacks of the present-day movement to be the absence of open polemics among those holding avowedly differing views, an effort to conceal the differences that exist over extremely serious questions."

These words offer a guide to revolutionary Marxists now. They will guide the conduct of the Alliance for Workers' Liberty. The fight for Marxism and for a Marxist labour movement is the fight to prepare the only force capable of taking humanity out of our age of neo-barbarism, the working class, for that task. It is for that task that the Alliance for Workers Liberty exists and fights.

As we were saying

15 lies against socialism answered

Sean Matgamna

"BUT SOCIALISM IS DEAD, DARLING!" This was one response on the street to the front page of Socialist Organiser [in 1991, after the collapse of the USSR] with the headline: "Stand up for socialism". And there were many similar responses, sad as well as gleeful. For sure, if the Stalinist systems were any sort of socialism, then socialism is dead, and it deserves to be dead. It was rotten and stinking for decades before its recent outright collapse. But Stalinism was not socialism. It was the opposite of socialism.

Throughout our existence, Socialist Organiser has championed the underground workers' movements and the oppressed nationalities in the Stalinist states. We have waged war on the idea — held by many in the labour movement — that the Stalinist states were socialist in any sense or in any degree. It is the same idea being peddled now — but from the other side, not by confused would-be socialists, but by bourgeois propagandists who insist that Stalinism was socialism because they want to discredit socialism and bury it.

If socialists hold their course then we will find the collapse of Stalinism and the discrediting of its bureaucratic falsifications of socialism has cleared the ground for a new flowering of unfalsified socialism. Socialist Organiser is one of the bearers of the seeds of this new growth of socialism. Fighting the lies that socialism and Stalinism are identical, and that Stalinism was the same thing as the Bolshevik Russian Revolution, we will hasten the new growth of unfalsified working class socialism.

The first thing now is to answer the lies of the bourgeoisie and of the ex-Stalinists.

1. The system now disintegrating in Eastern Europe was socialist.

No it wasn't! It was a system of extreme exploitation of the workers and peasants, run by a backward bureaucratic ruling class with a monopoly of political and social power. It was that bureaucracy which decreed that their state should nationalise and control everything — not Marx, or, for that matter Lenin.

Far from representing the working class, the Stalinist systems were characterised above all by a savage repression of the working class, and

345

relentless persecution of working class dissidents, especially workers who tried to organise independent trade unions.

2. The most important thing is to defend the nationalised economies.

It will be a great defeat for the working class in Eastern Europe and the USSR if the collapse of the bureaucratically centralised economies leads not to workers' liberty but to their replacement by Western-style capitalist exploitation. Far better if the state-monopoly system is replaced by workers' democratic self-management, and democratic socialist working-class planning. Such a trajectory would avoid the long detour and the bitter class struggles that otherwise face the workers in Eastern Europe and the USSR.

Some would-be Trotskyists, on the other hand, argue that the preservation of the Stalinist nationalised economy is of great importance and its loss would be a huge catastrophe, dwarfing almost everything else. But the nationalised economy has been operated on the basis of the savage exploitation of the working class. What is most important of all for the workers in the Stalinist state is to gain the liberty to organise, to think, to discuss, and thus to learn. Suppose a section of the Stalinist bureaucracy tights to defend the state-monopoly system, while workers, for example in Solidarnosc, press for the extension of market forces. The view that the preservation of the nationalised economy is of overriding importance would logically lead socialists — and even "Trotskyists"! — to support the hard·line Stalinists against the workers.

Neither market forces nor a Stalinist state-monopoly economy serve the working class. The cardinal value for socialists must, be the free activity of the working class — even when, in the opinion of those who take the long historical view, the workers are muddled and mistaken. In all circumstances socialists must support the right of the labour movement to exist, irrespective of its political ideas.

3. All that is needed is to liberate the nations of Eastern Europe from Russian overlordship.

That is needed! Socialist Organiser and Workers' Liberty — in the tradition of the Trotskyist movement of the 1940s — have been very outspoken in demanding freedom for the nations of Eastern Europe. But that is just a beginning. The question is, what is to replace Russian overlordship? The terrible truth is that Eastern Europe and large areas of the USSR are mosaics or crazy pavements of fractured nations and peoples. State boundaries rarely coincide with the outlines of ethnic or linguistic groups or of national self-definition.

346

National conflicts and resentments have festered and become doubly poisonous under the clamp of Stalinist repression. Now they are emerging into the open.

There is almost civil war between Azerbaijan and Armenia, and between different groups in the Yugoslav federation. The idea of national self-determination — that is, national democracy — is only a rough guide to what must be done in these areas to secure a basis for coexistence between the different peoples. If self-determination is not linked with the ideas of socialist internationalism, then in these conditions it can be channelled into the most vicious and narrow chauvinism.

The socialist movement long ago answered these problems with such ideas as creating a Socialist United States of Europe and a Balkan Socialist Federation. Only the working class, fighting for socialism, can make these ideas a reality. Market forces in Eastern Europe and the USSR must inevitably accelerate the present trends towards fragmentation and ethnic and national antagonisms.

4. The collapse of the planned economies in Eastern Europe means the eclipse of socialism.

Quite the opposite. It means the renewal of socialism. The disavowal of socialism by the Stalinists will help free socialism from the Stalinist, statist taint which poisoned much of the socialist and communist movement for six decades.

Socialism is a good idea — but it is not just a good idea! It is rooted in the class struggle of the working class. That struggle continues. The collapse of Stalinism has already opened up space for the workers, long suppressed, to begin to organise independently and think for themselves. They will formulate their own ideas.

Marxists do not believe that the dominance of socialist ideas is inevitable among workers. The hard truth is that there are great obstacles in the way of workers becoming socialists when they have lived all their lives under a Stalinist totalitarian system disguised as socialism.

We see that now in Eastern Europe. In the ex-Stalinist states the working class looks to the West and to market economics for its solutions. It mirrors the way in which working class movements in the West have for decades mistakenly looked to the Stalinist East as a model of escape from the peculiar horrors of our own society.

Nevertheless the prospect in all the East European states is for an intensified class struggle. Many workers, faced with class conflicts, in the new conditions, will move towards a genuine working-class world outlook. They will understand that the free market is no acceptable alternative to Stalinism, just as Stalinism was never a genuine working class alternative to the free market.

The rebirth of a mass socialist movement, cleansed of Stalinism, is a certainty in these conditions. It is a hard road from now to then, and it may be a long and winding road, but there is no other road for workers who want to defend their class interests to take.

Just as in recent years we have seen the inspiring development of such working class movements as South Africa's non-racial trade unions and the Brazilian Workers' Party — and Solidarnosc too — in previously more or less fallow areas of class struggle, so we will see the emergence of new workers' movements in the opened-up ex-Stalinist states.

5. Leninism bred Stalinism, and is discredited with it.

This is the central pillar of the edifice of lies now agreed on if bourgeois and ex-Stalinists alike. It is the biggest lie of all. Lenin and the Bolsheviks led the workers to power. They fought ruthlessly against the bourgeoisie and the opponents of socialism. They smashed the walls of the Tsarist prison-house of nations. Far from substituting for the working class, the Bolshevik party, by its leadership and farsightedness, allowed the working class to reach and sustain a level of mass action hitherto unparalleled in history.

The Bolsheviks based themselves on a system of democratic working class councils (soviets). Their goal was working-class democracy. They never believed that they could make socialism in backward Russia, only that the Russian working class could take power first. They believed they had a duty to maintain their bridgehead for workers' revolution in the most difficult and arduous circumstances.

The Bolsheviks were fallible human beings, acting in conditions of great difficulty. Mistakes they may have made in the maelstrom of civil war and economic collapse are proper subjects for socialist discussion and debate. As their critic and comrade Rosa Luxemburg wrote in 1918, the Bolsheviks would have been the last to imagine that everything they did in their conditions was a perfect model of socialist action for everywhere at all times. But what the Bolsheviks never were was the root of the Stalinist counter-revolution, which amongst its other crimes, murdered most of those who were still alive in the mid-1930s.

When things began to go wrong the Bolsheviks stood their ground. The workers' risings were defeated in the West. Invasions and civil war wrecked the soviets. The Bolshevik party itself divided. One section took a path on which it ended up leading the bureaucratic counterrevolution. The surviving central leaders fought the counterrevolution on a programme of working class self-defence and of renewing the soviets.

Those Bolsheviks (Trotskyists) went down to bloody defeat. Stalinism rose above the graves of Bolsheviks, just as it rose hideously above the murdered socialist hopes of the Russian and international working class. By the late-1930s Stalin had slaughtered the leading activists not only from the Trotskyist, but also from the Right Communist and even the Stalinist factions of the Bolshevik party of the 1920s.

Stalinism was not Bolshevism, any more than it was any kind of socialism. Trotsky, who was to die at the hands of Stalin's assassins put it well and truly when he said that a river of working-class and socialist blood separated Stalinism from Bolshevism. The workers in Eastern Europe and the USSR will learn the truth about that now that the possibility of open debate and honest information has been opened up.

6. Even if the Stalinist states were not fully socialist, they were "post-capitalist". They represented a stage in transition from capitalism towards socialism.

Post-capitalist is precisely what they are and were not. Socialism grows out of the most advanced capitalism. All the Stalinist states were and are comparatively backward and underdeveloped.

If capitalism had continued to decline as it was declining in its heartlands in the 1930s, and if the USSR had maintained the dynamism it had then, then the historical relationship between the two systems would perhaps have shaped up differently. But in fact capitalism has expanded immensely since the Second World War.

After 1945, US capitalism had huge power, and reshaped the world market into something not too far from the "imperialism of free trade" dominated by British capitalism in the mid 19th century. Capitalism grew both in its heartlands and in new areas. The USSR began to lose its relative dynamism in the early 1960s. As Trotsky had pointed out, bureaucratic rule could import basic technology and create a crude industrial infrastructure, but was a great obstacle to a self-sustaining modern economy generating its own new technology. With hindsight, the Stalinist system can be seen to be an epiphenomenon of the world capitalist system. The tremendous upsets now shaking the Stalinist system are the direct consequence of its comparative inefficiency. It is not the inefficiency of socialism, or of the working class. It is the inefficiency of a system which suppresses all working-class initiative.

7. Capitalism is vindicated by the disintegration of "state socialism".

One of the most profound and heartfelt paeans of praise ever written about capitalism will be found in the Communist Manifesto, the founding document of the modern socialist movement. Capitalism gave a tremendous boost to human capacity to change and control our environment and thus created the objective possibility of humanity rising above its "pre-history" out of the social jungle into a classless socialist society.

Marxists criticise the waste and irrationality and savage inhumanity of capitalism, but at the same time see capitalism as the necessary forerunner of socialism.

Capitalism has not ceased to be irrational and inhuman, nor have market mechanisms ceased to be blind and wasteful, just because of the Stalinist experiment in "state socialism". Wage slavery and exploitation have not ceased to be at the heart and root of capitalism. The possibility and even the inevitability remains of capitalism plunging once again into devastating slumps as in the 30s — and there are three million unemployed in Britain alone right now. Capitalism still presides over regular mass slaughters by hunger which are an indictment of any social system.

In the United States, the richest capitalist country in the world, thousands of people sleep on the streets, or get a living only through the drug trade. In the private-profit counterpart of Eastern Europe — Latin America — unemployment runs at 40% in the big cities, workers' living standards have sometimes been halved since the debt crisis broke in 1982, cocaine gangsters rule huge areas, and malnutrition and even starvation are widespread. Capitalism is no alternative at all!

Stalinism was not an attempt to go beyond advanced capitalism on the basis of the achievements of advanced capitalism which has proved by its failure the hopelessness of all such attempts. It was an experience on the fringes of world capitalism, arising out of the defeat of a working class revolution, and stifling under its own contradictory bureaucratic regime. Stalinism was part of the pre-history humankind must grow beyond. So is capitalism!

8. Socialism is discredited because only a free market economy can give a secure basis for democracy. Without it you get state control, and state control inevitably stifles democracy.

Marxists do not want any sort of bureaucratic state, neither that of a country like Britain, where the bureaucratic state works in tandem with the bourgeoisie, nor that of the Stalinist systems where the bureaucracy was the sole master of society's wealth

We advocate a "semi-state" without a standing army, without an entrenched bureaucracy. The Bolsheviks wanted that, too. They could not create it because of the backwardness of the isolated USSR, but it would be entirely possible in a country like Britain, especially with modern technology. The idea that only the market system of the West can be the basis for democracy is the idea that only wage slavery for the masses together with the phenomenal concentration of wealth — and therefore power — at the top of society can be the basis of democracy! It is a prize example of the crazy logic satirised by George Orwell according to which war is peace and lies are truth.

Even such democracy as we have in the West owes its existence to decades and centuries of struggle by the working class. Democracy in capitalism is limited, imperfect, and normally not very stable. Mass self-rule by the producers, dominated neither by a bureaucratic state monopoly nor by the economic rule of the multi-millionaires and their officials, is a better form of democracy. It is socialist democracy.

9. The reason for the economic impasse of the Eastern Bloc is that centralised planning cannot work in a complex economy: therefore capitalism is the only possible system.

This argument too rests on the lie that Stalinism — the Stalinist command economy — was socialism. The attempt to have the state control everything served the Stalinists, not the working class. Marxists never believed that the working class could take power and simply abolish the market: in 1921 Lenin set the goal of Soviet government as that of occupying 'the commanding heights of the economy'.

Socialism, once the workers have taken power and abolished wage slavery by taking the major means of production from the capitalist class, would — probably for generations ahead — operate through a combination of planning and market mechanisms — within the broad framework of a flexible plan. There is a vast difference between an economy where the basic strategic decisions are made by democratic planning — which is certainly possible — and one where they are made by the crazy gyrations of the Stock Exchange.

How quickly a workers' planned economy will be able to make its planning more comprehensive, and move towards replacing the market altogether, must be an open question.

10. Events in Eastern Europe prove that you can get a peaceful revolution.

No, they don't! The Stalinists (or neo-Stalinists) in Eastern Europe have nowhere given up the state power. Even in Poland the army, the police, and the core of the state bureaucracy remain in the hands of the Stalinists. They are by no means a spent force.

What will happen to these state apparatuses, how much purging they will receive in future, is an open question. Right now to dismiss them as a threat is to say the least premature. Whether even a shift to market economics, curtailing the power and privilege of the bureaucrats but allowing many of them to retain much of it on a new basis, can be achieved peacefully, is still an open question. There is no reason at all to believe that the workers in Eastern Europe could take power themselves, abolishing all the power and privilege of the bureaucrats, without violent clashes.

And even if they could, that would not mean that a peaceful revolution is possible in Britain. The reason why we cannot hope for a peaceful revolution that would end capitalism in Britain is that the ruling class would fight to defend themselves, as any ruling class capable of doing so would. They have the army and the civil service, the judiciary and the police force. They plan their strategies far ahead, as they planned and prepared to defeat the 1984 miners' strike years in advance.

In Eastern Europe we have regimes imposed by foreign armies, with very little support in the population apart from those admitted to the perks and privileges of the ruling class circles. They have in the past proved capable of lethal violence against the workers. Demonstrating workers were shot down in East Germany in 1953. Hundreds were mowed down in Gdansk, in Poland, in 1970. In 1981 the Polish bureaucrats imposed martial law.

Erich Honecker reportedly wanted to massacre the demonstrators in Leipzig. His colleagues stopped him. Why? Because the Russian overlord had changed the terms under which the satrap regime operated and, faced with the prospect of revolt at home and abroad, was no longer willing to guarantee support. The East European bureaucrats are the puppet rulers of a retreating empire. That is why they have conceded demand after demand. There is no real parallel here with conditions of working class struggle against a relatively stable ruling class of the capitalist sort.

11. The "melting" of East European Stalinism proves that the Stalinist bureaucracy is not and never was a ruling class.

This is a "left wing" rather than a bourgeois piece of nonsense. This opinion is held by two distinct currents of thought. One current denies that the bureaucracy is a class, still less a ruling class, and asserts that the working class rules in the Stalinist states. The other current simply says that there is no ruling class in any of the Stalinist states! This position is especially associated with Hillel Ticktin, a left wing academic.

The idea that the working class ruled and rules in the Stalinist states is on the face of it a strange idea about states where the working class has been savagely oppressed and denied freedom of speech, press, assembly, sexuality — in short denied all the civil and human rights workers in Britain have won through hard struggle over the decades and centuries. The workers have been treated like this by a vast privileged and corrupt bureaucracy which has ruled over society and controlled the lives of its inhabitants in its own interest, owning the means of production collectively because it "owned" the state.

The view that, nevertheless, the working class rules in these societies is tenable only if we believe that a nationalised economy — the model initially created after 1928 by Stalin — is working-class per se; and that in the perspective of history, in the necessary succession of stages in the development of society, a nationalised economy like the classic Stalin model can only be working-class. Such a view is held in Britain by, for example, Militant and others who went so far with this perverse view of history as to support the Russian army's napalm and gunships war against the people of Afghanistan after the USSR's invasion of that country in December 1979.

At root, in this its only logical form, this is a Stalinist theory, even though it is also adhered to by anti-Stalinists who mistakenly think it was Trotsky's position at the time of his death.

Events have long shown it to be a nonsense. We have had a massive experience of Third World bourgeoisies using extensive nationalisation to develop backward economies — Egypt in the '50s, '60s and early '70s, for example. By now it is indisputable fact that a social group with most of the attributes of a ruling class has held and exercised power in the Stalinist states.

The other view, that there has been no ruling class at all in East Europe and China for forty to fifty years, or in the USSR for the last 60 years, since Stalin overthrew the rule of the working class, rests on complicated technical theories and assessments. According to these, the chaos within the nominally planned Stalinist economies has meant that there is no properly worked-out system whereby the privileged rulers "appropriate the surplus product" and therefore they could not, in Marxist theory, be a ruling class. This is a very similar idea to the workers' state theory of Ernest Mandel and others, except that Mandel goes on to fantasise that, despite all the appearances, the working class, although it is socially, politically and intellectually kept down is nevertheless the ruling class. Instead of Mandel's mirage "solution", which allows him to formally stay within Marxist categories, the proponents of this view reach conclusions more typical of mainstream bourgeois sociology than of Marxism.

That the Stalinist bureaucracy does not have the stability of the bourgeois class is incontestable, based as it is on collective ownership, by way of its control of the state, of the means of production. Nevertheless it does rule the economy in its own interest, it does organise the population to work in its projects and for its goals, it does siphon off a vast part of the wealth of society for its own private consumption.

Bureaucrats can and do accumulate vast private wealth, as well as enjoying the right to live like billionaires while in office — the exposure of vast corruption has been one of the consequences of "openness" everywhere, from China to the USSR, and now East Germany. Children of the bureaucrats do not inherit ownership of factories, but they do inherit, by way of educational privilege, special access to the portals of the bureaucratic ruling class, "contacts", etc., places in the bureaucratic ruling class: a working class child even in Thatcher's Britain has a far better chance of a higher education, and even of becoming a capitalist, than a Russian working class child has of higher education or entrance to the ruling bureaucratic elite.

The whole of history — after the end of primitive communism — is the history of societies divided into classes under a dominant ruling class, more or less stable, more or less efficient at running society.

Vast areas of Stalinist society are shrouded in darkness after decades without freedom of information, or freedom of scientific sociological investigation. Much about the Stalinist societies and how they function is simply unknown. But it is perverse in face of this situation for Marxists to jump to the conclusion that the Stalinist states are the exception to the whole recorded history of human society! No they are not, no they can't be! All of recorded history — not to speak of Marxism, which codifies it — tells us that it is absurd to say that these societies have existed for decades with no ruling class, and that the typical all-powerful totalitarian Stalinist states which have tyrannised over the lives of countless hundreds of millions of peoples for decades have not been class states!

Should the analysis of Stalinism force Marxists to such a conclusion, then we would not be able to confine our conclusion to the experience of Stalinism. If societies can exist for decades with no ruling class, and if states can exist and do what the Stalinist states have done to the peoples over which they have had dominion, and yet still not be class states, organs of ruling classes, then you have a vast breach in the fabric of Marxist theory woven over the last 150 years out of the whole experience of human history so far.

Inevitably, vast credence is thereby given to liberals, reformists and others who argue — despite all the evidence that the real rule of the bourgeoisie is the hidden hand within the glove puppet of our bourgeois-democratic system — that states like the British bourgeois-democratic state are not class states, nor organs of class rule. Look at the view of Stalinism which denies the bureaucracy is a ruling class from a slightly different angle, and you find yourself looking at the old reformist picture of bourgeois-democratic states like Britain! Its advocates might not want that, may not hold such a view of the British state, but logic does work itself through in these matters.

If the facts led us to such a conclusion then honest socialists working in the spirit of Marx, Engels, Lenin and Trotsky would not want to close their eyes to it. It is in the light of the undeniable facts around us that we say: such a conclusion about the British state is an obvious absurdity — as absurd as the view which denies that the Stalinist bureaucracy is a ruling class, and the Stalinist states ruling-class organs.

12. The Communist Parties have ditched Marxism and Communism, and they should know what they're talking about.

The Stalinist rulers in the USSR have created an ideology through which their interests and their immediate political concerns were expressed in stereotyped language derived from Marxism. Marxist analysis has been no part of that ideological process. Communist Parties like the British CP danced like performing bears to that official "Marxism". In the high Stalinist period, Moscow could say on Monday that Britain and France were democratic powers justly opposing ravenous German fascism, on Tuesday thats British and French warmongering imperialism were ganging up on peace loving Germany, and on Wednesday that it was Anglo-French democracy against German fascism again — and the CPs would jump accordingly. (They did that between September 1939 and June 1941).

CPs justified Stalin's terror and for decades lied systematically about the reality of the USSR. When told to, they collaborated with Nazis against socialists in Germany in 1931-33; co-ordinated Nazi-like campaigning against "Jewish Trotskyists" in Mexico in 1939-41 when Hitler and Stalin were friends; organised bloody counterrevolution against the workers in Republican Spain in 1937; and so on. The list is almost endless.

Later, the CPs softened up, accommodated more to the societies they lived in, and for a couple of decades past they have occasionally criticised aspects of Stalinist rule. In practical politics, the West's biggest Communist Party, the Italian CP, has long been to the right of the British Labour Party. These political whores and charlatans can speak neither for socialism nor for Marxism. The best service they can render to socialists and Marxists is to distance themselves from us, the more formally and explicitly the better. The air around us will eventually be a lot cleaner for their departure.

When the Italian ex-Communist Party decides to change its name, what is collapsing is not Bolshevism or Communism but the grotesque counterfeit of Marxism and socialism shaped and moulded by Stalin, and in part sustained by Stalin's wealth and power.

13. The collapse of Communism vindicates the reformist "social democratic" model of socialism.

Social democracy defined itself historically not against Stalinism but against Bolshevism. And the social democrats were wrong at every point against Bolshevism. They either supported their own bourgeoisie, even against the revolutionary communist workers, or temporised and hesitated and thus helped the bourgeoisie to win.

It was the social democrats who rescued German capitalism in 1918 and thereby isolated the Russian Revolution. By betraying socialism or dithering in countries like Germany and Italy, the social democrats played the role of historic stepfather to Stalinism. The Bolsheviks did not lead the workers to power believing socialism could be rooted in Russia; they led the Russian workers on ahead believing the European workers would follow. The socialist leaders in the West left them in the lurch, amidst the Russian backwardness, where Stalinism was eventually to grow up. Whatever about this or that error made by the early Communist International, the international Bolshevik current was entirely right against reformist social democracy.

The reformists' criticisms of Stalinism have often, of course, been correct. They have been right on the same questions bourgeois democrats have been right on. The disintegration of Stalinism cannot lead logically to the conclusion that reformist social-democracy is the answer — unless we also accept that Stalinism was socialism, and that its collapse therefore shows us that capitalism is the best we can ever hope for.

Reformist social-democracy is not a different strategy for achieving socialism. Socialism is the replacement of wage-slavery and the capitalist system built on it by a different mainspring — free co-operative self-administering labour. What has that got to do with the achievements of social democratic reform?

The fight for welfare-state reforms, and the defence of existing welfare state provision, is indeed necessary for socialists. But socialists cannot stop there. And very often today the reformists do not even defend the welfare state. The fight to defend welfare state provision is often a fight against reformists in power — as it was in Britain during the last three years of the 1974-9 Labour government. The socialism of the reformist social democrats is like the smile on Lewis Carroll's Cheshire Cat.

Since the 1920s, social-democratic parties have abandoned even a verbal commitment to fighting for a socialist system defined as something radically different from capitalism. They aspire at most to modifying capitalism, with a few welfare measures. In the 1980s, social-democratic

356

leaders in France, Spain, Australia, New Zealand and Italy have become no better than pale-pink Thatcherites.

The only model of socialism restored to its proper shape and colour by the disintegration of Stalinism and the open disavowal of socialism by the Stalinists is the only model of socialism that ever deserved the name — the fight to organise the working class as a clear conscious force, a class for itself, to break bourgeois state power and abolish wage slavery, and establish a comprehensive, democratic self-rule throughout society.

14. The notion of a Leninist party is completely discredited. Stalinism and Bolshevism are the same, and the working class does not need such parties.

The opposite is true. It was the absence of organisationally coherent, disciplined, clear-headed and determined revolutionary parties in Germany, Italy, Hungary and France just after the Russian Revolution that left the Russian Revolution isolated and prey to bureaucratic counter-revolution. That same absence, by allowing capitalism to survive in the West, also prepared the way for Italian and German fascism, and for the millions of dead in World War Two.

If revolutionary organisations like the Bolsheviks existed now in Eastern Europe, then the mass movements could probably avoid the bitter clashes that are likely as market forces cut into the lives and living standards of the people. The workers could be organised now around the idea that their real interests, and the only possibility of creating a democracy that is not a hollow mockery of their aspirations, lie in substituting for discredited Stalinism not market economics but rational socialist planning of the major elements of the economy, confining market mechanisms to secondary things.

No such parties exist, though they may come into existence relatively quickly. Because they do not exist, the great mass movements crying out for democracy, with most of their supporters probably opposed to the growth of inequality and insecurity that is in fact inseparable from market forces, are going in a social and political direction which will produce nothing like what they want. They follow priests and intellectuals whose hopes and ideas centre on West European capitalist civilisation.

Human beings make their own history, but in conditions they do not choose and usually do not understand, with the consequence that the result is not what they want or aim for — that is what Marxism teaches us about human history so far.

Socialism is about overcoming that limit, and introducing conscious control by humanity of itself and its societies. A Marxist party which knows history, knows the experience of the working class, and knows the options in a given situation, can make the difference between a mass movement blundering into an outcome it would not choose and the same movement achieving the goals it sets itself.

The mass movements for democracy in Eastern Europe — within which tolerance and even a welcome for the development of capitalist modes of operation are so strongly allied with the desire for a classless democracy — have a great deal in common with historically pioneering movements like the movement of the masses in the French Revolution of 200 years ago.

In 1789 it was not possible to know better. Today it is. It is possible for the inspiring movement in Eastern Europe to learn from history, and reach its goal. But for that, an organisation is necessary which can help the working class to develop an independent world-historic viewpoint, a viewpoint which incorporates not just the experience of Stalinism and a negative recoil from it but also the experience of world capitalism, and an independent working-class programme derived from the world-wide experience of the working class. Without such an organisation, even a heroic working-class activist like Lech Walesa — who was an underground trade union activist when that was dangerous and unprofitable work and, for all he knew, might not bear fruit for decades — degenerates into someone touring the world trying to organise a more efficient form of exploitation for his fellow Polish workers. Not for many years have events given such a powerful proof that a Marxist revolutionary party, modelled on Lenin's and Trotsky's party, is irreplaceable for the working class if it is to act as a class for itself.

One of the most reactionary of the many reactionary features and consequences of Stalinism in power was that — by police-state terror and wholesale lies — it systematically prevented the working class from thinking for itself, from learning the lessons of its own history, and from organising. The consequences of that are felt now in Eastern Europe, where the working class is submerged in a series of vast national-popular movements for democracy — movements which cannot by their nature satisfy working-class demands or even survive in their present form.

The working class needs a revolutionary party — not a party to control the working class, but a party ultimately controlled by the class while having an existence of its own as an ideological selection. The working class needs such a party to make its mass action purposeful, effective, and capable of reaching the goals it aspires to. Hypocrites, cynics, and petty-bourgeois sharp-shooters say that such a view of the need for a revolutionary party is elitist. It is not. Such a party serves the class, it does not aim to dominate it or rule over it. One-party rule was no part of the Bolshevik programme, and arose in the civil war as a temporary measure, later preserved and made rigid by the Stalinist counter-revolution.

We are not elitists. A Marxist party can lead the workers only to the degree that it wins their freely-given confidence. But we say that this is how reality is: that the working class needs its own party to help it realise its own potentialities as a class and to help it free itself. Without such a party, the working class will suffer needless defeats. Unlike the cynics — who accept the real elitism of the capitalists, with their entrenched wealth, their galaxy of specialised intellectuals, their control of the State — we do not wish to live with capitalism. We want to help the working class to overcome it.

15. We are now entering an era of peace and stability, forever. The End of History has come.

What is likely to succeed the dead weight of the melting Stalinist icecap in Eastern Europe and the USSR is not bland liberal democracy, but a maelstrom of nationalist conflicts. Wars are probable.

The retreat of the Russian Empire is a sort of undoing of the outcome of World War Two. But History will only "stop", or, rather, move on to a higher plane, when capitalism stops, that is when the working class takes power and begins to "construct the socialist order" world-wide.

The words in quotes are Lenin's, from his speech to the Congress of Soviets just after the Bolsheviks' seizure of power in 1917. Circumstances and events ultimately defeated Lenin. The working class will yet start to "construct the socialist order" in better and more favourable circumstances. We do not know when, but for certain the disintegration of Stalinism will bring that day closer.

Is socialism utopian?

DEBATE: SEAN MATGAMNA AND KENNETH MINOGUE

Sean Matgamna

WE ARE DISCUSSING "IS SOCIALISM DEAD?" because of the collapse of Stalinism in the Soviet Union. The question there is: what, if anything, did the Soviet Union have to do with socialism? Yet there is a more immediate reason why we are discussing this issue in Britain. For ten years now the British working class has suffered a series of defeats. If we had not had those defeats we would not have the climate of ideas we now have, and we would not be discussing issues in this way. Quite likely, there would be euphoria in most of the labour movement about the collapse of Stalinism.

We are Trotskyists. We are in Trotsky's tradition. Unfortunately, "Trotskyism" today means very little. You need more information other than the word itself. To us it means that we are with the people who stood against the rise of Stalinism. We are with the people who were in Siberia, in the labour camps. Who organised hunger strikes in Stalin's prisons. Who tried to defend the Soviet working class against Stalinism. Who defended working-class freedom in the USSR in the 1920s. We are also with the people who made the Russian Revolution. We do not attempt to ingratiate ourselves with the bourgeoisie. We are with the people who shot the Tsar and who used the state against the capitalists. We stand for genuine Marxian socialism.

The idea that Stalinism has anything to do with socialism is based on a series of misrepresentations. We do not want state socialism. Marxists believe that ultimately society will be organised without coercion, without the state. The real roots of bureaucracy in British capitalist society and of bureaucratic tyranny in the USSR are in the fact that both these types of society are ruled by a minority. This minority cannot tolerate real democracy. At best it will concede — as in Britain — shallow forms of democracy. These societies cannot allow real self-rule by the people. Because real self-rule cannot be allowed, we get bureaucratic rule — although the levels of bureaucracy differ, sometimes greatly. Marxists believe that once the rule of the bourgeoisie is smashed and the self-rule of the people is a reality, we will not have a state in any of the old senses. We will not have the type of bureaucratism characteristic of Stalinism.

Marxist socialists believe socialism can only come out of advanced capitalism, that it can not come from anywhere else. Trotsky and Lenin did not believe that you could take a backward part of the world, the old Tsarist empire, cordon it off and build a viable utopian socialist colony there. Marx laughed at people with basically similar ideas — people who wanted to build socialist colonies in America. The Russian Stalinists tried to build a vast quasi-utopian system counterposed to capitalism. That collapsed because it was not possible for a backward country to overtake and outstrip the power and the might and the wealth of the world bourgeoisie.

The Bolsheviks led a workers' revolution in a country where socialism was not possible. They were right to take power. They wanted to see a European and a world movement of the workers taking power. They wanted advanced, capitalist Germany, which was ripe for socialism, to be taken by the workers. In 1917 socialists understood that socialism was not state tyranny: socialism was the elimination of the capitalist system, of wage slavery and the substitution of co-operatively organised society, with a real democracy.

One of the central criticisms Marxists make of capitalism is that it develops ideas it cannot make good on, cannot deliver. Capitalism suffers from a giant flaw: capitalism means private ownership of the social means of production, so real equality is impossible in capitalism. We have formal equality — for example, equality before the law. But economic inequality disrupts and destroys the possibilities for social equality.

If, ten or 15 years ago, someone made a socialist speech like this, the speaker might well be saying that it does not matter if the democracy that existed in Britain were suppressed; that it would not be a bad thing to have a Stalinist system instead. I am not saying that. I think the sort of liberty we have in capitalist Britain would be worth defending against the "stormtroopers" of capitalism who, in all probability, at some time in the future, will come — as they came to Germany under Hitler and to Chile, in 1973, under Pinochet. Nevertheless, British democracy is a great deal short of real self-rule.

The Russian revolution was made by Marxists with the full knowledge that socialism could not be built amid Russian backwardness. The collapse of Russian Stalinism is a vindication of Marxism. That does not lessen the triumphalism of the bourgeoisie at the collapse, or lessen the pressure on fainthearted people.

Mr Minogue attacks the bureaucracy we find in Britain. Minogue attacks the waste of a welfare state, which of course is superimposed on the capitalist system. But to a considerable extent, when Minogue attacks these things, calling them socialism, what he is actually attacking is the evolution of capitalism itself. The sort of statism which has been attacked by the so-called libertarian right is itself the product of capitalism. Monopolies long ago developed across the capitalist world, and the state and industry began to combine — for war and the plundering of colonies — a century and more ago. Into this development have come the demands of the labour movement, for example, for welfare reforms. Desirable and good goals — like a welfare state — have been strangled with bureaucracy arising out of the conditions of the British capitalist class society. Much of what Minogue and people of his outlook attack is bureaucratic monopoly capitalism — for which they then blame the socialists. This is a species of ideological card-sharping.

And there is more cheating about the legacy of Stalinism. Stalinism did not exist in the world on its own. During the long period of Stalinist rule in various countries, the bourgeoisie was the dominant world force. They are now realising their fullest domination with the collapse of Stalinism. Throughout this period many of the horrors of Stalinism can be traced to capitalism. For example, there are few things more terrible than the rule of the Khmer Rouge in Cambodia. They treated a large part of their own people as Hitler treated the Jews. Yet how were the Khmer Rouge produced? This psychotic social formation arose after the modern, democratic, bourgeois USA bombed Cambodia "into the Stone Age". Stalinism cannot be taken in isolation from the capitalist world in which it existed. Even Stalinism in the Soviet Union did not happen in isolation from capitalism. Fourteen states, including Britain, invaded Soviet Russia between 1918 and 1921. That was one of the factors which, by its effects on the economy, led to the rise of Stalinism.

One argument we meet is this: despite all the imperfections of capitalism, nevertheless this system is the best we can get. "Anti-utopianism" is very fashionable now. If we want to achieve a better society we are "utopians". And, comrades, "utopianism" is dangerous! Apparently it leads to Jacobin terror and Stalinism. Of course, Marxists do not condemn capitalism totally. The Communist Manifesto contains a great paean of praise, by Karl Marx, to the capitalist system. He truly says that the capitalists have done wonderful things.

Capitalism is progressive in history. It creates the conditions whereby capitalist ideals of liberty and equality can actually be realised — though the bourgeois class cannot do it. From this point of view, capitalism has been progressive. In previous epochs of history class society was necessary. In ancient Greece, when Aristotle argued in favour of slavery, he was arguing for a necessary condition for their actual civilisation.

I would concede that the capitalism we have in Britain is better than Stalinism. Indeed, it is nearer to socialism. Yet capitalism is still a dog-eat-dog system. Capitalism can work. It can continue for a long time. But in the 20th century it survived only by destroying large parts of the means of production in the Great Slump, creating mass unemployment, and by going into world wars. We hear about the horrors of Stalinism. I do not excuse them. But in this century we witnessed the near destruction of European civilisation — by forces arising from capitalism. If you walk down the streets from the London School of Economics, where Mr Minogue works, you find people asleep in doorways. In Lincoln's Inn Fields, nearby, there are hundreds of people camped. We live in a world where homelessness is nowadays considered almost normal. A world where culture is degraded to the lowest common denominator by the profit motive. Where the mass of the population is not educated to have the possibility of realising real self-rule. All these horrors are rooted in the fact that there is private, minority ownership of the means of production and everything is geared to exercising, justifying and maintaining the rule of that minority of big capitalists. Capitalism has its horrors, too.

Right now, we can see the outlines of three great trade blocs emerging: America, Japan and Europe. If capitalism once again slows down, and there is no reason to presume it will not, eventually, there is the possibility of conditions something like those of the 1930s. The nightmare scenario of an eventual "1984" world with three great warring powers. Capitalism is not a stable system. Capitalism is progressive, historically, allowing the creation of a working class. But then the working class must seize its historic destiny and put itself in conscious control of society. The alternative will not always be a bourgeois democracy like the one we have in Britain now.

It is arguable that we can not completely do away with the market. Who needs to do such a thing? But what we can do is eliminate the private ownership of the means of production and the wage slavery that is inseparable from it, and introduce real, democratic self-control in all spheres of society, including the economic.

Is socialism dead? No, and it will not die until capitalism is dead. Socialism is a product of and an answer to capitalism. The capitalists can win victories in the class struggle, but they cannot eliminate the working class. The class struggle will continue and the workers' movement will revive. Socialism will revive.

We are witnessing the purging of socialism of all the encrustations of Fabian statism and Stalinism. This is the purification of socialism. We are seeing the emergence of the opportunity for real socialism to expand. This is not the end of history. This is a new phase of history where real socialism will have a far better chance than it had when our heroic comrades took power in Russia in October 1917.

Kenneth Minogue

A lot depends on definitions. There are a lot of packaged words: capitalism, socialism, workers' power, democracy. These have been shuffled like a packs of cards. When Sean Matgamna says "Stalinism was never what socialists believed to be socialism" he is simply wrong. This is a matter of historical fact. Great numbers of people fought for the defence of the Soviet Union as the homeland of socialism. It is only as the project has more obviously failed that they gave it up.

I was struck by a story from the Tiananmen Square episode. It was repeated in Moscow. In both cases some luckless person said: "Now I know what fascism really means". Now why did these people choose the word "fascism"? These people were communists, not fascists. I think this illustrates one of the ways in which socialism is a type of perpetual virgin, never touched by experience. In Islam, the reward of warriors going to paradise is to meet women for ever reconstituted as virgins. Socialism is like this.

Sean Matgamna says that socialism is sometimes regarded as an ideal which is too good for us. It is a marvellous idea which we can not actually achieve. Matgamna believes it can be achieved. I believe revolutionary workers' socialism is pretty dead. All forms of socialism ought to be dead. I would like to see a stake through its heart. It has caused more death, unpleasantness and boredom than almost any other doctrine. Socialism involves a curious conception of society: a society in which there are no rich or poor; no aristocratic or bourgeois; no people dying for love or dreaming of getting rich; no scandal, gossip, monarchy — all the things which keep us enthused. We have little comrades slotted into a society where their needs are perfectly satisfied. This happens not to be the type of world I would like to live in.

If we ask: what is the opposite of socialism?, the obvious answer is capitalism. Capitalism is one of those packages containing everything. Capitalism contains the experiences in this hall, a type of socialism within capitalism. All over Britain you will find Hari Krishna people trying to worship at Stonehenge. You find a vast number of activities. The point about capitalism is that a great number of people do a vast number of different things with a great number of conflicting beliefs. This plurality distinguishes capitalism from socialism. You have to believe in socialism in order to live in a socialist society. You do not have to believe in capitalism to live in a capitalist society. According to quite respectable opinion you better not have a religion in a socialist society. The Russians set up the League of the Godless to remove all the nonsense from people's minds. The contrast is therefore between socialism as a single way of life, right through society, and capitalism as immensely plural.

How did the notion of capitalism as a single thing ever get going? The answer is that Marx, recommending a single way of life to a set of people who were already accustomed to a great plurality of ways of life, for rhetorical purposes had to present capitalism as a unity. Marx said: you may think you are as free as the birds, but in fact capital determines everything about you — it is a single system. This is a major mistake underlying Marxism. If you ask: what is the opposite of socialism?, the answer is individualism. Individualism is almost unavoidably the type of life you live in a modern society. What people in modern society do is to distinguish themselves from others, select their clothes, wear jewellery which contrasts with others. In thousands of ways individual endeavour is central to humans in a modern society. We go through these vanities — then we die. Dying is important people think a lot about it. What did Marx say about death? He writes a single sentence: death is a biological accident. This is an interesting comment which tells you a lot about Marx.

The way I would interpret it would be to connect it with other texts where Marx says there is no such thing as human nature; this is an ideological mystification, humans are essentially historical creatures without any essential nature. What I take Marx to mean is that a human being is social input plus organic transferences. Man is simply matter on which society makes its imprint. Marx's view is that a human being is the matter out of which societies are constructed. Now this is a significant part of Marx's doctrine I think Marx imagined a communist society to be rather like a giant computer. Every individual, no longer alienated, would have the great power of society available. By contrast to the present world, what he hated about capitalism is that we as individuals are alienated from each other, we have shames. It is the thing Christians mean by original sin.

Some types of socialist are people who have a vision of society and who think that the only valuable thing is a society which is lived in a certain sort of way. In order to do this there has to be "engineering". Just as in any fabricating you may well want to dispose of unsuitable material, what every socialist or communist ruler who has come to power has found is that large numbers of human beings are extremely unsuitable. That is why a lot of people die. In some cases tens of millions of people die when the project of constructing a Marxist society is embarked upon. I am obviously not saying that Marx told people to kill. It is just a matter of combining this philosophy with absolute revolutionary power.

The power which socialists want is not the power to be in Downing Street according to the constitution, it is what is described as "workers' power". You take this seriously. I do not. There is no such thing as workers' power. Any power which is exercised is done so by specific people over specific other people. The pretensions about "workers' power" is patter for the gullible.

If the rulers of a society start taking an interest in political theory, god help you, they should not. But if they do, they should read Plato or Rousseau or St Augustine. If they read Marx, get out, trouble is coming. The Marxists, supposedly on behalf of the proletariat, take the power to improve the condition of the poor. This is the promise made by all the Marxist rulers. This has also been betrayed by all the Marxist rulers. Every revolution is betrayed.

An interest in the poor is an unhealthy taste. It may be that the people with an interest in the poor are philanthropic and care sympathetically for these people. If you go through France you often see pictures of St Martin, the French saint who, coming across a poor man who was shivering, gave him half his coat. But it is difficult to imagine Ulyanov doing this. What they would say is that the pain and shivering of the poor is part of the machinery of changing the system.

If it is not a philanthropic and loving interest in the poor, we have to go back to the rather Platonic attitude of Marx. People are understood to be the matter of society. The point, for Marx, is that the proletariat are so far outside of society that they are less marked by the prejudices and illusions of bourgeois society and are therefore the matter out of which the new society will be constructed. The interest in the poor is one of the most significant features of revolutionary parties. These parties are actually looking to exploit the poor.

I am trying to draw out the contradictions of socialism. For example, socialists purport to hate capitalism and to love socialism. In many places, socialist societies have arisen which, despite what Sean Matgamna says, were plausibly socialist. People defended the socialist sixth of the world with enthusiasm. No-one in a capitalist society ever wanted to live in these places. The numbers who want to leave socialist societies for capitalism are very great indeed. The Vietnamese boat people are not trying to leave for China or Cuba. They go to Hong Kong, a great bastion of capitalism.

A Marxist in the West imagines him or herself to be an independent-minded struggler against all the bourgeois illusions which are thrust upon them. The others are lost in false consciousness. The Marxist has the true consciousness. When, however, the revolution actually arrives, the Marxists settle very easily into being apparatchiks. The independence of Marxists, the illusion of courage, comes from the fact that you have the splendid destiny of actually living in a capitalist society.

Another contradiction is notionally the doctrine of the liberation of the proletariat from their working class condition. They will eventually become socialist. If the members of this working class decide they do not want socialism, they are simply abused as traitors to their class. What appears to be liberation is in fact a prison. A proletarian, in Marx's terms, better think proletarian thoughts, supplied for them by the bourgeois Marx. There is an attitude of imprisonment inside the pretence of liberation.

A further contradiction: Marx's theory deplores the supposedly atomised condition of people living in capitalist society. The notion is that we are all so cut off from each other that we are all selfishly grabbing for our own benefits in a rat race. Now, it turns out that after what Sean Matgamna calls the "Stalinist system" that these collectivist systems atomise far more thoroughly than anything conceivable under capitalism. There are so many informers and secret police that people are afraid to talk freely. All institutions of civil society — trade unions, churches and so on — have to be instruments of the one single system of socialism. Socialism is unity or solidarity.

Finally, revolutionary Marxist doctrine is for the moment dead, although I can see many forms of socialism and collectivism coming up on the horizon. I am reminded of a story Arthur Koestler tells in his autobiography. It is from his communist days in 1942. He was working in Germany for a communist newspaper in danger of being closed down by the Nazis. He says they used to tell the story of a Chinese executioner whose duty it was to cut off people's heads. He was a perfectionist whose dream in life was to cut off a head so perfectly that the person would not realise it had happened. Years passed. One day a prisoner said: when are you going to do it? The executioner smiled and said: just kindly nod. Koestler said they used to say to each other: just kindly nod. That is my message to you socialists.

Kenneth Minogue sums up

There is a lot of trying to make water run up hill in your socialist arguments. You say life is pretty dull and dreary in a capitalist factory. That may well be right. All I can say is that not many people flee from capitalist factories into socialism or socialist countries. A lot of people from other countries and other systems try to get in. The problem the capitalist system has is not people fleeing from the horrors of it, but trying to keep people out who want to get in.

One speaker talked about mass movements for struggle and liberation. The biggest mass movements are movements of immigration of individuals moving from situations they hate to situations they prefer. Often they have illusions, but by and large America, that hated dollar sign of capitalism, is an immense success story. Again, the problem is not that people want to get out, but that people are trying to get into it. The lady who said "as long as we're oppressed we will fight and struggle" will find struggling doesn't really get you anywhere. If you imagine you are in a class war then I suppose you engage in the things called fighting and struggling. But fighting and struggling is a metaphor. What you are actually doing is sitting around here, listening to me, or each other, or other people. You're not actually out there doing any real fighting. You may occasionally go on a demo. But you largely live in a fantasy world, describing what you do in terms of military metaphors. It would be even worse if you actually did it, because it wouldn't produce anything.

Out there in the world, there is an economic system. I hate the word "system" because it is extremely misleading in many ways, but whatever happens, 55 million Britons are producing buildings, food, beer, vast numbers of things. That is presumably helping somebody to do something. Whether fighting helps them to do anything is another question.

The chap who suggested I misrepresented Marx said Marx was a terrific individualist. The question then becomes no longer what is socialism, but what is individualism? A lady said it would be nice if everybody could go to the opera and Covent Garden. Most people would be bored stiff by the opera. And to sit in the library at the LSE, I imagine, would not be a madly popular option either, except for those poor cripples like myself who have a taste for that sort of thing. The notion of individualism involved here is simply that people have a lot of wants. You might call it consumer socialism — an idea that the future will be for everybody what an inhabitant of Mayfair with two houses in the country now lives. That's not anybody's very serious conception of the future.

A socialist conception of human beings, as I understand it, is an organismic one. A man said that Marx believed that there was a human nature — people need food, they need shelter. Of course, Marx certainly agreed that human beings are organisms. The contrary view which, in fact, derives from Christianity, however remote it may be from the theology, is that life is a challenge. It includes what some economists call positional goods. In other words, it includes quite a lot of things which logically cannot be universalised. The things called capitalist privileges cannot be given to everyone, because to some extent they result from competition, and in competition some people win and some people lose. The good thing about capitalism is that it is so extensively pluralistic that some people winning in one direction are losing in terms of some other set of values.

I think death is quite an important thing to think about in this context. I would emphasise that what I am concerned with is states not in war, and the instance of the Gulf War seems to raise quite separate issues. The question here is what kind of society people want. Adolf Hitler wanted a racially pure society, and he was a collectivist, exactly like Stalin. The image you have of people is of great masses; collectivists even talk of elites and masses. The word masses is a contemptuous expression, I take it. It indicates a lot of people who have no significance except that an awful lot of them have weight.

Any collectivist view of that kind seems to me to dispose people who also are in the situation of having a lot of power over them to move very rapidly to the view that you cannot make an omelette without breaking eggs — and people who have a lot of power have a very strong disposition to make omelettes. As they say in Moscow these days it's easy enough to turn an aquarium into a fish soup, anybody can do that, the real trick is how you turn a fish soup back into an aquarium.

Sean Matgamna sums up

Mr Minogue says it is fantasy to talk about "fighting" and "struggle". But Mr Minogue is fighting the class struggle in one way, and on behalf of people who fight the class struggle in many other ways. For example, Mr Minogue is on the same side as the police who fought the class struggle with batons in their hands against the miners in events like the Battle of Orgreave in 1984. There's a continuing battle. I don't want to insist on this or that metaphor, although I think the battle metaphor is a very accurate one that sums up a lot of things. But Mr Minogue's criticism strikes me as essentially obtuse. I'm sure Mr Minogue knows what he is doing here — fighting a battle of ideas. He might not like the metaphor, but that is what he is doing, describe it as he may.

If I were to accept his picture of socialism, if I accepted the picture of socialism as the ant-hill society (as somebody called it), then I would certainly be anti-socialist. Even if you are rather badly off in this society, would you prefer to be a well-fed ant? Leon Trotsky, when he was a lad aged about 17, before he became a Marxist, was a Populist. In his biography of Trotsky, Isaac Deutscher talked about a scene where Trotsky denounces Marxism as a dry, economistic, inhuman doctrine which he hates. If that's what we are talking about, then I can understand the point of view of the other side.

But it's not what we are talking about! We are talking about changing the fundamental framework of social life. We're not talking about regimenting social life, we're not trying to reduce human beings into so much input of food or electricity, or whatever. We are talking about changing the basis of life from one where individual development, individual liberty, intellectual development, and so on, are the privilege of a minority. We're in favour of individualism. We want more individualism. We want all the people — all the working class — to have the chance to develop as individuals. We advocate a different arrangement of fundamentals in society to allow that to happen. We locate the reason why capitalist society has immense potential for doing the sort of things we want — many of which capitalism itself originally proclaimed — but doesn't do what we want, in the contradiction between the social means of production and their private ownership by capitalists, and all that follows from that in the way of keeping the workers down and exploiting them. We are for the development of individuals. We see the road to that as being the destruction of the system we live in, in which individual development is reserved for a very small minority.

Now, Hitler, Nasser, Ben-Gurion and Clement Attlee were all "socialists". So "socialist" is rather a meaningless term. But our definition of socialism is the Marxist definition. Marx's analysis of socialist possibilities within capitalist society indicated that socialism comes after advanced capitalism, and was impossible in conditions like Russia. We can use two ways of judging alleged socialism: against what Marx argued, and by what the working class experienced in the alleged socialism. On those two fundamental criteria, Stalinist "socialism" was simply not socialism at all. It was not socialist according to the Marxist premises which pre-date the modern labour movement, and pre-date the Russian revolution, and it was not socialist according to the way it treated the people. This seems to me to be a fair way of dealing with this question. We are not people who were, yesterday or the day before, pro-Stalinist, then suddenly discovered that Stalinism has failed, that it was only an alternative form of exploitation, and concluded that we should adapt to the bourgeois form of exploitation. We are the continuators of a political tradition that fought Stalinism all the way through its history. In fact, we fought Stalinism when the bourgeoisie lauded Stalinism, when "Uncle Joe" (Stalin) was a great favourite of papers like the *Daily Express*, when Hollywood was making movies such as *Mission to Moscow* glorifying the Moscow Trials.

As for Mr Minogue's argument about death — I don't think Marxism believed that human beings are so many battery hens, which is how I vulgarise what I heard Mr Minogue say. You can argue that human life is fundamentally tragic. We are leaves on the biological tree. We will cease to exist very quickly, all too quickly, and we become conscious of the reality that our lives are fundamentally tragic. But what do you conclude from that? Do you conclude that nothing is of any importance? If you are religious, you may think that nothing is of any importance except preparing for the future life. But if you are not religious, what do you say? What you do say if you're a reasonable being is that you make this life better, not just better in the sense of better for yourself, but better for human beings in general. You transform this life. That seems to me to be what Marxism says about how we relate to death.

If you read Victor Serge's account of the way the Cheka behaved, the way they massacred people, then during the Russian revolution — at a certain stage of the bloody, brutal civil war, and the wars of intervention — you could say that such state organs as the Cheka became death obsessed. If we do say that, we must do it critically, and look at what created the atmosphere in which they could slaughter people so casually or recklessly. It was created by the bourgeoisie in World War I.

Right now, almost 75 years ago, the Battle of the Somme was coming to an end. In the Battle of the Somme around three-quarters of a million people were killed. Germans, French, English and others were killed fighting for a few hundred bloody yards of land. Wave after wave of them were sent to their deaths by the savages who ruled Germany and England. That situation and the culture extrapolated from it and many similar things was not created by the Bolsheviks. If you believe they became infected by it, then they caught an infection from the bourgeoisie. Another example, personally close to me, Ireland. In the middle of the last century the British ruling class saw famine in Ireland and were pleased at the thinning-out of the population. The *Times* newspaper, watching a million people starve to death while the bourgeoisie exported food, could write that soon the native Irish would be as scarce on the banks of the River Shannon as a Red Indian on the banks of the Hudson River in New York. They let a million people starve to death. Where do the people who defend this system get the right to talk about socialist bloodlust? The first great massacre in relation to a communist revolution didn't involve communists murdering bourgeois. It took place in Paris, after the defeat of the Commune in 1871. Ten to fifteen thousand of our people were murdered in cold blood after the bourgeoisie won. We want to fight the culture that is death infected.

Capitalism has possibilities which it cannot realise them because of the class structure inseparable from capitalism. Capitalism grew up in the womb of feudalism, and socialism is ripening in the womb of capitalism. Real capitalism now is not thriving individualistic capitalism, but massive monopolies, a concentration of social wealth that is the property of a minority. Socialism is about converting that social wealth into socially owned and controlled property.

In the capitalist world of today, we can already see the outlines of future capitalist conflicts — possibly future capitalist world wars, almost certainly capitalist trade wars. The old way of putting the alternative before humankind — that there is a choice between socialism or barbarism — is still with us. This is the world in which socialist ideas are being renewed. Thank god a large part of the political barbarism on earth — Stalinism — is falling to bits! That is good. We are fighting for a socialist, humane, democratic control of the means of life, which can lead to a tremendous flowering of real, mass human liberty, individualism and self-development. Those who advocate the worship of the established fact, and the "hidden hand" that supposedly guides capitalism are as remote from reason as the devotees of some pagan cult.

The Aztec priests cut out living human hearts for their gods. The Thatcherites in their 12 years of rule have cut out an awful lot of human hearts. They have created mass poverty and barbarised part of a whole generation of young people. We represent the future. The working class cannot be beaten definitively. The class struggle cannot be contained. It is a necessary part of the capitalist system. While capitalism lives, so does the class struggle and socialism.

The debate between Kenneth Minogue and Sean Matgamna took place at the "Stand Up for Real Socialism" conference sponsored by the Alliance for Workers' Liberty on 2 November 1991.

Planning: what, how, whose?

DEBATE: DAVID MARSLAND AND MARTIN THOMAS

Martin Thomas

THE FREE MARKET is a cruel and unequal system. In a whole epoch of human history, nonetheless, it played a progressive role. Now it is possible to do better. The free market is a system of inequality fundamentally because of one exchange which takes place within it, the exchange between worker and employer. On the face of it, this is a free and equal exchange. Selling your labour power is much like selling a sack of potatoes. The difference is that when you sell your labour power, the employer then controls the bulk of your life. He decides what you do with your skills, your energy, and a large part of your time.

He has the power to destroy your health, even sometimes to destroy your life. In Japan, they now have a new word for death from overwork, because it so common. That is not a particularly backward capitalist country. That is the most dynamic capitalist economy in the world today. The sale of labour power is not like just exchanging one good for another. It is a fundamentally unequal exchange, and the root of that inequality is that the means of production are in the hands of a small minority.

The free market is also a system of inequality because, built into it, is a varying, but always substantial level of unemployment — that is, a number of workers who cannot even become wage slaves. Unemployment means poverty for those who cannot sell their labour power and insecurity for those who can — for the moment.

It means that the idea of the free market being the best way of enabling individuals to plan their lives is nonsense. All your plans can be destroyed from one week to the next. If you lose your job, you can lose your home. You can lose everything. The inequality of the free market goes wider than that. The free market system also generates huge inequalities between countries and regions. In the free market system, investment goes where it is most profitable, and that is a place where there is already a good infrastructure of communications, a healthy, educated workforce, good relations with suppliers, ample markets and so on, i.e., a place which is relatively developed economically already. Thus, in the world today, and for the last 200 years, most investment has gone to the advanced capitalist countries and a few selected areas in the underdeveloped countries. We get huge inequalities at an international level.

The free market is not just an unequal system. It is an inhuman system. I do not think that anybody, given a choice, would say that the millionaires of western Europe and the USA having that little bit extra is more important than feeding the millions of people in the world who live constantly in danger of starvation. In the free market, money buys everything — and human need buys nothing. If you're hungry, in a free market system, that is no entitlement at all to food. If on the other hand, you are quite well-fed and have lots of money, you can buy lots of food on a whim. Your whim is more important, in the free market system, than the desperate needs of the poor.

Further, the free market system counts or recognises as important considerations only what can be packaged as commodities for individual consumption. If you have the money, you can buy a house, a car, all sorts of gadgets. You cannot buy a healthy environment. You cannot buy the preservation of the world in a state where it will be safe for our children and grandchildren. You can buy hospitals full of high-tech equipment, you cannot buy preventive healthcare. You can't even buy decent drains. The free market is inherently unequal and inhuman. It systematically rejects what is social in favour of commodities for individual consumption. That is a good reason for looking to see if something better is possible.

David Marsland argues that most of the evils of the free market system exist in other known systems, and generally in worse forms. That is true. But if it is true that poverty on a great scale existed in all previous cultures, I do not think that is good reason for saying that we must stick with what we have today. Poverty has not been eradicated. The living standards of the poor have been going down. In the US, the average level of real wages has been going down since the 1970s. In many parts of the Third World, real wages have gone down by 25-30% since the debt crisis of the early 1980s. In Eastern Europe and the USSR, there is a mass pauperisation. Poverty today is not a marginal consideration. Even if you think it will decrease, how many generations are you prepared to see live out their lives in these conditions?

Why did this poverty and this inhumanity exist in previous systems? Until quite recently, the level of human industry and technology was not sufficient to meet the needs of the entire population. If you took what was produced and shared out equally, it would not provide a comfortable life for all. That was true for thousands of years. If there is not enough, then either you have an overlord deciding who gets enough and who does not; or you have a more impersonal system such as the market. Historically, the market was the mechanism which produced progress. It was more progressive than having an overlord decide. However, the precondition does not hold now. If you took the total production of the world now, and divided it up equally you would get an average amount per head roughly equivalent to the average national income of Portugal. The average better-off worker in Portugal is not starving. They are not living in splendour, but they have the basics. There is enough produced to give everybody the basic necessities of comfortable life. That is true now. It was not true before.

Now, the market system was shaped by the struggle for the basic necessities of life. And food and clothing lend themselves well to the use of market mechanisms. They can be divided into discrete units consumed by individuals. They can be dealt with well by independent market transactions. The market begins to break down even for housing. It breaks down even more if we look at things that make life more than just physical survival. In the developed capitalist countries today, the proportion of the labour time of society needed to produce basic food and clothing is very small. That basic production used to take almost all the labour time of society. With modern technology, it takes very little. It is no longer necessary for our lives as human beings to be dominated by an unequal system shaped by the struggle for the basics of food and clothing. A more equal system, based on democratic planning, is possible.

That new system will require other things apart from productive capacity. It demands that people have formed a habit of working together in co-operative units. It demands that we have a relatively high level of literacy and good provision of information, so that people know what is going on sufficiently to plan. It requires a certain level of culture and civilisation. It is not possible to plan an economy democratically where the majority of the people are illiterate and do not know what is going on outside their own village — or even if they did know, they would not have the level of education and knowledge to make any useful judgements on it. It requires a certain level of information and education. It requires also, the will to make society different.

Those preconditions are all created by capitalism, or are functions of capitalism. I have argued that the free market system is an unequal and cruel system. For a whole epoch of human history, however, it was progressive in terms of what was possible then, but conditions have been created now where something better is possible.

The obvious objection is that the better system has been tried, in the Stalinist states, and those states show the failure of socialist planning. I would argue that, whatever it was called, Stalinism was not even an attempt at socialist planning. To argue this is not a matter of saying "it went wrong" after the event. If we look back at the criteria and conditions that Marx saw as necessary for the development of socialism, we see that the practices and models of Stalinism were denounced by socialists long before they were ever put into practice.

If we go back a century to the beginning of the mass Marxist movement, one of its main arguments and polemics was against what they called "state socialism". They argued against people who thought that socialism meant control by the state, bureaucratic manipulation of the economy and bureaucratic nationalisation like that being carried out by Bismarck in Germany.

Marxists argued, not after seeing what would happen under Stalin, but in the 1880s and 1890s, that "state socialism" had nothing to do with their socialism. Socialism, they said, was about democratic planning controlled by the working class. Bureaucratic planning, contrary to the interests of the workers, was anti-socialist. They did not even give qualified support to Bismarckian nationalisations, let alone see them as socialism. Marxists further argued that the idea of developing socialism in a single country, particularly in a backward country, such as Russia was in 1917, was out of the question. Socialism could only be developed on the basis of the most advanced capitalism, and in a much broader framework than a single country. Again, that argument was not a get-out after the experience of Stalinism. It was argued before anybody in the socialist movement had ever heard of Stalin or Stalinism.

Finally, when Stalin launched into his Stalinist economic policy — and at the start, not after seeing the results — Trotsky and other Marxists condemned the policy as bureaucratic, over-centralised, and foolish in its attempt to do away with market mechanisms far too quickly.

Socialist planning does not mean that we want to do away with free markets straight away. We recognise that free markets played a huge role in human development, and cannot be dispensed with overnight. After a socialist revolution we will have to use markets quite considerably. It will take generations to eliminate them. On the evidence, Stalinism was not an attempt at socialist planning. It was bureaucratic planning. It was a form of economic organisation which — Marxists had argued long before — represented no advance over capitalism. Moreover, Stalinism was shaped not by socialist ideas, but much more by economic competition with and emulation of the capitalist West. Stalinism was trying to develop the industry of the Soviet Union in competition with that of the West. If we want to give credit or discredit for shaping the Stalinist system to socialism or capitalism, then the discredit must go to capitalism.

If socialist planning is nothing to do with Stalinism, how then do I define it? What would socialist planning be, if not "state socialism"? From a socialist point of view, the main purpose of socialist planning is quite different. Stalinist planning was about industrial development in competition with the capitalist world. Socialist planning is not primarily about faster economic growth. It is not even primarily about increasing control over the economy. It is primarily about decreasing the control of the economy over human lives. Up to now, economic affairs have dominated human life. For a whole epoch, the low level of technology and industry meant that the struggle to get the essentials of life had to dominate human life. Under capitalism it doesn't matter if enough of this or that is produced. There is always a drive for more profit, for this or that new profitable line of production, for increased pressure on the worker to work more. In Japan, they have the most tremendous technology, and they could produce the basics of life with a relatively small effort. It would be possible for people to have a relatively leisured and dignified life. Despite that, something like 70% of Japanese workers say that they constantly feel physically exhausted and mentally exhausted. That is their lives. Their lives are dominated by being exhausted for the sake of profit.

Socialist planning is aimed at ending the dominance of economic concerns over human life. How is that to be done? The first thing is to cut the working week to a level which enables everybody to have free activity, not to have their lives dominated by what an employer tells them all to do, still less by what the state tells them to do! We must reduce the drudgery necessary to produce the basics of life. We cannot do away with drudgery, but by mechanisation and automation we can continue the process already developed by capitalism, of reducing the necessary drudgery to a small amount. We should share that drudgery out equally, so that we don't have some people overworked, some people in idleness and rich, and other people in idleness and poor as under capitalism.

The organisation of that drudgery is the area where planning operates. Socialist planning is not about state planning of people's whole lives. And even in the area of basic production, we will not be able to plan social needs straightaway. It will take generations before the level of technology, the degree of information and culture, and the spirit of co-operation have developed enough to make the planning of basic economic essentials just an administrative question. Under socialist planning everybody would be required to do their share of the drudgery. When they have done that they have free time. That free time would not be the enforced idleness of many under capitalism. It would be free time on the basis of having the essentials of life and on the basis of access to education, culture and so on. It would be free time we could use for study, for sport, for handicrafts, for conversation, for friendship, or if we like just for idling.

Free time — time which is not dominated by economic consideration — is the core of socialism. It would release the time for people to plan their lives decently. They would not have their lives decided by the free market, where your life can be ruined from one week to the next, and not even by your own fault — not because you are an inefficient worker or an idle worker, but simply because of some shift in demand for your employer's products.

That is how I see socialist planning. Is it utopian? That question really comes down to: is human nature sufficiently elastic that it can develop the spirit of co-operation and solidarity necessary for such re-organisation? It is impossible to say yes or no for sure because it has not been tried yet. We will find out whether or not it is possible by trying. Then the question is, is there a force which will try? Yes, there is. One of the most important and progressive things about capitalism is that it generates the desire to improve society. It does not just generate that desire in general, it generates it in particular among a particular class, the working class.

The working class in capitalist society is the basic toiling class, similar to the toiling classes in other forms of society. But it is also different. It is the only basic labouring class in human history which has developed permanent organisations based on the principle of solidarity.

We are well aware of the deficiencies with which those developments have been marked — the deficiencies of the existing working class movements, the way in which they exist. But in a broad historical view, the remarkable thing is that capitalism generates a class which has this capacity to organise, and consciously to set itself the tasks of firstly changing its conditions within the old society and eventually substituting a new society.

The working class is a class which finds itself all the time, like it or not, in class struggle with the owners of the means of production. It finds itself in that struggle irrespective of what we, or anybody else, wish. That class struggle is going to continue, whatever people say about socialism being condemned by the experience of Stalinism. In that class struggle, there is the force which is going to try — at least — to re-organise society on a basis which is not as unequal and as cruel as the free market.

David Marsland

THERE IS NOTHING wrong in principle or in general with planning. It depends who is doing the planning, what for, and how. Individuals and families absolutely need to plan the personal project of their lives carefully and long-term. It is a primary function of the capitalist ethos and an enterprise culture to encourage this. Many do, but, alas, too many of us have been discouraged from the need for it by the Welfare State, which pretends to make it unnecessary. Big Brother does people's planning — for their children's education, for the family's health care, for pensions, and so on — very ineffectively. Only the people whose project it is can plan properly for themselves, since no one else can know or understand their wishes, needs, and situation.

Organisations also need to plan if they are to carry out their proper tasks effectively. The larger the organisation the more difficult it is to plan well, so it should be devolved as far as possible, with the centre handling only strategic planning. Even then there are difficulties due to the inaccessibility, unreliability, and fluctuating state of relevant planning information. Hence the key role of markets, as a source of information — about demand and consumers' preferences — to assist organisations in their planning.

The crucial importance of the market as a handmaiden to organisational planning is demonstrated by the general inadequacy of planning in organisations operating outside any sort of market. A major reason for the gross inadequacy of planning in health care or in education in Britain is their protection within a top-down, command-mode, state-centralist cocoon which insulates them from the information they need and blunts the awareness of managers of the need to plan.

Thus, quite contrary to the socialist analysis, a market is necessary to encourage long-term, strategic thinking. Only when power is devolved to relevant operational levels — schools, hospital trusts, etcetera — and when at least a quasi-market is established, is rational planning at the level of the organisation feasible. Planning, then, is necessary for individuals, groups, and organisations, and beneficial provided that relevant sorts of information in terms of which to ground planning decisions are available. Planning beyond those limited spheres — in state and society — is where the serious difficulties and the key theoretical and political arguments appear.

Both at local state and especially at central state levels grave problems about planning are inevitable, for three distinct reasons. First the scale of activities involved. The larger the context of action, the more problematical planning becomes. Secondly the nature and range of tasks for which the state is responsible. Generally speaking, the less appropriate for state capacities the tasks taken on by the state, and the wider the range of such tasks, the less effective does planning become. Thirdly, the infeasibility of states operating in a market. State capitalism is a contradiction in terms.

In general terms, wherever states take over tasks better handled by other agencies and a wider rather than a narrower range of tasks, in these conditions the essential planning tasks of the state — and of course there are such, for the internal and external protection of citizens, for relations with the governments of other states, and for the management of the law and money — are likely to be handled badly. Thus at state level too planning is essential and beneficial, but only provided that it is done in a minimal state context, and even then only if it is modest and cautious in the extreme.

In general, subsidiarity requires that state planning should be restricted to tasks in relation to which individuals and groups cannot plan for themselves, and which cannot be handled by organisations independent of the state and operating in markets, preferably real markets. The grounds for this restriction of the state's planning role are two-fold. First, economic: the state in general plans badly, lacking both the personal involvement and understanding of individuals and groups, and the task specificity and market-driven efficiency of independent, profit-oriented organisations. Secondly, political: if the state, even a democratic state, is allowed control of planning outside its proper sphere, liberty is bound to be dangerously threatened.

Thus there is a perfectly proper and very important role for planning in a free society by individuals, by groups, by organisations, and by the state as well. However, planning should be located appropriately, and at state level limited to essential modest tasks. The economy narrowly defined should be left largely to independent organisations and the market. So too should much of the economy broadly defined — the production and distribution of goods and services, which of course includes much of what we have been schooled by socialists to call welfare.

This analysis leaves the state with an important but restricted planning role. The importance of planning by the state, within its proper sphere, is unapologetically acknowledged. A free society needs a strong, confident state capable of carrying out on behalf of its citizens its vital role — including the planning required by that role — effectively and efficiently in a world of unpredictable challenges and dangers.

Despite this, socialists will read it as an expression of an extreme and intolerable market-orientated ideology. Certainly it goes beyond the level of marketisation achieved even by a decade of Thatcherism. It challenges absolutely the concept of the "mixed economy" of the Butskellite era, which postulated considerable state control and planning. And of course it must seem absolutely unacceptable to real socialists of whatever specific persuasion, as a contradiction of their basic principles.

Yet it is, I suggest, a modest proposition. The supporters of capitalism have never suggested that the market should replace planning entirely, or denied the importance of planning by the state in pursuit of its proper objectives. "Unfettered capitalism" is a socialist concept intended to subvert liberal capitalist societies, not a liberal concept at all. By contrast, socialists can never in principle be satisfied with controlling or managing the market. The principled aim of socialism is to supersede the market with alternative mechanisms, expropriate it entirely, and install a planned economy within a planned society. Capitalism requires modest but effective "fettering" of the market: socialism relies on "unfettered command", that is to say the replacement of the market by planning.

And of course we know why socialists want this. Their analysis exposes markets as inherently inefficient and unjust. It reveals profit as inevitably exploitative. It condemns competition as wasteful and as destructive of the character of those involved in it. It condemns capitalism, defined essentially by profit-driven competitive markets, as incapable of serving people's real needs, as requiring and reproducing intolerable inequality, and in short as a morally repugnant system serving the real interests of no one save capitalists.

My answer to this socialist challenge to capitalism, and to the demand for comprehensive planning deduced from and justified by it, is twofold. First a response in terms of theory and principle concerning the feasibility of planning. Secondly a pragmatic and practical response in terms of the demonstrated benefits of markets and the consumer sovereignty on which they rely.

However, there is one logically prior point. There is no need to justify markets in principle or in practice if the socialist critique of capitalism is fallacious or substantially exaggerated. I suggest that, despite the continuing popularity among intellectuals here and in other free societies of socialist ideas, the analysis of capitalism which provides their only justification is erroneous.

The socialist critique manages — despite the patent contradiction involved — to condemn capitalism for sustaining and aggravating poverty, and at the same time for maintaining its illegitimate power by bribing and corrupting the people with the fruits of economic progress. Perfectly absurdly, as it seems to me, accusations of creating poverty comprise today, as they have for more than a hundred and fifty years, one of the main lines of critique of capitalism.

Yet no civilisation throughout history, no other type of society, past or present — among modern societies neither self-proclaimed socialist societies, nor fascist societies, nor military dictatorships, nor dynastic despotisms, nor revolutionary theocracies, nor any others have succeeded in providing and sustaining such wealth as the tiny minority of capitalist societies have entirely reliably produced. None of these alternative systems has raised the general standard of living of whole populations to the high and continually improving levels which even the so-called poor in Britain take entirely for granted. Only capitalism destroys poverty.

Whether measured in terms of life expectancy, real incomes, distribution of property, leisure spending, or whatever, the material condition of the British population — even in general recession — is good and continually improving. "Trickle down" is altogether too modest a characterisation of recent improvements in standards of living. Capitalism has produced in Britain a veritable cornucopia of wealth which has cascaded right across society. This has transformed the standard of living and the quality of life in material terms beyond what was even conceivable except by a tiny minority as recently as 1945.

None of this is contradicted in the slightest by the persistence of economic inequalities, or even by their increase from time to time. Inequalities are required as the engine of the economic progress which increases living standards all round and destroys poverty. They are a major source of incentive, aspiration and ambition. They are also widely accepted in moral terms, and they are in a strict philosophical sense natural, being liberated by capitalism, as Hayek has shown, most notably in *The Fatal Conceit*, as a key component of the market which defines it. Challenge the shifting inequalities of capitalism, and economic progress is destroyed.

Of course this is miscomprehended by capitalism's critics and even by some of its more luke-warm supporters. The Poverty Lobby's spurious identification of economic inequality with poverty, and its dogmatic determination to eliminate by socialistic measures and mechanisms the very dynamic which has rendered real poverty obsolete, are an index of the poverty of socialist analysis and of the timidity of the pro-capitalist intellectuals who are their supposed opponents. Certainly their efforts provide not the slightest justification for believing other than that, as George Gilder has demonstrated in *The Capitalist Revolution,* on the material front at least, capitalism has succeeded and is succeeding triumphantly.

The second line of socialist critique is what I call the "materialist slander". It comes in many distinct versions, but they share a common incli-

382

nation to find in the styles of life, in the forms of character, and in the values required by capitalism for its success, a gross underestimate and a hideous deformation of human potential. It is the charge that capitalist culture is altogether and merely materialistic; the claim that competition is inherently destructive, the charge that property divides and subjugates, the accusation that individualism, or at least capitalism's possessive individualism, inhibits co-operation, the critical presumption that economic inequality precludes citizenship and even fraternity; the belief that pursuit of profit inhibits altruism and prevents genuine service; the widespread view even among moderate critics of capitalism that markets destroy community. Yet most even of the worst features are even worse by a big margin in pre-capitalist and post-capitalist societies. The scope for effective reform and improvement without structural change is patently enormous. Empirical studies of people's lives — as reported, for example, by Gilder and by Michael Novak in *The Spirit of Democratic Capitalism* — clearly and definitely suggest high levels of satisfaction at work, at leisure, and holistically; improving levels of education, sophistication, and civilisation; and consistent movement overall towards a far greater degree of personal and interactional expression and development than we have any right — given a realistic view of the past and of man's infinite capacity for evil — to expect.

Moreover, the supposedly destructive features of capitalism which it is alleged are responsible for all the problems — property, profit, competition, inequality, and the rest — turn out to be precisely the mechanisms which directly, in and of themselves and indirectly through their sustenance of freedom, are making positive human development possible.

Immigrants flood, where they can manage it, away from all sorts of primitive and evil societies, into capitalist societies, pursuing an escape from poverty certainly, but also and equally freedom, and the dream, which is no mere phantasy, of a good life for themselves and their families in the broadest and deepest sense of the concept of good so far available. Thus, in material and moral terms alike, even those capitalist societies such as Britain which have been most gravely weakened by socialist intrusions, including especially excessive planning and regulation, are succeeding to a degree which makes the proposal for substituting the plan for the market unnecessary and implausible.

Moreover, on both the economic and the moral front, those central features of capitalism which socialists would displace by installing a planning regime — competition, profit, enterprise, and consumer choice — are demonstrably playing a key role in securing this success.

Planning is unnecessary then; but in any case it can't work. This seems to me to have been adequately demonstrated in Hayek's refutation of Oskar Lange's thesis of the possibility of socialist calculation. Lange claims that all the information available to capitalist entrepreneurs which is necessary for them to make optimal decisions about resource allocation is available in practice to socialist planners. Given this data, they can then plan the socialist economy rationally. Or as Heilbronner, following Lange, puts it: "A central planning board would receive exactly the same information from a socialist economic system as did the entrepreneurs under the market system". This assumption — strengthened in some quarters recently by developments in information science and technology which speed up the flow of any sort of information and make it potentially much more comprehensive — is required by even the most modest sorts of planning, and is absolutely essential to systematic detailed planning such as would be required to replace the market. Hayek's response is as follows:

"I am afraid this is a blatant untruth, an assertion so absurd that it is difficult to understand how an intelligent person could ever honestly make it. It asserts a sheer impossibility which only a miracle could realise. In the first instance: most of the information which the capitalist entrepreneurs have consists of prices determined on a competitive market. This knowledge would not be available to anyone in a socialist economy where prices are not provided by the market. So far as the particular case of the production function is concerned, the relevant production functions which guide the competitive market are, of course, not (as the theoretical models simplifyingly assume) relations between general, generic categories of commodities, but very specific relations showing how, in a particular plant under the specific local conditions, changes in the combinations of the particular goods and services employed will affect the size of the output". (*Journal of Economic Affairs* Vol.2 No.3, 1982).

Moreover, even if the information were available — which by definition it cannot be in a socialist society — there is still no way it could be collated and analysed by a planning unit or by a single person or by any other means than the infinite complexity of the market itself. Dispersed market knowledge simply cannot be mobilised centrally. Even on more modest and substantially oversimplified assumptions about the range and particularity of the knowledge required, such that a kind of "accountancy planning" could be possible, it couldn't work in practice. As Hayek says:

"The mere idea that the planning authority could ever possess a complete inventory of the amounts and qualities of all the different materials and instruments of production of which the manager of a particular plant will know or be able to find out makes the whole proposal a somewhat comic fiction. Once this is recognised it becomes obvious that what prices ought to be can never be determined without relying on competitive markets. The suggestion that the planning authority could enable the managers of particular plants to make use of their specific knowledge by fixing uniform prices for certain classes of goods that will then have to remain in force until the planning authority learns whether at these prices inventories generally increase or decrease is just the crowning foolery of the whole farce ". (Ibid.)

This is why all planning systems — but only some markets — fail. A competitive market system capitalises naturally on a complex interaction of individual decisions which cannot be adequately recorded, let alone reproduced in the abstract by any artificial means. This is why Central Europe, and now Russia and the Ukraine, are simply having to marketise fully.

Without a market, economic decisions are bound to be guesswork and commonly — and cumulatively — mistaken. This is also why rational planning within the Welfare State is so difficult, why state functions which cannot be privatised such as defence are so expensive and inefficient, and why it is at those boundaries between national economies which are not made transparent by free trade that major dislocations of economic efficiency and dynamism occur.

In the absence of a market, there is simply no rational basis available for resource allocation decisions. If a plan, of whatever sort, is used instead, systematic resource misallocation is inevitable. Moreover reactions to the consequences of these errors will multiply them still further, resulting sooner or later in complete economic collapse — in an economic crisis such as socialists have long expected in capitalist societies but actually occurs only in socialist societies, or at least in those societies which have defined the competitive market as the essential characteristic of capitalism and replaced it by the plan.

Even the much more modest and commonsensical notions of planning typically recommended by socialists in Britain — for example organising the health service either nationally, or even regionally, in terms of prescriptions derived other than from a market, or distorting the natural flow of regional investment in order to supposedly protect economically weaker regions — are subject to the same fundamental errors. Socialist planning, however desirable it might seem to be, is simply not on. In addition to these problems of principle about planning, there are also grave practical difficulties. I can best make what I mean clear by spelling out the reasons why market systems — that is to say, modes of organising the production and distribution of goods and services which are responsive via prices and profits to consumer sovereignty — are generally effective.

All the eight advantages of competitive markets I will spell out are matched by correlative disadvantages in any non-market planning system. Similar disadvantages would also of course appear as a result of private monopoly, though these are worsened by state monopoly, and worsened further again by the comprehensive state monopoly of a planned socialist society.

Sooner or later private monopolies are defeated by innovative competitors. A state monopoly, by contrast, will persist — and grow progressively more inefficient — until the state can no longer afford it either economically or politically. A socialist society — a planned monopoly of planned monopolies — will simply go on and on, getting worse and worse at everything, until it collapses.

In the absence of free markets:
- Prices go up or fail to reduce.
- Supply is reduced and shortages follow.
- Innovation is blocked.
- The quality of service is reduced.
- The state incurs costs — for running nationalised industries or for subsidies — instead of benefits from taxes. Why does this happen? The main reason is because the only alternative to a competitive market — the only other way of organising the production and distribution of goods and services — is a command system. The central planning essential to a command economy simply cannot, in its nature, answer consumers' needs effectively as a competitive market system in most cases can. There are eight reasons why this is so.

1. Consumer tastes and needs vary over a wide range and unpredictably. Only markets, that is to say, mechanisms specifically answerable to consumer demand, can address this variety effectively.

2. Consumer tastes and needs are subject to rapid unpredictable change. Only markets can adjust with reliable rapidity to such change.

3. Entrepreneurs and technologists tend — unless they are prevented — to produce innovations and improvements. Only a market answerable to consumer preferences allows reliably for effective testing and implementation of such improvements.

4. Only those forms of organisation of the production of goods and services which are oriented to consumer preferences and subject to consumer sovereignty are likely, through competition, to minimise costs and prices.

5. Only those forms of organisation of the production of goods and services which are oriented to consumer preferences and subject to consumer sovereignty are likely, again through competition and the effects

of prices, to reduce waste and more generally to maximise efficiency.

6. Only consumer sovereignty is capable of determining optimum levels of investment and expenditure. In its absence investment and other expenditure is likely to be artificially and damagingly either held down or exaggerated.

7. Only consumer sovereignty within a competitive market prevents the need for excessive and dangerous political controls, ramifying bureaucracy, and rationing in one form or another.

8. Only organisations which are answerable to competitive markets and consumer choice are capable of resisting exaggerated trade union demands.

For all these reasons, a market, involving real competition between a number of producers and suppliers of goods and services, is likely in most cases to be superior to any command or planned economy in delivering the quantity and the quality of what people want.

The states belonging to free societies need to plan if they are to do their proper work effectively. However, this should be modest in scope and scale, cautiously handled, and limited to the decisively restricted sphere of operations which are appropriate to the state in free societies. Any extension of state planning beyond these limits is bound to be both ineffective and counter-productive. Extension of state planning as a counter-weight to or a substitute for the normal and natural operation of the free market cannot in any circumstances be other than gravely damaging to the real interests of the whole population.

When liberal capitalist societies like Britain are faced by recession, or challenged over the longer term by successful competition from other nations, there is a powerful temptation to believe that state planning and state intervention can provide an antidote. All our experience in Britain since the Second World War refutes this optimistic notion. Interference with the market, however modest and well-intentioned, simply makes things worse.

The real answer is not more planning, but less, not an increase in state intervention, but a radical reduction. The success of the British economy depends entirely on the capacities of entrepreneurs, managers and workers to invent, produce and sell products and services at a profit on the global market.

I have argued here that, beyond very modest parameters, planning is unnecessary, infeasible in principle, and ineffective in practice. It may seem that the progressive application of human intelligence to social affairs must inevitably counsel adoption of a comprehensive planning mode in relation to every sort of human problem. This is how it is being argued currently, for example, in relation to environmental problems and "green" issues. But in this important instance and generally this conception is mistaken.

Human intelligence and advancing knowledge ought, on the contrary, to advise us that the market is a powerfully productive institution, evolved naturally over generations, with which we should interfere as little as can be managed. The better part of intelligence is to marvel at the market's gifts to mankind, to protect and facilitate its operations, and to resist the impatient clamour of the planners tooth and nail. The commitment of socialists and others to planning is indeed, in Hayek's memorably precise phrase, a "fatal conceit".

Martin Thomas

CAPITALISM ENCOURAGES AND allows individuals to plan for themselves; socialism means planning by Big Brother, which is unfree and anyway does not work. So David Marsland argues. In fact planned cooperation on a large scale was introduced into human life by capitalism, not by socialism. Modern methods of production involve intricate networks of cooperation linking thousands of people. Under capitalism all that planned cooperation is shaped and regulated by the competing drives for profit of a minority of wealthy owners; and the planning is done despotically, from above, by those owners. Working-class socialism certainly does not mean replacing "unfettered command" by private capitalist owners with "unfettered command" by the state. It means making the planned cooperation social and democratic; and regulating it so as to provide for every citizen comfort, security and, by cutting work time, free time.

David Marsland argues that planning on such a large scale cannot work. The central administration cannot conceivably gather all the relevant information fast enough. A market economy, by contrast, provides information where it is necessary in a decentralised way.

There is some truth in this argument. In the dispute which David Marsland cites between Hayek and the maverick socialist economist Oskar Lange, I think Hayek was right. Lange's scheme, where the socialist administration is supposed to act like a socialist version of that theoretical fiction of academic economics, the "Walrasian auctioneer" who simultaneously finds prices to balance supply and demand in every market, is unworkable. But Lange was a maverick. Marxian socialists have long argued that, because of the difficulties of centralising information, a workers' government would have to combine broad strategic planning with the use of markets (real markets, not Lange's pseudomarkets) for a long time. Only the broad patterns of investment, social provision, and income distribution would be planned. Not all that planning would be centralised, any more than big capitalist corporations do all their planning in their head offices.

There would be tensions in the combination of planning and markets. A lot of experience from capitalist societies, however, shows it would be workable. Some highly successful capitalist systems, such as Japan's or South Korea's, have had effective government planning of major investment. It has been capitalist government planning, done bureaucratically, undemocratically, corruptly, and in the interests of profit. There is no reason to suppose that democratic planning would be less workable.

And then the working class, the great majority of the people, would no longer toil only to enrich the top 10 per cent, who in Britain own 53 per cent of all marketable wealth and almost all land and shares. Everyone could have a decent job, and the excess of what the workers produce over their own direct consumption would go to social provision and to socially-controlled investment. We could get rid of the vast waste and duplication arising from capitalist competition — and its offshoots, such as advertising, excessive packaging, and so on — and economise on the labour currently used to provide luxuries for the rich. Cutting the competitive drive for profit would also cut the roots of conflict between nations, and open the way to redirect the huge resources currently spent on preparations for war.

We could ensure decent public services, health, education, child-care, transport. With improving technology, the working week, and thus the control of the economy over human life, could be cut, to allow free time for a society which is a free association of free individuals. How fast the use of markets could be reduced, and when and how it could be reduced to nothing, is a more difficult question. That reduction, I think, presupposes that the burden of drudgery to meet our material wants is cut to a low level, and that those material wants themselves become stable and are satisfied. As Trotsky put it, it awaits the time "when the steady growth of social wealth has made us bipeds forget our miserly attitude towards every excess minute of labour, and our humiliating fear about the size of our ration".

The argument of Hayek, and other apologists for capitalism, rests on the axiom that it will never be possible to remove that "fear about the size of our ration" — that it is unchangeable human nature always to want to consume more, sooner. A competitive scramble for rations is therefore inevitable, and the market is a more flexible, dignified and efficient way to organise it than policemen and queues.

That argument, to my mind, is circular: it takes the patterns of behaviour shaped by capitalist economics, calls them human nature, and then triumphantly concludes that capitalism fits human nature! Obviously no one can say for sure when, or if, a cooperative commonwealth could erode the anxious greed for property bred into us by capitalism. But even if it never could, even if socialism could never get beyond an uneasy compromise between democratic planning and markets, we need to get rid of capitalism.

For David Marsland's claims for capitalism do not stand up. The best gloss that can be put on his claim that capitalism encourages and allows individuals to plan for themselves is this: that the market informs those individuals of the limits put on them by the need to fit into a society based on large scale cooperation (as capitalism is), and does it in an efficient way, allowing the individuals to make dignified choices within those limits. If that claim be true, it amounts only to saying that the market is a good way of telling workers that they are condemned to scrape by, in a life of drudgery and worry, largely shut out from access to the wealth and culture built on their labour. No doubt the discipline of the market is preferable to the slave driver's whip, and it does leave the worker some choice about how to scrape by.

But capitalism disrupts workers' plans for their lives even within those limits. With high interest rates and unemployment, some 80,000 people lost their homes last year through mortgage repossessions; there must have been hundreds of thousands who avoided repossession only through desperate scraping by. Any plans you make in a capitalist economy can be ruined from one day to the next when you are thrown out of work; and millions are thrown out of work, forced on to the dole queue or into marginal jobs, all the time.

Marx put it like this: "The sphere of commodity exchange is a very Eden of the innate rights of man. It is the exclusive realm of Freedom, Equality, Property, and Bentham... Bentham, because each looks only to his own advantage... When we leave this sphere, a certain change takes place in our dramatis personae. He who was previously the money owner now strides out in front as the capitalist; the possessor of labour-power follows as his worker. The one smirks self importantly and is intent on business; the other is timid and holds back, like someone who has brought his own hide to market and now has nothing else to expect but — a tanning." David Marsland claims to defend capitalism. In fact he — like all the others who have undertaken the same grim task, Hayek, Friedman, so on — defends only an idealised picture of "the sphere of commodity exchange".

Marx was only half ironic. Free market capitalism as compared to serfdom or slavery does bring a real expansion of freedom and equality. But capitalism is not just a system of individuals making free and equal exchanges in a market-place. Behind that market-place stands a system of production where the worker is unfree and unequal. The apparently free and equal exchange between buyer and seller of labour-power means in fact that in return for a routine pittance, scantier or more ample as it may be, the workers have to labour under the dictatorship of the capitalist and to increase the wealth of the capitalist.

And, real capitalist markets do not correspond with the "ideal" of efficient, reliable balancing of supply and demand. At almost all times outside wars, capitalist economies generate vast armies of the unemployed and marginally employed, people defined by the system as "excess supply" of labour-power. Two and a half million people are jobless in Britain today even according to the government's rigged statistics; the true figure must be well over three million.

David Marsland identifies capitalism with "consumer sovereignty". The idea is that the market, by transmitting signals from final consumer demand, ensures that the economy develops as consumers want. At best this would mean only that capitalism satisfies the wants which capitalism creates — for our wants are in large part created by capitalism. It is not as if there were wants embedded in human nature, right back to the Stone Age, for BMW cars, Nintendo games, and, for that matter, volumes of Marxist theory, and now at last capitalism has satisfied them.

In fact capitalism does not satisfy the wants which capitalism creates. Signals are sent through the market only by consumers with money, not by human wants or needs. The whim of the rich is satisfied; the desperate need of the poor is not. Capitalism does not even satisfy the most basic physical needs of millions. An increasing number of people in the world today — some hundreds of millions — live on the edge of starvation. The poor countries of the Third World are just as much a part of world capitalism, with its patterns of uneven development, as are the relatively rich countries of the West.

Moreover the big strategic investment decisions which shape the course of the economy are not dictated by consumer demand. At best market signals convey information only, about now, not about the time, five, ten or fifteen years away for which those big investments must be planned. Even enthusiastic supporters of free-market capitalism worry about its tendencies to "short-termism", or going for short-term gains at the expense of the long term. Social needs which cannot be satisfied by the selling of individual commodities to individual people — such as the need for a sustainable relation to the environment — generate no market signals at all.

The real driving principle of capitalist economics is not consumer demand, but profit. Clearly there are human wants more or less independent of the prevailing mode of production, and those wants influence consumer demand which in turn influences profits; but consumer demand is also shaped and limited by the drive for profit. The market is not the only way to provide people with choice about what to consume. A public library can offer a better choice of books than a capitalist bookshop; a good, subsidised works canteen can offer better choice than a streetful of capitalist fast-food places.

David Marsland argues that "inequalities are required as the engine of economic progress... They are a major source of incentive, aspiration, and ambition." In the idealised free-market economy made up of millions of small workshops or farms, this argument would have force. By making sure that the efficient workshop did better than the slovenly one, the market would promote progress. It is also true that a workers' government would at first need inequalities. Skilled and conscientious workers would get more than unskilled and idle ones.

But the idealised free-market economy has never existed, and never will exist. Even if it did exist, it would be a cruel and arbitrary system for those many whom it recognises only as "dependents" — those too old or sick to work, housewives, and children (that is, everyone in a large and important part of their lives). And the major inequalities in capitalist societies today have nothing to do with differentials between more and less productive workers. A series of excellent books — all written by supporters of capitalism — have recently told us a lot about what the rich actually do, and how they get rich. Read *Liar's Poker*, *Barbarians at the Gate*, or *Maxwell: the outsider*!

People who are very skilled and diligent at caring for children or the old, or educating, or scientific research, or engineering, or even production management, do not get rich. The skills and efforts encouraged by huge "incentives" under modern capitalism are those of the huckster and the wheeler-dealer. No doubt the skills of the energetic dealmaker and the fixer will be needed in a cooperative commonwealth, as they are needed in the labour movement today. But why should those skills be rewarded by huge riches? Why do they need to be? Moreover the evidence is that when those skills are rewarded by huge riches they are corrupted rather than refined. The Robert Maxwells, the John Gutfreunds, the Henry Kravises, the Ross Johnsons, become foolish, self-indulgent despots, if not outright crooks.

Nevertheless, argues David Marsland, "capitalism destroys poverty". He argues this in a capitalist world where 1,500 million people in two subcontinents, sub-Saharan Africa and South Asia, have an average food consumption of only 2200 calories per head, while the World Health Organisation sets the minimum for health at 2600 calories! That the poorest countries often have governments calling themselves "socialist" does not lift the blame from capitalism. From Nigeria to Bangladesh, these are capitalist countries, shaped over centuries by capitalist rule and capitalist trade.

In Britain people do not starve. It seems to me rather sick to give great credit to capitalism for this fact, when technology today allows only five per cent of the workforce to produce more than enough food for everyone. Even in relatively rich Britain a survey published in June last year found that hundreds of thousands of small children go without enough to eat at least once a month because their parents are short of cash; well over a million have "nutritionally poor" diets. Diseases of poverty such as rickets have reappeared. Some hundreds of thousands — no-one knows exactly how many — are homeless. Yet David Marsland asserts that "real poverty," is "obsolete", and the illusion of poverty is sustained only by "the Poverty Lobby's spurious identification of economic inequality with poverty".

No-one equates poverty with economic inequality. A millionaire and a billionaire are economically unequal, but the millionaire is not poor. However, a homeless family in Britain today living in a council-provided bed-and-breakfast place is poor, even if their food, their clothing, their amusements, and even the squalid room they live in, would look like wealth to a medieval peasant. Human beings are social animals. Human life is not just biological survival, but life in society. To get out of poverty means more than not starving or freezing to death; it means being able to take a normal and dignified part in society.

Capitalism does create poverty. Regularly and routinely, workers are paid no more than the value of their labour power, which is defined by a "living wage" adequate to keep the working class fit for work. Regularly and routinely, workers are poor relative to the riches they produce for the capitalist class and its hangers-on. And, while the averagely paid worker generally scrapes by in modest comfort, regularly and routinely capitalism throws millions out of their jobs. Capitalism cannot work without unemployed people, and without those unemployed people being unable to maintain even a working-class standard of living.

The pauper existence of the unemployed may mean starvation, or it may mean only discomfort and misery. It matters which. Capitalism modified by reforms imposed by the labour movement is better than unmodified capitalism; liberal capitalism is better than capitalism mixed with archaic or semi-feudal survivals; prosperous capitalism is better than stagnant, backward capitalism.

None of that should make us "marvel at the market's gifts to mankind" — or tolerate the fact that under capitalism so many human beings have to give up so much of their dignity, their energy, their hopes and their happiness to a cruel and inhuman market.

The debate between Martin Thomas and David Marsland took place at the "Stand Up for Real Socialism" conference sponsored by the Alliance for Workers' Liberty on 2 November 1991. The tape recording of the summations of Marsland and Thomas at that event was indecipherable. The second contribution here from Martin Thomas was written after the event as a response to David Marsland's opening speech on 2 November 1991. David Marsland was offered the opportunity to write a response to the response, but chose not to take it up.

Fact file

IN BRITAIN, INEQUALITY OF WEALTH and income has grown since Margaret Thatcher's Tory government took office 38 years ago. This inequality increased further under New Labour, though not as fast as under the Tories.

By 2014, chief executives of top companies (FTSE 100) were paying themselves 179 times as much as the median full-time worker in her or his job for at least a year. (Source: High Pay Centre).

Britain is also at the bottom of the league for social mobility, among the richer countries — along with the USA, another country where free-market economics and union-bashing have been unleashed with exceptional force. In Britain, if A's dad has twice the income of B, then A is likely to end up with 40% more income than B.

It's difficult to get exact measures, because it's impossible to take a snapshot, but according to an official parliamentary report in 2010, social mobility has either worsened or not improved in recent decades. Around 1980 poorer men died 5.5 years before the well-off; now the gap is 7.5 years. The gap has grown despite improvements in housing and food availability, and despite a decline in heavy manual work. Income inequality has been increasing since the early 1980s in a wide range of countries. (Source: Thomas Piketty, *Capital in the 21st Century*).

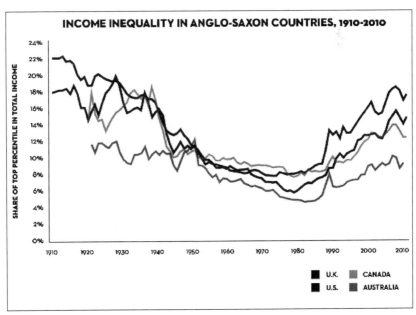

INCOME INEQUALITY IN ANGLO-SAXON COUNTRIES, 1910-2010

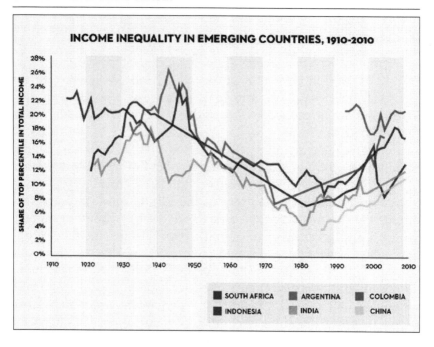

World-wide, 0.5% of adults hold 36% of household wealth. (Source: Credit Suisse Research Institute, *Global Wealth Report*, October 2010).

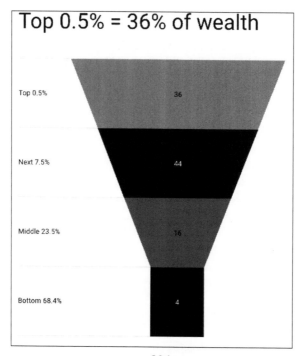

In Britain: the top 10% of households hold 44% of household wealth (Source: Wealth and Assets Survey 2006-8).

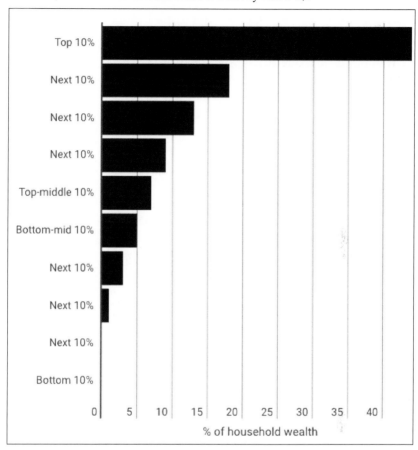

Privatisations have frequently been a large transfer of publicly-owned wealth to private profiteers. For example, the water utilities in Britain were sold off in 1989, and by 1995 the shareholders had clocked up a gain of £10 billion — the shares for which they had paid £4 billion were now priced at £14 billion — plus dividend payouts.

Voucher value of Russian companies privatised in 1990s compared with market value (in million U.S. dollars)		
Company	At Voucher Auction Prices (1993-1994)	At Russian Stock Market Prices (August 1997)
Gazprom (natural gas)	250	40,483
Unified Energy Services (electricity)	957	17,977
Lukoil (oil)	704	15,839
Rostelecom (telecom)	464	4,172
Yuganskneftegaz (oil)	80	1,656
Surgutneftegaz (oil)	79	6,607
Data compiled by Paul Klebnikov		

Index

We only want the Earth

Some men, faint-hearted, ever seek
Our programme to retouch,
And will insist, whene'er they speak
That we demand too much.
'Tis passing strange, yet I declare
Such statements give me mirth,
For our demands most moderate are,
We only want the earth.

"Be moderate," the trimmers cry,
Who dread the tyrants' thunder.
"You ask too much and people fly
From you aghast in wonder."
'Tis passing strange, for I declare
Such statements give me mirth,
For our demands most moderate are,
We only want the earth.

Our masters all a godly crew,
Whose hearts throb for the poor,
Their sympathies assure us, too,
If our demands were fewer.
Most generous souls! But please observe,
What they enjoy from birth
Is all we ever had the nerve
To ask, that is, the earth.

The "labour fakir" full of guile,
Base doctrine ever preaches,
And whilst he bleeds the rank and file
Tame moderation teaches.
Yet, in despite, we'll see the day
When, with sword in its girth,
Labour shall march in war array
To realise its own, the earth.

For labour long, with sighs and tears,
To its oppressors knelt.
But never yet, to aught save fears,
Did the heart of tyrant melt.
We need not kneel, our cause no dearth
Of loyal soldiers' needs
And our victorious rallying cry
Shall be: we want the earth!

James Connolly